Bobo Newsom

Bobo Newsom
Baseball's Traveling Man

JIM MCCONNELL

Foreword by MARK LANGILL

McFarland & Company, Inc., Publishers
Jefferson, North Carolina

LIBRARY OF CONGRESS CATALOGUING-IN-PUBLICATION DATA [new form]

Names: McConnell, Jim, 1948–
Title: Bobo Newsom : baseball's traveling man / Jim McConnell ; foreword by Mark Langill.
Description: Jefferson, North Carolina : McFarland & Company, Inc., Publishers, 2016. | Includes bibliographical references and index.
Identifiers: LCCN 2015042162 | ISBN 9780786497843 (softcover : acid free paper)
Subjects: LCSH: Newsom, Bobo, 1907–1962 | Baseball players—United States—Biography. | Pitchers (Baseball)—United States—Biography.
Classification: LCC GV865.N484 M43 2016 | DDC 796.357092—dc23
LC record available at http://lccn.loc.gov/2015042162

BRITISH LIBRARY CATALOGUING DATA ARE AVAILABLE

ISBN 978-1-4766-1959-0 (ebook)

© 2016 James E. McConnell. All rights reserved

No part of this book may be reproduced or transmitted in any form or by any means, electronic or mechanical, including photocopying or recording, or by any information storage and retrieval system, without permission in writing from the publisher.

On the cover: Bobo Newsom (National Baseball Hall of Fame Library, Cooperstown, New York)

Printed in the United States of America

*McFarland & Company, Inc., Publishers
Box 611, Jefferson, North Carolina 28640
www.mcfarlandpub.com*

For Diana, Laura and Irene

N is for Newsom,
Bobo's favorite kin.
If you ask how he's here,
He talked himself in.

—From "Lineup for Yesterday, an A-B-C of
Baseball Immortals" by Ogden Nash (1949)

Table of Contents

Acknowledgments		ix
Foreword by Mark Langill		1
Introduction		3
One	Hartsville, South Carolina (1907–1927)	9
Two	Raleigh to Brooklyn, via Greenville, Wilmington and Mobile (1928–1929)	22
Three	New York to Los Angeles, via Brooklyn, Jersey City, Mobile, Little Rock and Chicago (1930–1933)	31
Four	St. Louis to Washington, D.C. (1934–1935)	49
Five	Washington to Boston (1936–1937)	67
Six	St. Louis to Detroit (1938–1939)	85
Seven	Detroit (1940)	102
Eight	Detroit to Washington to Brooklyn (1941–1942)	128
Nine	Brooklyn to St. Louis to Washington (1943)	146
Ten	Philadelphia to Washington (1944–1946)	161
Eleven	New York to Hartsville (1947–1948)	179
Twelve	Chattanooga to Birmingham to Washington to Philadelphia (1949–1953)	189
Thirteen	Baltimore to Washington to Winter Park to Hartsville (1954–1962)	205
Epilogue		214
Chapter Notes		219
Bibliography		237
Index		239

Acknowledgments

Befitting its subject, this biography took a long and convoluted path to completion, beginning in 1970 with the author's interview with Jack Fournier.

In the course of interviewing former major leaguers (eventually, over 200 of them), one question used to break the ice was, "Who were some of the more colorful players you played with or against?" When asked of players from the 1930–1950 era, the vast majority came back with Bobo Newsom as the answer, accompanied by stories of Newsom's bizarre behavior.

Most of the credit for this book has to go to the former players who were willing to take the time to be interviewed, either by phone or in person. No one refused an interview, and many were extremely helpful. The author appreciates the trust that was placed in him by these individuals, many of whom are now deceased, and hopes that this book is worthy of that trust.

Originally, the Bobo Newsom story was just one of a dozen in the author's book on the St. Louis Browns, but it quickly became clear that Bobo deserved a book of his own.

This biography could not have been attempted, let alone completed, without the able assistance of Art Mazmanian, the late John Scolinos and the late Ron Squire. The author was exceptionally fortunate to have worked for all three of these distinguished college baseball coaches as a statistician, and that experience proved invaluable. Special thanks to Mazmanian, for reading the manuscript, correcting errors and making suggestions, to Scolinos, for his insights into what professional baseball was like in the 1930s and what it was like to play in the St. Louis Browns organization, and to Squire, for his wisdom on the art of pitching a baseball.

Acknowledgments go to three professional broadcasters, the late Don Bradley, the late Ron Menchine and the late Bill Welsh. Their input was vital to the sections pertaining to Bobo Newsom's aborted attempts at a career in broadcasting. Bradley supplied the author with his collection of old-time radio shows and tapes of his interviews with former players, all of which proved invaluable. Menchine gave his insights on being a play-by-play radio announcer, and on Newsom's time as host of Baltimore's Knot Hole Gang show. Welsh was most gracious in sharing information on Johnny Carson's kids' show host routine, and in explaining the perils of live broadcasting in the early days of television.

Vital to this book regarding Newsom's time spent barnstorming with Satchel Paige were the author's interviews with the late Buck O'Neil, the late Piper Davis, the late Joe

Black, and Don Newcombe. O'Neil was a national treasure. Davis was particularly insightful regarding the integration of baseball and the need to resist the deification of Branch Rickey. Black and Newcombe provided insights into the changes that swept through baseball in the immediate post–World War II period and the reluctance of teams to employ African Americans.

In addition to Fournier, Black and Newcombe, the following former major league players were interviewed for this book. Most are quoted directly within the text, a few are not, but all made important contributions to furthering the author's understanding of a time and place largely foreign to him: Hank Arft, Johnny Berardino, Ewell Blackwell, Lou Boudreau, Roger Bowman, Al Campanis, Ray Coleman, Babe Dahlgren, Cliff Dapper, Rod Dedeaux, Jim Delsing, Bob Dillinger, Clem Dreisewerd, Ryne Duren, Red Embree, Woody English, Jesse Flores, Dee Fondy, Owen Friend, Mike Garcia, Ned Garver, Lefty Gomez, Jack Graham, Tommy Henrich, Babe Herman, Earl Johnson, Tom Jordan, Spider Jorgensen, Don Lenhardt, Johnny Lindell, Don Lund, Frank Mancuso, Mickey McDermott, Charlie Metro, Les Moss, Irv Noren, Joe Ostrowski, Marv Owen, Roy Partee, Eddie Pellagrini, Jimmy Reese, Bill Rigney, Fred Sanford, Frank Saucier, Joe Schultz, Jr., Ray Shore, Roy Sievers, Enos Slaughter, Tuck Stainback, Chuck Stevens, Lou Stringer, Johnny Sullivan, Keith Thomas, Mickey Vernon, Al Widmar, Ted Williams, Ken Wood, Al Zarilla and Gus Zernial. In addition, long-time minor league player Frosty Kennedy was particularly helpful. Kennedy met Bobo Newsom in 1950 and remained in touch with him until Newsom's death.

Former baseball executives the late Lee Scott and the late George Goodale also assisted with this project. Scott was interviewed on the events leading up to the Dodgers players' mutiny in 1943. Goodale was interviewed on the assembling of a broadcast team for the 1961 Los Angeles Angels.

As Bobo Newsom would say, sometimes you get lucky. The author's interview with Red Skelton in 1983 was supposed to be about an exhibition of Skelton's paintings at a Pomona (CA) art gallery. It turned out Skelton was angry at gallery management for some real or imagined slight and did not want to talk about the exhibition, his paintings, or Pomona. In desperation, the author turned the conversation to Skelton's movie career. A portion of the interview appears for the first time in this book.

The author wishes to extend a Size 50 thank you to George Fergusson. Fergusson was kind enough to share his unpublished biography of Bobo Newsom, and that work was particularly helpful in tracking Newsom's accomplishments during his stints in the minor leagues with Macon, Little Rock, Chattanooga and Birmingham. Fergusson also provided key research on the dramatic 1940 American League pennant race. It is the author's sincere hope that "Homestretch," George's wonderful portrait of the final, hectic month of the 1940 American League season, will soon find its way into print.

Thanks also go to Kathy Dunlap and staff at the Hartsville (SC) Museum, Doris Gandy and staff at the Darlington County (SC) Historical Museum and Wayne Wilson and staff at the Amateur Athletic Foundation/Ziff Library (now known as the LA84 Sports Library) in Los Angeles. Their professionalism helped propel this project to completion.

Key to telling Bobo Newsom's story was the "Hartsville Connection." The author extends his heartfelt appreciation to Tallulah Williams, John Newsome, Bob Shirley and Ernest "Hoot" Gibson for their willingness to be interviewed regarding Newsom's time in his hometown. Sadly, as happened with many of the players interviewed, Newsome died prior to this book's completion. More than the information he willingly supplied, John's enthusiasm for the book was contagious.

The following also made important contributions to this project: Mel Bailey, Dave Bartlow, Carlos Bauer, Dick Beverage, Clarence "Lefty" Blasco, Mary Brace, Carl Bruner, Helen Hannah Campbell, Terry Cannon, Drew Case, Patric Doyle, Wirt Gammon, Sr., Goodwin Goldfaden, Chris Gutierrez, Bob Hoie, Paul Jarrell, Mark Langill, Dave Larson, Dorothy McConnell, Paul McConnell, Larry McReynolds, Ray Medeiros, Jerry Mezrow, Jerry Miles, Rick Obrand, Evo Pusich, Art Richman, Lester Rodney, Jim Russo, Meg Ryan, Mark Sandstrom, Brent Shyer, Eric Stone, Jim Vitti and Joe Wayman.

No one could ask for a better team behind him. Any errors in the text, either of commission or omission, are solely the fault of the author. Likewise, this book's conclusions regarding Bobo Newsom's life and career are solely those of the author.

Foreword
by Mark Langill

Colorful nicknames fill the history pages of Brooklyn Dodgers lore, the grown men at Ebbets Field working under such titles as Pee Wee, Campy, Duke, Oisk, Preacher, Cookie, Newk, Shotgun, Dazzy, Casey and Popeye. But the "Bobo" moniker attached to pitcher Louis Norman Newsom conjures images of a player who never quite found his footing during his two tenures in Brooklyn, which wasn't surprising because the oft-traded right-hander was best known for his suitcase. And his mouth, which made him popular with sportswriters and inevitably got him in trouble with management.

In an era before free agency, Newsom actually took advantage of his vagabond ways, negotiating deals and staging salary holdouts. When World War II began, Newsom didn't have to worry about getting drafted because he was married with two children—a point he subtly reminded reporters of in spring training 1943 when announcing why he was worth $20,000 per annum coming off consecutive records of 12–20 and 13–19.

The Brooklyn franchise was floundering in the second division in 1929 when the 22-year-old Newsom was promoted from the minors for the final weeks of the season. By the time he returned in September 1942, the Dodgers were reigning National League champions and Newsom was a grizzled veteran with World Series experience. Holding a modest three-game lead, manager Leo Durocher declared he wasn't worried about the second-place St. Louis Cardinals.

But team president Larry MacPhail didn't share Durocher's confidence. The bombastic executive frequently clashed with his manager, even firing him on the day Brooklyn clinched the 1941 pennant because of a misunderstanding over the Dodgers train skipping a stop, leaving MacPhail waiting on the platform. MacPhail thought Durocher snubbed his moment of glory, while "The Lip" explained he feared the players would slip off the train in the second-to-last stop before Brooklyn to avoid a mob scene.

With a larger lead in August 1942, fans dreamed of bigger parades. But MacPhail had predicted they would lose the pennant unless his players' attitudes changed. If the Dodgers assumed another World Series appearance, so did their new pitcher when he joined the team on August 30. "I'm pennant insurance," Newsom announced.

Alas, Newsom didn't join the ranks of Dodgers postseason heroes. He didn't even reach October. The Dodgers finished the 1942 season with a 104–50 record and an eight-game winning streak. Newsom went 2–2 with a 3.38 ERA in six games. But St. Louis (106–48) won 30 of its last 35 games, including a 12–1 dash to the finish line.

The landscape of the Dodgers' front office changed when MacPhail accepted a commission in the United States Army, prompting the Dodgers to hire Cardinals executive Branch Rickey. MacPhail wasn't afraid to spend money, having borrowed from the banks to purchase quality talent from other teams. Rickey had pioneered the farm system during his early days in St. Louis, signing hundreds of amateur free agents across the country for modest salaries. But Rickey wasn't known for throwing big money on established players. After holding out, Newsom managed to finagle a bonus clause in his 1943 Dodgers contract, which set the clock ticking on his Brooklyn tenure.

Unlike future Dodger Ralph Branca living with a fateful pitch to the Giants' Bobby Thomson in the 1951 NL Polo Grounds playoffs, Newsom's July 1943 drama didn't play out on a public stage. It began when Newsom and catcher Bobby Bragan weren't in synch during a game against Pittsburgh, resulting in a dropped third strike. Bragan thought it was either a spitter or a knuckleball. Newsom said it was a low fastball.

The pebble soon rolled into an out-of-control boulder when Durocher seized on the incident to accuse Newsom of not following instructions on pitching to hitters. Newsom informed Durocher where he could go, and the Dodgers players staged a revolt against Durocher for perceived mistreatment of Newsom. A week later, the headline "Rumblings Follow Dodgers' Storm" topped the front page of *The Sporting News*.

Newsom ignited a storm that tested the baseball futures of both Rickey and Durocher. If Rickey couldn't control this controversy, what would happen three years later if he approached the team's Board of Directors with the idea of signing Negro Leagues ballplayers? And if the players walked out on Durocher, would any other team give him a chance to manage?

Despite a 9–4 record and a 3.02 ERA, the odd man out had to be Newsom. There was too much at stake for either Rickey or Durocher to let the pitcher publicly question their respective authority. The backdrop of World War II meant patchwork rosters, blood drives for the community and just trying to keep Major League Baseball going for the duration. When Newsom was traded to the St. Louis Browns, it was revealed that he was in line for his $5,000 bonus if he was still a Dodger as of July 15. The trade to the Browns was executed on July 14, costing him the big payday.

Newsom and the Dodgers wouldn't cross paths again until the 1947 World Series, when Bobo was a member of the Yankees. He started Game Three at Ebbets Field and was knocked out in the second inning of a 9–8 loss. Newsom thought he had the last laugh when the Yanks won the Series in seven games. But the Yankees players voted Newsom just a three-quarters share of the World Series money, and soon thereafter his tenure in the Bronx was also over.

Bobo's misadventures in Brooklyn and elsewhere in the baseball universe are all contained in Jim McConnell's biography. It's a rollicking read of a one-of-a-kind character of a type long gone from the game. So sit back and enjoy the ride.

Mark Langill is publications editor and team historian for the Los Angeles Dodgers and the author of Game of My Life: Dodgers *(Sports Publishing, 2007) and three titles in the Arcadia Publishing Images of Baseball series:* Dodgertown, Dodger Stadium *and* The Los Angeles Dodgers *(all 2004). He has worked for the Dodgers since 1994, following a career that included a stint as sportswriter for the* Pasadena Star-News.

Introduction

Louis Norman Newsom, aka Buck Newsom, aka Bobo Newsom, found himself pitching for the Washington Senators in the spring of 1937. He hit a rough patch and Shirley Povich of the *Washington Post* reported the following: "The Senators' $12,500 pitcher is winless in his first two starts."

Newsom was incensed.

He cornered Povich the next day in the Senators' locker room.

"You're dead wrong, Bobo!" Newsom yelled, calling Povich his catch-all nickname for half the human race. "This Bobo don't pitch for any club for $12,500. I've been getting big dough for two years now, so get that straight."

A chastised but curious Povich took the elevator up to the Senators' business office and checked Newsom's contract status. Newsom was right. He wasn't working for $12,500. He was working for $11,000.[1]

Welcome to Bobo's world. Rule No. 1: Never tell the truth when a lie will get you more attention.

Newsom was paid varying amounts to pitch baseballs for parts of four decades, from 1925 to 1953. Over the course of those years, Newsom became the most traveled player in major league history. He played for nine major league teams, in his lifetime a record. In 20 years in the majors, he changed teams during a season eight times, a record he still holds. Newsom pitched for the Washington Senators on five different occasions, another major league record. He also had three turns with the St. Louis Browns and two each with the Philadelphia Athletics and Brooklyn Dodgers. He pitched on three pennant winners, the 1932 Chicago Cubs, the 1940 Detroit Tigers and the 1947 New York Yankees. He also pitched for two of the worst teams in major league history, the 1939 Browns and 1946 A's. In one three-year stretch, 1942–1944, Newsom was traded or sold five times. In his 28 years of pitching professionally, he changed teams 30 times.[2]

All of which testifies to the fact Newsom was talented enough to be wanted but a sufficient pain in the ass to become quickly unwanted.

It was talent—not bombast—that placed Newsom at many of the pivotal points in the game's history. Sometimes, he even made history. A series of games with Satchel Paige in the winter of 1933 was both daring and innovative. Also in 1933, Newsom was one of the first ballplayers to double as a play-by-play radio announcer. He also played the starring role in one of the most dramatic moments in World Series history, in the aftermath of which he became the highest-paid pitcher in the game.

Unlike most players of his era, Newsom was never shy about demanding more money, more fringe benefits and better working conditions. He wound up being well-paid, but his salary demands also hastened his exit from at least six major league teams. Along the way, he was among the first to test baseball's reserve clause successfully, by declaring himself a free agent and forcing the Philadelphia Athletics to release him in 1946.

Newsom battled baseball's establishment to no worse than a draw for nearly 30 years. His efforts clearly expanded the field of vision for players' rights, even if Newsom did not pitch, or live, long enough to see those rights become a reality.

Sadly, Newsom's athletic accomplishments are now largely forgotten. Remembered are the odd nickname, his off-beat behavior and his truly bizarre career path. But that would be okay by Newsom. He was ready, willing and able to accept fame in whatever form it arrived, even if it meant playing the country bumpkin or hitching a short ride on someone else's coattails.

For a game on August 20, 1946, at Griffith Stadium, Senators owner Clark Griffith dreamt up a sure-fire promotional scheme. Cleveland Indians right-hander Bob Feller, attempting to set a strikeout record, would have his legendary fastball timed before the game using a device invented by the War Department. Obtaining use of the device and setting it up at home plate was child's play compared to convincing the financially astute Feller to participate in the experiment. Griffith finally talked Feller into going through with it, playing on Feller's sense of fair play to not cheat the crowd, numbered by game time at some 20,000. Feller's sense of fair play was considerably heightened when Griffith wrote him a personal check for $700 to participate in the stunt.

Feller made five pitches into the maw of the machine, the fastest of which was clocked at 98.6 miles per hour. The crowd loved it, especially when Feller's final pitch hit the sturdy wooden frame of the device and splintered it.

Taking all this in on the top step of the Washington Senators dugout was Bobo Newsom. For the past ten years, he had pitched in the shadow of Feller. Here was an ideal time for a little payback.

As Feller arrived at his dugout, Newsom sprang from his. The crowd recognized him immediately—at 6-feet-3 and 230 pounds and wearing 00 on the back of his uniform, he was hard to miss—and launched into a rhythmic cheer. Newsom took to the mound, toed the rubber and stared in at the device. Then he went into the most elaborate windup in baseball, triple-pumping his arms, reaching far back, extending his arms above his head, kicking his left leg high in the air, and pausing for a full second before letting the ball fly.

However, instead of his best Sunday fastball, Newsom released a blooper pitch. It sailed into the humid night air, seemingly hung there forever, and finally floated through the machine's window and into the catcher's glove.

Newsom's toss totally flummoxed the device, which failed to come up with a reading on the ultra-slow pitch. The crowd didn't care. D.C. fans gave him a standing ovation as he sauntered back to the Senators dugout.[3]

Given such antics, Newsom was called many things, not all of them flattering, by his contemporaries. One sportswriter dismissed his career as that of a poor man's Dizzy Dean. Newsom would accept that label, quite literally. Dean became a wealthy man;

Bobo died virtually penniless. As to their pitching skills, Dean might have had a slight edge in ability, but Newsom had him beat nine ways to hell in terms of durability. The reality is that the *Baseball Encyclopedia* contains many one-year wonders and pitchers who put together two or three outstanding years and then flamed out, the victims of injury, ego or "WWS" disease, as in wine, women and song. There have been only a handful of All-Star-caliber pitchers who were able to extend their major league careers beyond 20 years, and with few exceptions all are in the Hall of Fame except Newsom.

A trait Dean and Newsom shared was an addiction to bragging. "He's the only man in baseball who can strut sitting down," Arthur Daley of the *New York Times* said of Newsom, sounding the sentiments of nearly every other sportswriter who encountered Bobo.[4] But the reality was that the younger Newsom—then known as Buck—won 20 games for three straight years (1938–1940) in a talent-laden American League. There was plenty worth bragging about, especially in 1940 when Newsom almost single-handedly pitched the Detroit Tigers to a world championship. At that point, no one in baseball or the media would have doubted that Newsom was headed for the Hall of Fame. Even the older Newsom—the one now known as Bobo—had his moments, including a brilliant stretch of pitching for the 1947 champion New York Yankees. And the accomplishment of playing pro ball for nearly 30 years looms larger and larger. Given the facts, it's fair to say Newsom didn't brag enough.

Shirley Povich, who covered Newsom's antics for the *Washington Post* for over 20 years, sized up Newsom in the spring of 1935 and never had reason to back away from his evaluation. "What manner of man is this Buck Newsom?" Povich wrote in his "This Morning" column on May 30. "Methinks he is no jabbering jack-wit, nor yet a supreme egoist who is as great a pitcher as he'd have you believe. I think he's a smart guy, a fair-to-middlin' pitcher, and a consummate showman who knows how the money can be made in the big leagues.... When he wins, the other club is a bunch of semi-pros. When he loses, the other club was lucky. You can't beat him. You can't even tie him."[5]

While a gifted fabulist, Newsom was (like most athletes) a lousy historian. He could be wildly entertaining and supremely able to bend the truth to make for a better punch line, but his was definitely a selective memory. Considering what is now known about Newsom's life, the bragging and tale tales appear to be a symptom of insecurity, a defense mechanism designed to hide heartbreak.

It bears mentioning that Newsom, born in 1907 in South Carolina, was a true son of the post-bellum South, raised in the wake of the region's bitter defeat in the War Between the States. Paul Hemphill, in writing about country music legend Hank Williams (another talented, broken-hearted soul), notes that the "psychic fallout from the South's loss was overwhelming in places like rural Alabama." And in Newsom's rural South Carolina. Those like Williams and Newsom who entered the public arena in the first half of the 20th century were "burdened with a sense that they were inferior to other Americans," claims Hemphill. Hank Williams' reaction to that inferiority complex was to write and sing. Newsom's was to pitch and talk.[6]

Psychologically, Williams and Newsom would no doubt agree on one thing: If my pay envelope is fat enough, I'm the equal of any man.

For an individual who took the nickname Bobo and often adopted a bumpkin persona, Newsom was anything but a fool. Those who thought they could take advantage of him soon had reason to regret it. Every owner and general manager who argued salary with him would attest to his tenacity. He was far ahead of the curve in terms of baseball's economics, and in some interviews articulated themes that would not be heard again until the time of Marvin Miller. Of course, for Miller it was a question of fairness. For Newsom, it was a question of getting all he could get while he could get it.

"I'd rather be lucky than good," Newsom told Arthur Daley. "Pitching good ball is important, but good luck is even more important."[7] Newsom's luck, in baseball at least, was remarkably bad.

Newsom was certainly unlucky to have played in an era when managers and general managers were notable for a near-absolute absence of a sense of humor. Lacking the ability to laugh off much of what Newsom did and all of what he said made managing him an impossible task. In addition, the unpleasantness of his relationship with his father no doubt prevented any subsequent authority figure from reining him in. As far as Newsom was concerned, pro baseball existed only for his own entertainment and financial gain. Anyone who threatened either of those goals was going to catch the full blast of Newsom's fury.

Newsom also had the misfortune to pitch at a time when ballplayers were expected to keep their egos in check. In contrast, Newsom had the gift—or curse—of turning every conversation onto paths of his own interests. His was a self-interest of immense size, and it made him a very difficult teammate (and husband and father). Despite the length of his career, he formed few lasting relationships with fellow players. Virtually all the players interviewed for this book expressed thoughts similar to Johnny Sullivan, a teammate of Newsom's on the 1940s Senators: "I thought he was great, but he was like that purple cow. I'd rather see one than be one."[8]

A story told by longtime Newsom crony Bob Shirley perhaps explains why.

> We were out driving in one of Buck's great big Cadillacs. We buzz through a small town and Newsom sees a bum sitting with his head down on the curb. So he decides he's gonna help this guy.
>
> He stops the Caddy, gets out and gives the bum a long pep talk. Then he gives him $5 and tells him to go to the diner across the street and get a good, hot meal. He gets back in the car and is talking about what a good deed he's done when he looks in the rear-view mirror and sees the bum making for a bar instead of the diner.
>
> Buck lets out a yell, jumps out of the car, grabs the bum and drags him into the diner. Then he orders a meal for him, and we sit there the whole time until the bum has eaten every single bite. He tells the bum, "When Buck Newsom buys you dinner, you God-damned well are gonna eat it!"
>
> It was all pointless kindness ... but to Buck it meant something. Even in giving, he wanted it on his own terms. You either accepted his behavior or you stayed the hell away.[9]

Newsom was definitely a rara avis. The success he did have in baseball was almost in spite of himself. He could be loud and ill-behaved. He could also be overbearing, petulant, whiny and stubborn. Author John Lardner, in the best profile in print of Newsom, called him an "erratic natural force" whose behavior and pitching could "fluctuate swiftly from the sublime to the unspeakable."[10] If his ego was of epic proportions, his over-indulgences were positively Ruthian. But, always, he was Bobo. Introspection was never high on his list of things to do. If he had any deep regrets, they were never made public.

What is notable, from a 21st-century viewpoint, is just how far ahead of his time Newsom was. His career more closely resembles that of a modern-day rock star rather than a professional athlete. He grasped that the only reason a sane person would pay money to see an inept baseball team was the promise of seeing someone do something so outrageous it would remain a memory long after the final score was mercifully forgotten. Newsom consistently delivered, putting on a show even in meaningless exhibition games or late-season outings with only a few hundred fans rattling around the ballpark. He knew his worth exactly and forced owners to pay him accordingly or suffer the consequences. Those consequences could be quite painful, financially and psychically. He firmly believed he wasn't crazy, but had no qualms about driving others to that state. For all his quirks, while he toiled he made the major leagues a brighter place. Most remarkably, in spite of everything, he was a damn good country pitcher.

Certainly, he was an anomaly within his own family. Kinfolk learned to maintain a certain distance, to the extent that more than one surviving Newsom relation describes Bobo as "the black sheep" of the family.[11] It was from his family that Newsom, at a very early age, sought to flee. Once he began the journey, it never ended until the end of his days. The game of baseball took him to hundreds of places. It brought him fame, and for one brief moment he was the most famous baseball player in the world. The journey also brought heartbreak, for nothing Newsom ever did was small.

Bobo's travels ended long ago. Only the memories of those who knew him remain. And they do remember, for Bobo Newsom was unforgettable.

One

Hartsville, South Carolina (1907–1927)

Louis Norman Newsome was born on the evening of August 11, 1907, in his parents' home on a farm near Hartsville, SC. No birth certificate marking the event has been found, and it is doubtful one was ever issued. But a handful of legal documents do exist that confirm the date and location, which is important because Louis Norman Newsome spent considerable time and effort in his adult years attempting to obscure the issue. It was merely one of his many idiosyncrasies.[1]

At an early age, he decided he didn't care for Louis and preferred to be called Norman. When Norman was 12, his uncle J. R. "Jake" Newsome gave him the nickname of

Bobo Newsom's birthplace, Hartsville, South Carolina. The brick façade is a later alteration. The structure now houses the offices of Drew Case, an engineer and land surveyor. The current address is 304 East Bobo Newsom Highway (author's photograph).

Buck, claiming he resembled one of the sharecroppers working their fathers' farms.[2] That stuck with him, so much so that his own family always called him Buck, never Louis or Norman.[3] When he reached a point in life when he could select his own nickname, he chose Bobo. He also opted to knock the last "e" out of Newsome, on the rationale it was always being left out of the box scores anyway.

No one is absolutely sure where the nickname Bobo came from. It is true that, as an adult making his mark in baseball, the man then known as Buck Newsom had great difficulty remembering names, and eventually took to referring to those of the male half of the human race as Bobo. The most likely explanation for the label is that Newsom used "bo"—short for boy—as a greeting, and since he had a tendency to stutter it came out as bo-bo.[4] It has also been suggested that "bobo" was the young Norman's corruption of "bubba," a standard Southern version of brother. Then there's the fact that in Spanish, bobo translates to "fool"; it's likely that Newsom eventually became aware of this. Newsom also became aware that a bobo, in carnival lingo, means a hanger-on, or more specifically, a big, dumb person willing to do the heavy lifting. He also knew that a bobo, in boxing parlance, is a human punching bag. There are elements of all these meanings in Newsom's use of Bobo to describe himself and all other males. Mainly, it was a very catchy appellation and Newsom found it useful. Everyone remembers a Bobo. A possibly revealing trait is that when Newsom signed autographs for his many admirers, he rendered the nickname as "Bo-Bo," a reflection of his oft-stated wish for a double helping of everything life has to offer.

By the late 1930s, he came into his own as Bobo Newsom. By that point in his life, he earnestly desired to put as much distance between himself and his father as humanly possible.

Louis and Norman were family names, one from each side of Bobo's antecedents. His mother Lillian, maiden name Hicks, was a native of South Carolina, as were her parents and grandparents. His father, Henry Quillion Buffkin Newsome, was also a native of South Carolina, as were his parents and grandparents. The Hicks and Newsomes had migrated to the Hartsville area, in the northeast corner of the state, during the 1890s. There, H. Q. B., known to his family as Quill, met and married Lillian. He was 27 and she was 19 when they were married in the Methodist church in Hartsville on June 26, 1899. By then, Quill had already established a prosperous cotton farm on the southern outskirts of Hartsville Township. Lillian's father was the town's only pharmacist. She never quite adjusted to life on the farm, although the couple worked hard at producing crops and children, not necessarily in that order. A son, Marion, was born in 1900, and a daughter, Aline, in 1904. A second son, Louis, came along in 1907, and a second daughter, Lillian Belle, was born in 1915.[5]

The principle crop on the H. Q. B. Newsome farm was cotton, although Quill also experimented with other cash crops including peanuts, potatoes and peaches. Like all the surrounding farmers, Quill also maintained a vegetable garden and various livestock to sustain his family. It was a way of life deeply ingrained in the area and still in evidence today. Cotton was definitely king in Darlington County, and Hartsville cotton was especially prized due to its large bolls and soft texture.[6]

Quill and Lillian did not lack for companionship on the farm, even though it was five miles removed from the center of Hartsville. They were literally surrounded by

Newsomes. Quill's brothers owned farms on three sides of his, and the Newsome name eventually became quite prominent in the Hartsville phone directory. In fact, the junction of state highways 15 and 151, on the western boundary of Quill Newsome's property, came to be known as Newsome Corners.

"There are Newsoms and Newsomes everywhere you look in Hartsville," said John Newsome, a cousin of Bobo.

> It's a rather large family tree. It would take an expert in genealogy to sort it all out, but in Hartsville it all started with the four Newsome brothers settling here back in the 1890s. There was Quill, J. R., who everybody called Jake, George and Willington, who everybody called Willie. Eventually, two of the brothers dropped the "e" from Newsome and the other two kept it. No logical reason that I know of, just a personal preference.
>
> In the case of Buck, the baseball box scores were always dropping the final "e" anyway and supposedly he just got tired of it and dropped it himself. The rest of his side of the family followed suit. The family saying is, you're a Newsome until you become rich or famous, and then you become a Newsom.[7]

The home where Louis Norman Newsome was born in the summer of 1907 still stands. The farm surrounding it is long gone, but the farmhouse is still there. It now contains the offices of Drew Case, a surveyor and realtor. Case said,

> From looking at records, the house was built in 1894. It's had several owners since the Newsome family last owned it in the 1940s. It's been added on to and remodeled, and all the outbuildings are long gone. But the living room, parlor and kitchen are pretty much as they were in 1907, when Bobo Newsom was born here.[8]

The home's current address is 304 East Bobo Newsom Highway. It remains outside of the city proper.

> The Highway 151 bypass, which they now call the Bobo Newsom Highway, was nothing but a one-lane dirt road when Bobo was growing up here. Back then, I don't think it even ran all the way through to the county seat at Darlington. Of course, if it rained the road was impassable anyway. So this was really out in the country back then.

It quickly became apparent that farm living wasn't the life for Norman Newsome. As an adult, he described Daddy Quill's farm as a plantation, complete with 13-room mansion and servants aplenty.[9] This was clearly fanciful, an attempt to create a dreamland out of the drudgery that was the Newsomes' lot in life. A hyperactive child, Norman lacked the patience of the true farmer. Family legend has it that Norman, when still a small boy, once planted a peach pit on the property, hoping to soon sink his teeth into the tasty fruit. When he came out the next day and nothing had sprouted, he dug up the offending pit and tossed it far into the adjoining field. The notion of planting a crop and nurturing it for several months, then painstakingly harvesting it and bargaining to sell it to the highest bidder was completely foreign to Norman's impulsive nature.

Another family legend is even more revealing of Norman's distaste for the rural lifestyle. By the time he was a teenager, Norman found day-to-day duties on the farm boring, and his father's dictates insufferable. By 1920, Quill's operations had become successful enough for the farm to support a few sharecroppers. Norman grew attached to them, so different from his own family. Tallulah Williams, another of Bobo's cousins, said,

> At that time, the sharecroppers were black families, of course. They lived in shacks to the north of Quill's farm. So there came a day when work was over that Buck marched off

north with a family of sharecroppers instead of heading south back to his home. He and his daddy had a big argument, both were very stubborn individuals, and Buck wanted to get in the last word so he told his daddy he'd rather stay with the sharecroppers than go home.

Daddy Quill just let him go. A couple days later, the father of the family came up to him and said, "Mr. Quill sir, you have to take Mr. Buck back now. I can't afford him anymore. He eats more than the rest of my family put together."

It was certainly true that young Buck hated working on that farm. He was looking for a way to escape. Fortunately for him, he found it in baseball.[10]

A failure as a farmer, Norman also wasn't a natural-born scholar. Sitting in a stuffy classroom was his idea of cruel and unusual punishment. He attended Hartsville public schools, on and off, for several years and had a bright, inquisitive mind. But he felt claustrophobic trapped inside a schoolhouse, and lacked the ability to focus on a teacher's lecture for longer than a few minutes.[11]

There were those, including some of his own family members, who regarded the young Norman as both lazy and dumb. Thus it is perhaps all the more remarkable that he made his reputation in baseball by being a tireless worker and gifted conversationalist. In later years, when Newsom spun a tale of having attended prestigious Georgia Tech, most teammates and even sportswriters believed it.[12] In reality, Norman started cutting class sometime around the fourth grade and stopped attending school altogether shortly thereafter. He would head off in the morning in the general direction of Hartsville Public School, but rarely reached that destination. Instead, he was far more likely to wander around town, taking in the sights and talking to the merchants.

By 1915, Hartsville was a bustling place. In addition to rail service, Hartsville had a cotton mill, a saw mill, a paper plant and a furniture factory. The downtown area featured dozens of shops. A favorite roosting place for Norman became the barber shop. There, there was talk aplenty, most of it about baseball or boll weevils, as well as well-thumbed copies of *The Police Gazette, Baseball Magazine, The Sporting News* and *Sporting Life*.[13]

Southerners were very much in the minority in major league baseball ranks in the pre–1920 period. However, two of the very best players were Georgia's Ty Cobb and South Carolina's Joe Jackson.[14] In the decade from 1911 to 1920, a frequently heard barber shop argument was over whether Cobb or Jackson was the best hitter in baseball. Cobb had the higher batting average, but Jackson had the better power numbers. The high eminence of Cobb and Jackson unquestionably inspired many a Southern boy to take up baseball in the years leading up to World War I.

Newsom's interest in baseball was certainly sparked by the likes of Cobb and Jackson, and further when he discovered major league players were paid, sometimes very well indeed, to play the sport. No doubt Newsom's vision of the big leagues as a staging ground for individual glory was formed at this time. Also likely formed at this time was his belief that outstanding athletic performance must be rewarded. Ty Cobb, by virtue of his talents and aggressive negotiating come contract time, had become the highest-paid player in baseball.[15] Newsom absorbed that lesson, as well as the legend of Greenville's Joe Jackson. Countless baseball fans, then and later, embraced the myth that "Shoeless Joe" was so underpaid that he was forced to throw games in the 1919 World Series in order to make decent wages.[16] Jackson's alleged plight no doubt stuck with Newsom, for as an adult he engaged in seemingly endless arguments with team owners and general managers over money, the arguments always boiling down to "you got it and I need it."

Later on, when the lad everyone now called Buck entered his teen years and began his baseball playing in earnest, Texas native Rogers Hornsby was tearing up the National League, winning batting titles from 1920 through 1925. Hornsby became a Newsom idol, especially so because Newsom enjoyed being smack-dab in the middle of things playing second base, the position Hornsby played for the St. Louis Cardinals.

As an adolescent, Newsom was also fascinated by the exploits of Babe Ruth, as was virtually all of America in the 1920s. It was of particular interest to young Norman that (a) nobody called Ruth by his given first name of George, and (b) Ruth, by virtue of his extraordinary talent and flamboyant nature, became the center of attention in everything he did. The notions of teamwork and humbleness might be all right for farmers and run-of-the-mill ballplayers, but they would never do for Newsom. He would either be the star of the show, or a no-show.

By age 8, Norman was hooked on baseball. In contrast, his father had absolutely no interest in the sport, and very little interest in anything other than running the family farm. Quill's enterprise had become quite profitable, especially when cotton prices escalated dramatically due to increased demand during World War I. In later press accounts, Quill is frequently referred to as a "prominent" or "prosperous" farmer, and clearly he was successful at his chosen profession, as were his brothers. The price of success was that the farm needed constant attention, and Quill had no time for something as trivial as a baseball game, even if it involved his son.[17]

Occasionally, Norman could indulge his baseball fancies by talking his older brother Marion into playing catch or taking him to see a local game. Usually, Marion was kept too busy with his chores to entertain Norman. Despite lack of encouragement from Daddy Quill, it quickly became apparent to Marion and others that Norman was something of a child prodigy at baseball. Already large for his age, he often played with boys in their teens, and more than held his own. At age nine, he could throw a baseball as fast as someone twice his age. This Marion found out, the hard way, when he and Norman were playing catch and Norman reared back and let go with his best fastball. The pitch broke through the flimsy webbing on Marion's glove and struck him in the face, breaking his nose. That was the end of Marion's baseball-playing days. "After that, he was afraid of the ball," Bobo claimed. "Once you get that little bit of fear in you, you can't play worth a damn."[18] John Newsome said,

> It's safe to say that Buck was an outstanding athlete. You don't get to the major leagues unless you're pretty darn good. Funny thing is, no one else that I know of in the entire family was any great shakes in sports. So it wasn't like it was in the genes for Buck to become a great ballplayer. Who knows where his ability came from? Likely it was just sheer determination, determination to be something that sets you apart from everybody else.
>
> The one thing I'm sure Buck did inherit was his gift of gab. That definitely runs in the family. It's no surprise that several Newsomes have become very successful used car salesmen. And I'm not letting out any family secrets when I tell you that our family reunions can be pretty lively events, with everybody talking at once. Newsomes love to talk.[19]

Fortunately for Norman, there were plenty of other kids who were willing and able to take to the sandlots in and around Hartsville to play baseball. It never took Norman long to talk his way into a game. "Buck never met a stranger," Tallulah Williams said. "He had absolutely no fear of going up to folks and introducing himself. So he usually wound up as the leader of whatever activity he got involved with. And that activity was usually baseball, since playing baseball was his favorite thing to do."[20]

Norman simply tucked his glove and cap into his back pockets and took to the road, looking for games. If no kids were handy, sometimes he joined in games with grown men, sometimes with teams of African American players. Blacks constituted the majority of the population in Darlington County, and Newsom literally grew up in their midst. While many of Quill's generation viewed "colored folk" as scapegoats for every bad thing that had happened to the South since the War Between the States, including famine and boll weevils, Newsom grew to identify with them, as one outsider to another. It's doubtful he ever considered them equals—who of his race, generation and background did?—but there is ample evidence from his baseball career that he didn't see the simple act of sharing a baseball glove or bat with an African American as the ruination of the South.[21]

Quill Newsom, not exactly thrilled with his youngest son's dismal attendance record at school, was positively appalled at Norman's fascination with baseball, and his willingness to rub shoulders with all and sundry. To the elder Newsom, education was important, baseball was a waste of time and mingling with non-family members usually led to no good. Bob Shirley, a longtime acquaintance of Newsom's in Hartsville, said,

> Bobo's old man was all business, he had no time for stuff like baseball. He'd send Bobo out into the field to do plowing or picking and Bobo would cut out. He had his baseball glove and baseball cap hidden in a tree stump, and he'd fetch 'em and off he'd go, looking for a ballgame.
>
> Sometimes Daddy Quill would catch Bobo running off and take out his razor strap and cut Bobo's ass. Bobo said his dad always told him, "You're never going to amount to a row of beans with that ball glove tucked in your back pocket." Truthfully, Bobo and his dad just didn't get along, and the baseball playing was only a part of it. Daddy Quill was proud of what he did, farming, and wanted his sons to do exactly the same thing. Bobo hated farming, hated everything about it. So it's not hard to see why those two were always at odds.[22]

In temperament, Norman clearly took after his mother Lillian. He much preferred staying in the kitchen and helping his mother prepare meals. Lillian was emotionally fragile and increasingly unhappy with the day-to-day drudgery of her life. The kitchen was the first and last stop on the farm assembly line, and the place where Lillian was the least unhappy, because the kitchen was the one place where she was the undisputed boss. Bobo's love of food, and food preparation, undoubtedly stemmed from the many hours he spent helping his mother in the kitchen. Lillian had a habit of muttering as she prepared pies, cakes and roasts, and Bobo absorbed the practice, later subconsciously putting it to use as he labored on the pitcher's mound. His sense of humor and love of exaggeration were also obtained from his mother, who used humor in an attempt to brighten her lot in life.[23]

Another of Newsom's favorite activities as a child was sitting next to the large window in the front parlor and watching the dirt road in front of the house for signs of travelers. Occasionally his efforts were rewarded by the sight of a horseless carriage. These were quite the novelty in the rural South during Bobo's childhood, enough of a novelty to make them eye-catchers. And ear-catchers, their noise being in marked contrast to the quiet clip-clop of a horse and buggy. Norman was thrilled when he saw an automobile, and he developed a love affair with cars that lasted the rest of his life. The speed, sound and fury of the automobile had instant appeal. As a boy, he equated owning a car with success, and endeavored to own the biggest, brightest model in town. In this quest he was ultimately successful.[24]

Other than the annual cotton auction and an occasional traveling minstrel show, baseball was the chief form of entertainment in Hartsville during Bobo's childhood. Very few households had the primitive crystal-set radios, and even Victrolas were scarce. But baseball could be played from ages five to 50, and required little other than open land and sunny weather, both of which Darlington County has in abundance.

Newsom spent every spare hour playing baseball in some form or fashion. Occasionally, on weekends in the summer, he hitched a ride all the way west to Columbia to watch the Columbia Reds of the South Atlantic League play. The Reds featured the best brand of baseball available in the Carolinas, plus the excitement of a big crowd in a real stadium. The experience definitely helped define Newsom's dream of playing pro ball, so much so that when he decided to turn pro the Columbia Reds were the first team he tried out for.

In Hartsville, the best ball teams were those at the high school and the Sonoco paper plant. By the time he was 15, Newsom was playing for both, despite the fact that he wasn't a student at Hartsville High School or a Sonoco employee. For, by age 15, Newsom was arguably the best player in town. Already six feet tall and a solid 160 pounds, Newsom could run, hit and throw like a grown man. His most prominent features—wide shoulders, long arms and huge hands—were already in evidence.

"Oooh, he could throw a ball," remembered L. L. "Luke" Sparrow, who played with him on the Hartsville High and Sonoco teams. "You had to have a thick mitt to protect the pocket, and if you didn't it would burn you. Most of the time, I'd put in some kind of sponge in the glove to cushion it. He could just burn it up."[25]

Newsom's baseball skills made him much in demand on Saturdays, Sundays and weekday evenings during the spring and summer months. The Sonoco team was a well-run semi-pro outfit, playing its games in the Palmetto League. Newsom was paid for playing for Sonoco, his first gainful employment. In addition to the standard $2-a-game stipend, for stars of a big game fans would pass the hat afterward and reward their chosen favorites with fistfuls of cash. Often as not, Newsom (now going exclusively by the nickname of Buck) was the star of the games he played in, making the experience of throwing, hitting and catching a baseball a lucrative one.

All this activity on the diamond came at the expense of both Norman's studies and his chores on Daddy Quill's farm. This made for heated discussions at the Newsome dinner table, on those occasions when Norman made it home in time for dinner.

While records are sketchy at best, Newsom apparently played at least two seasons with the Hartsville High team before someone—no doubt the coach of a rival team—complained to the high school principal about his highly questionable amateur and academic status.[26] Dr. William Thornwell, the Hartsville principal, summoned Newsom to his office, only to discover that Newsom was not only not in school that day, he had never been sighted anywhere on campus other than the baseball field. Finally located

The Sonoco company baseball team, 1922. The much-older-looking 15-year-old Norman Newsome is third from right, front row. The team played in the semi-professional Palmetto League (courtesy Hartsville Museum).

in town and ushered into Dr. Thornwell's office, Newsom was lectured on the importance of education and the need to attend classes. His response? "Shoot, doc, I can't do that. That would take away from my time playing baseball. Why should I go to school anyway? Hell, right now I'm probably making more than you are."[27]

Given the state of public education in South Carolina in the 1920s, this may have been one of Bobo's tamer exaggerations. The upshot of the conference was that Newsom said no to school and Dr. Thornwell said no to any further appearances by Newsom in a HHS uniform.

However, before he was barred from the ranks of the Red Foxes, as the Hartsville High team was known, Newsom had a couple of interesting experiences, both of which foreshadowed the triumphs and travails of his major league career. He was the starting second baseman for the Red Foxes, and over the course of several games took to harassing the Hartsville pitcher, who was having great difficulty getting batters out. Finally, on a day when Newsom was already riding the pitcher mercilessly as he took his pre-game warmups, the offended hurler challenged him with that classic line, "If you think you can do any better, you try it." Newsom, given the start on very short notice and having never before pitched in an actual game, proceeded to strike out 17 batters. According to Newsom, he still lost the game, 1–0, when the opposing team scored a run in the ninth inning on a pair of errors by the Hartsville second baseman—the same player who had challenged Newsom to change positions in the first place.

The other classic Newsom story regarding the Hartsville High team came when the Red Foxes were set to face their arch-rivals from neighboring Lydia. In the run-up to the game, Newsom had been taking a fair share of good-natured ribbing from some of the older Hartsville players. Newsom took exception to the remarks and when it came time to board the bus at the high school for the trip to Lydia, he was nowhere to be found. The Hartsville players waited as long as they could, but no Buck Newsome. So they traveled southwest to Lydia. Upon arrival, they saw the Lydia team taking infield practice, and off to the side the Lydia starting pitcher warming up for the big game. And that starting pitcher was none other than Buck Newsome. He beat Hartsville that day (in some accounts, he pitched a no-hitter) but the hard feelings were patched up afterward and Buck returned to the Hartsville nine in time for the next game.

His experiences with both the Hartsville High School and Sonoco teams did teach Newsom an important lesson: Not only was the pitcher the center of attention, he also commanded the biggest payday. While position players could fetch only $2 to $5 a game, a top-notch pitcher was always in demand and could ask for, and receive, upwards of $20 a game. While Newsom loved playing second base, he definitely could see the possibilities that pitching presented.

The Hartsville, South Carolina, High School Red Foxes baseball team, 1923. The 16-year-old Norman Newsome is second from left, front row (courtesy Hartsville Museum).

"He did want you to agree with him," Luke Sparrow said of the teen-aged Newsom. "[If you didn't agree] he would get mad at you. He could be very domineering that way. He had a very high opinion of himself and expected you to see things the same way."[28]

By the time of Newsom's 16th birthday, his father despaired of curing him of the "bad habit" of playing baseball. Since Buck was no longer maintaining the pretense of attending public school—"he just didn't have education on his mind" was the way Sparrow put it—Daddy Quill decided to ship him off to Carlisle Fitting School.[29]

Despite its fancy name, Carlisle School, located in Bamberg due south of Columbia, had more than its share of incorrigible youths, boys who had washed out of public school. Some even referred to it as a "reform school." Whether or not that is a fair assessment, it must have seemed like prison to a free-spirited youth like Louis Newsome.[30] Carlisle administrators attempted to have the all-male student body maintain military discipline (in 1932 the institution became a full-fledged military school). The idea was for Carlisle students to progress academically and socially to the point where they could qualify to enter nearby Wofford College as freshmen. Newsom got no closer to Wofford than the front gate. He stuck it out for a few weeks at Carlisle before running away and finding his way back home to Hartsville. In later years, Newsom told sportswriters he served time on an "honor farm" in South Carolina; likely, he was referring to his brief stint at Carlisle. Oddly enough, from his first days in pro baseball Newsom freely gave out the information that he had attended Carlisle (in contrast, he never claimed to be a graduate of Hartsville High).[31]

Education, baseball and family squabbles were all pushed forcibly into the background in late 1924. Lillian's "spells" had become more frequent, and Mr. and Mrs. Newsome agreed to see a specialist "in female problems" in Darlington on December 19. It is not known what the doctor told Lillian that day. She had turned 44 earlier in the year and it may well be that the onset of peri-menopause added one more burden to her litany of physical and mental woes.

Riding back from Darlington with her husband to the family farm, Lillian fell, jumped or was pushed from the car. Since no one was traveling in the car with Quill and Lillian and no other motorist witnessed the event, it will never be known exactly how it happened that Lillian tumbled out of the car. What is known is that she struck her head on the pavement and was run over by the car's rear wheels. By the time Quill stopped the car, Lillian lay dead on the pavement of Highway 151.[32]

Quill's version was that Lillian must have accidentally leaned against the door handle, the door flew open and she fell out of the car. In the absence of any other evidence to the contrary, that was the version eventually accepted by the authorities. Tallulah Williams said,

> Frankly, I'm not sure even to this day how Lillian died. I doubt if it was accidental. Did she jump out? Do I think she was pushed out? I don't know. I do know the topic of her death was whispered about at family reunions for a long time after it happened. I suppose the most logical explanation is that she took her own life. It was a very strange thing, people don't just fall out of cars out on the highway. It was definitely our family scandal, and I'm sure it had a huge impact on Lillian's children.[33]

No one was impacted more by Lillian's bizarre death than her youngest son, Louis. Unlike the authorities, he blamed his father for his mother's death, and the event strained an already tenuous relationship to the breaking point. At age 17, Buck ran away from the farm and became something of a hobo, reportedly spending time with a carnival as it toured the South. He later told teammates he learned how to pitch while manning the knock-down-the-milk-bottles booth at a carnival. Many of his favorite expressions were of carny derivation, including the nickname Bobo. More importantly, his philosophy of life seems to have been cemented in place at this time. His obsession with self-promotion, his difficulties in establishing lasting relationships, his suspicion of those in authority, and the sense that he always needed to stay on the move likely stemmed from his troubled teenage years.[34]

In truth, were it not for his remarkable gifts as a baseball player, Louis Newsom would no doubt have been lost to history. Baseball gave him a safety net in life, something he could always fall back on.

In the summer of 1926, still very much on the outs with his father, Newsom caught on with a semi-pro team in Cheraw, SC. Cheraw played its games in the Sand Hill League, one of several semi-pro leagues in the Carolinas that offered a highly competitive brand of baseball. The Sand Hill League served as both a springboard to organized baseball for youngsters and a final stop for older men who had already played in the minor leagues.[35] Newsom quickly became the pitching star for Cheraw, for the first time expanding his fame beyond his hometown of Hartsville. During the course of his first season with Cheraw, he met a young lady named Lucille Arant who regularly came out to watch the games. Eventually, the teenagers began dating, and throughout the winter of 1926–1927 were a "steady item."[36]

Despite the fact that Lucille knew the uncertain lives of ballplayers, and had to

Downtown Hartsville, South Carolina, circa 1925. W.W. Shirley's barber shop, a favorite hangout of the teen-age Newsom, is located in the row of buildings to the left (courtesy Hartsville Museum).

know after a few dates with Buck that he wasn't exactly prime husband material, the pair became engaged and, on February 17, 1927, were married in Lucille's hometown of Chesterfield, 15 miles northwest of Cheraw on the South Carolina-North Carolina border. They set up housekeeping in a boarding house in Cheraw, and with the advent of warm weather Newsom resumed his baseball activities.

Daddy Quill made one final pitch to his youngest son in an attempt to get him to drop baseball and take up farming, offering Buck and his new bride free room and board at the farm in return for their labors. However, Buck brought an "agent" to these negotiations in the person of his Uncle Jake. Jake, unlike his older brother, was both a big baseball fan and far more sensitive to Buck's true desires. Jake argued in favor of letting Buck pursue his baseball career. Daddy Quill, outnumbered 2-to-1 in the debate and outgunned by the considerable vocal power of his son, grudgingly agreed to allow Buck (at age 19, still technically a minor when it came to signing contracts) to play on, with the stipulation that, by leaving the farm, he was forfeiting any and all rights to the property or the profits derived from it. As would happen so many times in his adult life, Buck opted to leave a secure financial position for the uncertainties of new horizons.[37]

Newsom, by this time, was playing the outfield when not pitching for Cheraw. He had matured into an imposing physical specimen, a shade over 6-feet-2 and weighing 175 pounds. He appeared to possess all the "tools" necessary to play in organized baseball—he could run, hit and throw. Thus, it seemed only logical that he should take that next step and try out for a minor league team. Naturally, he chose his favorite, the Columbia Reds. A tryout date was arranged, a hat was passed among Cheraw's baseball fans to raise money for the Newsoms' room and board while in Columbia, and on a hot July day in 1927 Buck and Lucille set out for the South Carolina capital in a Ford Model T, borrowed from a family friend.

The Columbia Reds were managed by Gabby Street, a former major league catcher. They were affiliated with the St. Louis Cardinals of the National League, which meant if Newsom could catch on and make good in Columbia he would be on the fast track to the major leagues. It had to seem like a very promising opportunity for Buck and his new bride.

Street, well-versed in the workings of pro ball, arranged to have Newsom throw batting practice to the Columbia players. This saved the arms of his own pitchers and allowed Street to see how Newsom fared against real ballplayers, not those hicks from the Sand Hill League. The 19-year-old Newsom, for one of the few times in his life, was uneasy in his surroundings. After warming up, he began pitching batting practice but was unable to throw strikes. After a few minutes watching Columbia players bob and weave to avoid Newsom's errant deliveries, Street became agitated and began barking instructions. This helped not at all, as the next two Newsom deliveries completely missed the batting cage. The second one came within a whisker of hitting Street, who was standing next to the cage. That brought an abrupt end to Newsom's audition and led to his unceremonious exit from the Columbia ballpark. In Newsom's later recounting of the event, he pointed out that Street didn't even bother to leave him tickets for that afternoon's game.[38]

It was a turn of fate that would have convinced most men to find another line of work. But Newsom was not easily deterred, especially since the alternative to playing baseball for a living was returning to Daddy Quill's farm and admitting defeat. So back to Cheraw went Norman and Lucille, back to the cheap boarding house and the rigors and low pay of the Sand Hill League.

A story Newsom later told about his alleged time at Georgia Tech featured the revelation that he was ordered to throw a game by gamblers, refused and was attacked by a knife-welding thug afterward. This incident likely did happen, but not during Newsom's mythical stint at Tech. It is far more likely that it occurred while Newsom was pitching for Cheraw. Gamblers at the ballpark were a fact of sporting life throughout America in the pre–World War II period, and some of them would stop at nothing to make sure the game's outcome was favorable to their wager.[39]

Also at this time, Newsom discovered that fans always enjoy buying the star player a drink or two after the game. The pattern of his social life was thus set: baseball during the day, socializing at night. It was a pattern that plagued his marriage and eventually hastened his death.

Newsom's efforts for the Cheraw team finally paid off late in the summer of 1927. After an impressive pitching performance, he was cornered by a representative of Raleigh of the Piedmont League and signed to a contract, calling for him to report for spring training in March of 1928. A small signing bonus, undoubtedly less than $500, was negotiated.[40] Newsom welcomed the chance to show his abilities on a bigger stage. The contract did present the promise of steady wages for most of 1928, as well as reinvigorating his dream of ultimately playing in the major leagues like his boyhood heroes. It was also proof that Daddy Quill had been wrong about this baseball business. A man could really amount to something playing the game, and might even get to go to a few places beyond the sand hills of South Carolina.

Two

Raleigh to Brooklyn, via Greenville, Wilmington and Mobile (1928–1929)

Contrary to stories he later told, Bobo Newsom did not show up at training camp for Raleigh in the spring of 1928 riding a mule and with hay in his hair. However, he was naïve in the extreme as far as organized baseball was concerned. He brought Lucille with him, assuming she would be welcome to go wherever he went with the Raleigh team. And he assumed the team would pick up her tab for room and board. Neither assumption proved correct.

Raleigh was only 250 miles, as the crow flies, from Hartsville but it was a foreign land for Bobo—at this time referred to in press accounts as Norman Newsome. Raleigh was a bustling metropolis compared to sleepy Hartsville, and the Piedmont League was definitely big-time baseball. Even though the Piedmont was classified as only a C league on the then-existing scale of AA to D, Newsom quickly discovered that every player on every Piedmont team had been the star of his own hometown squad. And every player had the same desire: Make the major leagues. This wasn't a friendly little neighborhood game. It was cut-throat competition. Newsom wasn't ready. He barely knew how to pitch out of a stretch, change speeds on his pitches or field his position, and he lacked the discipline to learn.

It was a rough ride from the start for Newsom with the Raleigh Capitals. Newsom pitched 11 games in the Piedmont League that spring, with no wins to show for it. He was charged with five losses. In 53 innings, he gave up 64 hits and 46 runs, walking 33 batters and striking out only 21.[1] Despite his lack of success, it came as a complete surprise to Newsom—and Lucille—when he was released on May 20. Fortunately, a Raleigh teammate took pity on the couple and referred Newsom to Hal Weafer, the manager of the Greenville (NC). Tobacconists in the Eastern Carolina League. The ECL was Class D, the bottom of the organized baseball chain, but at least the towns in the league were closer in size to what the Newsoms were accustomed to. So Bobo and Lucille reported to Greenville, where Weafer not only added Newsom to the roster but agreed to put the Newsoms up at the Weafer family homestead. The latter proved to be a tactical mistake. Being around Newsom on the ball field was quite sufficient penitence for any manager; being around him 24/7 qualified as cruel and unusual punishment.[2]

At age 20, Newsom was highly sensitive, and his lack of success at Raleigh made him even more so. Weafer's attempts at tutoring were met first with indifference, then insolence and finally by open warfare. There was no such thing to young Newsom as constructive criticism—you were either for him or against him. Newsom later told writer John Lardner that he and Weafer fought on and off the ball field, and every night after dinner. At one point, Newsom was suspended for a couple days for throwing a beanball at Weafer during batting practice. According to Bobo, Lucille arranged a special reconciliation meal in an attempt to mend fences. That night, the fight began earlier than usual, right at the dinner table.

Weafer had enough problems keeping another opinionated right-hander on the Tobacconist staff, future major leaguer Johnny Allen, in tow. Allen and Newsom on the same club was simply two too many nonconformists.

After a month of combat, Weafer concluded that Newsom was more trouble than he was worth—the first but not the last of Newsom's managers to make that determination. That Newsom was winless in seven games with Greenville certainly factored into Weafer's decision. For the second time that spring, Newsom was cut loose. According to Newsom family legend, his contract was sold to fellow Eastern Carolina League member Wilmington for $18 and two slightly used baseball bats.[3]

Newsom's professional baseball career was only two months old and already he had been released, suspended and traded, with the sum total of zero wins to show for it. Most men would have given up the dream at that point and headed back home, but to Newsom home was infinitely worse that losing baseball games. At least in pro baseball he was getting paid to quarrel with authority figures. Back on the farm, he would again be under Daddy Quill's thumb—something he found intolerable in the extreme.

At Wilmington, the Newsoms decided to split up for the time being. Lucille went home to her parents in Chesterfield, while Bobo stayed for a last-ditch attempt to save his chosen career. Perhaps Lucille's departure removed a distraction, or perhaps the urgency of his situation finally dawned on Bobo. Whatever the case, when the weather warmed up so did his pitching. With his career at an early crossroads, he caught fire. He went 15–3 for Wilmington the remainder of the 1928 season, including 12 wins in a row. For the season in the ECL, Newsom finished at 15–6, pitching 172 innings and allowing only 155 hits. He also occasionally played the outfield, for the Norman "Buck" Newsome of 1928 was a remarkable athlete, tall and trim, who could run like his namesake and hold his own with the bat, at least against ECL pitching. He hit .340 that year, the highest batting mark he would ever compile in pro ball. His tumultuous 1928 season, his first in organized baseball, would have been exceptional for anyone else. For Bobo Newsom, it proved to be the norm.

Newsom's heroics with Wilmington caught the eye of major league scouts, the so-called "bird dogs" that were vital to baseball until the installation of the amateur draft in 1965. In the winter of 1928–1929, Newsom's contract was purchased by Brooklyn of the National League. Lost to history is who recommended Newsom to the Dodgers, but it might even have been Weafer, who later in life was named a full-time Dodgers scout.[4] Another account has it that Newsom was recommended to John McGraw, manager of the New York Giants. McGraw had a network of scouts throughout the U.S., so it is certainly possible one of them tipped him off to Newsom. McGraw had no interest in acquiring the headstrong youngster, but someone in the Giants front office slipped the recommendation to Wilbert Robinson, manager of the Dodgers. However it happened, Newsom was now property of the Dodgers and was proud to let everybody know about it back in Hartsville.[5]

The Dodgers, realizing full well that Bobo wasn't ready for the major leagues, assigned him to Macon (GA) in the South Atlantic League, or "Sally League" as it was called by newspaper scribes. The Class A Sally League represented a huge jump up the baseball ladder for Newsom, only a couple rungs below the majors. Virtually all Sally League players had either already played in the majors or were on option from major league teams. It was fast company for the 21-year-old Newsom, but he had no doubts he belonged.

In spring training with Macon, Newsom almost immediately clashed with his manager, Tom "Shotgun" Rogers. Rogers, 36, a highly touted prospect in his prime, had pitched in the American League from 1917 to 1921. His nickname arose from his high-velocity fastball and his inability to direct it accurately. Based on his own experience, Rogers clearly knew what it would take to get Newsom ready for the top level of competition.[6]

For starters, Rogers opined that Newsom needed to develop another pitch to go with his fastball and to abandon his sidearm delivery for the more conventional overhand delivery. Newsom rejected both bits of advice, and the battle was joined. At the midway point in training camp, Newsom decided he was ready for the regular season and stopped attending daily workouts. This didn't sit well with Rogers or the other Macon players. When Newsom finally did show up after missing a few days, Rogers informed him he was being shipped back to Wilmington.[7]

The news reduced Newsom to tears. Still a boy emotionally, he was honestly shocked to hear he was being demoted. Newsom's tale of woe, including as it did the shocking death of his mother, apparently struck an accommodating chord in Rogers, himself the victim of tragedy. While pitching for Nashville in 1916, a Rogers delivery had struck and killed a batter. The batter, Johnny Dodge, happened to be a friend of Rogers, and Rogers was haunted by the memory the rest of his life, a life blighted by the realization of unfulfilled talent and shortened to 44 years by alcoholism. Perhaps Rogers saw an image of himself in the hard-throwing but psychically fragile Newsom. However it happened, "Bobo" managed to convince "Shotgun" to keep him around a few more days so he could prove he could adhere to training rules.

During those days, Newsom redoubled his promotional efforts, so much so that he was able to talk Rogers into starting him in the Peaches' most important exhibition game of the season, against the touring St. Louis Cardinals. The Cardinals were not merely major leaguers, they were defending National League champions. They were a hard-hitting, take-no-prisoners bunch. Rogers must have believed he was sending a sacrificial lamb to the slaughter, but perhaps a good beating would help straighten Newsom out and convince him he needed to work harder at his craft. For Rogers, the worst-case scenario would be Newsom quitting the club. Or maybe, considering Newsom's truculence, it was the best-case scenario.

The Cardinals' arrival at the Macon ballpark on April 5 had to render even Newsom silent. After driving up to the park in a chartered bus, St. Louis players piled out wearing expensive warm-up jackets over their fancy uniforms and carrying a bountiful harvest of first-class baseball equipment. For each of the Macon players, one glove and two bats was about it. The Cardinals seemed to have an abundance of each. Even in the simple activity of warming up, every throw by a Cardinals player seemed faster than the one before. In batting practice, nearly every Cardinal was able to send the ball over the most distance fences. And in infield practice, the Cardinals were like a machine, executing plays that Macon players could only dream about.

For Newsom, not only was St. Louis the first major league team he would pitch against, it was the first major league team he had ever seen. In spite of his confidence level, he must have been unnerved before the game. Adding to the afternoon's tableau was the presence of the Cardinals' Grover Cleveland Alexander, one of Newsom's boyhood idols. On this day, "Alex the Great" would spend the afternoon at leisure in the bullpen, but just being in the same ballpark as him had to rattle Newsom to some extent.

So who was this unknown kid about to take the mound against the powerful visitors from St. Louis? The Buck Newsome who pitched that spring day in Macon had a very different physical appearance from the Bobo Newsom, rotund of belly, full of face and graying at the temples, who was baseball's elder statesman in the 1950s. The Newsom of 1929 was 6-feet-2 and 175 pounds soaking wet. He was built like an inverted pyramid, wide shoulders and narrow hips and legs, with exceptionally large hands and feet. Like another big man, Babe Ruth, none of his body parts seemed to fit, but they worked together perfectly. At this point in his life, Newsom bore a definite resemblance to his Daddy Quill. (Later on, as he put on weight, he looked more and more like his late mother Lillian.) He was described in the account of the Peaches-Cardinals game in the *Macon Telegraph* as "gangling."[8]

However, in most ways the Newsom of 1929 was exactly the same individual who was to brighten the big league scene for 25 years. He loved to talk, was not adverse to bragging, and was totally uninhibited. He told everybody he met to call him Buck. They did, and the Macon media quickly picked up on it and unfailingly referred to him as "Buck Newsome" in all stories. Those stories also unfailingly mentioned his brashness and unaffected enthusiasm. Before the start of the season, Newsom cornered one of the Macon sportswriters and asked the identities of the better hitters in the Sally League. The scribe, flouting his knowledge, proceeded to tell Newsom who they were and what their strengths and weaknesses were. This was a bit more than Newsom cared to know, and he cut off the writer with "Aw hell, I'll just pitch to their strong points and strike 'em all out."[9] As always, there was nothing premeditated about his boasting. He was, borrowing a billing from his days in the carnival, the one and only Newsom the Great.

The St. Louis lineup Newsom faced included three future Hall of Famers—first baseman Jim Bottomley, left fielder Chick Hafey and second baseman Frankie Frisch. It also included established major leaguers center fielder Taylor Douthit, right fielder Ernie Orsatti, shortstop Andy High and catcher Earl Smith. Pitching for the Cardinals was "Wild Bill" Hallahan, who threw just as hard as Newsom. It was a daunting task for Newsom, but he pitched valiantly. He gave up 11 hits and four walks, and the Cardinals took full advantage of his inexperience to steal six bases, two of them by Frisch. The Cardinals led, 6–2, entering the bottom of the ninth, and no one in Macon, not even Newsom, would have been disappointed if the game had ended that way. Newsom had held the mighty Cardinals pretty much at bay for the full nine innings, and with better defense behind him—and a better pickoff move to first base—he would have given up only three runs.

Macon manager Rogers pinch-hit for Newsom in the ninth, and pinch-hitter Gene Alford ignited a rally off Hallahan with a bunt single. Second baseman Rosy Ryan capped the rally with a bases-loaded double, driving in three runs and giving the Preacher a dramatic 7–6 victory over the Cardinals.

The ninth-inning uprising and Newsom's pitching were the talk of the town for several days afterward. Certainly, there was no longer any question as to whether or not he would stay with the Peaches for the Sally League season. He had made the team and secured a reputation as a genuine major league prospect.

Newsom did not get the starting call on Opening Day for Macon on April 15. The Peaches unveiled their new ballyard in Central City Park that afternoon before a crowd in excess of 3,000. (The park, now called Luther Williams Park in honor of a former Macon mayor, is still in use.) Macon lost to the Charlotte Bees, 6–4, but it proved to be a big day for Newsom. He relieved the Macon starter with his team down, 5–0, and held Charlotte to three hits and one run in 6⅔ innings, providing the biggest thrill of the afternoon for Peaches fanciers.

By April 22, the *Macon Telegraph* was running a feature on Newsom, with the headline "Watch This Boy."[10] He was clearly one of the most promising players in the Sally League. Other up-and-coming youngsters with the Peaches were 21-year-old infielder Ryan, on his way up to the majors for a six-year stay which included being the starting shortstop on the 1933 World Champion New York Giants, and 19-year-old third baseman Paul Richards, who later switched to catcher and played eight seasons in the majors as a prelude to a distinguished career as a manager in the American League. Another top "prospect" in the Sally League was future Hall of Fame umpire Cal Hubbard. Hubbard went on to umpire for 25 years in the AL, working behind the plate for many of Newsom's pitching appearances.

Umpires were usually mortal enemies of Newsom, but he and Hubbard hit it off from the start. Hubbard, a huge man who once played tackle in the National Football League, was a gentle soul who was rarely bothered by Newsom's incessant whining. In fact, when he missed a call he was usually the first to say something, as in "Safe! [slight pause, then in a quieter voice] Damn it, Buck, I sure missed that one." To which Newsom would shoot back, "Damn it yourself. Call 'em right!" At which both men would break out in laughter.[11]

In contrast, Newsom did not get along with Richards. Their differences possibly stemmed from Richards' defensive deficiencies at third base, coupled with Newsom's shameless grandstanding. The youthful Newsom was not above criticizing a teammate's play, on the field and loud enough for everyone to hear. Richards took exception to this behavior, and the two remained in opposing camps the remainder of their baseball careers. Unfortunately for Newsom, this was to have undesirable results in the 1950s when he needed a job and Richards was in a position to give him one.[12]

"If Buck took a dislike to you, he could be a real son of a bitch," said Bob Shirley, a longtime acquaintance of Newsom's from Hartsville. "He was world-class at holding a grudge. Here he was, this big tough guy, but he could be very sensitive to any kind of criticism. And once you got on his bad side, that's where you stayed."[13]

Likely inspired by the favorable article in the *Macon Telegraph,* Newsom went out the next day (April 23) and beat Knoxville, 7–4. He struck out 11 Smokies and walked only two, allowing seven hits in going the route. *Telegraph* sportswriter Jimmy Jones heaped on the praise, writing, "Newsome treated the crowd to one of the best pitching exhibitions ever turned in on a Macon field." Jones called Newsom "the big boy with the iron arm and the nerve of a lightning rod salesman." For the record, an error by Richards at third base led to two of the Knoxville runs.

Newsom developed into a definite gate attraction at Macon, even if he had yet to develop into a polished professional. By July, he was clearly a big man in town, and on July 19 he and his teammates were guests of the management for a vaudeville show at the Grand Theater in Macon. The theater manager stopped proceedings long enough to sing Newsom's praises and ask him to come up to the stage and take a bow. This Bobo did, to a standing ovation. As always, he was at ease in the limelight.[14]

Still, Newsom's pitching appearances could be wildly inconsistent. A route-going performance might be followed by an outing in which he was driven to cover in the second inning. The best thing that happened to him was that Rogers had no qualms about sending him to the mound. The Peaches were going nowhere in the standings— they finished seventh in an eight-team league—and Newsom was always ready and willing to pitch. In fact, he begged to pitch, the bigger the game and crowd, the better.

Newsom finished with a 19–18 won-loss record for the Peaches. He pitched in 45 games (he also occasionally was used as a pinch-hitter or pinch-runner) and racked up 298 innings. He was at the top or near the top of the league in all pitching categories, leading in runs allowed (167), earned runs allowed (128) and walks (173). He also struck out 149 Sally League batters and had a respectable 3.87 earned run average. His batting average fell 100 points, to .240. It was increasingly clear that Newsom's future was tied to his strong right arm.

There were definitely highlights along the way. One occurred the same week as Newsom's "theatrical debut." On July 22, Macon traveled to South Carolina to play the Columbia Reds. Lucille arranged for the occasion to be a sort of early birthday party/happy homecoming for Bobo, and invited a large number of Newsom kin and friends to the state capital to watch Bobo pitch. The turnout from Hartsville was impressive that day, and Lucille pulled off a major coup by getting Daddy Quill to attend. It was the first time the elder Newsom had seen his son pitch, and would be the last until 11 years later. If his father's presence affected Newsom psychologically, it certainly didn't bother his pitching. "The Pride of Hartsville" (as the *Macon Telegraph* game story referred to him) turned in a complete game in an 11–4 victory. The victory had to be doubly satisfying for Newsom, for it occurred nearly two years to the day of the Columbia tryout debacle in the same ballpark.[15]

Another highlight of the season for Newsom took place on Flag Day, June 14, when he faced Asheville before a sellout crowd at Macon. The festive occasion was made more so by the presence of Commissioner Kenesaw Mountain Landis. Landis and Newsom were to meet again on many other occasions, not always under favorable circumstances for Newsom. On this day, Newsom enjoyed himself to the fullest, including his greeting to Landis as they met for a pre-game handshake—"Hiya judge! Wait 'til you see me pitch!" Being in the presence of celebrities never intimidated Newsom; if anything, he was emboldened.

Newsom was able to back up his boasting, pitching the Peaches to a 3–2 victory and striking out 11 Asheville batters. Suffice to say, he made an impression on Landis.

The Peaches' season ended on September 6, capped by Newsom being named the team's Most Valuable Player. All indications are that Bobo and Lucille were packed and prepared to return to Hartsville on that date. Instead, a long-distance call from New York changed their plans and Bobo's life.

The Dodgers still owned his contract, and management decided to have a look-see. The Dodgers were locked in the second division and had nothing to lose except Newsom's train fare in bringing him up to the big club. He reported to the Dodgers in Cincinnati on September 9, and manager Wilbert Robinson immediately informed him that he would start against the Reds on September 11 (exactly a month past his 22nd birthday) against veteran right-hander Red Lucas, a 19-game winner for Cincinnati that year. Newsom (still referred to as Newsome in the Cincinnati and New York papers) was about as raw a rookie as the National League had seen in many years. In fact, the trip to Cincinnati marked his first time ever north of the Mason-Dixon Line and his first look at a major league ballpark.[16]

Jack Ryder, covering the September 11 game for the *Cincinnati Inquirer*, wrote the following:

> Newsome, who has been with the Robins less than a week and never before had placed his ample Southern hoof on a big league mound, forced the Redhead [Lucas] to go the limit. The big right-hander had informed his teammates that he was sure to make good when he got the chance, and his exhibition makes it look as if he may know what he is talking about.

The game turned out to be a remarkable microcosm of Newsom's baseball career. He bragged about how he would win, went out and pitched admirably (if not always intelligently), but was foiled by teammates' miscues. According to Ryder, "[Newsome] had plenty of good old stuff on the pellet and the Reds were unable to upset his supreme confidence."

Newsom's initial big league game opened on a discouraging note. The first batter he faced, Evar Swanson, hit a check-swing double to right. Newsom then struck out Hugh Critz and enticed Curt Walker to hit an easy fly to Babe Herman in right field. Unfortunately, Herman dropped the ball, allowing Walker to reach safely and Swanson to advance to third. Newsom bore down to strike out George Kelly, the Reds' cleanup hitter, for the second out. But while he pitched to the next batter, Walker took off for second and catcher Hank DeBerry's throw sailed into center field, allowing Swanson to trot home with the game's first run.

A botched play on a bunt by Newsom led to the Reds' second run in the third inning. Newsom slipped while trying to make a play, putting runners at first and third. Swanson was then able to score as Walker was hitting into a double play.

Inept Dodgers defense, and a Newsom mental miscue, again reared its ugly head in the seventh. With the Reds clinging to a 2–1 lead, Reds catcher Johnny Gooch enticed a walk, Newsom's only free pass of the afternoon. Gooch, possibly the slowest man in the National League, caught Newsom and DeBerry completely off guard, stealing second without a throw. One out later, he scored on the Reds' fifth, and last, hit off Newsom. Manager Robinson opted to pinch-hit for Newsom in the top of the eighth.

The Dodgers rallied late against Lucas, but fell one run short. The 4–3 final score tended to obscure just how well Newsom had pitched. Three runs, two of them unearned and all of them tainted, and five hits, three of them of the scratch variety, in seven innings, with five strikeouts and only one walk, was a memorable major league debut by anybody's standards.

The *New York Herald-Tribune* account of the game, by Murray Tynan, was effusive.

> The Robins didn't win today, but strange to relate they found a lot to cheer about.... The philosophical band of athletes from Flatbush started Louis (Buck) Newsome, a youngster from Macon with a reputation for being a wild man.... In spite of two silly errors in the first innings he pitched efficiently until he retired for a pinch hitter in the eighth.... [Newsom] has a lot of what managers call stuff. He also indicated that he knows what to do with that stuff.

Roscoe McGowen, writing for the *New York Times*, was considerably more subdued. "Buck Newsome, Brooklyn rookie pitcher ... gave a good account of himself." McGowen, then 43, was to remain on the Dodgers' beat for the next 25 years, long enough to cover Newsom's final season in the majors and to become an expert on Newsom lore.[17]

McGowen's customarily clean box score provides a clear snapshot of the contest. The game was played in one hour, 37 minutes. Swanson led the Reds' attack with three hits and three runs scored. There were no triples or home runs in the game. Brooklyn first baseman Del Bissonette made ten putouts. The home plate umpire was George Magerkurth. Other than being Newsom's debut, it was a thoroughly unremarkable game between two unremarkable teams. No players or coaches on either team were still around the major leagues in September 1953 when Newsom was to make his final pitch.

Newsom's impressive big league debut came as no surprise to Jimmy Jones, sportswriter for the *Macon Telegraph* who had covered his accomplishments with the Peaches that summer. From Jones' September 14 column: "It isn't often that a pitcher with Buck Newsome's color drifts into the major leagues. And it is exceedingly rare when one strikes a youngster with his supreme poise and confidence.... Newsome, like Rube Waddell and Art Shires, is nobody's shrinking violet."[18]

According to Jones, when the New York sportswriters interviewed Newsom that September, he told them that, after seeing some of the pitchers winning games in the National League, he had a lot higher opinion of his own talents. No doubt Newsom said it innocently enough, but such braggadocio wasn't heard in the majors and the writers ate it up and asked for more. Newsom was glad to oblige.

Newsom didn't have long to bask in the glow of his first game with the Dodgers. In his second start, this time against the powerful Chicago Cubs on September 15, Newsom was royally rocked. He was removed by Robinson after going only two innings, allowing six runs on seven hits and four walks. The Cubs (who had already clinched the NL pennant) went on to record a 13–4 victory. One final appearance, this time in relief, on September 24, wasn't any better. He worked only two-thirds of an inning, allowing three runs on three hits.

Still, the two bad outings weren't about to cast a pall on what had been a remarkable season. The 22-year-old Newsom had made the rare jump all the way from Class D to the majors in less than two years. He left Brooklyn that fall with a major league contract for the 1930 season in his pocket, and with absolutely no reason to believe his confidence in himself had been misplaced.

For Newsom, the Dodgers contract meant he didn't have to go back to work on Daddy Quill's farm. In fact, he used the contract to beg off any sort of manual labor, telling his father he couldn't risk an injury. This touched off one final argument between the two, ending with Bobo (and Lucille) moving out of his parents' home for good. Whatever happened from that point onward, he was no longer Norman Newsom, son of Henry Quillion Buffkin Newsome. He was now Buck Newsom, baseball pitcher deluxe.[19]

Three

New York to Los Angeles, via Brooklyn, Jersey City, Mobile, Little Rock and Chicago (1930–1933)

Bobo Newsom's first major league spring training camp established the tone for his spring training camps to come for the next 25 years. Newsom quickly became convinced that training was more trouble than it was worth. He enjoyed palling around with fellow ballplayers and the warm spring weather of Florida, but the training part always rubbed him the wrong way. He disliked the repetitious drills, the long hours of running to go nowhere, and pitching for no good purpose other than strengthening his arm. He already knew that he could run and throw. Adding significantly to Newsom's dislike for training camp was his discovery that major league players were not on salary during the spring. Besides, he had shown the Brooklyn Dodgers what he could do in his brief stint with the team in September of 1929. Now all he heard was talk of making the team. Hadn't he already made the team?[1]

The chief trespasser on Newsom's comfort zone was Dodgers manager Wilbert Robinson. The 66-year-old "Uncle Robbie" knew the 1930 edition of the Dodgers likely represented his last chance to win another pennant. His health was failing, as was the financial health of the franchise. Increasingly, Robinson was at odds with the Dodgers' front office, and lasted only one more season in Brooklyn before being fired. A desperate man, he drove the players hard in spring training camp, held in Clearwater, Florida.

Robinson had managed the Brooklyn Dodgers since 1914, long enough for the team to be called the Robins by the New York media. An overweight, blustery fellow, Robinson had a tendency toward impulsiveness that made him a "good quote" for sportswriters. Unfortunately, that same tendency carried over to his managerial duties, where Robinson was known to get caught up in the excitement of the moment and forget to flash a sign, or flash the incorrect one. His managerial approach remained a carryover from his playing days with the rough-and-ready Baltimore Orioles of the 1890s. Those teams were also the springboard of the managerial career of the New York Giants' John McGraw, and the two men were virtual mirror images in terms of baseball strategy. Where McGraw differed from Robinson was that McGraw possessed the quickest mind in baseball, a mental nimbleness bordering on ESP. Robinson had no such genius, and while he was able to earn his players' respect, he never earned their trust, the trust that the correct decision would be made at just the right time.[2]

"McGraw managed an inning ahead and Robinson managed an inning behind," was the way former Dodger Babe Herman remembered it.[3] Fresco Thompson, who played for Robinson in 1931, described the experience as being "akin to being aboard a floating insane asylum minus the compass.... When [Robinson's] dentures fitted properly you could even understand him. He missed by many miles being a baseball genius."[4]

Adding to his other foibles, as he aged Robinson became increasingly impatient with younger players, subscribing to the old adage that rookies should be seen and not heard. Since managing the likes of a Bobo Newsom required infinite patience and turning a deaf ear to a litany of complaints, spring training of 1930 proved difficult for both men.[5]

The Buck Newsom of 1930 was, if anything, even cockier than in his later years. He had no doubt about his abilities and no reservations about touting them. Robinson would be the first of seven Hall of Fame managers Newsom would play for, and he failed to excel for any of them except kindly Connie Mack. In truth, the best—indeed only— way to handle Newsom was to not handle him at all. In the case of Robinson, Newsom listened to his directions, but quickly discarded those that did not fit his own philosophy. One spring afternoon, Robinson was instructing his pitchers on how to hold runners on base. Newsom had little interest in the session, reckoning the easiest way to solve the problem was to concentrate on striking the batter out. Since Newsom, when bored, tended to sound off even more than usual, it wasn't long before "Uncle Robbie" found his patience frayed and his fuse lit.

Newsom was also resistant to Robinson's insistence that he throw strikes consistently. Newsom still held dear to his own theory that if the batters weren't hitting the ball, everything would eventually work in his favor. Camp had been in session for only a few days when Robinson and Newsom clashed. Newsom was throwing batting practice and was wilder than usual, which, in his case, was very wild indeed. Dodgers hitters were complaining, which made Newsom throw harder, which only served to aggravate his lack of command of any of his pitches. Finally, Uncle Robbie had seen enough.

He ordered Newsom off the mound and took him to an isolated area behind a storage shed. There was a practice mound and, 60 feet away, an automobile tire hung by a rope at strike zone level over home plate. "Throw the ball into the tire!" Robinson commanded.[6] Newsom made a series of pitches, none of which made it through the tire and most of which weren't even close. "God damn it, you couldn't throw a strike if I paid you!" Robinson exploded. Newsom responded in kind, and the two were off on a wild argument that ended only when Robinson bet Newsom $20 that he couldn't throw 20 straight pitches through the tire. Twenty dollars was a princely sum in 1930. A player could eat, drink and be merry for a week on $20.

Newsom rose to the occasion, as was to happen so often in his career, and promptly fired off 20 pitches, each of which touched nothing but air as it sailed through the hole in the tire. Newsom proved his point and was $20 richer, but his accuracy infuriated Robinson even more. Robinson paid the $20, grudgingly, but strongly suspected Newsom had hustled him. The incident set an unseemly tone to the pair's working relationship, not helped along when sportswriter Roscoe McGowen found out about the bet and filed a gussied-up account of it back to the *New York Times*.

Among a number of Robinson's not altogether rational theories on pitching was one that held that the bigger the man, the harder and longer he could throw. Thus, he had a definite attraction to oversized pitchers. Newsom would seem to fit this "wish list" perfectly, but when asked by sportswriters about Newsom, Robinson replied, "Sure, I like big pitchers. But this guy's head is *too* big."[7]

It appeared the Dodgers, with or without Newsom's large cranium, had a good shot at supplanting the Chicago Cubs at the top of the National League standings. While the roster of the 1930 Dodgers now reads like a cast of characters from a W. C. Fields movie, at the time Robinson had high hopes for the group.

Del Bissonette was at first base, where he hit .336 that season. Second base duties were divided between D'Arcy "Jake" Flowers, who hit .320, and Cornelius "Mickey" Finn, who hit .278. At shortstop was Glenn "Buckshot" Wright, who hit .321, while third baseman Wally Gilbert hit .294. The starting outfield consisted of Floyd "Babe" Herman, who hit .393, Johnny Frederick, who hit .334, and Raymond "Rube" Bressler, who hit .299. Catching was handled by Al Lopez, who hit .309. He was backed up by Hank DeBerry, who hit .295.

The undisputed ace of the pitching staff was veteran Dazzy Vance, who posted a 17–15 win-loss record. Other pitchers included Dolf Luque (14–8), Ray Phelps (14–7), Watty Clark (13–13), Jumbo Elliott (10–7), Ray Moss (9–6) and Hollis "Sloppy" Thurston (6–4).[8]

It was an experienced team and, like their manager, a rowdy bunch. Even the rookies on the roster, other than Newsom, had spent long years in the minor leagues honing their craft and fighting for a chance to get paid big-league money. The 22-year-old Newsom, with only a couple of years in organized baseball under his belt, failed to bond with his Brooklyn mates, and his time spent with the team proved to be an unhappy experience.

Thurston, who had already been in pro ball for ten years, was about the only teammate Newsom associated with. That liaison had a couple of fringe benefits. From Thurston, Newsom learned that it helped to have a catchy nickname. (Thurston's unusual moniker

Bobo Newsom with his first new car, a 1930 Ford Model A. He purchased this with proceeds from his 1930 contract with the Brooklyn Dodgers (courtesy Hartsville Museum).

came about because he was a snappy dresser; ballplayers love irony and turned that trait around so he became "Sloppy.") Newsom also learned from Thurston, who grew up in Los Angeles, the charms of playing in the Pacific Coast League. Thurston tipped him off on a way to make big money in the off-season, the newly formed California Winter League. Sloppy told Bobo that a pitcher could make thousands of dollars in the loop, the only caveat being "you have to play against colored guys." To Newsom, that was no deterrent. He had been there and done that.[9]

For all of his bluster, Robinson's assessment of his club proved sound and the Dodgers hovered around first place the entire season. They were atop the NL standings as late as September 15 before faltering over the final two weeks. As a team, the 1930 Dodgers hit .303 and had the lowest earned run average in the league. However, that ERA was 4.03. The statistic reflected the fact that the season of 1930 was to go down in baseball annals as the "Year of the Hitter." Amazingly, the Dodgers' team batting average was exactly the same as the league batting average. While their pitching was as effective as any in the league, with the starters turning in 74 complete games out of 154 starts, the lineup lacked the fire power of the other pennant contenders, and placed sixth in the NL in runs scored. They hung tough, but eventually fell short. The Dodgers finished at 86–68, in fourth place. The St. Louis Cardinals won 92 games to edge out the defending NL champion Chicago Cubs, who won 90. The New York Giants were third, with 87 wins.

The late September swoon added greatly to Robinson's grief. As some consolation, Robbie did not have to put up with Newsom for the second half of the season. Newsom made the team coming out of spring training, but Robinson felt the only way he was going to be a consistent winner in the majors was to throw strikes and develop an effective breaking pitch to go with his fastball. Robinson decided that Newsom should model his delivery after Brooklyn ace Dazzy Vance. What worked for Vance should work for Newsom, Robinson reasoned. It might have, except that Newsom wasn't about to model his style after anyone else, and Vance wasn't about to help a younger man knock him off a top perch on the pitching staff.

"Mr. Vance had no interest in helping Mr. Newsom," Dodgers outfielder Babe Herman recalled. "They just weren't sympatico. [Dazzy] tried to convince Robbie it was an impossible task but Robbie insisted."[10]

Vance had struggled in organized baseball for ten years before finally hitting it big with the Dodgers. During that time, he had developed a sharp-breaking curveball to go with his extraordinary fastball. He refined his mechanics so that he could throw both pitches overhand, from exactly the same delivery. He augmented those pitches with a natural aggressiveness, pitching hitters tight and using every possible advantage.[11] He was infamous for wearing long-sleeved undershirts even on the hottest days. Somehow, the right sleeve always managed to become frayed, and by the third or fourth inning it would flap in the breeze during Vance's delivery like a pennant on a flagpole. His overhand delivery, with the ball hidden until the last possible moment, made it difficult to pick up his pitches. The flapping sleeve made it virtually impossible. Vance made doubly sure the sleeve would unravel by cutting an inside seam ever so slightly with a razor blade prior to each start.[12]

Robinson quickly ran out of patience trying to coach Newsom in the Dazzy Vance style of pitching. So he called upon Vance himself to tutor Bobo. It was not a match made in heaven. The 39-year-old Vance criticized everything the 22-year-old Newsom did, a situation very close to the relationship Newsom had with his father. A reluctant teacher and a non-receptive student usually results in a failed lesson plan, and such was the case with Vance and Newsom. Since Newsom was still using a sidearm motion, he faced some major adjustments to convert to Vance's overhand delivery. He never did get the hang of it, nor did he acquire Vance's sharp-breaking curveball. After a few training sessions with Newsom, Vance had made exactly zero progress. Finally, the sessions ended one hot spring day in Clearwater with a very loud, very long and very profane shouting match.

Brooklyn teammate Babe Herman, his attention drawn to the fracas, decided to apply the needle to Vance.

"How are things going with your star pupil, Dazzy?" Herman inquired.

"If that dumb son-of-a-bitch keeps throwing that way, he'll break his God-damn arm," Vance replied. "And it can't happen soon enough to suit me."[13]

Newsom, now sans tutor, was reduced to sitting in the dugout and watching once the regular season began. He stayed on the Dodgers roster for two months, pitching a total of two games. The more notable of the two occurred in Wrigley Field in Chicago on May 7, when he held the heavy-hitting Cubs to no runs and one infield hit in two innings.

To Newsom, the lack of activity was akin to a slow death. Nothing in his young life prepared him for the role of spectator, and he became so frustrated at one point that he went to Robinson and pleaded to be allowed to play the outfield. While Newsom frequently bragged about his batting prowess, the reality was he would have never made it in the majors with the bat.[14] In 1930, he possessed remarkable running speed—Burleigh Grimes recalled Bobo as being the fastest player in camp—but you can't steal first base.[15]

Newsom was constantly adjusting his batting style and later in the 1930s even tried switch-hitting, but he was never more than a Punch-and-Judy hitter with little power. He finished his long major league career with a .189 batting average and exactly one home run. Off-speed pitches usually left him flailing helplessly, and teammates recalled more than one occasion when he took a hefty cut at a pitch and wound up falling down at home plate. Late in his career, he became so frustrated trying to hit the fluttering knuckleball deliveries of George Caster that he threw down his bat, reached out and grabbed the slow-moving pitch with his bare hand before it could reach the catcher's mitt.[16]

In the spring of 1930, it did not help Newsom's mood that it was cold in Brooklyn. He hated cold weather. Nor did he ever figure out the Big Apple's transportation system or its residents. For someone accustomed to the laid-back lifestyle of South Carolina, even the simplest things—ordering a meal or getting a haircut—seemed like a chore in New York. Newsom was also unhappy that Lucille elected to stay home in South Carolina. While he eventually grew to appreciate the excitement New York offered, he never felt truly at ease in the city.[17]

Finally, on the date to trim rosters, June 15, Robinson decided to demote Newsom to Jersey City in the International League. He gave strict instructions that Newsom was to continue to throw overhand and work to perfect the Dazzy Vance technique. Newsom made one start with Jersey City, completing the seven-inning game, the nightcap of a June 19 doubleheader. However, he gave up seven walks and lost, 4–3, to Montreal. Two subsequent relief efforts were much worse, as he gave up eight hits, two walks and ten runs in three innings.[18] Clearly, he wasn't going to be the next Dazzy Vance. A thoroughly bothered and bewildered Newsom pulled up stakes and headed home to Hartsville. When someone broke the news to Robinson back in Brooklyn, he offered the opinion that the circus must have gone through Jersey City heading south and that Newsom went with it.[19] Suffice to say, "Uncle Robbie" was not exactly heartbroken over Newsom's unscheduled departure.

Newsom's baseball career might have ended right there. Fortunately, cooler—and more financially savvy—heads in the Dodgers front office decided that he was still too valuable a prospect to lose. Team officials were able to convince him to report to Macon to finish out the last two months of season. This proved agreeable to both parties, the selling point for Bobo being retention of his major league salary.

Newsom's second go-around in Macon was one of continued experimentation, including a long, unrewarding stint in the Macon bullpen as well as duties as a pinch-hitter, pinch-runner and occasional outfielder. Finally, late in the season and with no prospect of being recalled by Brooklyn, Newsom went back into the starting rotation and resorted to his old delivery. He was able to win five of his seven starts, all complete games. There was a noticeable improvement in his control—he walked only 29 batters in 89 innings—and he finished with an excellent 2.43 earned run average. Was it enough to land him another shot in the majors? The answer was no.

That winter, the Dodgers failed to protect Newsom in the draft, and the other 15 major league teams all passed on acquiring his services. In the Dodgers 1931 spring training camp, Newsom was very much the forgotten man. Worse, he wasn't even the oddest bird in the bush. That honor went to a pitcher named Clyde "Pea Ridge" Day. Day wasn't much of a pitcher, but he was a champion hog caller in his native Arkansas. After a good inning, or striking out a batter, Day was likely to launch into his specialty, his swine serenades easily heard throughout any ballpark. Newsom may have been a rustic, but Day was downright primitive. Still, it was Day who was destined to stay in Brooklyn and Newsom who was headed for Arkansas.[20]

On April Fools' Day, the Dodgers sold his contract to Kansas City of the American Association, which in turn sold it to Little Rock of the Southern Association. This came as stunning news to Newsom, who told acquaintances in Hartsville he was through with pro baseball. But there was a depression spreading across the land that, coupled with the latest round of quarrels between Newsom and his father, greatly reduced Newsom's employment opportunities. On April 15, he reluctantly reported to Little Rock for the 1931 season. It wasn't the big leagues, but at least it was the Southern Association, the league he followed closely as a youth.[21]

The Little Rock Travelers were one of the "have-nots" of the Southern Association, fielding a roster filled with castoffs from other organizations and playing at a home field that was literally falling apart. Little Rock was also one of the smaller cities in the Association, its population standing at 75,000 in 1931. It was about as far from the bright lights of Broadway as you could get, but it put Newsom in an environment where he could once again focus on baseball.[22]

Three. New York to Los Angeles (1930–1933)

In what turned out to be a relatively uneventful season for Newsom, one event readily noticeable from the stack of Newsom press clippings is that there was, finally, a standardization of his first and last names. Newsome and Newsum gave way, unequivocally, to Newsom. And Louis or Lou or Norman or Bucky were gone, rarely to return. From this point forward into the 1940s, press accounts unfailingly referred to Buck Newsom. Newsom himself was undoubtedly the source for the change. Altering the spelling of his last name meant he had an excuse to approach any and all sportswriters with the "exclusive" scoop—a tactic Dizzy Dean later employed while pitching for the St. Louis Cardinals.

Newsom was far from the star of the Travelers. That honor went to centerfielder Walter French. The 32-year-old French had been a starting outfielder for the Philadelphia Athletes in the 1920s but was now on the downside of his career. With Little Rock, he had a banner season, hitting .346 and leading the Southern Association with 230 hits and 51 stolen bases.[23]

Little Rock, with six of its everyday players hitting over .300, possessed a powerful attack, but came up short in the pitching department. Newsom, still basically a one-pitch pitcher, was used extensively in relief, and several of the games he started were the second games of doubleheaders. The idea, obviously, was to have him pitch in the late afternoon, when shadows made it tougher for batters to pick up his fastball. His fastball was regarded as the best in the league, but his season was definitely a mixed bag. He pitched a league-high 51 games, 29 starts and 22 relief appearances. He also appeared in five games as an outfielder and pinch-runner, and finished with a .301 batting average. He led the Southern Association with 152 strikeouts while posting a 16–14 win-loss record. He pitched 271 innings, so there was no question that his arm was sound. But in those 271 innings, he walked 150 batters (also a league high) and allowed 289 hits. His earned run average was 5.05.

Little Rock's season record hovered around the .500 mark until August, when the Travelers caught fire and won 32 of their final 42 games to finish second to Birmingham. Sparking the Travelers' late-season surge was a rookie outfielder from Chicago named Bruce Campbell who hit .377 for the Travelers and went on to a ten-year career in the major leagues. He also became a life-long friend of Newsom and his future teammate on the St. Louis Browns, Detroit Tigers and Washington Senators.

One lasting legacy from Newsom's 1931 season at Little Rock was documented proof of his foot speed. He and French represented Little Rock in a series of races against players from other Southern Association teams. The players would compete in a 70-yard dash, a popular pre-game attraction of that era. Newsom won several of these races, a feat he bragged about for years afterward. He won numerous bets with teammates, incredulous that the 200-pound-plus Newsom could have possibly outrun any two-legged athlete, by producing the yellowed press clippings detailing his winning dashes.[24]

Newsom, still a young man at 23, was reasonably content pitching in the Southern Association. For the first time in his career, he didn't jump the team, or threaten to jump the team, or engage in a physical or verbal altercation with his manager. His efforts for Little Rock may have been less than awe-inspiring, but they caught the interest of Rogers Hornsby, manager of the Chicago Cubs. No doubt Hornsby also remembered Newsom's brief but impressive stint against the Cubs in May of 1930. He urged Cubs

President Bill Veeck, Sr. to acquire Newsom. Under the rules of that time, the Travelers had to make Newsom available for the major league draft, set for September 30. Several teams passed on him, but the Cubs did not. Newsom was once again headed for the major leagues.[25]

Ironically, in light of how their relationship ended, in 1932 Newsom held Hornsby in high esteem, and Hornsby was a great booster of Newsom's talents. Hornsby had been young Newsom's favorite player, back in those days in Hartsville when Newsom still saw himself as a second baseman. Newsom was actually looking forward to playing for the man they called "The Rajah." Hornsby, in addition to being Newsom's boyhood idol, was much younger than Wilbert Robinson, and a fellow Southerner to boot. Add in the fact that the Cubs were a first-class organization and it all gave rise to great optimism on the part of Newsom as he prepared for the 1932 season.

Buck Newsom warming up for an appearance that never came prior to a 1932 game at Wrigley Field. Cubs manager Rogers Hornsby used Newsom once, in relief, prior to demoting him to the International League (the Ray Medeiros collection, used by permission).

Unfortunately, with Newsom unbridled optimism always seemed to lead to unmitigated disaster. Back in Hartsville for the winter, Newsom brought with him from Little Rock two things: a fairly sizable bankroll and a new, powerful Chrysler roadster. He had definitely acquired a taste for automobiles, the bigger and faster the better.

"Back then, Buck wasn't much of a drinker and he didn't chase after the ladies," said Bob Shirley of Hartsville, who knew Newsom from Shirley's childhood up until Newsom's death. "His big thing was cars. He absolutely loved 'em. Fast cars, and playing pool and cards. Those were his vices, if you want to call 'em that."[26]

"Like just about all of us southern boys, Buck started out with a [Ford] Model T," said Hoot Gibson, another longtime Newsom crony from Hartsville. "But he gradually worked his way up to better cars. He always wanted to have the biggest, fastest car in town. He loved to drive, and was a good driver. But he had a lot of dare-devil in him. I think, if he had been born 25 years later, he would have become a NASCAR driver instead of a ballplayer. He loved his automobiles."²⁷

Another Hartsville acquaintance, L. L. "Luke" Sparrow, recalls a story from this era. It seems Newsom was driving from Hartsville to Rockingham via Cheraw, exceeded the speed limit by a considerable margin, and was pulled over by a Cheraw police officer. An argument ensued, not over Newsom exceeding the speed limit but over the merits of his driving. Finally, Newsom asked the cop what the fine was for speeding. When told it was $10, Newsom peeled off a $20 bill from his roll, threw it at the cop and told him, "There, that'll cover my round trip."²⁸

By this point in their marriage, Lucille had little success keeping Newsom home for more than one or two nights a week. Usually, he was out driving, frequently into the big cities of Columbia, Charleston or Charlotte, always in search of a friendly pool hall or hot game of poker. He also took up a little amateur action running moonshine down from the hills of North Carolina to thirsty compadres in Hartsville and vicinity.

In May of 1932, as a member of the Chicago Cubs, Newsom posed for the first of many photographs by noted Chicago photographer George Burke. Initially, Newsom was reluctant to pose, knowing that Burke was in the business of selling his finished product to the players, often in the form of postcards. Later, as Newsom changed teams nearly every year, he actively sought out Burke to "shoot him" in his new uniform (the Brace photograph collection, used by permission).

The new Chrysler was ideal for this purpose, having plenty of room for storage of the jugs and an engine Newsom had altered to outrun all but the most foolhardy Revenue agent.

It was on one of his moonshine runs, in January of 1932, when Newsom's baseball career, and life, nearly came to an end. Accompanied by his cousin Rex Newsome, the Chrysler skidded off the icy pavement and plunged down a steep embankment on U.S. Route 25 north of Asheville, near Walnut, NC. Bobo and Rex had been sampling their stock, and such was their mental state that neither was absolutely sure, in the aftermath of the crash, who had been driving. What was certain was that Bobo was badly hurt and unable to extricate himself from the wreckage.²⁹

Rex Newsome suffered only minor injuries in the crash, and was able to walk several miles to Walnut to summon help. The worst of Bobo's many injuries turned out to be a pair of broken legs. This necessitated a weeks-long stay in the hospital. Newsom family tradition has it that the very same day of the car crash, Newsom's 1932 contract from the Chicago Cubs arrived in the mail, calling for him to report to spring training in California in mid–February.

Newsom was in no condition to go to California, or anywhere else. In fact, it was generally assumed by his doctors that his baseball-playing days were over and that he would be lucky to walk again. At one point in his rehabilitation, doctors had to re-fracture one of the legs since it was healing incorrectly.

Came time for Newsom to be in the Cubs' training camp, held in the exotic setting of team owner William Wrigley, Jr.'s Catalina Island, and he was nowhere to be found. There commenced a series of communications between Cubs manager Rogers Hornsby in California and various and sundry Newsom kin in Hartsville. Bobo couldn't bring himself to tell the team he had busted up both legs while running moonshine and might not be able to pitch that year, or ever. So, while he struggled to strengthen his leg muscles, family members, the family minister, the family lawyer and the family doctor were all recruited to answer Hornsby's increasingly frantic letters and telegrams. Hornsby was not a patient man and quickly grew exasperated at what he regarded as defiant behavior.

It was during this time that Newsom created a colorful account to explain how he re-injured his leg. In this version, after getting out of the hospital he went with his Uncle Jake to the state fair at Columbia. There, while examining a prize mule, the animal hauled off and kicked Newsom, re-fracturing his left leg. When someone pointed out that he had no business standing next to the business end of the mule, he embellished the story further, claiming the mule had broken loose and was about to run down a little girl and that he jumped in to save her, incurring the fractured femur in the process. In later retellings of this tale, he changed the mule to a raging bull. However it was told, it made for an entertaining story for members of the Chicago media but did nothing to enlighten Hornsby as to when Newsom might possibly show himself at the Cubs' training camp.

As things turned out, Newsom missed the entire training camp. He also missed the start of the regular season. It was May 1 before he was finally well enough to drive north and join the Cubs in Chicago. However, he was barely able to walk, let alone pitch. According to Newsom, his first act upon walking into the Wrigley Field clubhouse was to throw his crutches into a trash can. Hornsby was unimpressed with Bobo's dedication to his craft and definitely did not feel his pain.[30] "The Rajah" was riding a winning ballclub and didn't need a problem child like Newsom.

Newsom was left behind in Chicago to work himself into proper condition (and nurse hurt feelings because the team refused to pay his salary from April) while the Cubs took an eastern road trip. When the Cubs returned home, Newsom was relegated to pitching batting practice. He later claimed Hornsby made him pitch batting practice for 22 straight days. Hornsby, if anything, proved to be even more unapproachable than Wilbert Robinson. The rest of the Cubs pitching staff, led by veterans Charlie Root and Guy Bush, ostracized Newsom, a not uncommon reaction to someone who is attempting to take your job. A month dragged by in this fashion before Newsom finally appeared in a game, pitching one inning in relief on June 4 against Pittsburgh.

By then, two things were clear: the 1932 Cubs were definitely a pennant contender, and Newsom wasn't going to break into their pitching rotation. On June 5, he was optioned to Reading in the International League.

Still struggling physically, Newsom also took a bad attitude along with him to Reading. He was unhappy at being demoted, and being sent to the chilly climes of the Northeast was like being exiled to Siberia. He was unable to take Lucille along with him and didn't know a soul in Reading. A few weeks after he joined the team, the franchise went bankrupt and was forced to shift operations to Albany to finish out the 1932 International League season. It all made for an unpleasant and unproductive summer for Newsom.

Newsom's pitching duties at Albany were confined to appearances in relief for the

A rare photograph of a smiling Rogers Hornsby. Most likely, he was getting paid for the radio interview. Newsom claimed Hornsby forced him to pitch 22 consecutive days of batting practice for the 1932 Chicago Cubs after Newsom missed all of spring training due to injuries sustained in a car wreck (the Ray Medeiros collection, used by permission).

first few weeks. Gradually he worked his way into the starting rotation, but was still not in tip-top condition and was able to complete only four of 22 starts. He finished with a very ordinary 7–7 win-loss record in 34 appearances and 145 innings, with a 5.28 earned run average. He struck out only 84 batters in those 145 innings. Clearly, he was not the ace pitcher the Cubs thought they were getting.

A chastened Newsom returned to Hartsville for the winter of 1932–1933. In retrospect, he probably should have sat out the 1932 season and allowed his legs to heal, but he felt he needed to impress Cubs management with his willingness to pitch while injured. The experience taught him, once and for all, that pro baseball was a business, and you had to look out for yourself. From this point onward, Newsom and nobody else was going to decide when he would pitch.

The leg injuries from the car accident took away his vaunted running speed and ended all hopes of making the major leagues as anything other than a pitcher. Thus, that winter, Newsom rededicated himself to his chosen profession, throwing a baseball, and renewed his vow to battle all authority figures to a fare-thee-well.

His new attitude became apparent when he refused to accept the Cubs' contract offer for 1933. It is believed the contract called for a $4,000 salary, the same figure Newsom received in 1932. It was a decent wage, certainly by standards of the economically challenged 1930s, but was $1,000 less than Newsom had received from the Dodgers in 1930. He wrote back to the Cubs, explaining the contract was unacceptable and that he could make more by staying home in Hartsville and helping Daddy Quill run the family farm, or "plantation" as he insisted on calling it. That he had done little or nothing around the farm for several years was for him to know and the Cubs to find out. After a month of negotiations, the Cubs grudgingly added a couple of hundred dollars to their offer. With time running out before the start of training camp, Newsom decided to sign the contract and report to California.[31]

Newsom's brief holdout, coupled with his unproductive 1932 season, helped alter the Cubs' plans. Newsom was regarded as a failed project of Rogers Hornsby, who had been fired by the team after 97 games of the 1932 season. The Cubs were now managed by Charlie Grimm, who had little rapport with Newsom. Besides, the Cubs had pitching aplenty. They were, however, always on the lookout for young prospects, a label that no longer quite fit Newsom. Chicago had a working agreement with the Los Angeles Angels of the Pacific Coast League, and during games between the Cubs and Angels in training camp a young Angels outfielder named George Tucker "Tuck" Stainback caught the eye of Cubs management. Thus an exchange of contracts was engineered, the Cubs receiving the rights to Stainback and the Angels gaining the rights to Newsom. Another door to the big leagues had been slammed in Newsom's face.

This time, there were certain mitigating circumstances. When Bobo and Lucille arrived at Los Angeles Union Station in mid–February, with two suitcases of cold-weather gear in tow, they were delighted to find the thermometer resting at 80 degrees. As they explored the City of Angels, they were equally delighted to find that the Depression had touched only lightly in the area. And they were positively ecstatic when, upon finding an apartment to their liking, the landlord refused to take their first month's rent, based on Newsom being a big-league ballplayer.

It turned out that former Dodgers teammate Hollis Thurston was correct. Newsom had landed in exactly the right place at exactly the right time. Assignment to the PCL Angels meant the Newsoms would spend the year in L.A. It proved to be a bit of a paradise for the young couple and was certainly the happiest time in their otherwise stormy marriage. For starters, both were accepted by the L.A. citizenry. Los Angeles was a city where everyone was from someplace else. The Newsoms were no more, or less, out of place than their neighbors.

The city was also baseball crazy, especially for the hometown Angels and the Cubs, who had trained in the area since 1921. Newsom was now fully recovered from the injuries sustained in his car wreck and motivated to prove his pitching skills were second to none.

Still, fate traversed a white-water course in Newsom's life, and his 1933 spring training began with a rocky ride. The first order of business was to get to Catalina Island where the Cubs and Angels trained. Most players took a seaplane the 26 miles from Long Beach across the channel to Avalon Harbor. Newsom tried it, but the plane had a rough flight and even rougher landing, and he vowed never again to set foot inside a plane. Coming back, he took the boat ... and got horribly seasick.

All that rocking and rolling was but a prelude to Newsom's next adventure. On March 10, the Cubs returned to L.A. for a highly anticipated exhibition series the weekend of March 11–13 against the Giants at L.A.'s Wrigley Field. They took up residence at the posh Biltmore Hotel (also owned by the Wrigley family). On the evening of March 11, Newsom decided he would enjoy one of the perks of being a Cubbie, a free shave and touch-up at the barber shop located in the basement of the Biltmore. The barber lathered up his ample face and was poised to apply the straight razor when an earthquake hit. And not just any quake; this was a 6.4-magnitude temblor that shook the hotel with a fury and destroyed much of nearby Long Beach. When the shaking started, Newsom bolted from the chair, dodged the razor, dashed upstairs, ran across a busy street and hid under a tree in the adjacent Pershing Square. That happened to be where L.A.'s political radicals and the more outgoing members of the gay community hung out. Under the circumstances, wild-eyed, his face covered with lather and still wearing the bright red barber's gown, Newsom was only slightly more conspicuous than the other denizens of the park.[32]

Newsom clung to the tree through a couple of aftershocks before Cubs manager Charlie Grimm finally managed to track him down. Grimm persuaded him to return to the hotel lobby, where the other players had gathered. There it was announced that Saturday's game was canceled.

The Cubs and Giants were finally able to play on Sunday at Wrigley Field, and as his luck would have it, Newsom pitched in relief in the game and was singularly unimpressive. This was not surprising, since he hadn't slept since the quake hit.

The earthquake triggered a couple of baseball aftershocks. The Giants were supposed to remain in Southern California the rest of the month; instead they pulled up stakes and fled, manager Bill Terry vowing never to return. For the Cubs, the natural disaster definitely disrupted spring training, and most Chicago sportswriters later blamed the Long Beach quake and its aftermath for the team's failure to defend its National League title.

Whether or not Newsom's less than courageous performance during the shaker had anything to do with the Cubs letting him go to the Angels is doubtful. Likely, the Newsom-Stainback transaction was already in the works by March 1. It became official on March 15, but that and other news was overshadowed when President Franklin D. Roosevelt declared a "bank holiday." The Great Depression had hit rock-bottom.

Joining the Angels provided a baseball angel for Newsom in the person of manager Jack Lelivelt. Lelivelt, a native of Chicago, had a rather nondescript six-year major league career (1909–1914) as an outfielder with three American League teams. He never achieved the status of an everyday player; a left-handed hitter, Lelivelt couldn't hit left-handed pitchers. But he was able to play with and against some outstanding baseball minds, including Frank Chance, Hal Chase, Ty Cobb, Tris Speaker and Nap Lajoie, and he learned all he could from them. It was said that "Lil" never forgot a play and had a strategy for any situation. Certainly, his 11-year stint as a manager in the PCL (1929–

1940) was nothing short of spectacular. He won 1,105 games while losing 811, a .577 win-loss percentage. He never had a losing team, and won four pennants.[33]

Lelivelt believed in establishing a set lineup and pitching rotation in spring training and maintaining that lineup throughout the season. He was also a keen judge of talent, and he quickly realized that Newsom possessed vast if untapped potential. Lelivelt made Newsom his No. 1 starter, and his confidence in his new right-hander never wavered. Lelivelt's approach was worlds apart from Wilbert Robinson or Rogers Hornsby and it paid huge dividends, for the Angels and for Newsom. "Old Lil" didn't care about appearances, he was only interested in results. Newsom could throw the ball overhand or underhand or anything in between, as long as he got batters out.

The Angels entered the 1933 season coming off a disappointing 96–93 campaign, but they quickly established themselves as the best team in the PCL. Anchored by speedy outfielders Tuck Stainback (who hit .335), Marv Gudat (.333) and Jigger Statz (.325), and the power hitting of third baseman Gene Lillard (.307, 43 home runs and 149 RBI) and first baseman Jim Oglesby (.313, 20 homers and 137 RBI), the Angels had plenty of sock. But where they really excelled was pitching and defense. Newsom had a break-out year on the mound, going 30–11. Right behind was teammate Dick Ward, who was 25–9. Fay Thomas (20–14) gave L.A. its third 20-game winner. LeRoy Herrmann went 16–9 and Win Ballou finished at 12–19.[34]

It was all good enough for the Angels to post a 115–73 record in the elongated PCL season and beat out Portland for the pennant by 6½ games.

Newsom started quickly out of the gate, winning four of his first five decisions. In May, he missed a couple of starts when an opposing batter lined a ball off his pitching hand. He returned to the rotation, nursing a sore thumb, but struggled, holding a 15–10 record as of July 23. From there, he took off like a rocket, winning 15 games in a row before losing to San Francisco, 5–4 in 11 innings, in his final start of the season. The winning streak gave him exactly 30 wins (although some sources credit him with 31).[35] Newsom was also used 16 times in relief, with outstanding results, saving six of those games. Thirty wins or 31 (in later life Newsom claimed he had actually won 33 games), it was a remarkable season, and Newsom reaped the benefits. He was named the PCL's Outstanding Player by *The Sporting News*, among a number of post-season honors. He led PCL pitchers in games (56), complete games (26), shutouts (7), wins (30), innings pitched (320) and strikeouts (212).[36]

It was also a rewarding season for Newsom financially. Still drawing his $4,200 base salary, he and Lucille discovered that they rarely had to pay for anything, once the vendors found out Newsom was the Angels' new star pitcher. Newsom also was able to talk Angels management into a series of cash advances, especially during his 15-game winning streak. Add in endorsements, appearance fees and a highly lucrative winter season—more on that later—and Newsom in later life claimed he made over $10,000 in 1933 in L.A.[37]

As early as April, the Los Angeles sportswriters were referring to him as "The Great Newsom" and comparing him favorably to Dizzy Dean. Newsom probably promoted most of that press, but a lot simply evolved from his effective pitching. Once Newsom got rolling that summer, he dominated the L.A. sports pages. Angelenos found Newsom fascinating, from his thick southern drawl to his colorful stories about down-home Hartsville to his overflowing confidence. In the motion picture capital of the world, Newsom seemed to have been perfectly cast as the star on the town's favorite baseball team.

Jimmy Reese, the second baseman on the 1933 Angels and a former roommate of Babe Ruth's on the Yankees, offered this observation:

> No doubt, Buck was larger than life, just like the Babe. They were always the center of attention wherever they went. They could say and do outrageous things and get away with it. One Babe Ruth or Buck Newsom on a ballclub is great, but thank goodness they were never on the same team at the same time. That would have set baseball back 50 years.[38]

While Newsom was having a career year, a rival for media attention suddenly cropped up, a 19-year-old outfielder with the San Francisco Seals named Joe DiMaggio (or DeMaggio, as his name was consistently misspelled all year long by West Coast sportswriters). DiMaggio tore into PCL pitching that summer for a 61-game hitting streak. Newsom bragged he could get the Seals slugger out and had a couple of chances to halt the streak but was unable to do so. DiMaggio had equaled Jack Ness' league record of 49 straight games when he faced Newsom on July 14. Newsom was quoted in both L.A. and San Francisco papers as saying he would "put a stop to the wop" but DiMaggio slashed a first-inning single to break the record.

Lee Stine, a teammate of DiMaggio's on the 1933 Seals, remembered a game during DiMaggio's 61-game streak, played at Wrigley Field in L.A. "[Bobo] knew Joe was going real good, so he knocked him down," Stine said. "His cap went one way and he went the other. On the next pitch, Joe hit it 440 feet. It was a line-drive shot. The brushback pitch didn't bother him one bit."[39]

It was the first of many battles between the two. DiMaggio almost always prevailed, as he did against virtually every pitcher. Newsom was as loud as DiMaggio was quiet, but it was clear they were the two best players in the PCL and destined for bigger things. Newsom and DiMaggio definitely gave a boost to attendance in the PCL that summer. A highlight in this regard for Newsom came on September 10 at Wrigley Field in L.A., when he notched his 27th win of the season (and 12th in a row), beating the crosstown Hollywood Stars, 9–1, before a sell-out crowd of over 20,000.

"Of the guys I faced in the PCL, Newsom threw the hardest," said Babe Dahlgren, who played for the Missions of San Francisco from 1929 to 1935. "Later on, I faced him in the majors and he wasn't throwing as hard, but had developed a better curveball. But there in 1933 you could tell he was definitely on the way way up."

Dahlgren also remembered that Newsom was already a unique character. In the days when most ballparks did not have a loudspeaker system, lineups, substitutions and public service announcements were made by a guy on the field with a megaphone. Dahlgren said that during one game Newsom ran out and grabbed the megaphone and announced himself as "Now pitching, Newsom the Great." "From him it just seemed natural, like the way Muhammad Ali was later on," Dahlgren said. "I didn't see it as showing up the other players at all."[40]

The above incident may have evolved in Newsom's mind into a story he later told about the 1933 season. In that version of events, he was warming up in front of his dugout, hurriedly getting ready to go into a game in relief of a beleaguered Angels starter. Supposedly, the starting pitcher walked in a run, but Newsom, while warming up, engaged in an exchange of insults with the runner coming in from third. Eventually, they went nose-to-nose between third base and home. Newsom then hollered for the game ball, promptly announced he was now pitching for Los Angeles, and tagged the argumentative runner out.

No one ever believed the bizarre story, although Newsom tried selling it to gullible teammates for the rest of his career. As late as 1960, he was still telling the tale, usually with the "hook" that truth is stranger than fiction. While many remarkable things actually happened to him, this particular tale was pure poppycock.[41]

An occurrence that did happen helped shape Newsom's attitude toward air travel. Early in the season, he was relating his unfortunate flight to Catalina Island. Angels teammate Orv Mohler was easily able to top that. That winter, he had survived a crash while riding as a passenger in a small plane. The crash took the life of the plane's pilot and another passenger. Mohler's morbid description of the fiery crash scene stayed with Newsom the rest of his life.[42]

The year in L.A. inspired Bobo's creative side in more positive ways. He was able to fulfill a couple of long-standing dreams during the season. Enthralled with radio, as was most of America in the 1930s, Newsom managed to talk his way onto it, helping out on a few sportscasts when not pitching.[43] He and several of his Angels teammates also did extra work at the Hollywood studios. Joe E. Brown recalled an incident involving Newsom, who was an extra in a scene in a movie Brown was shooting at Warner Bros. Newsom wouldn't shut up during the scene and was drowning out the dialogue. This resulted in the director having Newsom thrown off the set.[44]

Newsom's popularity didn't end with the PCL season. He was persuaded to remain in Los Angeles for winter league games. Since Lucille was pregnant with the couple's first child and a long trip back east to Hartsville would have been a physical hardship on her, the offer was most welcome. Further, weekend winter league contests in and around L.A. frequently drew large crowds during the area's balmy weather in November and December. Thus, he saw the chance to make some easy money, of the cash-on-the-barrelhead kind.

Going into the winter league campaign, Newsom knew that the league's biggest attraction was a touring team of all-stars from the Negro Leagues, led by Satchel Paige. Most of the PCL's best players skipped the series, and major leaguers, by decree of Commissioner Landis, could only participate until ten days after the World Series had concluded. Newsom, technically, wasn't on a major league roster, meaning he could play all winter. And that's what he set out to do.

Promoter of the winter league was Joe Pirrone, an enterprising sort who owned a successful nightclub and had arranged for a Paige-Dizzy Dean matchup on October 16 to kick off the season. The game drew a reported 10,000 fans. Inspired by that turnout, Pirrone saw definite possibilities for a series of games pitting Paige against Newsom, who by the fall of 1933 in L.A. was an even bigger drawing card than Dean. When Paige and Newsom met with Pirrone to discuss how proceeds would be divided, they discovered they had a lot in common besides being two of the top right-handed pitchers on the planet. Both were Southerners through and through, both were shameless self-promoters, and both had little use for anyone else's opinion, especially regarding baseball. They also agreed they should receive the lions' shares of the proceeds from the games.⁴⁵

Both were also true extroverts who loved to entertain. The Paige-Newsom series quickly became a showcase for the pair's considerable talents at pitching and clowning around. Their exchange of insults before and during the games prompted laughter from black and white fans alike. The attendance was impressive, the games frequently drawing more than 5,000 fans to White Sox Park, the so-called "colored" ballpark in south L.A.

The absence of PCL or big league stars was pure gravy for Newsom. Since he clearly was the only worthy opponent for the remarkable Mr. Paige, he could charge Pirrone whatever the traffic would bear for his personal services. The Paige All-Stars, as everyone called the team even though the actual name was the Philadelphia Royal Giants, had an outstanding lineup, including Cool Papa Bell, Willie Wells, Mule Suttles and Turkey Stearnes. After October 31, the Newsom All-Stars—technically Pirrone's All-Stars after the promoter—had little to offer other than Bobo himself. For the most part the Pirrones were royally thumped by the Giants.

Paige had first barnstormed in Southern California in the winter of 1931–1932, on a team that included Josh Gibson. Paige returned in 1932–1933. But the 1933–1934 tour was the first where he was the undisputed gate attraction, and the first that consistently matched him up against the best white pitcher available. The Paige-Newsom format proved so successful that Pirrone used it for series of games featuring Paige and Dizzy Dean in 1934 and Paige versus Bob Feller in 1937. While records of these winter games are incomplete, and it must be acknowledged that they were glorified exhibitions, Paige almost always bested his rivals.

This was certainly the case against Newsom. The pair went up against each other at least eight times that winter, with Paige winning seven of the matchups. In the six games between the pair in L.A. that can be fully documented, Paige won five of them. Newsom's only victory came in a wild 10–8 game played on Christmas Day, 1933. Perhaps the pair's most notable matchup occurred a week later, played at Wrigley Field and designated as Buck Newsom Day. Before a crowd approaching 20,000, Paige bested Newsom, 3–2, Satchel striking out 15 batters and Bobo 13.

Newsom had better luck against the Philadelphia Royal Giants when he wasn't matched up against Paige, beating the Negro Leagues stars at least three times. Based on available box scores, Newsom had reasonably good success against Cool Papa Bell and Willie Wells, but the power-hitting pair of Mule Suttles and Turkey Stearnes wore him out, both hitting well over .400 against Newsom's offerings.

The Paige and Newsom All-Stars battled on into January, when Southern California's rainy season arrived and brought an end to the series.

In retrospect, it was remarkable that Paige and the fans accepted Newsom as an equal. After all, for all his heroics in the PCL, Newsom had pitched only six games in the major leagues. But the matchup was a natural, between two talented, larger-than-life characters. For Newsom, the games were a life-changing experience. He learned much from Paige, not only about pitching but about setting himself apart from baseball's traditional team concept. It was a philosophy that fit Newsom perfectly, and one he adhered to the rest of his life.

Newsom, from all indications, never thought twice about facing a team of African

Americans. Jackie Robinson, who as a youngster attended at least one of the historic Paige-Newsom games,[46] had an on-point observation about the racial dynamics of the time: "The black and white Southerners had the basis for a much more genuine understanding of each other and realization of their absolute need for each other on a partnership level than the Northern blacks and whites."[47]

Newsom could never be described as a crusader for civil rights; the same could be said for Paige. But Newsom had grown up around blacks and was at ease around African American players. He didn't hesitate to shake their hands, pat them on the back and, yes, occasionally rub them on the head. While Newsom's and Paige's clowning during California Winter League games often had a racial tinge, and such behavior would be decidedly politically incorrect in the current age, it was all part of the show in 1933. Like Paige, Newsom was above the bigotry so common in American society at that time, simply because it got in the way of making money playing baseball.

Cool Papa Bell quotes Newsom as asking, "how can I pitch in the big leagues if I can't get these niggers out?"[48]

"I doubt that he said that," Newsom acquaintance Bob Shirley said. "I know what he told me. He said he knew he could pitch in the big leagues when he was able to get those colored boys out in L.A. Now, that may seem like the same thing but it isn't. Bobo had nothing but respect for the players from the Negro leagues. And he thought Satchel Paige was the greatest."[49]

About the only thing that clouded an otherwise balmy winter for Newsom occurred off the field. The Angels, with a roster of talented players, had to make at least one available in the major league winter draft under the rules then in effect. They gambled on putting Newsom on the chopping block, reasoning that major league teams would pass on a player who had washed out in trials with the Dodgers and Cubs. It was an ill-advised move, for the St. Louis Browns, with the first pick in the October 2 draft, selected Newsom.

The news did not set well with Newsom. He wasn't interested in playing for the lowly Browns, and especially wished to avoid further contact with their new manager, Rogers Hornsby. He made noises in the L.A. press all winter about how he would stay home on Daddy Quill's farm and pitch hay instead of baseballs. It was, of course, all a bluff. Newsom, by now, knew the rules of the game and knew the Browns held the trump card. He longed for Paige's situation, where Satch could and did change teams based on his own whims and not because of some piece of paper being sold from one team to another.[50]

Newsom also knew, deep down, that he belonged in the big leagues. If he was to make big money and a big impact in the game it would have to be on the major league stage. It would be sad to leave LA—especially for Lucille, who had grown to love California—but Newsom was convinced he would be welcomed back if things didn't work out with the Browns. If Satchel Paige said Newsom was great, who could argue with that?

Four

St. Louis to Washington, D.C. (1934–1935)

Members of the 1934 roster of the St. Louis Browns gathered for spring training in early March at El Varano Hotel in West Palm Beach, FL. Veteran or rookie, all viewed the upcoming season with trepidation. The team's principal owner, Phillip Ball, had died in the off-season, meaning one thing to the players: An already struggling franchise was now officially out of money and possessed little hope of raising any. Bankruptcy and the Great Depression were very much on the minds of those in the Browns camp, held directly across Lake Worth from ultra-posh Palm Beach. As a reminder, those players who wandered across the bridge to the Gold Coast to view the trappings of the rich and famous were invariably picked up as vagrants, escorted to the city limits and told in no uncertain terms not to come back. With some players making as little as $3,000 for the season—and no one on salary during spring training—the gap between the haves and have-nots was sharply defined.[1]

Brightening the gloom somewhat was the presence of Bobo Newsom. A fringe benefit of his successful winter league season in Los Angeles was that he reported to the Browns' camp in great shape, physically and mentally. He weighed in at less than 200 pounds, for one of the last times in his adult life. For a change, his marriage to Lucille had experienced a peaceful winter. Unlike most of his teammates, he was flush with cash and filled with confidence. While Newsom still had little desire to play for the lowly Browns or the tyrannical Rogers Hornsby, he knew the major league axiom: three strikes and you're out. Having failed in trials with the Dodgers and Cubs, he had to figure the big league portion of his baseball career was definitely at a crossroads, and washing out with the Browns would likely end it.

In point of fact, Newsom was deeper in baseball's limbo than he knew. The Browns owned the rights to his contract but still hadn't closed the deal. They had until May 15 to pony up the $7,500 draft price to the Los Angeles Angels. If they were unwilling or unable to do so, his contract reverted back to the Angels. Factoring into the Browns' indecision was Newsom's age; at 26, he was already an "old man" in conventional baseball wisdom.[2]

From Newsom's standpoint, it made sense to give the game another shot. The worst that could happen was going back to L.A. There, Newsom could (if he stayed healthy and reasonably sober) pitch for a decade in the warm glow of the Pacific Coast League.

Quitting baseball meant going back to Daddy Quill's farm and spending his final years in quiet desperation. He wasn't keen on either of those concepts.

During winter workouts in Los Angeles, Newsom hooked up with an unlikely ally in the person of George Blaeholder. Blaeholder, a native of Southern California, was about to enter his seventh season with the Browns, making him the team's elder statesman. He was also, by all accounts, one of baseball's most gentlemanly players. Virtually every player recollection of Blaeholder begins with "He was a nice guy."[3] A mini-biography, on page 82 of the 1933 edition of *Who's Who in Major League Base Ball* by Harold "Speed" Johnson, describes Blaeholder aptly: "A prince ... universally popular.... Never excitable, his work is machine-like rather than spectacular, but nonetheless effective as so many American League batters can testify." The quiet, polite Blaeholder and the loud, impolite Newsom palling around stands as yet more proof that opposites attract, for the pair quickly became fast friends and remained so up until Blaeholder's untimely death from cancer in 1947 at age 43.

A right-hander of unremarkable accomplishments (his 11-year major league career produced a 104–125 win-loss record and a 4.54 earned run average),[4] Blaeholder would be long forgotten by even die-hard Browns fans except for two things: He gave up Babe Ruth's 600th home run on August 21, 1931, at Sportsman's Park in St. Louis, and he has been credited as the inventor of the slider.[5]

In truth, the slider has been around since the game's infancy. Frequent historical references to "nickel curves" probably refer to the slider. What Blaeholder did was to refine the idea, locking and loading it so it became a formidable weapon in virtually every modern-day pitcher's arsenal. The concept Blaeholder came up with was that the slider had to work in concert with the fastball. To maximize its effect, the pitch needed to be thrown with the same arm motion and the same release point as a fastball. The difference, and what a difference it was, was that by adjusting the grip on the ball, the slider would "slide" or move late in the pitch, leaving a batter with little time to adjust. The pitch didn't need a big break, in fact the best sliders break no more than six to eight inches. But it did need to break late, and it had to be thrown so that the batter would not be able to see it coming. While a hitter with a compact swing might be able to react in time to fight the pitch off, a power hitter with a wide, sweeping swing was going to have serious problems. So it was, as Hall of Famers Jimmie Foxx, Joe DiMaggio and Ted Williams along with countless other big leaguers named the slider as the toughest pitch to hit.[6]

Indeed, what Blaeholder envisioned was a nearly unhittable pitch, a pitch that appeared to be a fastball but wasn't and appeared to be in the strike zone but would "slide" away from it. A pitcher with a very good fastball, a sharp-breaking slider and the correct mechanics could be a winner, even if he did not have pinpoint control with either pitch. Enter Bobo Newsom.

Newsom was the perfect pitcher for the slider. Before, he was attempting to augment his outstanding fastball with a big, roundhouse curveball, or by varying his arm angle, all the way from submarine to sidearm to three-quarters to straight overhand. With the slider, it all became simple. Two pitches, properly thrown, and Newsom was a winner. Since the key to the slider involves how the baseball is gripped, and Newsom had remarkably strong hands and long fingers, learning the pitch came quickly. By mid-

Four. St. Louis to Washington, D.C. (1934–1935)

Browns manager Rogers Hornsby, left, checks out Buck Newsom's grip on a new-fangled pitch called a slider during spring training in 1934 in West Palm Beach, Florida. The two were to eventually experience a rather colorful parting of the ways, something that happened frequently with Newsom and any manager he played for (the Ray Medeiros collection, used by permission).

season 1934, Newsom was baffling American League batters with his "nickel curve." In his prime, Newsom's slider came to be regarded by many as the best in the game. Blaeholder also convinced Newsom to stick to a three-quarters delivery and to quit tinkering with trick pitches. Newsom would eventually return to tinkering, but for the time being the "KISS" theory definitely worked in his favor. Movies of Newsom's pitching form, when viewed in slow motion, reveal how remarkably fluid his throwing motion was, more like slinging the ball rather than throwing it. Despite his elaborate "windmill" windup, Newsom's motion at the point of release put minimal strain on his shoulder and elbow. Based on the visual evidence, Newsom's claim that he never suffered a sore arm is quite credible.[7]

Sadly, Blaeholder was not able to benefit appreciably from his "invention." His own fastball (described as "room service" by former opponent Marv Owen)[8] wasn't good enough, no matter how good his slider was. The best hitters just waited him out, fending off the wicked slider as best they could until they got the fastball, on which they feasted. Fortunately for Blaeholder's legacy, Bob Feller gave him credit for developing the slider in an essay on pitching that was reprinted in the widely read *Fireside Book of Baseball*, edited by Charles Einstein. That notice secured "Gentleman George" a permanent place in baseball lore.[9]

Blaeholder also experimented with other aspects of baseball. He worked with Newsom and other Browns pitchers on a number of the finer points of pitching in the big leagues, including holding runners on, fielding the position and scouting the hitters. Blaeholder also devised a highly effective pickoff move to second base and taught it to Newsom. While the move didn't do Newsom much good while he was with the Browns, it paid handsome dividends when he was pitching for the Detroit Tigers from 1939 to 1941. Blaeholder's presence was especially important to Newsom, because Blaeholder was one of the few players on the team that Hornsby deigned to talk to. Since dealing with pitchers—and rugged individualists—was not one of Hornsby's strong suits, "Gentleman George" became the team's de facto pitching coach and chief mediator of disputes between Hornsby and Newsom. The latter role quickly became a full-time job.[10]

If he hadn't been thoroughly dislikable, Rogers Hornsby's managerial career could be described as tragic. He took the reins of the St. Louis Cardinals in 1926 at the prime of his playing career, to the detriment of his own considerable playing skills. Despite a series of season-long disputes with Cardinals owner Sam Breadon and team president Branch Rickey, and despite a roster with some notable deficiencies, Hornsby skillfully guided the Redbirds to the National League pennant and World Championship. His Cardinals beat a clearly superior New York Yankees team in a dramatic, seven-game World Series, thanks in no small measure to Hornsby's bold use of veteran pitcher Grover Cleveland Alexander.

From that remarkable start, Hornsby's stints as manager became increasingly varied, and ultimately unproductive.[11] His problem, according to virtually all those who played for him, was a total lack of people skills. Simply, he could not get along with anyone. He was unreceptive to advice and undiplomatic about rejecting it. He had no patience with players and no use for "new-fangled" ideas. He was also, it must be admitted, a bigoted, small-minded man who had a major problem, an addiction to gambling that destroyed whatever chance he had of duplicating his managerial success with the 1926 Cardinals.[12]

"He was a miserable human being," said sportswriter Art Richman. "He hated Jews, he hated blacks. Hell, he hated everybody. Funny thing was, he also hated ballplayers. His ideal team would have been nine robots. Painted white, of course."[13]

After bouncing from the Cardinals to the New York Giants to the Boston Braves, Hornsby appeared to have landed with a winner as manager of the 1932 Chicago Cubs. However, his gambling addiction blew wide-open that summer, with bookmakers pressuring him for payment and Hornsby pressuring his players for "loans" to pay off the bookmakers. It was probably the closest thing to the Black Sox scandal that the major leagues experienced under Commissioner Kenesaw Landis. It cost Hornsby his job in Chicago and very nearly got him banned from baseball. The Cubs players certainly didn't forget—they refused to vote Hornsby a share of their 1932 World Series pot.[14]

"He didn't know how to handle men," claimed Charlie Grimm, who took over for Hornsby as manager of the Cubs. "He refused to let players drink soda pop in the clubhouse, watch movies or read the newspapers—but you could see the Racing Form sticking out of his back pocket."[15]

Branch Rickey, in a moment of forgiveness, gave Hornsby a job as a player for the Cardinals in 1933—albeit at a greatly reduced salary. Rickey also made Hornsby promise to give up gambling, a promise he was unable to keep. "The Rajah" could still hit, but a serious ankle injury precluded him from playing even adequately on defense. In mid-July, the cross-town Browns (on their way to a 96-loss season) fired manager Bill Killefer. Rickey recommended Hornsby for the job and, reportedly, also paid his salary for the remainder of the 1933 season. The Browns named him manager on July 26.[16]

With Phil Ball's death on October 22, 1933, Hornsby suddenly became a key figure in the power struggle for ownership of the ballclub. He spent a busy 1934 season attempting to find backers to join him in purchasing the Browns, while also managing the team, pinch-hitting on occasion and serving as general manager and traveling secretary. In St. Louis, the Balls' family attorney half-heartedly watched over the troubled franchise. In reality, Rickey's chief lieutenant Bill DeWitt handled the day-to-day bill-paying and gate receipts for both the Cardinals and Browns.

The heavy workload may have been a blessing in disguise for Hornsby, because it forced him to concentrate more on the diamond and less on the racetrack. His only public tumble off the wagon occurred in spring training, on St. Patrick's Day. The Browns had an exhibition game scheduled that day at Wright Field in West Palm Beach, but a light morning rain was all the rationale Hornsby needed to cancel the contest. The real reason for Hornsby's action quickly became apparent: The Florida Derby was being run at nearby Hialeah Park that afternoon. Hornsby and several Browns players, including Newsom, made the trek southward to Hialeah. It was a very profitable trip for Hornsby, who bet a bundle on a 16-to-1 long shot in the Derby and it came home a winner. He couldn't resist bragging about his successful wager, and the entire incident wound up in the next day's newspapers. That led to an urgent phone call from Branch Rickey, lecturing "The Rajah" on the evils of gambling. It also prompted a warning from Commissioner Landis, who was especially irked that Hornsby had canceled the game in order to go to the track.[17]

From the spring of 1934 onward, whatever betting Hornsby did remained on the "QT" until 1937, when he was caught using a St. Louis bookie to place bets on the ponies. At Landis' direction, Hornsby was fired by the Browns.[18]

Under the circumstances, the job Hornsby did assembling and managing the 1934 Browns was commendable. For a team picked by most sportswriters to finish last and lose 100 games, the fact that the Browns posted a 67–85 record (good enough for sixth place in the American League) and were over the .500 mark as late as mid–June was surprising. Not only did the 1934 Browns have no future Hall of Famers on their roster (with the exception of Hornsby, who at age 38 had only 23 at-bats), they were forced to play untested rookies at both shortstop and third base. Going into the season opener, Blaeholder and Bump Hadley were the only proven pitchers. And there was absolutely no help on the horizon, since the Browns lacked a farm system and could ill-afford to purchase players from other teams. By season's end, Hornsby had used only 28 players, including himself and coaches Grover Hartley (age 46) and Charlie O'Leary (age 58), who made token appearances. From May 15 until September, the active roster consisted of only 19 players.[19]

Newsom was trying to crack a starting pitching rotation in which only Blaeholder and Hadley were assured of jobs. Blaeholder, the team's starter on Opening Day on April 17 and a workhorse throughout the season, finished with a 14–18 won-lost record. Hadley would eventually have the great good fortune to be traded to the Yankees, where he pitched on four world championship teams. In 1934, he was an unremarkable 10–16 for the Browns. Hornsby finally settled on Newsom as his third starter and Dick Coffman as his No. 4 starter.

Coffman, who hailed from Veto, Alabama, was one of a dozen Southerners on the team. This was in large part by design, since Texan Hornsby was still fighting the War Between the States and was unsparing in his criticism of "damn Yankees." Coffman posted a 9–10 record for the 1934 Browns. Paul "Ivy" Andrews, a native of Alabama, became the team's spot starter and finished at 4–11. Jack Knott, a native of Texas, was the team's most frequently used reliever. He finished with a 10–3 record. Ed Wells, the only left-hander on the staff and a native of southern Ohio, posted a 1–7 record in 33 appearances.

In his first trip into Chicago with the St. Louis Browns in the spring of 1934, Newsom poses for George Burke at Comiskey Park (the Brace photograph collection, used by permission).

Hornsby was able to acquire Ralston "Rollie" Hemsley to serve as his regular catcher. Hemsley had played for Hornsby in Chicago, where he was Gabby Hartnett's backup. With the Browns, Hemsley immediately became the top receiver and Hornsby's field general, calling the pitches and setting the defenses. He was a tough, no-nonsense guy who, like his manager, suffered from a serious addiction. In Hemsley's case, it was alcohol. His drinking problem made him expendable with the Cubs, and the Browns were able to acquire him on a waiver claim late in the 1933 season. Hemsley's alcohol-fueled escapades became legendary, but little remembered is that he was one of the few players of his era who was able to beat Demon Rum. Hemsley's sobriety—it is believed he was the first major leaguer to participate successfully in the Alcoholics Anonymous program—was achieved in 1939. His recovery enabled him to extend his major league playing career to 19 years and then continue in professional baseball in various capacities until his death in 1972.[20]

Hemsley's backup was Frank Grube. If Hemsley was tough, Grube was tougher. Grube played eight seasons in the majors, never being more than a second-stringer.

His athletic claim to fame came from football. He was an All-American at Lafayette in 1926 and played for two years in the National Football League before concentrating on pro baseball, because baseball paid considerably more than football.

Although he stood only 5-feet-9, Grube was a solid 190-pounder. He was someone no one wanted to tangle with, not even Hornsby. As with Hemsley, the Browns were able to get Grube cheap. He had come up with the Chicago White Sox in 1931 as a highly touted prospect. After that season, Grube participated with the rest of the Sox in the annual City Series against the Cubs. In one game, Grube touched off a near-riot when he punched out the home plate umpire. His career never quite recovered, and he was sold to the Browns in 1933. Grube's glowering presence made "The Rajah" downright uneasy, and he was traded away early in the 1935 season. For one supremely skilled at self-defense, it was ironic that Grube was shot and killed by a would-be burglar outside his New York City apartment in 1945.[21]

The presence of Hemsley and Grube, like that of Blaeholder, was fortuitous for Newsom. He needed a strong-willed catcher to stay on him and keep his concentration from wandering. Birdie Tebbetts put it this way in his autobiography, *Birdie, Confessions of a Baseball Nomad*: "I found out that if you fell for Bobo's sob stories his pitching was lousy, so I always brought him up short, then he'd get mad and throw like hell."

The 1934 Browns had veterans at first base, Jack Burns, and second base, Oscar Melillo. Neither hit much—Burns finishing at .257, Melillo at .241—although Melillo was regarded as one of the top defensive second basemen in baseball. Melillo played in the majors for 12 years, but is best known for his unusual nicknames—Ski (for his prominent nose) and Spinach. He had a serious kidney ailment and ate large portions of green vegetables to help overcome it. In tried and true baseball fashion, Melillo's health problems didn't generate much sympathy among the players but did generate a one-of-a-kind moniker.[22]

Hornsby opted to go with rookie Alan Strange at shortstop, backed up by rookie Ollie Bejma. Strange had several outstanding seasons in the Pacific Coast League, before and after 1934, but never quite fulfilled his potential at the big league level, especially with the bat. Like Melillo, Strange left behind a unique nickname—Inky. Bejma had been a big star at St. Paul in the American Association but also never made much of a splash in the majors. Long gone from baseball and largely forgotten, Bejma had his 15 minutes of fame in the 1960s, thanks to a series of "Peanuts" comic strips in which Charlie Brown named Bejma as his favorite player (Bejma had been a boyhood hero of "Peanuts" creator and St. Paul native Charles Schulz).[23]

Harlond Clift, another rookie, manned third base for the 1934 Browns. Clift was singled out for praise by Hornsby in spring training—a rare occurrence—and for the most part lived up to that advance billing. In 1934 and for several years thereafter, Clift was regarded as the Browns' top player, possibly the best third baseman in the league. He led the 1934 Browns in home runs with 14 (a surprisingly low total in a decade known for offense). Late in his career, when Clift was finally traded by the Browns, he had a chance to play on a pennant contender, the 1943 Washington Senators. However, he contracted the mumps and missed three weeks of action in September, during which time the Senators lost out on the pennant to the Yankees.

"Clift was a great player, but nobody knew that outside of baseball," said former

Browns teammate Johnny Berardino. "In St. Louis, he got almost no publicity. And he developed a lot of bad habits playing on those bad Browns teams. The losing really affected him and he just kind of lost the desire to play baseball. (Clift) is a good example of the type of guy who could have been a Hall of Famer if he had played with a first-class organization."[24]

Hornsby's regular outfielders were Sam West, Ray Pepper and Bruce Campbell, backed up by veteran Debs Garms. All four were regarded as potent hitters and average to below-average fielders. West, the team's token representative in the 1933 and 1934 All-Star Games, led the team in hitting at .326. Pepper, a Cardinals castoff, led with 101 RBI. Campbell, a native of Chicago and a teammate of Newsom's on the 1931 Little Rock Travelers, would be reunited again with Newsom in Detroit, in 1940, and Washington, in 1942. He survived an attack of spinal meningitis in 1935 to play through the 1942 season.[25] Campbell was a left-handed hitter and a tough out for right-handed pitchers. In the outfield, he had a strong throwing arm but was erratic on tracking fly balls as his back problems limited his range of motion.[26]

From this mix Hornsby was able to milk 67 wins, and it might have been more if he had been willing to pitch Newsom more frequently early in the season. As things developed, Newsom was lucky to avoid being cut at the conclusion of spring training.

Newsom was impressive in Florida and continued to pitch well after the Browns broke camp and headed north. The problem came when a sportswriter asked him about the upcoming City Series, a best-of-three affair at Sportsman's Park in mid–April that concluded the exhibition season. Newsom made the mistake of saying he deserved to start the opening game of the series and compounded it by comparing himself, quite favorably, to Cardinals ace Dizzy Dean. It all came out in the newspapers as Newsom issuing a challenge to Dean to find out who was "the best pitcher in the world." Likely Newsom hadn't put it quite that way, but then again it was a fairly accurate reflection of his true feelings. After all, he had taken on—and even beaten—the great Satchel Paige in Los Angeles, so he was more than willing to square off against Dean in St. Louis. Dean's response to all this, while not memorable, was expected: "Who the hell is Buck Newsom?"[27]

Dean and the Cardinals found out, as Hornsby decided the best way to defuse the debate was to pitch Newsom against Dean in the City Series opener. The Newsom-Dean exchange definitely hyped attendance; fans of both teams were suddenly clamoring for the matchup. Still, Newsom's impudence horrified Hornsby, who took the exhibition games against his former team very seriously.

The Cardinals, predictably, were all over Newsom the minute he stepped on the field for pre-game warm-ups. The "Gashouse Gang" was aptly named, and their razzing was world-class. Once the game began, the verbal abuse gave way to the real thing. Newsom, fired up for the occasion, promptly forgot how to pitch and attempted to strike out every Cardinals batter. Three innings and 12 runs later, a disgusted Hornsby removed Newsom from the game, to catcalls from the Cardinals and their fans. The Cardinals, who went on to win the world championship that season, demolished the Browns by a final score of 22–9.[28]

If there was a low point in Newsom's baseball career up until that time, this had to be it. Losing a game was one thing, but losing face was quite another. However, Dean made a point to console Newsom after the game—something Hornsby would never do—and offer words of encouragement. The two became friends, and Dizzy, like Satchel before him, remained an acknowledged role model for Bobo.

"There were other southern boys pitching well in the big leagues—like Wes Ferrell and Buck Newsom—but Dizzy was the one we followed," South Carolina native Kirby Higbe told author Donald Honig. "He was the one we wanted to be."[29]

Still, it is evident there was a certain cross-pollination going on in the case of Dean and Newsom. The similarities are striking. Both were hard-throwing right-handers. Both reached their peak of fame as players with outstanding World Series performances. Both were born in the years prior to World War I (Newsom in 1907, Dean in 1910). Both became so well-known by their nicknames that even their own family members had trouble remembering their given first and middle names (depending on the source you use, Newsom was either Louis Norman or Norman Louis; Dean was either Jay Hanna or Jerome Herman). Both told a bewildering array of stories about their childhood and early years in baseball, leaving it to future historians to sort out the mess. Both affected a country bumpkin persona when it suited their purposes, but both were highly adroit at the treasured Southern art of haggling. Both had a reputation for bragging, but as Dean himself said, "it ain't bragging if you kin back it up." Both were hard to handle for their managers, and nearly impossible to deal with for general managers. Both viewed professional baseball as a venue for individual glory, and neither could ever be accused of selling his talents short. And both were determined, come hell or high water, to avoid going back to the farm.[30]

Newsom and Dean were great innovators and masters at manipulating the media. Dean, by virtue of his outlandish behavior with Houston in the Texas League in 1930, became famous in baseball circles even before he set foot on a major league field. Newsom beat him to it, thanks to his antics with Macon in the South Atlantic League in 1929. Dean was one of the first major league stars to pitch in a series of games against Satchel Paige. Dean did this in 1934. Newsom beat him to it, in 1933. Dean was one of the first players to try his hand as a play-by-play broadcaster, in 1941. Newsom beat him to it, in 1933.

The major difference between the two men is that Dean knew when to quit. For all his quirks, he never burned his candle at both ends. Newsom not only ignited said candle at both ends, he placed a firecracker in the middle. Dean was also always able to rally the establishment around him. Never was this more evident than with his election to the Baseball Hall of Fame in 1953, an election in which he was the top vote-getter. No matter that Dean's big league playing career in essence consisted of only five seasons with the Cardinals in the 1930s before he injured his shoulder. By 1953, Dean was probably the most famous baseball personality alive. He had thousands of words written about him, and a major Hollywood movie was made about his life. Newsom, despite pitching professionally before Dean and continuing to pitch long after Dean retired, was the ultimate baseball outsider. The American public loved Dean, and the lords of baseball learned to tolerate him. Newsom had a psyche only a mother could love.

Hindsight is 20–20, and that is certainly true of Hornsby's reflections in his revealingly titled autobiography, *My War with Baseball*, published in 1962. In that book, Hornsby compared Bobo favorably to Ol' Diz. "Those two did more clowning around and silly stuff than the circus," Hornsby wrote. "Only Dizzy and Bobo always produced. Some do, most don't." Likely the fact that Newsom was on his death bed at the time Hornsby's book was being written mellowed his opinion, but it is interesting to note that Hornsby wasn't the only contemporary of Dean and Newsom who compared their pitching skills favorably. That list included Branch Rickey.[31]

In April of 1934, Newsom was definitely in Hornsby's casa canine. Hornsby's mood was improved somewhat when the Browns won games two and three from the Cardinals to take the City Series. It was not improved to the extent he was willing to forgive Newsom. When the regular season started on April 17 in Cleveland, Newsom was relegated to the bullpen. Hornsby went with Blaeholder, Hadley, Coffman, Jim Weaver and even Ed Wells as starters before finally relenting and starting Newsom in the seventh game of the season. Newsom was less than impressive in a 5–2 loss to the Chicago White Sox and was sent back to the bullpen. He started again, on May 4, but lost again.

With the May 15 date to trim rosters looming, Hornsby faced a decision. The Browns had acquired Weaver's contract from the Yankees. "Big Jim"—at 6-feet-6 the tallest player in the AL—won 25 games in 1933 for the Yanks' top farm club at Newark in the International League. However, like Newsom he had control problems, and like Newsom his age, 30, made him a bit more of a suspect than a prospect. The Browns simply did not have the money to keep both Weaver and Newsom; since the price tag on each was only $7,500, it was a true indicator of just how strapped for cash the Browns were.[32]

As was to happen frequently in the ensuing years, a game in which he was the losing pitcher helped boost Newsom's career immensely. On May 8 at Yankee Stadium, Newsom faced the fabled Yankees for the first time. He pitched extremely well and may well have come away with a win except for the antics of Hornsby. Newsom and the Browns held a 3–1 lead over the Yanks entering the bottom of the seventh, despite an ongoing series of disputes with home plate umpire Emmet "Red" Ormsby over whether or not Newsom's slider was sliding into or out of the strike zone.[33]

Front-and-center in the arguing was New York veteran Tony Lazzeri, who was caught looking at a slider for strike three in his first at-bat and complained bitterly about the call. Newsom and Hornsby answered in kind and the battle was joined. In his next at-bat, Lazzeri again struck out, this time swinging, on one of Newsom's hellacious sliders. In swinging at the pitch, Lazzeri lost control of the bat, which sailed out of his hands. In the words of the *New York Times*' James P. Dawson, "Lazzeri's war club narrowly missed the head of Lou (Buck) Newsom, the Browns' twirler." This may or may not have been intentional on the part of Lazzeri, but it prompted more choice comments from Newsom and Hornsby.

In his third at-bat, in the seventh inning, Lazzeri and Newsom continued their discussion, and not about the weather. This time, Lazzeri got the better of the debate, lifting a fly ball down the left field line that had just enough distance to clear the barrier. The question was, was it fair or foul? Umpire Ormsby ruled fair, and this brought an already angry Hornsby from the Browns dugout. Despite Hornsby's protests the call stood, and the Yanks had cut the Browns' lead to one, at 3–2.

But Hornsby wasn't through. He now was carping in earnest about every pitch, and clearly had become a distraction to both Ormsby and Newsom. In the top of the eighth, Ormsby had finally heard enough and banished Hornsby to the Browns' clubhouse. All this tumult had the net effect of breaking Newsom's concentration, and the Yankees broke through big-time in the bottom of the inning, scoring six runs to come away with an 8–3 victory. The go-ahead runs were driven in by Lazzeri. Fueling the New York rally were two throwing errors on bunts by a now thoroughly flustered Newsom.

Still, Newsom might have won with better officiating and with a less frantic manager. Win or loss, it was certainly a memorable debut in the Bronx for Newsom, and he never tired of telling the story about how he had lost the game on Lazzeri's "phantom" home run. The game also stuck with Yankees manager Joe McCarthy, who was now convinced the way to beat Newsom was to distract him. He continued to use that tactic for the next 15 years, and it must be said that it usually worked. The fact that McCarthy was managing clearly superior teams during that time should also be considered when viewing the bottom line.

Further enhancing Newsom's chances of sticking with the Browns were two subpar performances by Weaver, in games he started on May 9 and May 12. Hornsby, in what had to be a difficult call, decided to keep big-mouth Bobo and get rid of Big Jim. Aiding his decision was the fact that Hornsby had found a willing buyer for Weaver. Weaver was sent to Newsom's old team, the Chicago Cubs, who not only paid off the Yankees, they gave the Browns $5,000 for the rights to Big Jim's contract.[34]

Newsom finally knew where he would be, at least for the rest of the 1934 baseball season. Sportsman's Park, St. Louis, MO, would be his summer address. The park, home field for both the Browns and Cardinals, was only 25 years old in 1934 but was not aging gracefully. Red Smith, working in 1934 at the *St. Louis Star,* recalled the place as "a garish, country-fair sort of layout," its fences lined with advertisements and the streets bordering the park filled with vendors hawking everything vaguely baseball-related, including "Babe Ruth Condoms."[35]

Sportsman's featured spacious left and center fields, but a right field severely truncated at 300 feet down the foul line. To compensate, a 20-foot-high screen was erected. Behind the screen was the right-field pavilion, cheap seats frequented by gamblers who leaned on the screen and shouted encouragement, or profanities, at the ballplayers. In 1934, the park still lacked a public address system. Red Smith remembered that a rotund gentleman named Jim Kelly would stand at home plate and, using a megaphone, announce the starting lineups. Kelly would then amble down the left- and right-field foul lines, repeating the process. On hot days, and there were plenty of those, Kelly would limit his announcements to that day's batteries to the fans in the outfield seats. On really hot days, he eschewed the walk, and the announcements, altogether. Few complaints were lodged at Browns games, since by the dog days of summer there were few fans in the outlying stands.

For Newsom, springtime in St. Louis was the perfect time to show Hornsby and all the rest of those Doubting Thomases just how good he could be. A relaxed and focused Newsom started on May 18 against Boston at Sportsman's Park and came away with his first major league victory, 11–3. He came back on May 23 to beat the Washington Senators, 6–2, and finally secure a spot in the starting rotation.

A rematch against the Yankees on May 27, this time in St. Louis, was an even more bizarre affair than the May 8 game at Yankee Stadium. It was certainly an unforgettable day for Newsom. In what might be the oddest pitching line of his career, he survived giving up seven runs, ten hits and 11 walks (he struck out only one batter) to beat the Yankees, 16–7. The inspired Browns, playing before an unusually large and rowdy crowd estimated at 12,000, routed Yankees ace Red Ruffing. The Yanks took a quick 4–0 lead, but the roof fell in on Ruffing in the fourth as he gave up eight runs, the capper being a grand slam by Bruce Campbell. For the Yanks, it was an especially painful setback, their eighth in nine games as the McCarthymen fell behind pace-setter Cleveland in the pennant race.[36]

This time around, Newsom held Lazzeri to a two-run double in four at-bats. He also kept Lou Gehrig hitless in three at-bats. But, of course, the center of attention any time the Yankees of that era played was Babe Ruth. Newsom, pitching carefully to the Babe as instructed by Hornsby, held him to two harmless singles in four at-bats. Newsom had now pitched against Ruth ten times, and the aging slugger had yet to hit a ball hard against him.

Newsom followed the memorable May 27 game with strong starts on June 2, against Cleveland, and on June 7, against Chicago. Suddenly, Newsom was attracting the attention of players and sportswriters for things he did as well as things he said.

Thus it was that Newsom was even more cocky than usual when he faced the Yanks once again, on June 12 at Yankee Stadium. It was a rematch with Ruffing, and the Browns grabbed an early 1–0 lead on a home run by Debs Garms. It stayed that way until the last of the fourth. Newsom had again retired Ruth, this time on a tapper back to the mound, in the first. Facing the Babe to start the fourth and ahead in the count 0–2, Newsom decided that now was the time to abandon Hornsby's plan of throwing off-speed pitches and blow his fastball right past Ruth, fat and 39 and looking more than a tad hung over. In Newsom's later version of events, he yelled, "I'm gonna strike you out, old man!" prior to delivering the pitch. This could well be true. What is also true is that Ruth crushed his best fastball, the drive winding up some 500 feet away in the right-center field bleachers. As Ruth tootled around the bases, he yelled back at Newsom, "Not this time, kid, not this time."[37]

The game wound up being rained out in the top of the fifth, thus washing away Ruth's home run. But not from Newsom's memory bank. Forever after, he remembered it as the longest home run he ever gave up, in fact the longest home run he ever saw. Late in life, when instructing Baltimore-area Little Leaguers on the perils of the game, Newsom's favorite tale involved Babe Ruth's titanic home run, the price Newsom paid for lipping off to the great Bambino. So while the record shows that Newsom faced Ruth 16 times that season and held him to four singles and two walks, Newsom knew he had witnessed greatness and never hesitated to sing Ruth's praises.[38]

Since Newsom had pitched only four innings in the June 12 game, he was sent back out against the Yanks on June 15, but was less than sharp in a 6–3 loss. Inept fielding by the Brownies cost Newsom in this game, as Ben Chapman took full advantage of the shaky St. Louis defenders by (a) scoring from second on a ground out and (b) bunting for a double past Browns first baseman Jack Burns, the puny hit driving in the eventual winning run. Controversy eventually enveloped Chapman's career, but at the time the "Alabama Flash" was probably the fastest man in the league and was regarded as a rising star.[39]

Newsom rebounded by winning in relief at Boston two days later and beating the Athletics in Philadelphia on June 21, and the East Coast media was congratulating Hornsby on his exciting new pitching discovery. As the weather heated up that summer, the other Browns pitchers faded but Newsom got stronger and stronger. He loved pitching in hot weather, even the heat and humidity of St. Louis in July and August, as a story from Lefty Gomez illustrates. In his account, Gomez and the Yankees faced Newsom and the Browns on a furnace-hot day in St. Louis, likely referring to the game of July 26, 1934, in which the future Hall of Famer outpitched Newsom for a 3–1 Yankees victory.

Gomez's goal was to throw as few pitches as possible and get back to the dugout, where the team had wet towels and a little shade. Meanwhile, Newsom's goal seemed to be to take as much time as possible on the mound. In the sixth inning, Gomez led off and watched helplessly as Newsom took all his allotted warm-ups, and then proceeded to spend the next several minutes walking around the mound inspecting it, eventually getting down on all fours to groom the front of the mound to his liking.

> Finally our third base coach Artie Fletcher yells out, "Fer Krist's sake, get back on the damned rubber and throw the damned ball!" That gets Newsom's attention, and he glares over at Artie. Then he throws a pitch, damnest fastball you ever saw, right straight at my head. I hit the dirt, and of course my uniform was soaked anyway and all that dirt just sticks to it. Now, I'm mad. I yell over at Fletcher, "Dammit Artie, shut the hell up! You're gonna get me killed up here!"
>
> They call me Goofy, but that guy belonged in a looney bin.[40]

By July, Newsom was a regular in the rotation and was also frequently called on in relief. He finished the year with 47 pitching appearances (he also was used three times as a pinch-runner), 32 starts and 15 relief appearances. He won 16 games, tops on the team, and lost 20 games, tops in the American League. He also saved five games in relief. And he was the league leader in walks allowed, surrendering 149 in 262⅓ innings. Bases on balls remained the bane of Newsom's pitching, with the slider contributing to the problem. Like the hitters, AL umpires continued to have a tough time determining whether the sharp-breaking pitch was in or out of the strike zone.

A doubleheader in mid–September against Philadelphia at Sportsman's Park was a good indicator of the nature of the Newsom-Hornsby relationship. Starting the first game, Newsom walked the first four batters, prompting a quick hook by Hornsby and a whole lot of angry words from both parties. It was the shortest start of Newsom's career. Newsom sat in the dugout and stewed as the A's went on to post a 9–7 victory. Between games, he harangued Hornsby for another chance. Hornsby finally relented, on the condition that Newsom throw strikes from the get-go. Newsom took the mound for the nightcap and promptly struck out the same four batters he had walked to start the first game. From there, he went on to pitch a 5–2, complete-game victory.

Newsom's next start, on September 18 in St. Louis against Boston, was even more bizarre. In fact, it turned out to be one of the oddest games of the 1934 season or any other season. Newsom's mound opponent that day was the Red Sox ace, Wes Ferrell. One of the top right-handers in baseball, Ferrell also was known for his intensity and trigger temper. It didn't take long for that temper to come into play.

After a scoreless first inning, Boston got two runners on board via walks in the second inning. That brought up Ferrell, possibly the best-hitting pitcher ever. Newsom jumped ahead in the count, 0–2, and then threw a pitch that appeared, to Newsom and Ferrell and just about everyone else, to be outside. Not so, said plate umpire Lou Kolls, who called Ferrell out on strikes. This provoked considerable argument, fueled by the fact that Ferrell and all the Red Sox knew that Hornsby had a hard-and-fast rule for his pitchers: if they were ahead in the count 0–2, they were to waste a pitch. Penalty for not doing so was a $20 fine.

Ferrell yelled at Kolls. Newsom, knowing he had just lost $20, came down off the mound to join the discussion. Hornsby yelled at Newsom from the dugout. Ferrell yelled louder at home plate. Kolls yelled back. Out of the Boston dugout raced Red Sox catcher Rick Ferrell, Wes' brother. He joined in the fray, the Ferrell brothers reportedly jostling umpire Kolls to some extent as they rendered their respective opinions of his skills. Kolls, like the Ferrells known for his short fuse, threw both Wes and Rick out of the game and later reported to the league office that he had been pushed, punched and verbally abused. Regardless of what had really happened, Kolls was clearly in a fine fury. After succeeding in having the Ferrells escorted off the field, he turned his wrath on Newsom and threatened to toss him as well. Newsom opted to shut up and pitch. He got out of the jam, but was severely chastised by Hornsby when he returned to the dugout, both for the location of the 0–2 pitch and for the unseemliness of arguing to have it declared a ball. In Newsom's account of the affair, he claimed he had to pay Hornsby's $20 fine in spite of the way the game finished. The Ferrells' behavior netted them both fines and suspensions, courtesy of the American League office.[41]

Boston, suddenly in need of a pitcher, turned to veteran left-hander Rube Walberg. Walberg was once a star for the World Champion Philadelphia Athletics but now was just playing out the string. He finished the 1934 season with a lackluster 5–6 record. Unfortunately for the Browns and Newsom, on this day he pitched his best game of the season. The Red Sox picked up a run without a hit in the fifth inning, on a walk, a wild pitch and an error by the usually reliable "Spinach" Melillo. The Browns pushed across a run in the sixth to tie it up. It stayed that way until the tenth. Somewhere along the way, it dawned on Newsom and his teammates that he had yet to allow a hit.

In the tenth inning, Newsom walked the leadoff man. Then came an out. Then came another walk, his seventh of the game (he struck out nine). Then came another out. That brought up Roy Johnson, the Red Sox's top hitter. Johnson hit a hard ground ball up the middle that eluded Newsom. For a fleeting moment, it appeared either shortstop "Inky" Strange or second baseman Melillo might flag it, but the ball got past them and went into center field, the runner at second scoring without a play. Newsom retired the next batter, but his teammates failed to score off Walberg in the bottom of the tenth and Newsom was saddled with a 2–1 loss.

Despite Newsom's gem and the altercation pitting the Brothers Ferrell versus Kolls, the game story barely made the front of the next day's sports sections in St. Louis. The newspapers, and the nation, were fixated on the capture of Bruno Richard Hauptmann, main suspect in the kidnapping/murder of the Lindbergh baby. That the Cardinals were engaged in a dramatic pennant push—fueled in large measure by the colorful antics of Dizzy Dean—also dimmed interest in all things Browns, even a no-hitter. In fact, Dizzy's brother Paul pitched a no-hitter of his own three days later, further relegating Newsom's accomplishment to the back pages.

At the time, baseball's record-keepers regarded Newsom's feat as a no-hitter, with the notation that he had allowed a base hit in the tenth. Some 60 years later, Major League Baseball revised the record book to remove all except complete-game, nine-inning no-hitters. Thus, Newsom—although dead for 30 years—lost out once again. It was the only "no-hitter" pitched in the American League in 1934, and one of only six pitched in the majors in the 10-year period from 1927 through 1936. For the record, Wes Ferrell pitched one of the six no-hitters in that span, against the Browns in 1931.

Official no-hitter or not, the game was a real asset to the Newsom legend. He was never shy about claiming it as a no-hitter, and the hapless Browns managing to lose the game made for a much better story. Aiding Newsom's tale-spinning ability was the fact very few fans were actually in Sportsman's Park on September 18. While no "official" crowd count is available, sportswriters' estimates put the turnout for the midweek contest at considerably less than 1,000. Thus, if Newsom was challenged about details, he would say, "Were you there? If you were, I woulda seen you."[42] Once, years later, when Newsom was carrying on about the game to a group of sportswriters, a rookie scribe asked if he had ever pitched any other no-hitters. "No son, only one," replied Newsom, this time truthfully. "They don't come in bunches like bananas, you know."[43]

Newsom's next start following the phantom no-hitter might have been even better. Facing the American League champion Detroit Tigers on September 23 at Sportsman's Park, Newsom squared off against Tigers sensation Lynn "Schoolboy" Rowe (a 24-game winner that year) in a rematch of an earlier game in Detroit in which Rowe and the Bengals had prevailed. This time, Newsom outpitched his highly touted rival, winning 4–3. While he lost his final two starts of the season, including one on closing day September 30, Newsom clearly ended the year under a full head of steam.

It was a very happy homecoming in Hartsville, because this time Newsom came home a legitimate big leaguer. He celebrated by buying his first Cadillac. The vehicle was used, and he had to buy it on credit, but still it was a definite status symbol, a big, expensive car for a big, expansive man.

Unfortunately, that winter saw increasing discontent back in St. Louis. There, events were unfolding that were going to shorten Newsom's stay with the Browns considerably. The team still hadn't found a new owner, Hornsby falling short in his bid to form a syndicate of buyers. Despite the presence of Hornsby, an exciting rookie in Newsom, and a team that hustled and clearly overachieved, the 1934 Browns drew slightly more than 115,000 fans for their home games. That was an improvement from the announced 1933 season attendance of 88,000 but still left the franchise in dire financial straits.[44] Part of the blame falls squarely on the shoulders of the Cardinals' Branch Rickey and Bill DeWitt. That pair was also interested in purchasing the Browns, and there remains the very strong suspicion that they deliberately under-reported attendance, and overstated expenses, in 1934 and 1935 in order to drive down the Ball estate's asking price. Reportedly, the estate was asking $600,000 for the ballclub and $1 million for Sportsman's Park. Even on an installment plan, those amounts were too rich for Rickey's blood.[45]

At the very least, Rickey and DeWitt controlling the Browns' books represented a classic case of conflict of interest. Thanks to sales of players engineered by Hornsby, the 1934 Browns actually made a profit of $28,000, the first time the team had been in the black since 1923.⁴⁶ But that tactic obviously had limitations and served to further alienate the dwindling fan base. In addition, prior to the 1934 season Rickey made a decision that ultimately cost both the Browns and his Cardinals at the gate. Rickey pulled the plug on radio broadcasts of both Cardinals and Browns games, claiming they were hurting attendance. In reality, the broadcasts helped lure fans to the games, as even Rickey was later to admit.

The future of the Browns had never looked bleaker. One immediate impact of the ownership void landed squarely on the players: 1935 salaries were frozen at 1934 levels. Things were so bad that American League President William Harridge requested that the other seven AL teams pitch in and supply the Browns with surplus players, free of charge. Visiting teams suffered a total loss on the long western trips to St. Louis in the 1930s, there being virtually no gate receipts from the games to counterbalance the travel expenses. With no radio, no promotions, no advertising and no attempt to sell season tickets, it was almost as if the Browns had ceased to exist as far as the fans in St. Louis were concerned.⁴⁷ Understandably, AL owners were less than receptive to Harridge's call for charity. It became evident the only viable solution to keeping the Browns afloat was for the team to sell its best players. The exodus began in November when outfielder Bruce Campbell was sold to Cleveland; it continued in February when pitcher Bump Hadley was sold to Washington.

Once 1935 spring training began in March, Hornsby had a new problem to contend with: a roster filled with disgruntled, underpaid players. While nationally the economic picture had brightened somewhat, you could not prove it by the Browns' camp. Leading the way in complaints was, predictably, Bobo Newsom. He pointed out he had already taken a huge cut in pay to go from the Pacific Coast League to the Browns. Factoring in the money he raked in pitching winter ball in L.A. in 1933, Newsom reckoned he made over $10,000 that year. His 1934 salary with the Browns was less than $5,000, and his major league contract prevented him from augmenting that income by playing winter league ball, or barnstorming as it was known back then. Now that he was the Browns' top pitcher, he expected to be paid accordingly and was unimpressed with Bill DeWitt's explanations of debits and credits. Besides, Newsom had a wife and an infant daughter to support (Norma, named after her daddy Norman, was born in January of 1934). The brash Bobo would not be shushed on the question of salary and eventually managed to get veterans George Blaeholder and Oscar Melillo in his corner.

It did not help Newsom's state of mind when he was summoned to the office of Commissioner Landis in Chicago on April 10, just prior to the start of the season. On this occasion, he was joined by his new buddy, Dizzy Dean. It seems that Landis had gotten wind of payments the pair had received from an East St. Louis businessman, "bonuses" for games won. Dean had reportedly received $5,000 in 1934, Newsom $1,000. After some discussion, Landis let the players keep the cash, with the caveat that it was not to happen again.⁴⁸

Off the record, Landis admonished the pair on their barnstorming activities versus Satchel Paige, a much more serious matter that "troubled" the commissioner. Both Dean and Newsom agreed to curtail such appearances, under threat of lengthy suspensions. Eventually, they reneged on the deal but that was several years in the future.

Back with the Browns for the 1935 season opener, Newsom saw the team break slowly out of the gate. Terrible weather in April of 1935 forced a series of rainouts in St. Louis. When the team did play, Newsom in particular was a disappointment. He pleaded a sore arm but more likely the soreness was in his cranium. He blamed team management, specifically Bill DeWitt (and Branch Rickey, DeWitt's advisor) for "squealing" to Landis about the businessman's "bonuses." Then again, it was tough to play quality ball with a price tag on your head and a target on your back. Newsom was, by now, wise enough to know that he was one of the few players the Browns had that anybody else would want.

Hornsby, unconcerned about his players' fragile feelings and ailing bank accounts, opined publicly that many of his charges were giving less than their best effort. Whatever the cause, the unhappiness became evident immediately.[49]

Newsom, the Browns' Opening Day starter, lost a heartbreaker in 14 innings to the Cleveland Indians and Mel Harder, 2–1. Hornsby blamed the loss on Newsom's pitch selection. Newsom blamed the loss on lousy managing by Hornsby. That sent both men, and the team, off in the wrong direction. Newsom, the poster boy for the Browns' malcontents, was knocked around in his next five starts, all of them losing efforts. However, it was not his pitching or bitching that brought his relationship with Hornsby to the breaking point.

Hornsby had several quirks as a manager, one of them being that no one was allowed to speak to him during a game.[50] In the game in question, Newsom merely happened to be an innocent bystander when the Browns fell behind early. Hornsby began to pace back and forth nervously in the dugout. This action hindered Newsom's view of an attractive blonde sitting in the box seats across the way from the dugout. Normally, he would have addressed the situation with a few choice comments, but with Hornsby that was unthinkable. Instead, as Hornsby passed by Newsom's spot in the dugout, he spat chewing tobacco on his manager's shoes—an ancient baseball rite of passage for a rookie who might dare block the sight lines of a veteran. Hornsby, engrossed in the awfulness of the Browns' performance on the field, did not at first notice his shoes were being christened by Newsom's tobacco sorties. Finally, Newsom's aim was a bit off and the warm, sticky juice sprayed onto Hornsby's socks.[51]

"What the holy hell do you think you're doing?" yelled Hornsby. "Yer blocking my view," replied Newsom. "Get the hell out of here!" yelled Hornsby.

Hornsby, the former Bobo booster, now earnestly desired the removal of the recalcitrant right-hander from his sight, permanently. He hit upon the perfect solution to his personal problem and the team's financial dilemma, all in one fell swoop. On May 21, the axe fell. Newsom was sold to the Washington Senators for $40,000. He had company leaving St. Louis that day, for Hornsby also engineered the sale of fellow "conspirators" Blaeholder (to Philadelphia for $20,000 and two players) and Melillo (to Boston for $40,000 and Moose Solters). The transactions promptly balanced the Browns' books, while simultaneously dooming the team to another miserable season.[52] The deals also paved the way for the 1935 Browns to set two modern-day major league records unlikely to be broken: lowest paid attendance for a season, 81,000, and lowest paid attendance for a game, 34.

For Newsom, he was heading to the uncharted waters of the Potomac. He had little knowledge of Washington, D.C., or the Senators. But he did know two things: He had been royally cheated by the Browns, and if he ever saw "Rajah" Hornsby again it would be too soon. Certainly, his experience with the Browns crystallized his views on authority figures. From this point forward, he rarely had anything good to say about his managers or team owners. The exception to that rule proved to be the Washington Senators' Clark Griffith.

Five

Washington to Boston (1936–1937)

"Bobo looked on Clark Griffith like a father," Newsom once said in his third-person fashion. "He'd roar like a bull whenever Bobo asked for more dough, but Bobo always got it."[1]

"I would have loved to have been a fly on the wall when Bobo sat down to talk money with Mr. Griffith," said Johnny Sullivan, a teammate of Newsom's on the Senators. "Griff could be a very imposing character. But Bobo was able to smooth-talk the old man into giving him more money. How he did it, I have no earthly clue."[2]

One of baseball's most unlikely partnerships was formed in May of 1935 when Washington Senators owner Clark Griffith purchased Newsom's contract from the St. Louis Browns. Partnership is definitely the operative word, for Newsom never viewed Griffith as his employer. Instead, as many former Senators players noted, Griff and Bobo were more like father and son. Why the sane and sensible Griffith treated the anything but normal Newsom as kin is difficult to say. In Griffith's nearly 70 years in professional baseball, his attachment to Newsom would have to rank as his No. 1 guilty pleasure. Newsom took five spins on the Senators' merry-go-round—in 1935, 1942, 1943, 1946 and 1952. "I had more terms in Washington than FDR," he would brag in later years. Of course, Roosevelt was elected by vote of the people; Griffith had only himself to blame for the recurring presence of Bobo Newsom in the District of Columbia.

"Everyone knew that Bobo was Mr. Griffith's pet," Sullivan said.

> One day we were getting ready to go out and practice and someone sees ol' Griff heading our way. One of the guys yells, "Bobo! Here comes your sugar daddy!" And darned if Bobo wasn't why Griff was there. He wanted to "borrow Mr. Newsom" to play cards with him. So while the rest of us are out on the field sweating in the hot sun, Bobo is up in Griffith's office playing pinochle.[3]

While the mystery of what exactly attracted Griffith to Newsom will never be solved, there are clues in Griffith's background and baseball resume that indicate why he latched onto Newsom as a favored son.[4]

Griffith was the first big-league owner to provide entertainment at the ballpark consistently, correctly reasoning that his second-rate Senators teams were not sufficiently entertaining to lure most fans. For 20 years, Griffith employed not one but two baseball clowns, Nick Altrock and Al Schacht. Many still believe their routines, presented before games, between innings and between games of doubleheaders, represent the high point of on-the-field clowning. Many of their "bits" have since been lifted for use by others, from Max Patkin and Jackie Price to the San Diego Chicken and Phillie Phanatic. Included in the list of their many fans were movie comedian Harpo Marx and famed circus clown Emmett Kelly. Unfortunately for Griffith, Altrock and Schacht did not get along off the field, agreeing on only one thing: both were underpaid. Keeping the pair in harness became a chore for Griffith.[5]

Also for 20 years, Griffith had a reliable gate attraction in star pitcher Walter Johnson. "The Big Train," the best pitcher of his era and quite possibly the best of all time, was a consistent crowd-pleaser. Griffith set up the Senators' rotation to make sure Johnson pitched on Opening Day, weekends and holidays. This maximized attendance at Griffith Stadium. However, even "The Big Train" finally lost his steam and his attraction to D.C. baseball fans. Walter Johnson, a great ballplayer, was worth paying to watch. Walter Johnson, a mediocre field manager, was not. Thus, Griffith ended his association with Johnson after the 1932 season.

Schacht jumped ship after the 1934 season, sick of Altrock and tired of arguing with Griffith over money. So it is likely that Griffith saw in Newsom a rare combination of clown and ace pitcher. Being able to pay one man to play two roles had to be a very pleasant thought for the man they called "The Old Fox."

It's also possible that Griffith saw in Newsom a kindred spirit. Like Newsom, Griffith had something of a split personality regarding baseball and life. He remained very much a creature of his Southern-style upbringing in 19th century rural Missouri. Like Newsom, Griffith tried his father's occupation—the elder Griffith was a professional hunter—and rejected it before casting his lot with pro baseball. Like Newsom, Griffith was always a bit defensive about his hardscrabble childhood and lack of formal education. While Newsom stood apart by virtue of his outsized nature, Griffith stood apart due to his size—at 5-feet-6 and 150 pounds, he was small even by big league standards of the 19th century.

The parallels between the lives of Newsom and Griffith date back to their baseball beginnings. Griffith established himself as a pitcher to be reckoned with while playing on the West Coast. "The Old Fox," as he was known even then for his cunning, won 30 games for Oakland in the California State League in 1893 to earn a spot on a major league roster. Like Newsom, Griffith was also something of a rabble-rouser as a player, leading a brief players' strike while a member of the Oakland ballclub.[6]

From Oakland, Griffith rose to the big leagues and pitched for the Chicago Cubs of the National League until 1901, when he jumped to the Chicago White Sox of the fledgling American League. This made him persona non grata in the Senior Circuit, although it did strike an early blow in the battle for the rights of players. Griff finished his major league career with 237 wins (some sources credit him with 240), a Hall of Fame-caliber number that gives ample evidence to his skills on the mound. Once his days were done as a player, he stayed in the game as manager of the Senators and in 1920 became the team's principal owner, principally because no one else wanted the team.

In spite of his playing career, or perhaps because of it, Griffith was less a fan of the game than a practical businessman. He became increasingly cynical of "greedy" ballplayers and lived in fear that they might someday try to unionize, as he had once tried to do. Griffith could, on occasion, be remarkably generous to employees other than Bobo Newsom. At other times, he could be far more unreasonable about money than even his tight-fisted contemporary, Charles Comiskey.[7]

Johnny Sullivan told of the time, late in the 1943 season, when he was called into military service:

> I was summoned to Griff's office and figured he just wanted me to sign some legal papers. Instead, he handed me a check, his personal check, for $500. He told me he was sorry I had to go and wished me luck. And he apologized for the check, telling me "I wish I could do better by you." You know, to this day I honestly believe him. It seemed like he was a lot more upset about me having to march off to war than I was.[8]

Roy Sievers, star player for the Senators in the 1950s, had a different sort of encounter:

> You have to remember [Griffith] owned the franchise and it was his sole source of income. You'd go in to ask for a raise and say, "The team's gotta pay me more money." And Griffith would yell back, "It's NOT the team's money, it's MY money! You're trying to steal right out of my wallet!" And he would rant on, and of course drop the line about "we finished last with you, we can finish last without you." By the time he'd gone on for a while, you forgot all about your raise and were willing to settle for whatever you had been making. In fact, you'd probably thank the old man for not releasing your sorry ass.[9]

Griffith's attitude toward race relations also gives evidence to a split personality. His lasting legacy in baseball has to be as a pioneer at signing Latin American players (Cuba's Bobby Estalella was a member of the 1935 Senators team Newsom joined). However, Griffith negated the accomplishment by dismissing the many Cuban players he signed as "cheap labor."

The key personage in Griffith's virtual monopoly of Cuban talent was scout Joe Cambria. Cambria, a native of Italy who spoke fluent Spanish, developed contacts in Cuba that were unrivaled. In the 1940s and 1950s, he had carte blanche to sign Cubans to contracts, in most cases sans signing bonuses.

"[Cambria] pretty much had his pick of the best players down there right up until [Fidel] Castro took over in the late 1950s," Al Campanis, longtime Dodgers executive, said.

> Someone at some point asked Griffith about all these Cuban players and he said, "Oh, they're just cheap labor." That got into *The Sporting News* and the Cubans saw it and started to ask the American players about salaries and bonuses. They found out they were getting a lot less than the Americans. Naturally, it created a lot of resentment and put Cambria in a tough spot.[10]

Griffith was willing to allow Negro Leagues teams to use Griffith Stadium (for a price, or course), but wouldn't allow the players to use the locker rooms, shower stalls or toilets.[11]

Griffith also had to notice that, from the 1940s onward, African Americans were a big part of his fan base. Rather than reach out of these fans, he complained publicly that the Senators were going to have to leave town because the area around Griffith Stadium "was turning colored." Virtually until the end of his life—Griffith died on October 27, 1955—the stadium bearing his name remained D.C's Exhibit A of de facto segregation.

His final Senators team in 1955 had ten Cubans (several of whom were multi-racial) on the 40-man major league roster, but no African Americans. The Senators did not employ an African American player until pitcher Joe Black joined the team, briefly, in 1957. They did not have an African American in the everyday lineup until outfielder Lenny Green in 1959. After the 1960 season, Calvin Griffith, Clark's heir, moved the team to Minnesota.[12]

Griffith was far ahead of his contemporaries in the use of promotions, as evidenced by the presence of Altrock and Schacht as star attractions. Yet he was also one of the most outspoken opponents of promotional genius Bill Veeck and was a driving force in forcing Veeck to sell the St. Louis Browns in the fall of 1953, even though it put a rival American League team in nearby Baltimore.[13]

For years, Griffith rallied against installing lights at major league parks, but reversed course in the mid–1940s when someone well-placed in the government—probably President Roosevelt—pointed out that the many defense workers and military personnel in town could only attend Senators games if they were played at night. Griffith also came out publicly against live radio broadcasts of games, before becoming one of the first AL owners to set up a radio network, bringing back no less a personage than Walter Johnson to do the play by play.

Clearly, Griffith and Newsom led lives filled with contradictions. Neither ever let these contradictions dim his self-confidence.

Of the stadium that bore Griffith's name, journalist David Brinkley remembered,

> It was a modest place. There were green-painted steel and wood grandstands and bleachers, a lighting system that faded dangerously toward near-darkness in the far outfields. On the scoreboard in right field small boys changed the numbers by hand. There was not enough parking for the players and none at all for the customers. Griffith Stadium stood in the midst of one of the city's worst slums and looked as if it belonged in one of the minor leagues.[14]

Baseball, and stadium rentals, being his only source of income, money problems plagued Clark Griffith from the Great Depression onward. The Senators won the American League title in 1933, but had an awful 1934 season, artistically and financially. Season attendance at Senators games surpassed 600,000 in 1930; by 1935 it fell below 300,000. With no farm system, and a team clearly in need of better players, Griffith had to find creative ways to raise money, and fast. Late in the disappointing 1934 season, player-manager Joe Cronin married Griffith's niece, Mildred Robertson.[15] Ol' Griff came up with an excellent wedding gift for the newlyweds and also a viable solution to his stagnant cash flow by selling Cronin to the Boston Red Sox for $225,000, on the condition that Sox owner Tom Yawkey give Cronin a five-year contract at $30,000 per annum.[16]

The deal set up Mr. and Mrs. Cronin in style and enabled Griffith to re-enter baseball's talent market with a fistful of cash. He pulled off a series of player purchases, capped by his acquisition of Newsom from the Browns in mid–May.

"[Griffith] used to say that Bobo kept him in business," Jimmy Robertson said of his Uncle Clark's regard for both Newsom's ability to attract fans to the ballpark and his sustained value on the open market. "Uncle would say, 'I used to get Bobo cheap and then sell him like he was caviar.'"[17]

Still, "The Old Fox's" shell game with Newsom's contract could generate only so much income. Further, factoring in Newsom's unique ability to finagle advances on his salary, his skill at consistently beating Griffith at games of chance, his tendency to run up huge bills for room service, long-distance phone service, clothing and dry cleaning, and his talent for flat-out begging when he was short of cash, and it's fair to say that, bottom line, Newsom was no bargain. There was definitely something quaint about the Griffith-Newsom business relationship and in the way Griffith ran his ballclub. Try as he might, Griffith could not de-personalize his players. And Newsom was impossible to ignore. "Clark was trying to be a corner grocery store in a supermarket world," summed up sportswriter Shirley Povich on the occasion of Griffith's death.[18]

The 1935 Senators that Newsom joined were an interesting mix, none more interesting than field manager Stanley "Bucky" Harris. Harris is scarcely remembered in the 21st century but for over 40 years was part of the big-league scene. In 1975, the Veterans Committee selected him to the Baseball Hall of Fame. Part of that decision had to be a sympathy vote. Harris somehow lasted 29 years as a big league manager, guiding the fortunes of a couple of world championship teams but most of the time calling the shots for second-division finishers—such as the 1935 Senators team that Newsom joined. Harris wound up with a losing record as a manager—2,158 wins, 2,219 losses—and it could be claimed that his teams more frequently underachieved than visa versa. Still, since Harris had to cope with Newsom for six of those 29 seasons, he probably belongs in the Hall merely for not committing high crimes and misdemeanors against Newsom and/or himself.[19]

"I thought Harris was a great manager," said former Senators outfielder Irv Noren. "He had no rules, no clubhouse meetings, no curfews. He'd just let you play. He used to tell us, 'I don't care what you do tonight, just be ready to come back out here tomorrow and do battle.' He was a very easy-going guy to play for."[20]

Perhaps too easy-going. Former Yankees outfielder Tommy Henrich said,

> I liked Bucky as a person. But he left something to be desired as a manager. For one thing, on the Yankees he followed Joe McCarthy and was followed by Casey Stengel. McCarthy and Stengel were baseball geniuses. Harris wasn't close to being in that class. To me, he tried too hard to be a nice guy and wound up having problems handling some of the players.[21]

Harris' lasting contribution to the Bobo Newsom saga was in the nickname department. It quickly became confusing having both a Bucky and a Buck on the Senators. Beginning in 1935, Newsom gradually took on the Bobo persona, in part to set him apart firmly from Harris. Sportswriter Bob Addie claimed the Bobo moniker came from Senators equipment manager Frankie Baxter. Newsom heard Baxter use the term (definitely not one of endearment) when yelling at the players to pick up after themselves and liked it so much he adopted it as his own. However, some members of the Senators family assert that Baxter actually acquired the term from Newsom. Either way, "Bobo" became a big part of Newsom's vocabulary at about this time.[22]

Nicknames proved to be about the only subject on which Newsom deferred to Harris. He wasn't about to change his pitching style or lifestyle for Harris, even if Harris did own a World Series ring from the 1924 Senators. According to *Washington Post* columnist Shirley Povich, on the eve of Newsom's first start for the Nats, Harris spent considerable time with him, instructing him on how to pitch to Chicago White Sox hitters. Once the game started, "either Newsom's control was bad or his understanding of the King's English was sadly deficit," Povich reported. Whatever Harris had told him, Newsom was doing just the opposite. After that display, Harris decided to let Newsom choose his own way of pitching.[23]

On balance, Newsom's nature rubbed Harris just about the same way it rubbed Rogers Hornsby. Harris may have been an easy-going fellow, but he took his baseball seriously. His patience with Newsom quickly ran out. Understandably, Harris also became increasingly uneasy over Griffith's open-door policy vis-à-vis Newsom.

The 1935 Senators that Newsom joined featured some talented hitters—second baseman Buddy Myer led the league in hitting at .349 and outfielders John "Rocky" Stone and Jake Powell both hit well over .300—but were definitely deficient in pitching. As a team, the Senators hit .285, but the pitchers combined for a 5.25 earned run average.[24] Aside from Newsom, the staff's ace was veteran left-hander Earl Whitehill, who had a career year in 1933 to help the Senators to the AL pennant, winning 22 games. That was his only 20-win season in 17 years in the majors. A pre-teen Newsom had seen Whitehill pitch for Columbia (SC) in the South Atlantic League way back in 1920. By 1935, Whitehill was clearly on the down side of his career, although he finished with a respectable 14–13 record for the sixth-place Senators. Whitehill quickly became a role model for Newsom, in large part because he had fought Newsom's arch-enemy Ben Chapman during a game in 1934 after Chapman upended Myer on a hard slide. The ensuing fight spilled over into the runway to the locker rooms at Griffith Stadium, where Whitehill went after Chapman despite being outweighed by at least 40 pounds.[25]

Joining Whitehill in the starting rotation was Bump Hadley, acquired over the winter from the Browns. Unfortunately for the Senators, Hadley was a disappointment, going 10–15. Newsom finished with an 11–12 record, with the Senators, and after that there wasn't much to brag about. "Unknown soldiers" including Ed Linke (11–7), Leon Pettit (8–5), Jack Russell (4–9), Lefty Burke (1–8) and Hank Coppola (3–4) picked up the pitching slack as best they could. Even the uniquely named Beveric Benton Bean—

By mid-season 1935, Newsom was a member of the Senators. Thus, he sought out George Burke to have a photograph taken with his new team (the Brace photograph collection, used by permission).

Belve to his friends—took a shot in the rotation, appearing in ten games before being cut loose. About the only satisfaction for Newsom in an otherwise frustrating year was the fact the Senators finished the season one-half game ahead of Rogers Hornsby's Browns.

Going into his first start as a Senator, on May 24 against the Chicago White Sox at Griffith Stadium, Newsom predicted he'd pitch a three-hit shutout. Indeed, he did shut out the Sox, on five hits. Afterward, he issued an apology for the two extra hits, saying he "plum lost count." This arrogance came from a pitcher who was 0–6 on the season going into the game.

Newsom returned to the mound on May 28 against the Cleveland Indians. In the third inning of that game, Newsom decided to go against the book and attempt to sneak a fastball past Earl Averill, the Indians' top hitter. Averill, a left-handed hitter with a quick bat who always gave Newsom a bad time, was waiting for the "heater" (some reports claim Newsom yelled to Averill that he was going to strike him out on the pitch) and drilled it off Newsom's left kneecap. Newsom went down in a heap, and manager Harris rushed to the mound.[26]

Several versions of their conversation have been reported, although it appears clear that Harris and many of Newsom's teammates—along with Averill and the rest of the Indians—questioned Newsom's very audible claim that his "laig was broke." After struggling to his feet and hobbling around for a while, Newsom resumed pitching. Harris not only doubted the extent of Newsom's injury, he criticized his choice of pitch to Averill. Newsom now had a point to prove to his new skipper, so damn the leg, full speed ahead.

He finished the game, a 5–4 loss to Cleveland, all the while complaining about his "broke laig" to all and sundry. No one appears to have taken the claim seriously, least of all Senators trainer Mike Martin, until that night at the hotel when Newsom was clearly having great difficulty walking. A doctor was summoned, and after a cursory examination announced that Newsom had a fractured left kneecap. The injury forced Newsom to miss nearly six weeks and limited his effectiveness for most of the summer. The knee never quite healed properly and eventually led to Newsom being declared 4-F during World War II.[27]

Newsom extracted revenge on the Indians, if not Averill, late in the season with a 5–1, complete-game victory. The outing was typical Newsom, in which he gave up ten hits—four of them by Averill—and a couple of walks but consistently managed to pitch his way out of trouble.

Newsom nursed his broken knee in the Senators dugout for a couple of games before his constant comments and unsolicited advice drove Harris to distraction. Fortunately, Griffith was agreeable to Harris' suggestion of having Newsom watch the action with "The Old Fox" in the owner's box. There they bonded, a bonding helped along when Griffith agreed to raise Newsom's salary from $4,500 to $7,500. The raise was reportedly negotiated over a spirited game of pinochle.[28]

Newsom started earning his keep when he returned to action on July 7 at Griffith Stadium against the Yankees. A gimpy Newsom was pounded by New York, 11–1, but managed to liven things up for Senators fans by engaging in a prolonged shouting match with the Yanks' Ben Chapman. Chapman bunted his first two times at bat, allegedly to test Newsom's lame knee and rusty reflexes, and that set Newsom off. It was the pair's third on-the-field rumble in two years.

After that shaky outing, Newsom gradually rounded into shape. And he dealt out plenty of pay-back against Chapman and the Bronx Bombers, beating them twice late in the season to damage their pennant hopes. He also outpitched Boston Red Sox ace Lefty Grove twice, 4–2 at Fenway Park on August 11 (Newsom's birthday) and 2–1 in 14 innings at Griffith Stadium on September 1. He capped the season on September 10 with a 6–0 shutout of the soon-to-be World Champion Detroit Tigers, besting ace Schoolboy Rowe in the process.

Griffith began retooling in earnest over the winter, his major move being trading Hadley to the Yankees for pitchers Pete Appleton and Jimmy DeShong. Appleton and DeShong may not have been good enough to help New York, but they were definitely better than most pitchers on the Senators roster. DeShong won 18 games and Appleton 14 for the 1936 Senators. A now healthy Newsom won 17. It all added up to an 82–71 season for the Senators.[29]

Other than the addition of DeShong and Appleton, the major change in the 1936 team was in the outfield, where Jake Powell was traded to the Yankees in June for Chapman in a swap of two of the game's more disreputable characters. Griffith apparently decided it was better, and safer, to have Chapman in the Senators' fold than having him continue to torment the Nats. It definitely wasn't a case of forgive and forget for Newsom, who refused to shake Chapman's hand when he joined the team. The two never spoke to each other thereafter, in Newsom's case a genuine rarity.[30]

The 1936 Senators had an outstanding infield, probably the best foursome Newsom ever played with. Joe Kuhel was at first base and hit .321 with 118 RBI. Ossie Bluege, one of the few holdovers from the 1933 championship team, was at second base and hit .288. Cecil Travis was the shortstop, and hit .317. Buddy Lewis was the third baseman and hit .291. As a team, the Senators hit .295. Outfielder Rocky Stone led the way at .341. Chapman finished at .332.

Even so, the Senators finished 20 games behind the Yankees in the AL standings. The major difference between the teams? The Yanks were managed by Joe McCarthy and had a rookie center fielder by the name of Joe DiMaggio.

For Newsom, 1936 was a relatively peaceful year. Other than old nemesis Chapman, he got along with his teammates. For a change, he was happy with his contract. And he was now the proud pappy of a son, Alan having been born that winter. Adding to his enjoyment of life was the fact he was now reaping the fringe benefits of being in the big leagues. His likeness began appearing on bubble gum cards, and that summer an image even made it onto a Wheaties box. Newsom himself had little use for the boxes of bubble gum or the case of Wheaties these endorsements netted, although he didn't mind cashing the check from General Mills. Friends and family back in Hartsville were assigned the task of dividing up the gum and breakfast cereal; since Wheaties placed a distant second on a Southerner's breakfast table to grits, most of the flakes wound up in the hog trough on the Newsom farm.[31]

Newsom enjoyed the Senators' new training camp in Orlando, FL. Eventually, both Griffith and Newsom spent their winters there. When Newsom's playing days were over, he settled in the Orlando area year-round. Being in the vicinity of Griffith gave him an available partner for extended card games and discussions of glory days gone by. If necessary, he could also hit up Griffith for a loan.[32]

There was little doubt as to the Senators' starting pitcher on Opening Day 1936. Earl Whitehill, by virtue of seniority, should have gotten the assignment. But Newsom lobbied hard for the honor, knowing it was an extra special one in that Senators legend Walter Johnson traditionally started Game One of the season. Harris deduced it would be a lot easier to pacify Whitehill than Newsom, and gave Newsom the nod. It is likely that Clark Griffith also weighed in on the subject, an opinion that did Newsom's advocacy no harm.[33]

April 14, 1936, proved to be a memorable day on the Beltway, and politics had little to do with it. Pleasant weather, Newsom's presence on the mound, and the promise of both President Franklin D. Roosevelt and Vice President John Nance Garner in attendance combined to draw a crowd of over 31,000 to Griffith Stadium. FDR, per tradition, threw out the first pitch. Newsom, standing next to the VIP box, secured his reputation for the unexpected by yelling loud enough for the presidential party, and many in the crowd, to hear: "Sign that Bobo up! He's got a great arm!" FDR, who had been called a lot worse on the campaign trail, laughed it off.[34]

The game matched Lefty Gomez of the Yankees versus Newsom and it was a pippin, with the Senators prevailing, 1–0. Newsom, sailing along with a shutout, was nearly knocked from the game in the fifth inning. In fact, he nearly lost his life.

On a topper hit up the third-base line, both Newsom and third baseman Ossie Bluege broke for the ball. Bluege got there first, grabbing the ball with his throwing hand and, all in one motion, firing it toward first. Unfortunately, the throw intersected with Newsom, standing within ten feet of Bluege. Newsom had only the time and presence of mind to turn his head slightly before the throw struck him on the right side of his face, just below the eye socket. The ball ricocheted into foul ground while Newsom keeled over, eventually winding up on his back—like a beached whale, as one newspaper account described it. By the time his teammates reached him, he was unconscious, not surprising considering Bluege had one of the strongest throwing arms in the league. A whiff of smelling salts brought him back from La-La Land, but as far as Bucky Harris and trainer Mike Martin were concerned, it was time to get him off the field and into the nearest hospital. Newsom had other ideas.

Led from the mound to the dugout, a woozy Newsom caught sight of a solemn Roosevelt. That was sufficient motivation to reverse course. Newsom was center stage, the star of this show, and he wasn't about to turn the role over to an understudy. He charged from the dugout back to the mound and demanded a new baseball from the plate umpire. The crowd, taking in a dramatic scene worthy of Shakespeare—assuming Shakespeare was a baseball fan—began to roar. They roared louder with every Yankee that went down, and continued to roar after Newsom got the final out in the ninth inning to keep the Yanks scoreless. The Nats pushed across a run in the bottom of the ninth to win the game to their fans' delight. Then, and only then, did he consent to a trip to the hospital. The medicos determined his jaw was broken in two places. It was also determined the damage could have been much worse if Newsom had been hit flush in the face by the throw. Indeed, the blow could have been fatal.

Asked why he refused to leave the game, the answer was pure Bobo: "When ol' FDR comes out to see ol' Bobo pitch, ol' Bobo ain't gonna disappoint him." Lost to history is the reaction of Newsom's teammates to that bit of egotism. Nor, sad to say, do any of Roosevelt's diary entries or correspondence contain mention of the incident.

Not lost to history was the game itself, taking its place in Senators lore as a classic second only to the franchise's dramatic Game Seven victory in the 1924 World Series. The April 15 editions of the *Washington Post* devoted three pages to the opener. The game story, by Shirley Povich, had the following lead: "The ballgame belonged to big Buck Newsom." Povich quoted Newsom (rather fancifully) as saying: "Shucks twarn't nothin,' I kin lick them punks any time I want to." Whatever Newsom really said, or was able to say, didn't matter. Like the dead, he could not be libeled. The important thing was, the game secured his place in the D.C. media's temple of the gods. After that day, he could always rely on Povich and his cohorts for "ink."

Newsom spent the next few days on a liquid diet. He was also supposed to remain mum, which was like telling Al Jolson not to sing. Soon, Newsom was communicating; allegedly, his silence was broken when a pretty woman passed him by in a hotel lobby and he could not resist commenting on her assets. A couple days after Newsom's close encounter with Bluege's throw, Povich reported to his *Post* readers that Newsom was talking about half as much as usual, which was still twice as much as anyone else. Newsom was also supposed to refrain from throwing a baseball for a couple of weeks, but he tossed that advice aside and started five days after the incident. Of course, a big league pitcher has to eat, so he used the occasion of his return to duty to discard the doctors' carefully laid out liquid diet. The broken jaw left no lingering medical concerns, but the incident remained a vivid memory among Washington baseball fans. If everyone who claimed to have been at the 1936 season opener had actually been there, the crowd would have numbered well over 200,000. Even Richard Nixon mentioned witnessing the event, which would have been difficult since the future president was a student at Whittier College in California at the time.[35]

The remainder of the 1936 season contained several more Bobo moments, each one further endearing him to the Senators' faithful. On May 15, he defeated his former teammates the Browns by a 10–5 score, striking out 11 Brownies in the process. For Rogers Hornsby, the result was additional proof things had indeed turned sour in St. Louis, representing his squad's 23rd loss in 27 games.[36]

On Memorial Day, Newsom and Joe DiMaggio renewed their personal rivalry. To prove how far the two had come from their days in the sleepy Pacific Coast League, their "reunion" was held before 71,754 rabid fans at Yankee Stadium. As in days of yore in the PCL, Joe D. got the best of Buck, cracking three straight doubles as the Bronx Bombers and Red Ruffing drubbed the Senators, 6–1. Before the game, Newsom informed sportswriters that he knew DiMaggio's weakness and would have no trouble with the rookie outfielder (who had missed the first series of the year between the teams due to a foot injury). Afterward, when quizzed on his pre-game claim, Newsom replied: "I DID find his weakness. He's got a weakness for doubles."

Newsom and DiMaggio locked up again in the teams' rematch, a July 4 doubleheader. The twin bill drew the largest crowd in Senators history, as an estimated 35,000 to 40,000 jammed into Griffith Stadium. Newsom was saved for the second game, but again was bested by the powerful boys from the Bronx. With DiMaggio leading the way with a home run, a double and a single, New York came away with a 5–0 victory.

However, there was no way for Clark Griffith to look on the day as anything but a huge success. Thanks in large part to the Opening Day and July 4 SRO crowds, the Senators' home attendance rose to 380,000 in 1936, up from the paltry 255,000 the team drew the year before.

The July 4 loss was quickly forgotten when, on July 10, Bobo turned in the second near-no-hitter of his major league career. In a 5–0 victory over the Detroit Tigers, Newsom allowed only one hit, an infield single in the third inning. The play, a routine grounder to the right side of the infield, saw both first baseman Joe Kuhel and second baseman Buddy Myer break for the ball. Kuhel got it, but Newsom—as often happened—forgot to cover first base. Kuhel had to hold the ball as the batter, Jack Burns, reached safely. The only scoring of the play possible was base hit, the only hit of the afternoon for the Bengals.

Newsom loved matching up against the other team's top pitcher, whether it was Boston's Lefty Grove, the Yanks' Red Ruffing or Lefty Gomez, the White Sox's Ted Lyons, Detroit's Schoolboy Rowe, or the Indians' Bob Feller or Mel Harder. It was a taste acquired in the winter series in Los Angeles against Satchel Paige, and one Newsom retained. He reasoned that few would remember who won or lost, only that he had faced the best the other team had to offer. The trait was one of the factors that kept his win-loss record hovering near the .500 mark in 1936 and throughout his long career.[37]

For the season, Newsom posted a 17–15 record, leading the league in games started with 38, including four shutouts. He finished 14⅓ innings shy of 300 innings, despite badgering Bucky Harris to pitch him virtually every day late in the season in order to have a shot at 20 wins.

After some give-and-take, Griffith upped Newsom's salary to $11,000 for the 1937 season, a raise that put him in elite company among major leaguers. In the 1930s, a $10,000 salary was equivalent to $100,000 in the 1960s. Newsom felt he was largely responsible for the Senators' rise in attendance and wasn't entirely happy with Griffith's initial offer. For a brief time, he threatened to hold out and remain in Hartsville, telling visiting sportswriter Bob Considine, "I ain't signing this danged contract" and asking Considine to "tell the ol' goat [meaning Griffith, presumably] I'm fixin' to stay home all season if I have to."

Considine immediately wired the hot scoop back to the copy desk at the *Washington Herald* and continued the drive south on U.S. Highway 17 toward Orlando. Arriving the next day at the hotel where the Senators were staying, Considine was greeted by none other than the ol' goat, Clark Griffith, who joyously reported he had just received Newsom's signed contract in the mail.

Newsom arrived in camp the next day, explaining to an angry Considine that "I didn't want y'all comin' all the way down to Hartsville and leavin' without gettin' a story."[38]

Newsom's contract beef seemed rather cheeky to Griffith, considering Newsom had only three full years of big league service under his belt. By now, Griffith also wondered aloud about Newsom's increasingly frequent demands for "advances" on his salary. Newsom may have viewed Griffith as a father, but since he also viewed Daddy Quill with distrust, it was becoming clear that the grace period between the Ol' Fox and Ol' Bobo was over.

As Shirley Povich reported in his January 20 "This Morning" column in the *Wash-

ington Post, "Griffith knows ... that Newsom, when called to account for his utterings, will deny all and everything as blandly and naively as you please and vow to the heavens that he has been misquoted." Povich concluded: "Even Clark Griffith does not take Newsom's chronic kicking over his contract seriously anymore."

The shotgun marriage of Bucky Harris and Buck Newsom was also unraveling by the spring of 1937. Several times during the spring, Harris complained to the press about "rebellious" players and how the Senators must pull together to contend for the American League pennant. For Newsom, there no longer were calming influences around such as George Blaeholder or Earl Whitehill to keep his mind on baseball. He became alarmingly lax about things like workouts and curfews. He fell back on some bad habits on the diamond and developed new ones off of it. A medical report from Newsom's final year of life, 1962, indicates his alcoholism dated back 25 years, putting the beginnings in 1937.[39]

"I don't think Buck was ever a falling-down drunk," said John Newsome, his cousin. "But he was having marriage troubles and the more money he made in baseball the more pressure he felt to produce. Drinking was his way of coping with problems."[40]

With his teammates, Newsom's behavior veered toward the bizarre, with an emphasis on elaborate practical jokes. Senators teammate Johnny Sullivan said,

> Oh God, you had to watch him like a hawk. He'd try to pull the darnedest things. Tying your uniform in knots, nailing your shoes to the floor, giving hot foots, burning your jock strap. The thing was, you couldn't stay mad at Bobo. He could pull that stuff and everyone just accepted it. Once the game started, if Bobo was pitching he was all business and gave 110 percent. I believe he couldn't help himself as far as the practical jokes were concerned. He got bored real easy, and the jokes were something he did to relieve the boredom.[41]

Wavering concentration and a mistrust of others, two self-destructive traits Newsom displayed in abundance, went far to seal his fate with the Senators in 1937. During spring training in Orlando, he discovered that a teammate was deathly afraid of alligators. So Newsom played hooky from training one day and spent it in a nearby swamp, finally catching a three-foot-long gator. This he smuggled into the hotel in a sack and placed in the bed of the phobic teammate. Unfortunately, he got the room numbers mixed up and the gator wound up in the boudoir of Bucky Harris. That evening's repose at the hotel was broken by the screams of Harris, who did not have to stay up the remainder of the night figuring out who was responsible for his unwelcome bedfellow. Those bonds that still existed in the Newsom-Harris relationship were ripped asunder by the errant reptile.[42]

Once the season began, Harris was up to his hips in alligators, figuratively speaking. Specifically, the Senators lacked a reliable catcher. Six men took turns behind the plate during the early days of the 1937 season, and none rose to the level of adequate. Wally Millies, who hit .312 as a reserve in 1936, had the inside track on the starting job but never got untracked with the bat and finished with a paltry .223 batting average. Since the catcher in Harris' scheme of things was responsible for calling the pitches and setting the defense, lack of competence at the position was a glaring weakness.

Despite their talented infield quartet, the Senators stumbled out of the gate and by June 1 were effectively buried in the standings by the Yankees. In particular, 1936 pitching standouts Jimmy DeShong and Pete Appleton disappointed. DeShong slumped from 18–10 to 14–15 and soon vanished from the major leagues. Appleton dropped from 14–11 to 8–15.

It wasn't much better for Newsom. The struggles of DeShong and Appleton, coupled with his high salary, put pressure on Newsom to produce. But he was slow to round into shape and deaf to advice from Harris. That spring highlights in Newsom's outings for the Senators were limited to a 4–1 victory over the World Champion Yankees on April 30 and an 8–3 victory over Detroit on May 8. In that game, Newsom hit his first, and last, major league home run, off the Tigers' Jake Wade.

By the morning of June 11, Newsom's record stood at 3–4. The team was stuck under .500 as well, and Harris was finally able to convince Griffith that change was not only good, it was necessary. Specifically, Harris coveted Boston catcher Rick Ferrell, probably the premier defensive catcher in the league. However, to get Rick the Senators were also going to have to take his brother Wes. Wes Ferrell, once hailed as the second coming of Christy Mathewson and the best right-hander in the AL in his prime, was only 29 years old in 1937 (Rick Ferrell was 31). But Wes had incurred the wrath of Red Sox manager Joe Cronin late in the 1936 season, a dispute that culminated with Wes being fined for threatening to punch Cronin's lights out. Rumors of a trade swirled around the brothers Ferrell throughout the winter and spring. Not surprisingly, Wes struggled in the early part of 1937, possessing a 3–6 record on June 10.

Neither Ferrell was averse to holding out for more money or voicing an opinion as to a manager's shortcomings, but both were angelic compared to Newsom. They also preferred to remain teammates and had strongly hinted they would retire rather than be sent to different teams. Despite all the ramifications, Griffith and Red Sox owner Tom Yawkey were able to cook up the biggest trade of the 1937 season. The Sox packaged up the brothers Ferrell with outfielder Mel Almada and sent them southward. In return, Boston received Newsom and outfielder Ben Chapman. Cronin somehow convinced himself that Newsom and Chapman would be easier to handle than the Ferrells and the phlegmatic Almada. It was an opinion shared by almost no one else in baseball. The reaction voiced in a *Sporting News* editorial was typical and prophetic: "If restoration of harmony in the Red Sox family is supposed to be assured through the acquisition of Newsom and Chapman, then someone may have missed their guess."[43]

While Wes Ferrell has now faded into undeserved obscurity, he was one of baseball's biggest stars in the 1930s. In many ways, his life was a mirror image of Newsom's. They were born within six months of each other, on farms in the Carolinas. Both were big, hard-throwing right-handers who were regarded as difficult to handle and not at all shy about demanding a decent wage, even if it meant holding out to get it. Both were stars for second-division teams whose win-loss records were a misleading marker as to their effectiveness.

However, while Ferrell was known for clean living, Newsom was, by 1937, a party animal. And their careers were going in opposite directions. Injuries would rapidly curtail Ferrell's stay in the majors—he suffered the ultimate indignity of being released by the Senators in 1938—and that early exit no doubt cost him in future Hall of Fame voting.[44]

Cronin publicly praised the trade, especially after Newsom won his first start with the Sox, defeating the Tigers, 5–4, on June 12 before a crowd of over 40,000 at Detroit.

Privately, he soon had reason to doubt his ability to rein in the feisty Chapman, let alone the bombastic Bobo. No one consulted Newsom about the trade, of course. Had they asked his opinion, he would have told Griffith, Yawkey, Cronin and anyone else that he hated pitching in cold weather and never much cared for either Boston fans or Boston sportswriters. Or Ben Chapman.

Despite the fact that the Ferrells, Newsom and Chapman were All-Stars at some point in their careers, and Almada was still regarded as a promising prospect, the net result of the trade was negligible. Washington did get a reliable catcher; Rick Ferrell hit only .229 in 1937 but improved on that in subsequent seasons and remained outstanding on defense. He hung on in the majors for 18 seasons, long enough to serve as Newsom's catcher on the 1947 Senators.

Wes Ferrell was pretty much spent. Overwork and his herky-jerky pitching motion had combined to tear up his elbow and shoulder. He fell off to an 11–13 record with the Senators in 1937 and was released in August of 1938. He caught on with the Yankees but failed to hang on with them (or get along with Joe McCarthy) and by 1941 was gone from the big leagues.

Wes Ferrell certainly held no ill will toward Newsom. He always listed Newsom as one of his favorites, and until his death in 1976 enjoyed telling the story about a game where the two faced each other in 1937, shortly after the big trade. Both Ferrell and Newsom were of a superstitious nature. Ferrell believed that no one, including his brother, should speak to him before a game he was starting. On the day in question, June 30, a crowd of over 20,000 assembled at Griffith Stadium to see the matchup of recently traded right-handers.

Newsom decided to approach Ferrell in conversation as Ferrell was warming up. He had a wager to propose. Ferrell was having none of that and tried to shoo him away. Newsom was not exactly the shoo-able type and continued to insist on some sort of bet. Finally, an exasperated Ferrell hit on what seemed to be a win-win proposal. The bet? The first one to get a hit in the game would have his hand shaken by the victim. Since Ferrell was far and away the best hitting pitcher in baseball, and Newsom was something less than threatening with the stick, it seemed like a sure thing to Ferrell. Besides, what trouble could a handshake bring? Newsom, just happy having distracted Ferrell for a few moments, accepted.

Once the game started, Ferrell forgot all about the wager, for he and Newsom became locked up in a tight contest. The Senators jumped out to a 2–0 lead, but Jimmie Foxx clubbed a three-run home run off Ferrell in the fourth inning to put the Sox ahead. Boston led, 4–2, in the sixth inning when Newsom came to bat. Somehow, he managed to time a Ferrell fastball properly and whacked it up the left-center field alley, cruising into second with a stand-up double. Ferrell recalled in a 1973 interview,

> The big SOB is standing there at second base, and he's waving to me and calling out, "Wesley! Oh Wesley! Come to Bobo!" And then I remembered that stupid little bet. So what could I do? I stepped down off the mound and walked out toward second base to shake Buck's hand. Well, the funny thing was, the umpires (Lou Kolls and Bill McGowan) thought I was going out there to fight.... But all I did was shake his hand and say, "Nice hit, Buck." And he said, "Nice pitching, Wes." And that was the end of it.[45]

Ferrell claimed he didn't remember the game's outcome, but it's a cinch that Joe Cronin did. Newsom, nursing a 4–3 lead and still basking in the glow of his winning wager, faced Ferrell with the bases loaded in the bottom of the eighth. Ferrell gained revenge, and the margin of victory, with a two-run single. He held the Sox at bay in the ninth to come away with a 6–4 victory. The result, Newsom's first loss with Boston after three wins, soured Cronin on him. Cronin was not amused by Newsom's pre-game bet and felt (possibly with some justification) that Newsom hadn't taken the game as seriously as he should have. Their relationship headed rapidly downhill thereafter, sped there by a Newsom on-the-mound tirade late in the season in which he called Cronin a "nervous little old woman" for visiting the hill once too often.[46]

Almada, the least-known player in the trade, was in many ways the most talented. The first Mexican-born player in the major leagues—he was hailed as the "Mexican Ty Cobb"—the speedy left-handed hitter was able to spray hits to all fields. In retrospect, it appears Almada's career was impacted as much by racism as it was by injuries. When he played, he put up quality batting statistics, albeit with little power. He had a solid season with the Senators, finishing with a .295 average. He was traded to the St. Louis Browns early in the 1938 season, played every day in St. Louis, and hit .342. One year later, he was a reserve on the Brooklyn Dodgers. One year after that, he was out of the major leagues.[47]

"Mel was a great athlete, had all the tools to be a big league star but just didn't have that drive to be a pioneer, like Jackie Robinson did," said Ivo Pusich, a longtime major league scout who played with Almada in high school and in semi-pro leagues in Los Angeles. "He was a proud man and hated it when other players made fun of his accent or yelled racial slurs. Being shuffled from one team to another really messed up his confidence. I guess you could say he was overly sensitive, but I'm sure it was really tough on him."[48]

Eventually, Almada returned to his native Mexico, became a well-respected manager in the Mexican League, and was elected to the Mexican Baseball Hall of Fame.

Chapman already had a history with Newsom, and it wasn't a happy one. That they were still teammates did nothing to endear one to the other. "Battling Ben" had two quality years with the Red Sox, leading the team in hitting at .340 in 1938. Then along came Ted Williams and Chapman was traded away to Cleveland, earning him a permanent place in SABR trivia contests as the man "Teddy Ballgame" replaced. Like Almada, Chapman's career was blighted by racism—his own. His hatred of his fellow man proved excessive even by the low standards of the time, and eventually he was deemed unemployable in pro baseball. His stay in the majors ended in infamy in the late 1940s when, as manager of the Philadelphia Phillies, he became Jackie Robinson's chief tormentor. Long before then, Chapman was known as a hothead who would rekindle the Civil War at the drop of a wrong word or the hint of a slight.

The uneasy truce between Chapman and Newsom ended one summer day prior to a game at Fenway Park. Chapman overheard Newsom bragging about having once beaten "the great Satchel Paige" and became incensed, both by the bragging and the bracketing of "that God-damn nigger" with a white man. The two went at it in the clubhouse, Newsom reportedly getting the better of the fray. Cronin wrongly assumed it was Newsom who started the fight, and the incident helped hasten Newsom's exit from Boston.[49]

With the Bosox, in addition to Chapman, Newsom found himself trying to fit into a team that included Cronin, along with future Hall of Famers Lefty Grove and Jimmie Foxx. Their presence meant that Newsom was decidedly not the top dog in the clubhouse. His antics, which pleased fans and media alike in Washington, were mocked by Boston's sportswriters. Typical of the irritating comments generated by Beantown scribes was one by "Colonel" Tom Egan, who reported that the new Red Sox battery of Moe Berg and Buck Newsom combined for an IQ of 171. Since it was common knowledge that Berg's IQ was in the 170 range, it didn't take Newsom, or the readers, long to deduce that the "1" must belong to him.[50]

Berg, unlike his manager and most of his teammates, found Newsom both a humorous study and an entertaining presence. Their first meeting was memorable: Newsom came up to Berg and asked, "Hey Bobo, what are the signs today?" "My name is Morris," Berg replied. "OK, have it your way," said Newsom. "Bobo Morris, what are the signs today?"[51]

Berg, in his own way every bit as peculiar as Bobo, remembered Newsom's disconcerting habit of reading the *Daily Racing Form* and placing bets on the ponies, this on the bullpen phone while a game was going on. Berg eventually earned Newsom's respect, to the extent that he would check with Berg as to the wisdom of the wager before calling his bookie.[52]

In June of 1937, Newsom was traded by the Washington Senators to the Boston Red Sox. Once again, on his first trip into Chicago, he sought out George Burke to have new photographs taken. Here, he strikes a heroic if unlikely pitching pose before a sea of empty seats at Comiskey Park (the Brace photograph collection, used by permission).

Newsom, not surprisingly, did not agree with Cronin's strategy when it came to pitching. It was widely reported that Cronin's attempt to offer advice was greeted by "You get back and play shortstop, I'd do the pitching."[53] What wasn't reported was that it was exactly the same advice both Wes Ferrell and Lefty Grove gave Cronin and on more than one occasion. In reality, unlike Grove, Newsom didn't miss a start for the Sox until the season's dying days and never ducked an opponent, including the powerful New York Yankees.

By late August, the Sox were reduced to competing with Cleveland for fourth place in the AL. Boston came into Cleveland for a series that figured to decide the teams' final standings and, for the first time, Newsom was matched against the Indians' wunderkind,

18-year-old Bob Feller. In the run-up to the game, Newsom made quite a production about how he was going to put the kid in his place. However, it was Feller who prevailed, beating the Sox 8–1 on a four-hitter and striking out 16 in the process. Newsom was knocked out in the sixth inning, but hung around the dugout belittling Boston batters' efforts to catch up to Feller's fastball. Cronin, who struck out twice himself against Rapid Robert, found the experience distasteful and Bobo's conduct intolerable.

"Cronin was a nice guy, but not much as a manager," said Babe Dahlgren, who played for Cronin in Boston in 1935 and 1936. "He didn't give a damn about pitching or defensive alignments. His approach was, let's go out and score more runs than the other guys. When I was in Boston, Joe had Moe Berg decide the pitching changes. He'd just look over at Moe in the dugout. Thumbs down by Moe, Joe would yank the pitcher."[54]

Despite ill-timed losses to Wes Ferrell and Bob Feller, for the most part Newsom kept the Sox in all the games he pitched. He finished with a 13–10 record with Boston, giving him a 16–14 mark for the season. His off-the-field behavior was no more excessive than Jimmie Foxx, whose drinking and carousing rivaled Babe Ruth. And Newsom, for all his eccentricities, was easier to get along with than Lefty Grove, who rarely had a good thing to say when he won and was a holy terror when he lost.

Newsom stayed in a hotel while in Boston and supposedly kept a pair of pet rabbits in his room. The rabbits did what rabbits do best—multiply and chew—and completely ruined the suite. In fairness, ballplayers don't need rabbits to help them tear up hotel rooms, and Newsom was no more or less tidy than any of his contemporaries. It was also reported that Newsom billed food, drink and wardrobe to the team. Since there is ample evidence he did this everywhere he played, it shouldn't have come as a great shock to Red Sox management.[55]

Joe Cronin, another future Hall of Famer, was Bobo Newsom's manager with the Red Sox. Cronin had a decided disadvantage in that he was also Boston's starting shortstop. Thus, he could not escape Newsom's verbal blasts. After a half-season of listening, Cronin had heard enough and shipped Newsom off to baseball's Siberia—the St. Louis Browns (the Ray Medeiros collection, used by permission).

Then again, there was a special madness in everything Newsom did that could aggravate even the most patient of men. Perhaps inspired by his pets, Newsom adopted a new habit with the Sox. After each inning, he would hop on one foot down the dugout steps. Late in September, on a misty afternoon at Fenway Park, Newsom did his hopping, slipped on the wet concrete, and sprained his ankle. He was unable to continue his pitching duties, and apparently it was one hop too many for Cronin.[56]

About the only tangible benefit of Newsom's time in Boston came in the off-season, when he joined Foxx, Grove and several other big leaguers in a series of Sunday exhibitions against the Buck Leonard/Josh Gibson-led Homestead Grays in Baltimore. The games often attracted crowds approaching 10,000, with Newsom pitching the majority of innings for the major league stars. The games helped increase Newsom's bank balance and also helped him establish contacts in Baltimore that would pay off later in life.[57]

Back in Boston, by September there were already newspaper reports that he would not return to the team in 1938. The 1937 Red Sox finished a disappointing fifth, and the chief deficiency of the team was pitching. Grove finished at 17–9, Newsom and Ferrell's stats combined yielded 16 wins and as many losses, and Jack Wilson was 16–10 (the best year of his big league career). Beyond those numbers, there wasn't much to brag about. Not helping matters was Cronin's tendency to use his starters frequently in relief and his inability to stick with a set starting rotation—he would often alter it to accommodate Grove.

Bottom line, Cronin and Yawkey were uncomfortable with Newsom, for myriad reasons. In early December, he was traded to the St. Louis Browns, along with infielder Red Kress and outfielder Buster Mills, for outfielder Joe Vosmik. Even at the time, it didn't appear to be a coup for the Sox. Vosmik was a dangerous hitter but an indifferent fielder and, like Newsom, a bit of a rounder. As so often happened in Boston, it turned out the Sox didn't need an extra bat as much as they needed a reliable pitcher. But it was a final break in the Newsom-Cronin relationship. Although the Red Sox had several opportunities to re-acquire Newsom in future years, they consistently declined.[58]

For Newsom, it was back to St. Louis, back to pitching for the pathetic, penny-pinching Browns. It was a big step down the big league ladder, but it turned out to be a blessing in disguise.

Six

St. Louis to Detroit (1938–1939)

While Bobo Newsom was delighted to leave the Red Sox, he held no illusions about what awaited him in St. Louis: yet another awful Browns team. The only two things that set the 1938 edition of the Browns apart from the 1934 and 1935 versions that Newsom pitched for were that Rogers Hornsby was gone as Browns manager (fired during the 1937 season) and the Browns had a new ownership group, headed by Donald Barnes. Bill DeWitt was still running the front office, with Branch Rickey waiting in the wings to offer advice. That penny-wise combination meant Newsom was going to have to hustle to obtain a raise, let alone his customary "cash advances."[1]

Barnes, by all accounts, was a pleasant fellow who enjoyed watching baseball. While well-to-do (he made most of his money selling insurance and operating a finance company), he wasn't a candidate for the Fortune 400 list. He also had no knowledge of the game other than that of a fan, and was perfectly content to have DeWitt run the baseball side of the Browns operation.

For a field manager, DeWitt selected Gabby Street, 55, a former batterymate of Walter Johnson who gained a measure of fame by catching a ball dropped from the top of the Washington Monument. After his playing career ended, in part due to military service in World War I, Street worked his way back up the minor league ladder as a manager. Included in that stint was managing the 1927 Columbia Reds, where he became

One of the promotional issues by the Hartsville Museum was this postcard of Bobo, taken from a family snapshot taken at Detroit in 1939 (courtesy Hartsville Museum).

bête noire in Newsom's bio by tossing young Norman Newsome out of an aborted tryout. Eventually, Street was selected to manage the St. Louis Cardinals. His teams won National League pennants in his first two years, and the World Series in 1931. However, the Cardinals slumped to sixth place in 1932 and weren't doing appreciably better in 1933 when Street was fired by Rickey in mid-season. He was caught in a power struggle with Cardinals second baseman Frankie Frisch, who openly harbored managerial ambitions. Rickey, facing a decision of keeping Street as manager and alienating his star second sacker or firing Street and making Frisch a player-manager, took the obvious course and showed Street the highway.[2]

Street eventually resurfaced in St. Louis as a radio announcer. In the spring of 1938 he was hired to manage the Browns, at a reported $20,000 a year. He definitely had name value in town, but whether or not he possessed the skills to assemble a winning ballclub out of the available raw material was debatable. It was a question never answered, because Street never really tried.

"We're in spring training in San Antonio, and DeWitt calls Street over to talk to Donald Barnes," recalled Jack Fournier, the Browns' chief scout and advisor to DeWitt at that time. "So Barnes asks him how he thinks the Browns will do in 1938. And Street says, 'Well sir, if I can get these guys to bust their asses and if Billy Boy there can get me a couple more big league ballplayers, I see no reason why we can't finish in sixth place.' Thing was, he wasn't kidding when he said it."

Fournier also recalled a time, late in the season, when an argument broke out at home plate over balls and strikes, pitting batterymates Newsom and Billy Sullivan versus the home plate umpire. The umpire threw Sullivan out of the game and was about to do the same with Newsom, but still no sign of Street.

"Barnes and DeWitt, up in the owners' box, are looking around and there is Street down at the opposite end of the dugout, paying absolutely no attention to what's going on, shooting the shit with a couple fans," Fournier said. "So you knew that Gabby's heart just wasn't in it, and he wasn't going to be around much longer."[3]

For Street, a former catcher, assembling and handling a pitching staff should have been Job One. Instead, other than Newsom, the Browns pitching staff was a shambles from the start of spring training in Texas. The Browns were coming off a 108-loss season in which the "ace" of the staff was Jim Walkup with a 9–12 record. Other returning starting pitchers were Lefty Mills (10–12 in 1937), Jack Knott (8–18), Oral Hildebrand (8–17) and Julio Bonetti (4–11). No one in that group gave American League batters cause to quake in their cleats. Street evinced high hopes for a pair of New York Yankees castoffs, left-handers Russ Van Atta and Vito Tamulis, but neither contributed much. Other members of the staff, in alphabetical order, included Emil Bildilli, Ed Cole, Bill Cox, Fred Johnson, Harry Kimberlin, Glenn Liebhardt, Ed Linke, Les Tietje, Bill Trotter and Jim Weaver. They contributed even less.

Indeed, the Joe Vosmik trade that DeWitt had engineered over the winter proved to be the Brownies' saving grace, as it brought them Newsom, a starting shortstop in Ralph "Red" Kress and a starting outfielder in Colonel Buster Mills (his given name). This was the first in a series of DeWitt trades in which he attempted to swap quality for quantity; eventually, the trend would enfold Newsom.

For 1938, Newsom posted a 20–16 record. The rest of the pitchers won 35 games and lost 81. It doesn't take a stretch of statistical imagination to realize that if the 1938 Browns did not have the services of Newsom, they likely would have lost 106 games. With Newsom, the Browns lost "only" 97 and managed to avoid last place by two games over the Philadelphia Athletics, thanks in no small measure to the fact that two late-season games between the teams were rained out and not rescheduled. Thus, Street proved to be a better prophet than manager.[4]

Street's one stroke of managerial brilliance involving the pitching staff was to let Newsom pitch as often as he liked. "He likes to strut and make a lot of noise," Street told sportswriter Dick Farrington. "Some managers have tried to hold him down and show him who was boss, but I just let him pop off and be important."[5]

Just how important was Newsom to the team, and just how bad was the rest of the Browns staff? That staff led the majors in hits allowed (1,584), walks (737) and runs (962). The way things were going late in the season, Browns hurlers may well have given up 1,000 runs if the two games in September hadn't been washed away by rain. Bottom line, the Browns started virtually every game with the probability they would have to score at least six runs in order to have any chance of winning. Newsom appeared in 44 games and won 20 of his 40 starts.

For long-suffering Browns fans, all too typical of the caliber of pitcher the team employed was Fred "Cactus" Johnson. Johnson was 44 years old and had last pitched in the majors in 1923 with the New York Giants. He was old enough, in biological theory at least, to be Newsom's father. With the Browns, he managed to get into 17 games, with a 3–7 record and a 5.61 earned run average. Unbelievably, he returned to pitch briefly for the Browns in 1939.

Bildilli, at age 25, was the youngest member of the staff. He pitched in only five games for the Browns, with a 1–2 record and a 7.06 ERA. His chief legacy was his unusual last name and the rhyming nickname his teammates hung on him: "Hill Billy." Bildilli's birthplace was also notable: Diamond, Indiana.

Other than Newsom, the team's most effective pitcher in 1938 was Howard "Lefty" Mills (no relation to Buster Mills). Mills, like Newsom, debuted with the Browns in 1934. Unlike Newsom, he didn't produce for the team until 1938, when he posted a 10–12 record and a 5.31 ERA, completing 15 of 27 starts. Hildebrand was 8–10 with a 5.49 ERA, but Walkup, the 1937 staff leader in wins, slumped to a 1–12 record and a 6.80 ERA. Yankees castoffs Van Atta and Tamulis combined for a 4–10 record and a 6.26 ERA. The Browns bullpen was so unreliable that Street and Newsom decided early in the season that no matter how poorly Newsom might be pitching on a given day, he was still better than anyone Street could summon. Newsom wound up completing 31 of his 40 starts, both figures leading the league.

At this stage in his career, Newsom tended to "nibble" at the strike zone and frequently ran the count full. Add to that the fact the Browns' defense was deficient in many areas and Newsom compiled numbers in 1938 that aren't likely to be duplicated. He pitched 329⅔ innings, allowing 334 hits, 205 runs, and 186 earned runs, struck out 226 and walked 192. He faced 1,475 batters. Including exhibition games, Newsom's pitches in batting practice, warm-ups and actual combat likely totaled over 10,000 that year. Most amazingly, he won 20 games. His 5.08 earned run average is the highest ever for a 20-game winner.[6]

Newsom needed to win on the final day of the 1938 season, October 2, to reach that magic mark for the first time in his major league career. Street wasn't around to see it, having been fired by DeWitt two weeks earlier. Oscar Melillo, released as a player by the Red Sox earlier in the year, returned to St. Louis to finish out the season as Browns manager. The team went 2–7 under "Spinach"—both wins recorded by Newsom.[7]

Street was no doubt glad to leave the sinking Browns ship. He quickly resurfaced as a play-by-play radio announcer, a job he held until his death in 1951. Scarcely anyone now remembers him as a major league manager, for he has become noteworthy in baseball annals as Harry Caray's mentor and first broadcast partner in 1945.

"He was an OK guy, but definitely an old-school kind of broadcaster," Caray said in a 1987 interview. "He told me, if something happens in a game and you missed it or don't understand it, just fake it. Great advice, huh? This coming from a guy who actually managed a major league team. He'd just go along on the broadcasts, making stuff up."[8]

The Browns began the 1938 season with new starters at six of nine positions. Newsom, of course, was the Opening Day starting pitcher. George McQuinn, acquired from the Yankees, took over at first base. Don Heffner, also an ex–Yankee, took over at second. Kress was at shortstop, and Buster Mills was in center field. The Browns' new catcher was Billy Sullivan. Sullivan, the son of the longtime Chicago White Sox catcher of the same name, was acquired from the Cleveland Indians in February along with relief pitcher Ed Cole for catcher Rollie Hemsley. Sullivan had been around the big leagues for six years, with three different teams. A graduate of Notre Dame, he was regarded as a bit too independent by management but was well-liked by teammates. With the Browns, he quickly became Newsom's favorite catcher, mainly because he was as easygoing as Hemsley was gruff. Johnny Berardino remembered Sully, when quizzed by a rookie pitcher about what pitch to throw, saying, "Surprise me."[9]

Whatever his defensive shortcomings, the left-handed-hitting Sullivan was a tough out, hitting .277 in 111 games. His backup was Tommy Heath, who hit only .227 in 70 games and was returned to the minors to stay in 1939. He capped his baseball career with a 12-year stint as a manager in the Pacific Coast League.

The three holdovers from the 1937 Opening Day lineup were third baseman Harlond Clift and outfielders Beau Bell and Sam West. Clift, at age 25, was in the prime of his career and other than Newsom was the closest thing the Browns had to a star. He hit .290 with 34 home runs, 118 RBI, and 119 runs scored. Since he was the only power hitter in the Browns lineup, he drew 118 walks. Bell was coming off back-to-back years in which he batted .344 and .340, but disappointed in 1938, falling to a .262 average, although he did hit 13 home runs and drive in 84 runs. Still, that RBI mark was a long way from his 1937 total of 117. It was the beginning of the end for this "BoBeau." He was traded by the Browns in 1939 and was out of the major leagues by 1941. A Texan and protégé of Rogers Hornsby, Bell clearly suffered without the Rajah's tutoring. Bell's rapid decline—not unlike what Clift would experience—was one more case of "Browns disease": potential stars who grew discouraged at the team's low standing and low payroll and seemed to lose interest in the game.[10]

Red Kress and Don Heffner, the Browns' double-play combination, were at the tail end of their playing careers. Both turned into baseball lifers and eventually became longtime major league coaches who also had brief flings at managing in the big leagues.

In 1938, Kress hit .302 and Heffner .245, but age and nagging injuries had slowed both down defensively. They did manage to turn 100 double plays, but that was due to increased opportunities rather than exceptional skills. With the Browns' pitching staff, it seemed as if they started every inning with a runner at first base.[11] Jack Fournier said,

> With both the Browns and Cardinals using the field [at Sportsman's Park] DeWitt never had a chance to work on the infield. By June 15, it was hard as a rock and had a million divots. Then it would bake all summer long, and the clay wound up being like concrete. Any ball hit on the ground would just take off, and if you didn't have infielders with quick reflexes and great range every ball hit on the ground was going to the outfield.[12]

Buster Mills proved adequate in the outfield, hitting .285. Veteran Ethan Allen, still a skilled hitter at age 34, was the team's top pinch-hitter. However, Allen received an offer he couldn't refuse, to coach baseball at Yale, and quit the Browns in June. The Yale position represented a huge jump up in terms of prestige, pay and job security. In the wake of Allen's defection, rookie Mel Mazzera saw increased action and played in 86 games, hitting .279 in his best year of an otherwise undistinguished five-year big league career.

The other Browns outfielder on Opening Day, Sam West, had been in the American League since 1927 and with the Browns since 1933. West, at age 33, was still a potent offensive force. However, having West and Bell in the outfield at the same time was akin to a medieval torture chamber for Browns pitchers, since neither rose to the level of competence on defense. DeWitt put up with the situation until June 15, the final day for trades. On that date, he sent West to the Washington Senators in exchange for Mel Almada. Almada was an upgrade over West defensively and hit .342 for the Browns the rest of the way, scoring 77 runs in 102 games. But the "Mexican Ty Cobb" faded rapidly thereafter and was out of organized baseball by 1941, yet another untimely career demise that resists rational explanation.

Almada had a subpar 1939 season, hitting well under .250. By 1940, he was back in the Pacific Coast League. There, he bitterly complained to his older brother Louie, an established PCL player, about the racial climate in the major leagues.

"They threw at me every time at bat," he told Louie Almada. "They kept throwing at me because I'm Mexican!"

"No, Melo," his brother replied. "They threw at you because it worked. That's why you're not in the big leagues anymore."[13]

When the dust at Sportsman's Park settled on the 1938 season, the Browns as a team hit .281 and scored 755 runs. The pitching staff negated that number, and what the pitchers didn't spoil, the defense did.

"With that team," Fournier said, "you didn't see guys hustling and diving to make a play like you would see on the Yankees. It was the Browns, what can I tell you? Those 20 games that Buck Newsom won had to be the toughest 20 wins in history. He earned his keep that year."[14]

Newsom began seeking that keep in February of 1938, returning a Browns contract that called for the same amount of money ($11,000) that he made in 1937. After some rather tame negotiations, by Newsom's standards, he managed to talk DeWitt into a $500 raise, with another $1,000 bonus to come due at the end of the season if Newsom won 20 games. No Browns pitcher had accomplished that feat since Walter "Lefty"

Stewart in 1930 (and no one would again until Ned Garver in 1951). DeWitt had to feel the $1,000 was a safe bet, but he didn't reckon with Newsom's powers of concentration when it came to money. Newsom led the league in games started, complete games, innings pitched, hits, runs and earned runs. He would have also led in strikeouts and walks except for the emergence of Bob Feller in Cleveland.[15]

Feller, only 19, won 17 games, helping the Tribe become a surprise pennant contender. He also beat out Newsom in the strikeout race, finishing with 240 to Newsom's 226, and in walks, issuing a modern-day record 208. How Feller topped Newsom in the strikeout race provided a remarkable conclusion to Rapid Robert's season.

Newsom went into the final day of the season feeling optimistic about winning the strikeout title. He trailed Feller by only six, 222–216. His final start of the year, the first game of doubleheader against the White Sox at Comiskey Park in Chicago, started an hour earlier than Feller's game in Cleveland against the Detroit Tigers. Newsom pitched a complete game, winning 4–3 (his 20th triumph) and striking out ten Chicago batters in the process. For the time being, he held the league lead in Ks, had earned an extra thousand dollars for 20 wins and was feeling pretty cocky about it. Newsom returned to his hotel room to await word from Cleveland. Finally, a radio report said Detroit had beaten Cleveland, 4–1, but gave no further details. Newsom could wait no longer. He got on the phone and called the Cleveland clubhouse. Feller recalled,

> I had just struck out 18 Tigers to set a new major league record. So we are having a little celebration in the clubhouse, and I'm talking to sportswriters, and all of a sudden I'm called away for an "urgent" phone call. Turns out it was Bobo. "I got 10, how many did you get?" he asks. "18," I answer. Then there's this long pause, and then I hear "Damn! I wonder if I can still make this a collect call?[16]

The 1938 season was one wild ride for Newsom, from Opening Day to that final phone call. Coming out of training camp, there was little doubt that Newsom was going to be the Browns' starting pitcher in their season opener at Cleveland. Three days prior to the opener, by happenstance, Newsom bumped into Donald Barnes just after the Brownies had beaten the Cardinals at Sportsman's Park in the teams' annual City Series. Striking up a conversation, Barnes asked Newsom how he thought he would do in the opener. Newsom, of course, replied with words to the effect that he would murder dem bums. Barnes, impressed by a rare show of confidence on the part of a Browns player, replied that if he could indeed beat the Indians he would buy him a new suit when the team got back to St. Louis.

Came the opener and Newsom was on his game. He beat the Indians and Johnny Allen, 6–2, before a crowd in excess of 30,000 at Cleveland's Municipal Stadium. It was quite a thrill for Barnes, who wasn't used to seeing either (a) the Browns winning, or (b) more than 1,000 people in the stands. He sought out Newsom at the team's hotel to congratulate him. "By the way, my boy, here's the money for the suit I promised you," Barnes said. "Keep the sugar, Bo," Newsom answered. "I bought the suit already. The bill's gonna be on your desk when we get back to St. Loo."[17]

Somehow, the newspapers found out about the suit story, and it became the latest Bobo-ism. The incident featured an additional twist, not reported by the media. DeWitt, discovering Barnes' generosity and confronted with a bill for an expensive, custom-made suit (Newsom wore a size 52 coat) with two pair of pants, dress shirt and assorted accessories from the best men's shop in town, decided that stern measures were in order. From that point onward, DeWitt made it a point to steer Barnes away from Newsom, and visa versa.

A game on May 18 that Newsom didn't win, and was in fact routed, became the next big event for his chroniclers. It took place against the World Champion Yankees. Newsom later claimed he had the best stuff of his career that day. He recorded six consecutive outs via strikeout and had nine K's in the first four innings. But two home runs by Joe DiMaggio led the Yankees past the Browns, 11–7. Later on, Newsom, in recalling that day, always skipped over the negative and accentuated the positive, the six straight strikeouts against one of the most powerful lineups in big league history. It was an impressive feat and helped convince Yankees manager Joe McCarthy to add Newsom to the AL roster for the annual All-Star Game.

That year's Midsummer Classic was played July 6 at Crosley Field in Cincinnati. While Newsom was delighted to be selected to the AL team for the first time, he was less than pleased at the outcome of the game. The Nationals beat the Americans, 4–1, as McCarthy chose to go with his own Lefty Gomez as the starter, followed by Cleveland's Allen and Boston's Lefty Grove. Newsom, not surprisingly, felt he was better than those three and thus began a feud with McCarthy that continued for another decade. Like Newsom, McCarthy had a healthy ego. Unlike him, McCarthy ran the best ballclub in the business. What Newsom might have accomplished pitching in his prime for the Yankees is difficult to cognate, but his intemperate comments regarding McCarthy put the kibosh on whatever possibility might have existed.[18]

In addition to Newsom's break-out season, the 1938 American League season was enlivened by a dramatic development. The powerful Yankees were unexpectedly challenged by the upstart Cleveland Indians and their new manager, the hard-driving Ossie Vitt. Cleveland was actually in first place at mid-season and was still in the pennant hunt when it faced St. Louis in a doubleheader on August 11—Newsom's 31st birthday—at Sportsman's Park. He pitched the first game and was immediately the target of trash talk from the Cleveland dugout. He never hit it off with the Indians, perhaps stemming from the Earl Averill incident in 1935, perhaps from remarks by Indians general manager Roger Peckinpaugh about Newsom's diminished mental capacity.[19] Averill was still on the Tribe and was aided in his bench jockeying on this occasion by first baseman Hal Trosky and Vitt himself. Apparently, Vitt subscribed to Joe McCarthy's theory that if Newsom could be distracted, he could be beaten. The razzing that hot August day in St. Louis did strike a nerve in the birthday boy, although not the one the Indians were aiming for.

Just before Newsom was to deliver the first pitch of the game, he turned his back to home plate and with his spikes drew big letters on the front of the mound that spelled Y A N K S. "I hope you guys can read that!" he yelled to the Cleveland dugout. "Because that's the boys who are gonna whup your ass!" It was the Indians, not Newsom, who became rattled, and he pitched a complete-game victory over them. The Tribe also lost the second game and was subsequently swamped in the pennant race by New York.[20]

Another development that added interest to the season, especially in the waning weeks when the Yankees ran away from the rest of the pack, was Hank Greenberg's quest to surpass Babe Ruth's record of 60 home runs in a season. By mid–September it looked like Greenberg was a lock to accomplish the feat. But he never recovered his batting stroke after facing Newsom in late September. Over 40 years later, Greenberg still winced at the memory.

"When I was going for the home run title in 1938 and [Newsom] was with the Browns, I couldn't hit him," Greenberg told author Mike Ross. "He kept pitching me outside, low and away, and it was hard for me to pull a ball and hit a home run off him. When I look back at it I didn't hit more than one or two home runs off him in my whole career."[21]

Newsom, by now, had also learned that a hitter as talented as Greenberg could handle even his best fastball, so he fed "Hammering Hank" almost exclusively sliders, most of them winding up out of the strike zone. The late-season game in which he was held to one harmless single in four at-bats on Newsom's diet of "nickel curves" left Greenberg stuck at 58 home runs, two short of the Babe's mark.

Newsom faced the Tigers six times that year and won four of the games. It was an accomplishment that left an impression on Greenberg and the rest of the Detroit organization, as a story told to author Richard Bak by Charlie Gehringer testifies.

> I remember him pitching to Greenberg once. It's a hot day. He's got two strikes on Hank, and all of a sudden he just walks off the mound. He didn't even give the umpire a sign or anything, just took off for the dugout.... We see him going over to a big pail of water, and he's washing his face and he's toweling off. All this time, Greenberg's just waiting, probably thinking Bobo had hurt himself. Finally, after he's all washed up and dried off, Bobo trots out and throws one more strike and Greenberg's out. I've never seen anyone leave quite like that before. Or since.[22]

The incident Gehringer describes likely took place in St. Louis in the summer of 1938. Whether or not Newsom was acting on gamesmanship or impulse is impossible to say. Either is a possibility.

Newsom also rated the 1938 season a success in that he was able to talk Gabby Street into allowing him to start both games of a doubleheader against Philadelphia on August 7. Newsom went the distance to win the opener, but was knocked around in the second game and was kayoed in the fourth inning. "That's all right," he said afterward. "I'll two-time those babies yet."[23]

All in all, it was a satisfying campaign for Newsom, and the "Welcome Home Buck" celebration that October in Hartsville was especially spirited.

Adding to his fun was the news that he was set to make his feature film debut in January, in something called *The First Century of Baseball*. Sponsored by General Motors and produced by the American League, the film illustrated baseball then and now. A number of AL stars were recruited to appear, including Newsom in a segment showing how to throw a curveball. Unfortunately for him, once he finally saw the finished product, edited down to 39 minutes, his role was severely truncated. Even so, he didn't hesitate to include it on his broadcast resume in later years.[24]

Back in St. Louis, Bill DeWitt viewed the wreckage of another Browns season. His first task that winter was to find a new manager. Oscar Melillo was offered the job but declined it, although he did agree to stay on as a coach. After reviewing his limited options, DeWitt deferred to Branch Rickey, who recommended former Cardinals player Fred Haney for the job.

"Nobody really wanted the job, but DeWitt thought that Fred would be a good guy to work with our younger players," Jack Fournier said. "There in 1938, DeWitt and Barnes were thinking about moving the team to Los Angeles. Haney was an L.A. guy, and a pretty glib fellow, and he would have been a real good PR-type person for the team in L.A. That, and he was recommended by Branch Rickey. DeWitt rarely went against a Rickey recommendation."[25]

Newsom had played against Haney but didn't really know him. However, reports of DeWitt's desire to use younger players in 1939 were a concern. Newsom was 31, and that didn't exactly qualify him for April pullet status in the world of baseball.

A more immediate concern was Newsom's contract for the 1939 season. The Browns drew over 130,000 fans in 1938, last in baseball but still representing their highest attendance since 1931. Newsom felt the increase was solely due to his pitching. DeWitt attributed the increase, such as it was (the Browns had drawn 123,000 in 1937), to a stepped-up promotional campaign. The Browns also landed an exciting new player that year in first baseman George McQuinn. Dumped by the Yankees because they had Lou Gehrig and at least three other players in their minor leagues they felt were better, McQuinn put together an outstanding season with the Browns. He finished with a .324 average, 195 hits, 82 RBI and 100 runs scored. He was a standout defensively and assembled a 34-game hitting streak in July and August.

From DeWitt's standpoint, who could argue that the slight increase in attendance was due to McQuinn rather than Newsom? From Newsom's standpoint, the financial picture had changed. By the winter of 1938–1939, the Great Depression had lessened. Major league salaries had started to creep up, largely due to the demands of young players like Feller, DiMaggio and Greenberg. Lou Gehrig was getting $40,000 and deserved it. Jimmie Foxx was getting $30,000 and deserved that. But Feller, after only three years in baseball, was to receive a reported $20,000 for 1939, and Newsom saw no reason why he shouldn't also receive $20,000. The Browns offered $14,000, a mere $1,500 more than he made in 1938. There the matter rested throughout the winter, with Newsom unwilling to come down from his lofty asking price and DeWitt unwilling to up the ante.[26]

Newsom tried bombarding DeWitt and Barnes with letters citing "desperate circumstances." This may not have been entirely a lie. Newsom's tendency to spend money as rapidly as he made it always left him without a nest egg. Factor in a willingness to pick up the tabs for friends and assorted hangers-on, and by the time February rolled around he was usually broke. Bob Shirley said,

> Bobo almost always ran out of money in the off-season. He never worked in the winter and really didn't have much sense when it came to living on a budget. I remember one year, this was probably 1938 or 1939, he came home from the baseball season with thousands of dollars in cash, and by the time it came time to leave for spring training he was absolutely broke. He didn't have a pot to piss in or a window to throw it out of, as they say. We had to put together a benefit banquet here in Hartsville to raise funds for him.[27]

Newsom, by this time, also had a wife and two small children to support. He needed money and realized desperate times call for desperate measures. He increased his letter-writing campaign. For February 14, he even sent Barnes a Valentine's Day card. He called the Browns' front office and pleaded his case with DeWitt. Nothing worked.

Came March 1 and the opening of the Browns' spring training camp in San Antonio, and Newsom was still sans contract and still in Hartsville.[28]

Well, if the mountain wouldn't go to Muhammad, Muhammad would just have to go to the mountain. Newsom and family pulled up stakes and headed to San Antonio, where they took up residence at a motel on the outskirts of town. From there, Newsom opened up his personal public relations bureau, issuing daily media updates on the status of the contract talks and anything else that happened to cross his mind. For about three weeks, Newsom and the sportswriters covering the team enjoyed the routine. But the season opener was getting closer and closer, and the bills were piling up. Finally, Newsom agreed to a face-to-face with DeWitt. Whatever the pair said in private, and odds are they said plenty, the agreement they hammered out was pure compromise on the part of Newsom. Newsom was to receive $15,000 for 1939, only $1,000 more than the Browns' original offer. It wasn't exactly the bonanza he had in mind, and when the season opened he wasn't in the greatest of moods. Neither was DeWitt, when a few days later he received the motel bill for the Newsoms' stay in San Antonio.

Newsom also wasn't getting along with Fred Haney, the Browns' new manager. Haney, in his first go-around as a big league skipper, ignored the veterans on the ballclub, hoping to work his managerial magic on the younger players. He didn't have a lot to work with. In fact, the Browns' only notable trade over the winter was with the Yankees, St. Louis acquiring outfielder Myril Hoag and catcher Joe Glenn in exchange for Oral Hildebrand and Buster Mills. Sizing things up in San Antonio, Haney decided to begin the Browns' youth movement immediately and go with untested rookies Johnny Berardino at second base and right-hander Jack Kramer in the starting rotation. The team struggled from the get-go and Haney was soon talking about "cleaning house."

The bad start couldn't be directly blamed on Newsom, who won three of his first six starts, the Browns' bullpen blowing the lead in another. But Newsom's selfish attitude wasn't helping Haney maintain a semblance of discipline.[29] Matters came to a head on May 10 and, as so often happened with Newsom, they had nothing to do with his pitching. The Browns were playing at Sportsman's Park and starting pitcher Johnny Marcum was getting trounced by the Yankees. By the third inning, fans were calling for Newsom, who was not scheduled to pitch that day. For some reason, in the midst of this tumult Newsom decided he couldn't sit in the dugout any longer and strolled down to the Browns bullpen. Everyone in the park saw this (Newsom being rather difficult to miss) and assumed he was going there to warm up. Indeed, he began to play catch, likely just out of boredom. This act touched off high hopes among Browns fans that they would get to see him pitch in that afternoon's game.

Haney envisioned no such plans and regarded Newsom's antics with great distaste. In fact, he felt Newsom had deliberately shown him up. The incident resulted in Haney being roundly booed when he replaced the beleaguered starter with someone not named Newsom. Afterward, Haney demanded that Newsom be removed from the roster, by any means short of homicide. DeWitt was thinking along exactly the same lines.[30]

According to Jack Fournier, DeWitt figured the only Browns player any team would want was Newsom. The Browns tried working out a trade with the Yankees but they weren't interested, not surprising considering Joe McCarthy's distaste for Newsom. Finally, a deal was arranged with the Tigers, possessors of one of the top farm systems in baseball. Fournier said the two Detroit prospects the Browns wanted most were outfielder Chet Laabs and infielder Mark Christman.[31]

The trade, announced May 13, was a bombshell, certainly one of baseball's biggest transactions of the 1930s. The Browns sent Newsom—obviously the headliner in the deal—along with Beau Bell, Red Kress and Jim Walkup to the Tigers for pitchers Vern Kennedy, Bob Harris, George Gill and Roxie Lawson, along with Laabs and Christman. At the time, and for the next couple of years, DeWitt was roundly criticized for the deal.

"Unfortunately, the pitchers we got didn't do much the rest of the 1939 season and that's the main reason DeWitt got ripped for the deal," Fournier said. "But the reality was, we were going to finish last with Buck Newsom or without Buck Newsom. And Laabs and Christman turned into solid players for us."[32]

The immediate result of the trade was fan and media unrest in St. Louis. Browns attendance that year fell back to 119,000. On the field, Haney felt compelled to put Kennedy, Harris, Gill and Lawson in the starting rotation and keep them there. That quartet combined for a 16–48 record. DeWitt quickly cut his losses, releasing or selling Mel Almada, "Cactus" Johnson, Harry Kimberlin, Ed Cole and Russ Van Atta. The "new, improved" 1939 Browns proceeded to lose a team-record 111 games.

Regarding the Browns' plight, Newsom could not have cared less. He was now a Detroit Tiger.

Lucille Newsom balked at this latest in a series of gypsy-like moves. She had no desire to live in the nation's colder climes and took the couple's young children, Norma and Alan, back home to Hartsville. However, dealing with Detroit management was quite a different experience from what Newsom was accustomed to with the poverty-row Browns. In St. Louis, he had begun working a regular "gig" as a sports commentator on a local radio show. The job netted him only a few bucks a week extra, but he loved radio and was loath to leave it. He complained to Tigers general manager Jack Zeller that he wouldn't report unless he was "properly compensated" for the loss of the show. Zeller was savvy enough to doubt Newsom's claim but Tigers owner Walter O. Briggs wanted his new pitcher in town immediately and ordered Zeller to pay Newsom a

In June of 1939 Newsom joined the Detroit Tigers. Of course, upon arrival in Chicago he called his old friend George Burke to have new photographs taken. Note the Baseball Centennial patch on Newsom's left sleeve (the Brace photograph collection, used by permission).

$2,000 bonus. Since this represented considerably more than Newsom would have made behind a microphone, he readily accepted and agreed to report post haste.[33]

Newsom experienced another pleasant surprise when he reached Detroit. Thousands of Southerners had moved to the Motor City in the 1920s to work at the automotive plants, and the city had taken on a definite Southern flavor. He quickly felt at ease with the fans. His comfort zone was also enhanced by the fact that he found favor with his new teammates.

Managing the Tigers was Del Baker. A quiet man, Baker had a brief major league career (1914–1916) as a second-string catcher for the Tigers. He hung around baseball long enough to become a coach for the Tigers in 1933. He "lucked" into the Tigers' managerial job on an interim basis when Mickey Cochrane suffered through a serious illness in 1936, and again in 1937 when Cochrane's playing career came to an abrupt end as the result of a being hit in the head by a pitch. Cochrane was able to return to his managerial duties in 1938 but had a run-in with upper management and was relieved of his duties on August 6. Had Cochrane stayed healthy and held his temper in check, Baker likely would have never become a major league manager, for Baker wasn't a natural-born leader or the cheerleader type. Instead, his reputation was for "inside baseball"—the little things teams can do to win games.[34] "I liked to play for him," Charlie Gehringer said. "He was all baseball, morning, noon and night."[35]

According to many who played for and against him, Baker may have been the greatest sign-stealer ever. He also excelled at picking up opposing pitchers' pitches. If Detroit batters wanted to know what was coming, and most did, Baker could oblige. If a Detroit fielder wanted to know if the opposition had a play on, Baker could be counted on to tip them off.

"He was so quick at stealing signs or reading pitchers it was uncanny," said Tigers third baseman Marv Owen. "I swear, he had the pitch even before the catcher called it. It was part knowing what to look for and where to look for it, but it was also part that you just have to say was ESP."[36]

Tigers catcher Birdie Tebbetts seconded that motion. "Del Baker was one of the brainiest men in baseball," he said. "He was a great sign stealer."[37]

Del Baker was Newsom's manager with the Tigers. Baker, virtually unknown in baseball circles today, succeeded where many others had failed and turned Newsom into a consistent winner (the Ray Medeiros collection, used by permission).

Baker and Newsom hit it off from the start. Baker had no hard-and-fast rules for his players, in fact didn't want to deal with off-the-field matters at all. That suited Newsom just fine. Baker did two things for Newsom that proved helpful. He convinced him that he didn't need to pitch every inning of every game, that come September he was going to be much more effective by not having worn down during the long, hot summer. He also refined a couple of rough spots in Newsom's elaborate delivery. Other than that, he put Newsom in the starting rotation and let him pitch.

The 1939 Tigers that Newsom joined were a veteran ballclub with several players still on the roster from the Tigers' 1934 and 1935 pennant-winning teams. Greenberg, of course, was the team's biggest name. But hard-working veterans like second baseman Charlie Gehringer, shortstop Billy Rogell and pitcher Tommy Bridges also carried a lot of clout in the clubhouse. It was generally felt the Tigers had grown long of tooth, and indeed even with a boost from Bobo they finished at 81–73 in 1939, far behind the Yankees in the standings. Rogell was clearly at the end of the line and Gehringer was no longer the player he once was, creating uncertainty in the middle infield.[38]

Detroit did have several promising youngsters, the most promising being Rudy York. York, like Greenberg, had tremendous power. Unlike Greenberg, there was nowhere he could play. He had been tried at several positions, including catcher, and was found wanting at all of them. Wrote Red Smith: "No matter where he was stationed in the field, Rudy York always played the same position. He played bat."[39] In 1939 York hit .307 with 20 home runs in only 329 at-bats.

Greenberg, slowed by injuries, fell off from his 58-home run output of 1938 to 33 in 1939. Earl Averill, Newsom's old nemesis, was acquired from the Indians during the season but failed to provide much sock, hitting .262 in 87 games with ten home runs. Bell and Kress, picked up from the Browns with Newsom, were no better than reserves for the Tigers.

If not a world-beater, it was an interesting ballclub, made more so by the presence of Newsom. After trying several other players as roommates for Newsom, Baker decided to match up Bobo and Schoolboy Rowe. Since Rowe, known as "Schoolie" to his teammates, was a slow-talking, well-mannered gent who eschewed clowning around, it is possible Baker figured that opposites might attract. However, the arrangement was short-lived.[40]

Rowe had a set schedule consisting of early to bed, early to rise. Newsom's agenda did not include the concept of early. Their first night together in their Chicago hotel room, Newsom insisted on having all the lights on and the radio blaring at full volume, all the while talking about his two favorite subjects: baseball (he had won that afternoon's game) and women (he had spotted an attractive redhead in the hotel restaurant). The lights and noise made it almost impossible for Rowe to sleep, but he finally nodded off, well after midnight, while Newsom was in the middle of a description of his pitching prowess in that afternoon's game. About two hours later, Rowe had a bad dream and suddenly woke up. He found the lights still on, the radio still blaring and Newsom still bragging about how well he had pitched.[41]

The next morning, a bleary-eyed Rowe went to Baker and requested a change of roommates. After that, it was decided to let Newsom room by himself. Even so, Rowe remained in peril.

"[Newsom was] a great jokester," Charlie Gehringer told Richard Bak. "He was always pulling some trick, especially on Schoolie. Schoolie wasn't too quick with the repartee, so Bobo was always getting the best of him. Nailed his spikes down to his locker, things like that. Just drove Schoolie crazy."[42]

Thanks in part to Newsom's effective pitching and outlandish antics, attendance at Briggs Stadium surpassed 835,000 in 1939, second best in the American League and an improvement from the 800,000 the team drew in 1938. Newsom greatly enjoyed the crowds, having grown tired of pitching before the few brave souls the Browns and Senators were drawing.

On a staff that included aging veterans like Bridges and Rowe and untested youngsters like Freddie Hutchinson, Dizzy Trout and Hal Newhouser, Newsom quickly worked his way in as the team's top pitcher. He started 31 games for the Tigers and completed 21 of them. He also was used four times in relief, and twice protected a Tigers lead in the late innings. He won 17 and lost ten in Detroit, with an excellent 3.37 earned run average.

For the season, Newsom repeated as a 20-game winner, going 20–11. As in 1938, he notched his 20th win on the last day of the season, beating the Indians 1–0 in a game shortened to five innings by inclement weather on October 1 at Detroit. He once again led the league in games started (37) and complete games (24), but cut his innings pitched down to 291⅔, hits allowed to 272 and walks allowed to 126, resulting in far more efficient labors.

His status was definitely rising with baseball fans, in Detroit and all around the league. When Cleveland played the first night game in its history, on June 27 at Municipal Stadium, a matchup of Newsom and Bob Feller drew over 55,000. Feller was the victor on this occasion, winning 5–0 on a one-hitter. The hard-throwing Newsom and Feller represented a great test of whether or not batters could pick up the ball under the new lights at Municipal Stadium. Several sportswriters went so far as to predict that Feller's record of 18 strikeouts in a game would certainly be broken that night. As it turned out, Newsom left after two innings and Feller struck out "only" 13.[43]

Buck Newsom warms up for a start for the Detroit Tigers in 1939. The high leg kick was standard operating procedure for Newsom, as was hiding the baseball with his body until the last possible instant (the Ray Medeiros collection, used by permission).

Once again, Newsom was selected to the AL squad for the All-Star Game, played on July 11 at Yankee Stadium. And once again, he had to take a back seat to others. Perhaps as a result of the locale, Joe McCarthy loaded up the lineup with six Yankees and let five of them play all nine innings. Red Ruffing was McCarthy's choice as starting pitcher. After Ruffing pitched three innings, McCarthy chose to bypass Newsom in favor of his teammate Tommy Bridges. He then closed the game with Bob Feller, who was brilliant in a three-inning stint. The result was a 3–1 victory for the Americans and a wounded ego for Bobo.

Newsom vowed he would never again go to the All-Star Game and led the criticism of McCarthy for playing so many Yankees for so long. While Newsom held no grudges against Ruffing, Bridges or Feller, he clearly found it inconceivable that McCarthy would pitch them over him.[44]

A few days after the All-Star Game, on July 17, Newsom had a close encounter with Ted Williams, the slugging rookie outfielder for the Boston Red Sox. The story Elden Auker told about that day is that when Williams hit a home run off Newsom, Newsom found the sight of Williams' skinny frame running the bases so amusing he laughed out loud. The next time up, Williams really got into a Newsom delivery and hit it about 500 feet. As he was rounding the bases, he yelled at Bobo: "Laugh that off, you son of a bitch! That's to show you the first one wasn't an accident!" There is no question about Williams being a fierce competitor. However, this story is simply not true, at least not the way Auker recalled it.[45]

What actually happened was that when Newsom first faced Williams that year, on May 7 when he was still on the Browns, he struck out the Red Sox rookie three times and rubbed it in with some choice remarks. The Browns won that game, 6–3, stopping a seven-game Boston winning streak. Auker was the losing pitcher for the Red Sox. Then, on July 17 at Briggs Stadium, Williams hit a home run in his first

From his debut in the American League in 1934, Newsom found himself at war with New York Yankees manager Joe McCarthy. While McCarthy was skipper, the Yankees had several opportunities to trade for Newsom and consistently declined. What Newsom might have accomplished pitching for the best team in the majors is difficult to imagine (the Ray Medeiros collection, used by permission).

at-bat against Newsom and returned the taunting. That home run turned out to be the last he ever hit against Newsom, who went on to win, 13–6, once again stopping a Red Sox winning streak, this one of 12 games. Williams said in a 1970 interview,

> Ol' Buck was no picnic to hit against. He had a good fastball, [but] that didn't bother me. But his slider was hellacious. One mean [expletive] pitch. And he would never give me the pitch I was looking for. You always look fastball on a 3–0 or 3–1 count. But Buck was just as likely to throw that slider. And his pitches were always tough for me to pick up.[46]

The Tigers players, for the most part, accepted Newsom for who he was and managed to tune out much of what he said. Helping the situation tremendously was that Greenberg welcomed Newsom as a teammate, and Newsom responded in kind. Prejudice in Newsom's world always took a back seat to profit. The pair hit it off and even began to socialize, something that would have shocked many of Newsom's gentile neighbors back in Hartsville and many of Greenberg's Jewish neighbors back in the Bronx. Greenberg told author Mike Ross,

> When [Bobo] came to Detroit I had no trouble with him. [The only trouble] was something between Bobo and Slicker Coffman [a pitcher on the 1939 Tigers]. We were staying at the Cleveland Hotel and we were having dinner in the hotel restaurant. Well, Bobo was an overbearing kind of guy.... [He] had been a bit obnoxious and he and Slicker started going at it. We went into the bathroom, where they were going to settle it, and Slicker pulled a knife and said, "I'm gonna get you, you so and so".... Bobo was a little concerned when Slicker challenged him, he kind of turned a little pale.[47]

Oddly enough, Newsom had been a teammate of Slick Coffman's brother Dick on the 1934 Browns, and by all accounts that pair got along just fine. But Bobo the Verbose could have a strange effect on people, creating an urge to cut his throat or their own. Apparently, a combative streak was the dominant trait in the Coffman family, perhaps a legacy of their hailing from Veto, Alabama. Dick Coffman, who pitched in the big leagues for 15 years, has as his chief claim to fame the fact that he was the one player actually to punch out Rogers Hornsby. It happened in September of 1935, when the Browns were on a train going from Chicago to St. Louis. And it resulted in Dick Coffman being suspended. Ultimately, he was sold to the New York Giants.

George "Slick" Coffman, who pitched only 23 games and 42⅓ innings for the Tigers in 1939, was traded twice by the team in the winter of 1939–1940. The first deal, with the Philadelphia Athletics, was voided by Commissioner Kenesaw Landis. The second, in February, sent Coffman to the Browns for catcher Billy Sullivan. Whether or not the incident with Newsom factored into the Tigers' decision is not known, although teammates acknowledge lingering bad blood on both sides. Coffman started for the Browns against Newsom and the Tigers in the 1940 season opener and beat them, 5–1. It turned out to be the best game he ever pitched; after that day, he won only once more for the Browns and was out of the majors for good by 1941.

One thing was for sure: Newsom definitely kept his Tigers teammates loose. "Everybody took their baseball so seriously.... When we went out to the ballpark, it was like being in an operating room," Greenberg said. "Everybody had to be precise. Bobo brought some fun back into it."[48]

When the Tigers ended the 1939 season, there was a curious optimism in the clubhouse. If Del Baker could find somewhere to play Rudy York, if the young Tigers pitchers came through, if the team could stay healthy, perhaps they could make a run at the Yankees in 1940. New York seemed invincible, but then again their first baseman, Lou Gehrig, had seemed indestructible. Now he was out of baseball. Going into the 1939 season, talk about the Tigers overtaking the Yankees seemed foolish. But with the promise of Bobo Newsom's services for the entire 1940 season, maybe, just maybe, it wasn't so foolish to dream.

Seven

Detroit (1940)

Bobo Newsom reported to the Detroit Tigers spring training camp in Lakeland, FL, on March 1, 1940. He was in good spirits, having landed a contract calling for a $20,000 salary. Management also threw in two new cars: a Cadillac LaSalle for Newsom's personal use and a Plymouth station wagon for Lucille.

While the $20,000 salary was less than the reported $25,000 that Cleveland's Bob Feller was making, Newsom was a happy man, in large part because the cars were a very pleasant dividend and he could say, by adding up the vehicles' combined retail value, that he was actually making more than Feller. Being a devoted car buff, he discovered he had at least one thing in common with Tigers owner Walter Briggs, Sr., who made his fortune designing and producing auto bodies for Chrysler. When Jack Zeller,

the Tigers general manager, asked what kind of car Newsom wanted, he reportedly replied, "Oh, nothing special. I'll take whatever Mr. Briggs is driving." Thus, Newsom wound up with the latest model Cadillac LaSalle with all the trimmings, including automatic transmission, a novelty in 1940. Briggs was so amused by Newsom's request, and so pleased with his pitching in the later half of the 1939 season, that he threw the Plymouth into the deal.[1]

Newsom with the Detroit Tigers in his best season in baseball, 1940. Newsom wore uniform No. 12 with the Tigers, reverse 21 (he was a die-hard card player). He would change numbers frequently throughout his long career, usually in an attempt to snap a losing streak or when he changed teams (the Ray Medeiros collection, used by permission).

The 1940 Tigers team that Newsom rejoined in Lakeland was basically the same group of players that finished the year in 1939, with three notable exceptions. Zeller acquired Dick Bartell from the Chicago Cubs to play shortstop, Billy Sullivan to serve as Birdie Tebbetts' backup at catcher, and Bruce Campbell to play right field. Campbell's acquisition, on January 20 from the Indians in exchange for Beau Bell, was something of an afterthought. Zeller had earlier swung a deal for Philadelphia Athletics right fielder Wally Moses, but the trade was voided by Commissioner Kenesaw Landis. The fact that Campbell and Sullivan were pals of Newsom from their days with the St. Louis Browns no doubt factored into their acquisition. On paper, neither Bartell, Sullivan or Campbell figured to make a dramatic difference from what had been a mediocre 1939 Tigers team; in reality, they made all the difference in the world.[2]

But there was no getting around the fact that, even before spring training, the organization was dealt a blow on January 14 when Landis voided the Moses trade and released 92 of Detroit's minor leaguers from their contracts. Landis ruled that Zeller had been "hiding" the fact that the players were Detroit property by use of bogus documentation and gentlemen's agreements with minor league team owners. It was a controversial ruling at the time and created ill will between Briggs and Landis that lasted until Landis' death in 1944. Curiously, although several of the 92 "slaves" set free by Landis went on to play in the majors, none became a standout. The most highly touted player of the group, second baseman Benny McCoy, wound up with the Philadelphia A's where he proved to be a disappointment.[3]

In spite of off-the-field developments, or perhaps because of them, the Tigers quickly grew into a tight-knit ballclub filled with optimism. Not that anyone outside the organization gave them a ghost of a chance to contend for the American League pennant. Further, no sportswriter of note went on record predicting a pennant for Detroit, and a few even picked them for last place. The New York Yankees seemed invincible, and even if for some bizarre reason the Yanks faltered the Tigers would still have to climb over both the talent-laden Boston Red Sox and Cleveland Indians.

But the 1940 Tigers had two personages the other teams did not: Bobo Newsom and Del Baker. However improbable it may have been, the free-spirited Newsom became one of the top players in baseball that year and the mild-mannered Baker became one of the top managers. By 1940, after stops at five other major league teams, Newsom had finally found his comfort zone. And by 1940, the Tigers players had mastered Baker's system of relaying signs and pitches. "Newsom was the heart and soul of the 1940 Tigers," wrote Joe Falls in his history of the franchise, "and Baker was the brains."[4]

Baker quickly settled on a starting lineup and did not alter it throughout the season. The only platooning was done at catcher, where Tebbetts and Sullivan shared duties, and in right field, where playing time was divided between Bruce Campbell and Pete Fox. All four were veteran players, and all had solid seasons. Tebbetts hit .296, Sullivan .309, Campbell .283 and Fox .289. Neither Tebbetts nor Sullivan was a power hitter, and they customarily batted in the No. 8 position. Still, they combined for seven home runs and 87 runs batted in. Campbell and Fox combined for 13 home runs and 92 RBI.

The rest of the Tigers lineup was even more potent. That spring, Baker put York, a notoriously inept defensive player, at first base (he had previously been tried at catcher, third base and left field). This necessitated Greenberg, the team's undisputed star and highest-paid player, moving from first to left field, a position he had never played. "Hammering Hank" agreed to do so, spurred by a reported $10,000 bonus. Money aside, Greenberg's willingness to make the switch had a positive effect on the team and set the tone for the season.[5]

York wound up playing all 155 games at first base, and if not a Gold Glove candidate proved to be more than adequate defensively. Offensively, he had a career year. The man teammates called "Chief" hit .316 with 33 home runs, 134 RBI and 105 runs scored. He was particularly effective during the September pennant drive, in large part because of Baker's genius. York, of all Tigers hitters, was most effective when he knew what pitch was coming. Baker's ability to steal the other team's signs or "read" the opposing pitcher and relay the type of pitch to York proved crucial to the Tigers' cause.[6]

Greenberg also proved adequate defensively in left field. Offensively, he had a vintage season. Playing in 148 of the team's 155 games, Greenberg finished with a .340 batting average, 41 home runs, 150 RBI and 129 runs scored. Like York, "Big Greenie" was a terror to opposing hurlers down the stretch.

"The big deal about those 1940 Tigers was that York and Greenberg were deadly with men on base," said Tommy Henrich of the Yankees. "That September, I tracked their box scores and figured they must have hit about .500 with men on base. For that one month, they were the best one-two punch I ever saw."[7]

In a 22-game home stand in September that turned the Tigers' season around,

On the Tigers, Newsom became pals with Hank Greenberg. Reportedly, when Greenberg was drafted into the Army in the spring of 1941, Newsom asked, "Can I go wit' ya?" Clearly, Greenberg's absence was deeply felt by the 1941 Tigers, and in particular by Newsom, who turned from a 20-game winner into a 20-game loser (the Ray Medeiros collection, used by permission).

Greenberg batted .400 with 15 home runs and 39 RBI. York was almost as good, hitting .375 with eight home runs and 37 RBI. With that kind of run production, it wasn't surprising that the Tigers won 17 of the 22 games.[8]

Completing the Tigers outfield was Barney McCosky. McCosky was actually of Lithuanian-Polish ancestry (birth name Kwietniewski). He had grown up in Detroit and attended Southwestern High School in the city, where he was a sensational all-around athlete. Signed by the Tigers after his senior year in

1935, he quickly moved up their minor league ladder. He became the Tigers' starting center fielder in the spring of 1939 and held that job until he joined the armed forces after the 1942 season. A left-handed hitter, McCosky lacked power but was one of the fastest players in the league. He hit .311 as a rookie with 120 runs scored, and topped that in his sophomore season of 1940, hitting .340 with 123 runs scored. He led American League hitters with 200 hits and 19 triples, and was solid defensively. Until an injury late in the year forced him to miss five games, McCosky started every game for the Tigers. His roles, as the leadoff man and the go-get-'em guy in an outfield that included the lumbering Greenberg and the less than spry Campbell and Fox, were crucial to the team's success.

McCosky's career closely parallels that of the Dodgers' Pete Reiser. Both were regarded as great players prior to the war, but three years away from baseball and serious injuries thereafter drastically affected their careers. McCosky and Reiser were through as starting players by age 30; both wound up their playing careers as seldom-used reserves with the Cleveland Indians in the early 1950s.

On the infield, the Tigers had plenty of experience. Second baseman Charlie Gehringer, at age 37, was at the end of what proved to be a Hall of Fame career. Called "The Mechanical Man" for his fluid skills, Gehringer had been the Tigers' starting second baseman since 1926. By 1940, he was no longer the superstar he had been, and in fact seriously thought about retirement after 1939, when a back injury limited him to 118 games. In 1940, he was able to play in 139 games, hitting .313 with 108 runs scored. He made an excellent No. 2 hitter, coaxing 101 walks from opposing pitchers. With McCosky and Gehringer getting on base at the top of the batting order, the table was set for the Tigers' power hitters.

Defensively, Gehringer's range and arm strength were limited, but he was able to compensate by skillfully playing the hitters. Manager Baker "hid" Gehringer's weak throwing arm by having Dick Bartell take the bulk of the relay throws.[9]

Bartell, picked up from the Chicago Cubs in exchange for longtime starting shortstop Billy Rogell, was nicknamed "Rowdy Dick." It was a name that fit perfectly. Never a great player, offensively or defensively, Bartell was a battler, a 1930s version of Eddie Stanky. The trade was a calculated risk for the Tigers. Rogell, a key member on Detroit's 1934 and 1935 pennant-winning teams, was a hometown boy and well-liked by fans. Bartell was the starting shortstop on the NL champion New York Giants in 1936 and 1937 but was coming off two off-years.

As it turned out, Rogell was spent; he played sparingly for the Cubs in 1940 and then retired. Bartell, although he hit only .233 for the Tigers and committed 36 errors at shortstop, was able to play in 139 games. The intangibles he brought to the 1940 team never showed up the box scores, but proved to be a big factor in the Tigers winning the pennant. As an example, he convinced the Tigers pitchers to work with him on a pickoff play at second base. By Newsom's reckoning, the play caught at least two dozen opposing runners off second that season, an extra 24 outs. Twenty-four outs wouldn't mean much to a bad ballclub, but for the Tigers, who wound up in a pennant race that went down to the final weekend of the season, those extra outs quite possibly meant the difference between finishing first and third.[10]

Bartell also played in pain the entire season. His ankles were in sorry shape from

15 years of manning the middle infield and his back was almost as bad as Gehringer's. Even with physical limitations, Bartell was able to score 76 runs and drive in 53, batting in the No. 7 slot. Those were important contributions, especially because his understudies, Red Kress and Frank Croucher, combined for a sub-.200 batting average with one home run and 13 RBI.

Frank "Pinky" Higgins held court at third base. The native Texan had been a starting third baseman in the AL for the past eight seasons. He didn't have a great 1940 season for the Tigers, hitting a below-par .271 with 13 home runs and 76 RBI, but he was a feisty competitor with a knack for delivering in the clutch. Like the other three members of the Detroit infield, he had limitations defensively, committing 29 errors in 130 games. And, like teammates York and Newsom, Higgins enjoyed a long drink after a hard game. All three later developed serious problems with alcohol, and all died prior to their 60th birthdays. Despite his substance abuse, Higgins was able to play in the majors for 14 years and went on to serve as manager of the Boston Red Sox from 1955 to 1962.[11]

The 1940 Tigers reflected the selfless work habits of its manager and the city of Detroit—blue-collar workers who kept their noses to the grindstone. Individually, the defending champion Yankees had better athletes at six of the eight everyday positions; collectively, these Tigers were a formidable foe.

The pitching staff was a study in oldsters struggling to hang on and youngsters trying to learn their craft at the major league level. Newsom (21–5), Schoolboy Rowe (16–3), and Tommy Bridges (12–9) combined for a 49–17 won-loss record. The remainder of the staff combined for a 41–47 record. Of that latter group, the biggest contribution was made by Al Benton. Benton appeared in 42 games, all in relief. He posted a sub-par 6–10 win-loss record, but notched a league-leading 17 saves according to a formula applied retroactively in 1969. He was often used as the "closer" in games that Rowe and Bridges started, and was especially effective in that role. None of the Tigers' highly touted young pitchers—Johnny Gorsica, Hal Newhouser, Fred Hutchinson and Dizzy Trout—had a winning season. They were all maddeningly erratic, and Baker was forced to use them sparingly during the September pennant drive.

Rowe had been the team's pitching star in 1934 and 1935. Then he incurred some sort of injury to his throwing arm; exactly what was wrong with his right arm or shoulder was never quite determined. He was unable to pitch for long stretches and won a total of one game for the Tigers in 1937 and 1938. Eventually, Mickey Cochrane decided unwilling rather than unable was the operative word to describe Rowe's condition. Cochrane suspended Rowe for a month at the start of the 1937 season, supposedly for "breaking training" but actually because Rowe refused a pitching assignment. In 1938, he was demoted to the minor leagues. Had Cochrane remained as Detroit manager, Rowe would likely have never gotten back on the Tigers' roster. Fortunately for the man called Schoolboy, Cochrane was fired during the 1938 season and replaced by Del Baker. In one of his first acts, Baker insisted Rowe be recalled. Rowe recorded a lackluster 10–12 record for the 1939 Tigers, but at least he was pitching once again in the majors. For 1940, Baker promised to pitch him only on days when Rowe felt his arm was up to the challenge. It was a promise kept, and Rowe had one last outstanding season with the Bengals.[12]

Tommy Bridges had also been a star on the 1934 and 1935 Tigers. Like Rowe, his arm was no longer in great shape, and he needed a full four to five days off between starts. Bridges, at 5-feet-8 and 150 pounds, was a virtual dwarf by major league standards. He shared the unfortunate malady of alcoholism with teammates Newsom, York and Higgins and had an understandable tendency to wear down as the season progressed. By 1940, he no longer had much of a fastball, but his curveball remained the best in the business. Tigers teammate Marv Owen said,

> Tommy's curve was a thing of beauty. Late in his career, he would just show the hitters his fastball, usually threw it low and outside. His out-pitch was definitely the curveball. Later on, when I was a scout, for a kid who had a great fastball we would say he has a "Bob Feller" fastball, and if he had a great curve he has a "Tommy Bridges" curveball. Those were the gold standard for those pitches.[13]

With Rowe and Bridges requiring frequent rest, Newsom was the unchallenged ace of the staff. He started on Opening Day in April and started Game Seven of the World Series in October. And he had a career year. Prior to arriving in Detroit, Newsom hadn't been able to shake the curse of losing focus on the mound, resulting in him mindlessly throwing instead of thoughtfully pitching. With Baker and catchers Tebbetts and Sullivan working with him, constantly reminding him to keep his head in the game, he developed into a star of the first magnitude.

The Tigers completed their training at League Field in Lakeland in late March and began a barnstorming tour northward versus the Brooklyn Dodgers, playing nine games in nine days. The final contest was held at Nashville's Sulphur Dell ballpark on April 7. After that, the Tigers traveled to Knoxville to play the Knoxville Smokies prior to opening the season at home on April 16. Nothing that occurred in the exhibition season gave any hint of the "miracle" season to come.

Nor did the Tigers' home opener, on April 16 at a very chilly Briggs Stadium, bring promise of great things. Despite the weather, 49,417 fans showed up to watch Newsom pitch against his former ballclub, the Browns. Browns manager Fred Haney made a curious choice for his starter, going with former Tiger Slick Coffman. Coffman, perhaps motivated by revenge, perhaps by his nightclub altercation with Newsom the year before, pitched the game of his life, stopping the Bengals on seven hits and outpitching Newsom for a 5–1 victory. Newsom, who disliked pitching in cold weather, was adversely affected by the elements. He gave up seven hits and four walks in seven innings while striking out only two. It did not cheer Newsom one whit to find out that his arch-rival, Cleveland's Bob Feller, had pitched a no-hitter against the Chicago White Sox on the same day. Newsom and Feller, and the Tigers and Indians, were destined to be locked in combat for the entire season.

The Opening Day debacle turned out to be one of only a handful of sub-par starts all season for Newsom. Following April 16, he reeled off 13 wins in a row, almost single-handedly keeping the Tigers within clawing distance of first place. It was far and away his best stretch of sustained pitching excellence. Even though he pitched well for the Tigers in the later stages of the 1939 season, his extraordinary efforts in 1940 were a revelation to his teammates, especially the veterans who well remembered his unpredictable behavior while toiling for other teams.

"[Newsom] probably was on more ball clubs than anybody that ever pitched, but he certainly had a great arm and a great heart for the game," Charlie Gehringer told Richard Bak. "He had a big year. He really put it all out."[14]

"[I found] he wasn't always fooling around," Hank Greenberg told author Mike Ross. "He loved to pitch. Actually, I found him to be a good competitor. He wanted to show that his talent was good enough to offset your talent."[15]

The 1940 season for Newsom was marked by an absolute minimum of shenanigans. His only documented lapses occurred in July, while his winning streak was still going. He was selected to the American League All-Star squad for the annual Summer Classic, played that year at his old stamping grounds at Sportsman's Park in St. Louis. However, when Boston manager Joe Cronin (subbing as skipper of the All-Stars for an ailing Joe McCarthy) unveiled his plan to start the Yankees' Red Ruffing and not Newsom, Newsom announced he was quitting the squad.[16] That he had tangled with Cronin in Boston, and with McCarthy as a member of the 1938 and 1939 AL All-Stars, no doubt factored into Cronin's decision not to start him, and to Newsom's reaction to the "snub." "If I don't start, I don't pitch," Newsom told any sportswriter who cared to listen. "Bobo follows nobody."[17]

On this occasion, Commissioner Landis himself spoke to Newsom and convinced him to be in attendance for the July 9 game in St. Louis—or else. Newsom was able to justify rescinding his "resignation" on the grounds that Cronin's planned pitching rotation of Ruffing, Newsom and Feller still gave him billing over the Indians' Rapid Robert. However, he was not mollified by the outcome of the game. Ruffing went out and gave up a three-run home run to Max West in the first inning, and the AL stars were unable to rally, losing 4–0. For the record, Newsom pitched the fourth, fifth and sixth innings, shutting out the National's top players on only one hit.

Newsom's pre- and post-game comments may not seem outlandish by current major league standards, but in 1940 they were definitely controversial. Of course, Newsom never considered the long-term effects of any of his actions. In this case, it just so happened that his judgment was sound, even if his diplomacy was faulty.

The Tigers had a weekend series at Washington right after the All-Star Game. Newsom was quoted in the D.C. papers as to the mayhem he would inflict on the Senators lineup. Newsom later told John Lardner this was all pre-arranged hype to help old friend Clark Griffith attract a large crowd for the game. However, the media attention became especially intense; what else was there to write about in Washington with Congress not in session? Froth of the furor was a column by Robert Ruark of the *Washington News*, who reported that Newsom had been seen in the lobby of a Washington hotel berating loyal Senators fans, some of whom were of the female persuasion. While these press accounts may well have been fanciful, Newsom certainly had no one to blame but himself; his conduct had always veered toward the outrageous, and his attitude toward the press was best summed up by "Write whatever you want, just spell my name right." His well-publicized criticism of Joe Cronin—a former star with the Senators and still much-admired by Washington fans—did not assuage the situation.

Newsom had no serious quarrel with stories of his bragging but did object to Ruark's account of the alleged altercation at the hotel, on the grounds he would never accost a lady. On Friday, the day after Ruark's column ran, he and Newsom met face-to-face at Griffith Stadium following that day's ballgame. Newsom, drinking a bottled beverage which was likely beer but for some reason he forever after insisted was soda pop, took time out to call Ruark "an unchaste name," according to John Lardner. Ruark responded with fisticuffs. At least, that was his intent. But Newsom successfully held him at bay with his long left arm while his long right arm continued to hold the bottle, occasionally taking swigs out of it between comments relating to Ruark's parentage and sexual proclivities. Finally, Ruark took an exceptionally wild swing and tumbled over a bench, something of a technical knockdown for Newsom. Teammates then broke up the fight, such as it was.[18]

Newsom was quick to note that not a drop of his drink was spilled during the encounter. The only casualties were Ruark's pride and dress shirt, which was torn during the melee, and innocent bystander Shirley Povich, who took an elbow to the head trying to act as peacemaker. The Newsom-Ruark "war" was dutifully reported by other members of the press, and further served to foster heated feelings among the Senators faithful. For Ruark, the incident was persuasive evidence of the need for a career change to a safer profession. He gave up sports writing and became a big-game hunter in Africa. Eventually, he became a novelist of some note.

Saturday was another hot July day on the Potomac and destined to be even hotter at the ballpark. Before a howling crowd of approximately 25,000 (a huge turnout by Senators' standards), Newsom pitched a two-hit shutout. After recording the final out in the 4–0 victory, he left the playing field, but not before thumbing his nose at the noisy rabble. At least, Lardner reported he thumbed his nose. It is possible another digit was involved in his farewell salute to the fans.

The victory over the Senators was Newsom's 13th in a row. His next start was on July 17 at Fenway Park in Boston. In the fourth inning of that game, he was late covering first when Ted Williams hit a hard ground ball to first baseman Rudy York. York's feed to Newsom was also slightly off-course, resulting in Newsom having to reach for the ball while trying to tag Williams going by. They collided, and Newsom suffered a broken right thumb. That forced him out of the game and also forced him to miss three starts.[19]

Newsom was never one to stay idle, and he hit on a scheme to make some easy money while waiting for the thumb to heal. Calling on his show business savvy, he arranged a week of personal appearances at the Fox Theatre in downtown Detroit. All he had to do was walk on the stage, swap quips with the M.C. for a few minutes, take a bow and walk off—all the while wearing an oversized rubber thumb on his injured digit. It was corny stuff, but it paid very well. Newsom told friends he netted $2,000 for the week, which likely was fairly close to the truth.

Newsom also received a rare billing above Hank Greenberg when a quartet of Tigers visited the World's Fair in New York on July 21 to take part in an ongoing series of youth clinics at the Court of Sport. Somehow, Newsom rated billing by Fair officials over manager Baker and Greenberg, a NYC native. Billy Sullivan also took part for the Tigers and caught a few of Newsom's pitches for benefit of the kids. Newsom and his mates received a few hundred dollars for the appearance, but he would have been delighted to show off his talents gratis, especially since he wasn't doing any actual pitching.[20]

When Newsom resumed pitching for real, on July 28 at Detroit, his control was less than sharp and he lost a 9–5 contest to the Philadelphia Athletics in 11 innings, ending his 13-game winning streak. It was an especially frustrating loss in that Newsom couldn't hold a 5–2 lead and was finally routed by the light-hitting A's with a four-run 11th-inning rally.

After the game, Newsom returned to the Statler Hotel, where he and several teammates were staying, but the loss stayed with him, leading to one of his "purple cow" moments. He used a special salve on his injured thumb but couldn't locate the salve in his room. So, at 1 in the morning, he summoned the bellhop. Once the youth arrived, Newsom ordered him to go into town and get a can of the salve, giving him a 50-cent piece. The bellhop had to visit several all-night pharmacies before he finally located the special salve, all of which took over an hour.

"Where the hell have you been?" yelled Newsom once the youth showed up at his room. "Where's the salve?" The youth cautiously produced the can. Newsom took it and flung it across the suite. "And where's my change?"

The shell-shocked youth fished in his pocket and produced a dime and three pennies. "That's it?" yelled Newsom. "In St. Louis this stuff only costs a quarter!"[21]

No tip, no thanks. And for the rest of the season Newsom complained to his teammates about how bad the service was at that hotel.

Not that the salve made a difference. Some years later, Newsom revealed his right thumb never did heal properly and that he pitched in pain the remainder of the 1940 season. But pitching in pain was a Newsom specialty.

"Painful" was the way to describe the Yankees' 1940 season, certainly to their players. Heavily favored to win a fifth straight world championship, the Yankees struggled mightily in the early going. After a loss to Newsom and the Tigers on May 23, New York stood at 11–17 and in last place in the American League for the first time in 25 seasons. New York didn't get untracked until August, when the promotion of right-hander Ernie "Tiny" Bonham from the minor leagues finally gave them a consistent winner. Even so, the Yankees were in third place, five games behind the Indians and also trailing the Tigers on the morning of September 1. They cut that deficit to only one game on September 7, and a mere half-game on the morning of September 11. On that day, they won the first game of a doubleheader against the Indians to take the league lead by percentage points. Unfortunately for the Bronx Bombers, they lost the second game, and then five of their next six contests, seriously dimming their pennant hopes.[22]

After the doubleheader split at Cleveland, the Yanks lost two of three games at Detroit. Even so, entering games of September 15, the Yankees appeared to have as good a shot at the AL title as either Cleveland or Detroit, perhaps even better, since the remaining schedule favored them. They did not have to play either Cleveland or Detroit in the final two weeks of the season, while the Indians and Tigers were to play each other six times.

The Yankees were a confident bunch entering a four-game series at St. Louis. A sweep of the hapless Browns would likely vault the Bronx Bombers back into first place. Instead, the series was a disaster. The Browns swept a doubleheader on September 15, by scores of 10–5 and 2–1, and then pummeled the Yanks the next day, 16–4. The three losses put New York four games behind the league leader, which on the morning of September 18 was the Tigers, by a slender half-game over Cleveland.

"We just were never right there in 1940," said New York's Tommy Henrich. "We made a great run to get back in it, and then lost three games at St. Louis and that was that. Even so, if our front office had recalled Tiny Bonham a month sooner than they did, we would have won it all. You know what they say, we felt we didn't lose the pennant, we just ran out of time."[23]

Even more than the three embarrassing losses at St. Louis, the Yanks' fate may well have been sealed by one freak play in the September 12 game against the Tigers at Briggs Stadium. Trailing the Yankees 3–2 with one out in the bottom of the eighth, Charlie Gehringer worked Atley Donald for a walk. Hank Greenberg followed with a scorching one-hopper directly into Red Rolfe's glove at third base. Gehringer could no longer run much, and Greenberg could barely run at all. If ever there was a tailor-made double-play ball, this was it. Rolfe made an accurate throw to second baseman Joe Gordon to force out Gehringer. Gordon had all the time in the world to throw Greenberg out at first; "Big Greenie" was barely halfway down the line when Gordon touched second base. But, for whatever reason, Gordon rushed the throw to first. Maybe it was just force of habit, or maybe he forgot it was Greenberg running. The throw eluded Babe Dahlgren and wound up in the Detroit dugout. Instead of the Yankees getting two outs, the Tigers now had the tying run at second base.

Rudy York, as he had done all month long, came through for Detroit, driving in Greenberg to tie the game. York took second on the throw home. Bruce Campbell was intentionally walked, but Pinky Higgins delivered his most important hit of the year for the Tigers, singling to right to score York with what proved to be the game-winner.

Without Gordon's bad throw, or even if Dahlgren had been able to knock down the throw and keep Greenberg at first base, the Yanks likely would have won the game. Gordon and Dahlgren were regarded as outstanding defensive players, possibly the best at their positions in the major leagues. If the Yankees had held on to win, they, the Tigers and Indians could have finished the season in a flat-footed tie for first place. Rarely in baseball history did one lousy throw mean so much for so many. Dahlgren said,

> That's one of those plays that will always haunt me. I know it haunted Gordon.... Funny thing, with Greenberg running, I probably could have gone down the [right-field] line 10 feet to catch the ball and still have time to get back and touch the bag before Hank. Even so, if [Tommy] Henrich hadn't got hurt in September [he injured a knee in the game of September 7] and missed the rest of the year, we would have won it all.[24]

Dahlgren also believed frequent absences by manager Joe McCarthy hurt the team. He claimed McCarthy "just flat-out disappeared" for a couple of games at least two times that summer (McCarthy did miss the All-Star Game, citing health reasons). Not surprisingly, these unannounced absences created an unneeded distraction for the Yankees. At other times, McCarthy was in the dugout but seemed ineffective and distant while coach Artie Fletcher made most of the strategy decisions. Dahlgren said,

> The amazing thing was that the New York newspaper guys protected the guy like he was some sort of saint. Mac wouldn't be at the game and not Word One would be written about it. Compare that to what was going on with [Ossie] Vitt there in Cleveland. It seemed like every time he had a bowel movement it got into the Cleveland papers.

Indeed, the 1940 AL pennant race just might be the only major league season actually decided by newspaper coverage.

Oscar Vitt, hired by the Indians in 1938, never hit it off with the majority of the Cleveland players. He replaced Steve O'Neill, one of the most well-liked men in the game; he was an outsider, from the Yankees organization; he was definitely old-school in his tactics and approach to player-manager relations; and he had the misfortune of winding up with a group of young, reasonably well-paid and well-educated players who resisted his bullying tactics. Plus, as events in the summer of 1940 would dramatically reveal, he did not have the support of the Cleveland front office.

It wasn't surprising that Vitt had problems with outfielder Ben Chapman and pitcher Johnny Allen. Both were notorious hot-heads who would have given any manager grief. But he also ran afoul of the Indians' two undisputed stars, pitcher Bob Feller and first baseman Hal Trosky. Virtually all accounts of Cleveland's "Crybaby" players' revolt that summer agree that the turning point was when veteran pitcher Mel Harder joined forces with those seeking to have Vitt fired. Harder was anything but a rabble-rouser and was the team's elder statesman.[25]

Entering the season, many felt the Indians had enough pitching and defense to challenge the Yankees for the pennant. Indeed, their starting pitchers, anchored by Feller, held up quite well. Feller, still only 21 years old, developed into the superstar many had predicted, finishing with a 27–11 record and leading AL pitchers in innings pitched, strikeouts and earned run average. Al Milnar posted an 18–10 record, Al Smith was 15–7, Harder 12–11 and Allen 9–8. Joe Dobson provided effective relief.

The Indians also possessed the best defensive infield in baseball. With Trosky at first, Ray Mack at second, Lou Boudreau at shortstop and Kenny Keltner at third, outstanding plays were the norm. Catching was handled quite capably by veterans Rollie Hemsley and Frankie Pytlak. Roy Weatherly was the team's top outfielder, hitting .303 in 135 games. Veterans Ben Chapman and Beau Bell platooned in right. Bell, acquired from Detroit in exchange for Bruce Campbell, was something of a mixed blessing. He hit well enough, finishing at .279, but made a couple of egregious errors in the heat of the September pennant race that cost Cleveland dearly. Leftfielder Jeff Heath, of all the Indians' players, was clearly affected by his ongoing squabbles with Vitt and finished with a career-low .219 average.

Feller later described the Indians' season as one of black bitterness. It certainly started on a high note with Feller's no-hitter against the White Sox in the season opener. But somehow, the Indians were never able to put together a long winning streak to capitalize on the Yankees' woes in the first half of the season. The Indians also had more than their share of bad luck. Trosky missed five games in May when his infant son became deathly ill. That same week, the Tribe lost utility infielder Oscar Grimes for the season when he was struck by a line drive during infield practice.

Still, the main cause of the Indians' on-field inconsistency could be traced directly to Vitt. "Sometimes I feel that [Vitt's] decision to manage from the dugout in 1940 hastened the blowup," Feller wrote in his 1947 autobiography, *Strikeout Story*. "He was highly emotional and reacted strongly to the tide of a game. Out on the coaching lines he could yell and release his emotional stream. In the dugout, he paced up and down and delivered sarcastic comments. It was our feeling that he produced tension."[26]

Contrast the Indians' plight, with Vitt, and the Yankees' plight, with McCarthy, to the serene atmosphere on the Tigers, and it becomes obvious what an outstanding job Baker did. Newsom himself summed up the Tigers' success thusly: "We had a great manager ... and we were 25 men playing as one man."[27]

On June 13, a delegation of 12 players, led by Harder, paid a visit to team president Alva Bradley, demanding the firing of Vitt. It was supposed to be a confidential meeting, but the news quickly leaked out. Feller claimed he never found out who told the press about the meeting, but the likelihood is that leaks occurred from both the front office and from more than one of the players. News of the meeting touched off a media feeding frenzy, especially between the rival *Cleveland Press* and *Cleveland Plain Dealer*. From that point onward, the antagonism between the players and Vitt was to flap in the breeze like dirty laundry.[28]

From June 15 onward, the Indians were branded as a bunch of malcontents. The descriptive noun that became attached to them was "crybabies." In the world of manhood and sportsmanship, circa 1940, nothing was worse than a crybaby. It was a label that stung.

In baseball, bench jockeying is a specialized skill that, in the current era of mass media coverage and million-dollar players, has fallen out of vogue. In Newsom's era, the worst thing for any player to do was to give opponents grist for their name-calling mill. A classic example was the Tigers' Rowe. During his outstanding 1934 season, he was asked to guest star on the Eddie Cantor network radio program. During the show, broadcast live of course, Rowe became somewhat flustered while reading his script and blurted out, "How'm I doin,' Edna?" over the air, referring to his girlfriend who was listening back home in Texas. Until the end of his career in baseball, in the 1950s as a minor league manager, Rowe was destined to hear the "How'm I doin'" line from the opposition at least once in every game.[29]

For the 1940 Cleveland Indians, they were now "The Crybabies" to opposing teams and fans. The taunt was spurred on by newspaper coverage and spread like wildfire throughout the league. While major league players will deny having "rabbit ears" and claim name-calling has no effect on their playing ability, the evidence from 1940 certainly tends to refute that.

Had the players' blow-up with Vitt occurred in 1938, probably not a peep would have been heard about it from the Tigers dugout, filled as it was at that time with quiet, gentlemanly players. But the 1940 Tigers team had Bobo Newsom, one of the most accomplished and aggressive bench jockeys in the game. It also harbored Rowdy Dick Bartell and former Indians Earl Averill, Bruce Campbell and Billy Sullivan, a group ready and willing to heap abuse on any opponent.[30]

Vitt was an easy target, for he had always been an aggressive "jockey" even as a player. He also possessed all manner of nervous mannerisms that invited abuse, and those mannerisms became more pronounced during the blistering hot summer of 1940. By July, the verbal slings and arrows directed against the Indians were unrelenting. Interestingly, Feller remembered Yankee players and fans as being the worst offenders, although the Detroit contingent couldn't have been far behind.[31]

Fueling Newsom's anger against Vitt was an incident in August. Newsom had taped up his broken thumb in an attempt to ease the pain, but Vitt announced he would protest to the American League office if Newsom pitched against the Indians with the tape in place. Vitt's implication was that Newsom was a cheater, and while technically it was against the rules to have tape on his pitching hand, Newsom bitterly resented both Vitt's charge and his going public with it. Newsom removed the tape, but dramatically escalated his verbal attacks when the two teams met.

In spite of everything, the Indians were in good shape in the standings on the morning of Labor Day, September 2, leading Detroit by 3 ½ games and the Yankees by 4 ½. With Feller pitching every fourth day, they appeared to be slump-proof. The weather, which had set record highs in July and August, was cooling off, always good news to ballplayers in those days before lightweight uniforms and air conditioning. But the Indians lost a doubleheader that day, at home to the lowly Browns, and their agony began in earnest.

Of all the misfortunes that befell the Indians, the worst occurred on September 4 when star first baseman Hal Trosky, the team's only consistent home run and RBI man, suffered a freak injury. Trosky tripped on the base while rounding third and pulled a muscle in his leg. He missed a week and then was rushed back into the lineup by a frantic Vitt, but was definitely not the same player. During the Indians' final 16 games, Trosky hit just .140 with three RBI. His lack of production spread to the entire team; for September, the Indians hit .230 with only 11 home runs.

Vitt proved to be a better prophet than manager. "I look for this race not to be decided until the last week of the season," he told a writer from the United Press on July 6. "The club I fear more than any is Detroit. If Gehringer and Bartell can hold up all year they're going to be pretty tough."[32]

It worked out that way. Due to a fluke in the schedule, the Tribe and Bengals were to play each other nine times in the season's final 24 games. Six of those games were at Detroit. While the Tigers were playing mediocre baseball entering September, having won 12 of their last 25 games, they could not be overlooked.

Detroit had hit its nadir in late August. On August 21, the Tigers lost their third straight game at Yankee Stadium, on a bases-loaded walk by Al Benton in the bottom of the ninth. It was the team's sixth loss in a row, and their tenth in 12 games.

Following the rough series in New York, the Tigers traveled to Boston. Upon arrival at the Hotel Touraine, Newsom found a copy of the *Boston Herald* with a screaming 72-point headline: "Trotsky Dead." The headline was announcing the assassination of the exiled Bolshevik in Mexico, but Newsom quipped, "See? I told ya Vitt would get him sooner or later!" The reference to "Crybaby" first baseman Hal Trosky and the Cleveland manager broke the tension of the slumping ballclub.[33]

The next day, it was rookie Freddie Hutchinson giving the team a huge lift. Newsom started but was driven to cover in the second inning (his shortest start of the season) as the Bosox took an 8–2 lead. However, Hutchinson entered and held Boston scoreless the rest of the way. Detroit rallied, and Hutchinson himself eventually drove in the winning run in the tenth inning, giving his team a 9–8 victory. Detroit's pennant hopes were revived, and Boston's were banished.

Now it was September, and the first of the nine games to make or break Detroit's and Cleveland's seasons was set for September 4 at Briggs Stadium. Baker and his Tigers were ready.

The wily Baker made sure the infield grass at Briggs was thick and ankle-high to keep balls from scooting past the Tigers' slow-of-foot defenders. He also, by this point in the season, knew every one of the Indians' signs and knew how to "read" every one of their pitchers. While the Indians suspected that someone in the outfield scoreboard was stealing signs and relaying them to Baker, that sort of covert operation wasn't necessary. Baker could see all he needed to see, from his customary seat in the Tigers dugout or from the third base coaching box.[34]

Moreover, Baker knew Vitt like a brother, had played with him on the Tigers and had managed against him long enough to be able to out-guess the Indians skipper at every turn. Vitt might yell and wave his arms and pace back and forth in the dugout, but Baker didn't need to do any of that. He was the ultimate baseball voyeur, looking for the slightest hint of movement—the muscles on a catcher's arm twitching as he put his hand down to give a sign, the index finger on a pitcher's throwing hand as he gripped and re-gripped the baseball, the left foot of an infielder as he set himself for the upcoming pitch, the way a batter's shoulders either slumped or rose as he received a sign from his manager. This was to be Del Baker's shining hour.

The Tigers smashed the Indians in the three-game series at Briggs, winning all three and outscoring Cleveland, 28–10. Newsom pitched the third game, securing the much-needed sweep with a 10–5 victory. Trosky was injured in the first game of the series, forcing the Indians to play Beau Bell at first base. Bell, never an accomplished defensive player, played a key role in the 10–5 game. With the Tigers clinging to a slender 4–3 lead in the bottom of the fifth inning, two-out walks to Greenberg, York and Tuck Stainback by Al Milnar loaded the bases with Bengals. Billy Sullivan followed with a grounder to Bell at first which he promptly booted, allowing Greenberg to score. He then made a belated and awkward throw to Milnar, covering first base. Milnar, caught off-guard by the throw and no doubt disgusted by Bell's error on the routine ground ball, showed his frustration by holding the ball while gazing into the outfield. York saw this and broke from third, scoring without a throw from the shell-shocked Milnar. Birdie Tebbetts followed with a two-run double and the Tigers had a four-run rally, on only one hit, and an 8–3 lead. That was more than enough of a cushion for Newsom.

The Indians had their chance to bury the Tigers. Instead, by virtue of the sweep Detroit was now only one game out of first place. The pennant race was definitely on. When the Indians lost to the White Sox on September 9, they fell out of first place for the first time since August 12.

The Tigers had their chance to KO the Yankees by sweeping the Bronx Bombers in a three-game series at Detroit on September 12–14, but after winning the first two games Newsom had one of his worst outings of the year, getting shelled by the desperate Yanks for five runs in the fourth inning. New York went on to a 16–7 victory. The only good thing about the game, from Newsom's standpoint, is that he made relatively few pitches before leaving in the fifth inning. After the game, he immediately went to Baker and reported that his arm was fine and he was ready to pitch again as soon as possible. This Baker did, as he started Newsom on one day's rest on September 16. Newsom responded with brilliance, stopping Washington on five hits in a 9–2 victory, his 19th of the year.

Schoolboy Rowe followed that with another nifty performance against the Senators in a 6–3 victory on September 17 to improve Rowe's record to 15–3. However, he left the game in the seventh inning, reportedly because his right shoulder stiffened up. In reality, he had felt something pop in the shoulder and was in severe pain. Baker successfully hid this information from the media and opponents, but it was doubtful if

Rowe would be able to pitch again that season.[35]

Tommy Bridges was the next veteran to give the Tigers a lift, pitching a complete game in a 14–0 victory over the Philadelphia A's in the first game of a doubleheader. However, rookie Johnny Gorsica blew a 6–4 lead in the ninth inning of Game Two, the A's scoring nine runs to win, 13–6. Obviously, Baker was going to have to select his starting pitchers with great care in the season's final two weeks.

Baker rolled the dice the next day in another doubleheader against the A's. The last-place A's would be playing their eighth and ninth games in five days, due to make-ups of games that had been rained out during the miserable weather of April. Connie Mack was out of pitching, and his everyday lineup was exhausted. Baker sensed the time was right to start a virtual unknown, Floyd Giebell, in Game One. Giebell had just been recalled from Buffalo of the International League, where he had posted a lackluster 15–17 record. He had pitched briefly for the Tigers early in 1939, exhibiting an above-average curveball, a below-average fastball and a lack of command of either pitch. Now, the tall, skinny right-hander was back with the big club and in the midst of a red-hot pennant race.[36]

With Baker counseling him after every inning, Giebell responded with a quality start, going the distance to beat the A's, 13–2. Baker followed that by using rookie Dizzy Trout in Game Two, and Trout was even better, beating Philly, 10–1. It was Trout's third, and final, win of the year.

The sweep of the A's left the Tigers and Indians in a flat-footed tie for first place at 85–61, with eight games remaining on the schedule. After 146 games spread over five months, after swapping the league lead 17 times since late June, the Tigers and Indians were neck-and-neck with only one week to go. The beleaguered Indians had climbed back into the race by winning nine of 12 games. Meanwhile, the Yankees had fallen four games off the pace, leaving them with only the ghost of a chance to win the pennant. It was now obvious to all that the race would be decided between the Tigers and Indians, especially since the two teams would play each other in six of their eight remaining games. If either team could win even four of the six, that likely would be good enough to secure the pennant.

The Detroit fans were out in force with diapers, baby bottles and even a baby carriage strategically placed next to the Cleveland dugout for Game One of the three-game set at Briggs on September 20. Nearly 25,000 were in the stands, and all of a like mind—to belittle and harass the Cleveland players and their manager. The game matched Newsom, going for his 20th win of the season, against Mel Harder, chief spokesman for the "crybabies."

It was a chilly afternoon, and Newsom had his customary problems pitching in cold weather. He struggled into the sixth inning, giving up four runs and 11 hits, before being replaced. Meanwhile, the wily veteran Harder, a sinkerball specialist, was pitching a gem. Entering the bottom of the eighth, Harder held a 4–1 lead and had allowed only three hits. The agile Cleveland infield gobbled up ground ball after ground ball, and when Billy Sullivan grounded out to begin the eighth the Tigers were suddenly down to their final five outs.

Then Harder did something uncharacteristic. He walked Barney McCosky. Charlie Gehringer, just as wily a veteran as Harder, followed with a single to right, McCosky racing to third. The crowd came alive, for the middle of the Detroit lineup was now going to get its licks with men on base. Vitt could have stayed with Harder, certainly not an unreasonable move. At the very least, he could have gone out and talked to Harder. Instead, he did something that ultimately doomed his fate as Cleveland manager and the Indians' pennant hopes. Vitt had his ace, Bob Feller, sitting in the bullpen all day, and now he decided to use him. Feller's great fastball figured to be tough to see in the late afternoon. However, Feller was not expecting to pitch, having had only one day of rest since a complete-game victory, and wasn't warmed up. Vitt waved him in anyway.

So in comes a power pitcher, and he isn't completely loose. What's he going to throw? A fastball, of course. Baker called Hank Greenberg over to remind him, although Greenberg, being a heady player, scarcely needed the heads-up. Feller's first pitch was indeed a fastball, and Greenberg laced it back up the middle, scoring McCosky as Gehringer raced to third. Rudy York was next up, and after failing to connect on two Feller deliveries he managed to lift the third into shallow right field. Right field happened to be where Beau Bell was playing this day. Bell misjudged the ball, broke late, and it bounced in front of him. Tigers fans roared as Gehringer scored. Bell fumbled the ball and the fans roared even louder. York, seeing Bell fumbling the ball, took off for second. Greenberg, who had reached third, took off for home. For Bell, the only play had to be at home plate, on the lead-footed Greenberg representing the tying run. But the crowd's roar made it impossible for him to hear his teammates yelling to throw home. Instead, Bell hesitated and then threw to second base, too late to get York as Greenberg lumbered home with the tying run. Of all the plays in all the innings of the 1940 season, Bell's blunder (actually, three blunders rolled into one) proved to be the ultimate pennant-decider.

Feller, no doubt beside himself by what had transpired, tried to sneak yet another fastball past Pinky Higgins. Higgins slapped it into left field, and York was just able to beat the throw home, sliding in with the go-ahead run. In this gamble, Vitt had rolled snake-eyes. He slowly walked to the mound to remove Feller, amidst the noise of the fans and the yelling and screaming from the Tigers dugout, much of it generated by Newsom, including the cutting comment "Just put some tape on him, Ossie!" The Tigers added another run in the inning, and held off the Indians in the ninth to win, 6–5.

For giving Harder the quick hook, Vitt was roasted in print by the Cleveland sportswriters and more than a few of his own players. It got no better for him the next day. Before a Saturday afternoon crowd in excess of 42,000, Baker called on the sore-shouldered Schoolboy Rowe, and Rowe pitched a gem, using all his guile in holding the Indians to only five hits in a 5–0 victory.

Leading the Tigers' cheers from the dugout was, of course, Newsom. Despite the non-stop crowd noise, Newsom's voice had an unusual carrying quality, and it represented a particular annoyance to Vitt. Newsom had an abundance of material to aim at the Cleveland skipper, who opted to man the third-base coaching box for the crucial series. Further riling the Cleveland skipper, early in the game someone fired a roll of adhesive tape out of the Tigers' dugout, directed toward Vitt in the coaching box. Vitt argued with umpires to have Newsom—the most likely culprit—ejected, but none of the umps had seen the tape thrown.

The crowd was even larger for the Sunday game, well over 50,000. Vitt, now with no choice, went with his ace, Bob Feller. Feller was dog-tired but managed to pitch a compete-game victory, the Indians routing Tommy Bridges early in a 10–5 triumph. That left the Tigers with a one-game lead in the standings.

Both the Tigers and Indians had Monday off. The Tigers had two games scheduled with the White Sox before ending the year with three games at Cleveland. Needless to say, Detroit could not afford to look past Chicago. On Tuesday, a day-long downpour forced the postponement of the Tigers-White Sox game, but Tigers' spirits were definitely lifted by news from Cleveland, where Elden Auker of the Browns beat the Indians, 7–2. It marked the fifth time that year that Auker, the former Tiger, had beaten Cleveland. If rules permitted, Tigers players would have likely voted the personable Auker a share of their subsequent World Series pot.

More stormy weather awaited the Tigers and White Sox on Wednesday, when a doubleheader between the teams needed to be played at Briggs Stadium. Skies were gray and temperatures were in the low 50s for the 1 p.m. start of Game One. Baker started Bridges, though the veteran was clearly near his breaking point. The Tigers gave him a 4–1 lead, but the White Sox knocked him out of the box with a six-run fifth inning. Dick Bartell made it a 7–6 game with a two-run home run in the sixth, and an RBI triple by Higgins followed by a Pete Fox sacrifice fly enabled the Tigers to regain the lead, 8–7, in the seventh. Chicago stormed right back, scoring twice in the eighth off Dizzy Trout to go ahead, 9–8. The Tigers tied it in the bottom of the eighth on Charlie Gehringer's RBI double.

The Tigers had squared the count, but appeared to be out of relief pitchers. At that point, legend has it, Bobo Newsom bolted from the dugout, told Baker he was gonna pitch, like it or not, and took the mound. Actually, Baker and Newsom discussed the situation the day before and Newsom willingly volunteered for bullpen duty. Unlike Feller, Newsom had plenty of experience pitching in relief and did not need long to get loose, even on a cold day. Thus it was that he took the mound in the ninth inning, to the absolute delight of the 22,000 Tigers fans in attendance. He retired the Sox in order in the ninth. The Tigers failed to score in the bottom of the ninth. He retired the Sox again in the tenth. This time, the Tigers' offense came through. The speedy McCosky started it by beating out an infield grounder. Gehringer moved him to second with a perfectly placed sacrifice bunt. Greenberg was intentionally walked, but York smashed a long drive off the wall in left field, easily scoring McCosky with the game-winner. The dramatic 10–9 victory gave Newsom his 20th win of the season, his third straight 20-win season. The question now was who would start Game Two for the Tigers?

Newsom was the scheduled starter, but whether he could answer the bell seemed doubtful. For Bobo, there was no doubt. He had pitched doubleheaders before, he would pitch them again. He felt good, his team had won, and now they needed him one more time. It was a scenario made to order for Newsom the Great.

Newsom marched out to start Game Two against White Sox ace Johnny Rigney. The Sox scored first, on a two-run home run by Larry Rosenthal in the second inning. Rigney was still clinging to a 2–1 lead when Greenberg batted for the Tigers in the last of the seventh. "Hammering Hank" was having a tremendous month of September, with clutch hit after clutch hit, but none was more clutch than what he did against Rigney, slamming a curveball into the left field seats to tie the game. Rigney was primarily a fastball pitcher, and it is highly likely that Baker picked off the signal for the curveball and let Greenberg know what was coming. The "inside baseball" that Baker had been working on all during his stint as Detroit manager paid off, big-time.

Now on equal footing, Newsom retired the White Sox in order in the top of the eighth. In the bottom of the eighth, Rigney finally weakened, likely aided by more pitch-calling from Baker. Back-to-back singles by the pesky McCosky and Gehringer put runners at first and third. Greenberg, not surprisingly, was intentionally walked, but York came through with a fly ball to deep right, enabling McCosky to tag up and score the go-ahead run.

Newsom held off the Pale Hose in the top of the ninth, and the Tigers had the win and a sweep of the twin bill. Even though the Indians won their game in Cleveland, Newsom's heroics enabled the Tigers to take a two-game lead into their season-ending series at Cleveland. The Indians had to win all three games to win the pennant.

Neither team was scheduled to play on Thursday, September 26. The Tigers spent that night at their hotel in Cleveland, preparing for an onslaught from Indians fans. To get to the hotel, they risked the wrath of an angry mob that met them at the train station. Cleveland police wanted the Detroit contingent to exit the station via a back door and an adjacent alley. Newsom wouldn't hear of it. "I'm going out the same way I always have, the front door of the station," he reportedly proclaimed. Most of the Tigers followed his courageous example and made it safely to the hotel. Once there, Newsom happily signed autographs in the lobby and chatted with all and sundry.[37]

Up in his hotel room, Baker faced a decision, the biggest baseball decision of his life. He did an interesting thing, certainly something that Vitt or McCarthy would never think to do. He called several veteran players to his room, including Newsom, to discuss who should pitch the next day. The consensus, ironed out over a two-hour gabfest and drinking session: the Tigers would go with rookie Floyd Giebell. It may have seemed like folly, but the reasoning was sound. The Indians had no choice but to go with their ace, Bob Feller. Should worse come to worse, and the Indians rout Giebell, the Tigers would still have Newsom, Bridges and Rowe to choose from for games two and three of the series. But there was more to it than that. Giebell was the one Tigers pitcher the Indians had never faced. His off-speed pitches figured to give the over-anxious (and possibly over-confident) Cleveland hitters problems. Further, at age 30, Giebell had been around long enough to have a certain maturity the other young Tigers pitchers lacked. While the tale changed over time and depending on who was telling it, it appears that Baker informed Giebell late that night that he would be given the start.[38]

For the media, Baker had a very different story. The scheduled Tigers starter for Friday's game was Schoolboy Rowe. Baker didn't tell the media he wouldn't start Rowe, but didn't say he would, either. "I won't make up my mind until about a half-hour before game time," he said. In reality, the Tigers coaching staff spent a couple of hours before the game with Giebell and his batterymate, Billy Sullivan, going through the Indians hitters' strengths and weaknesses. Giebell had experienced problems with first-string catcher Birdie Tebbetts, a hyper sort, in his previous start and asked Baker if the easy-going Sullivan could catch him instead. It wasn't a request a rookie would dare make to Vitt or McCarthy, but to Baker it made sense.

Baker's deception worked. No one in the ballpark except the handful of Tigers who attended the previous night's meeting could believe it when the Tigers' battery for the game was announced as "Sullivan catching, Giebell pitching." According to Giebell, "The fans thought Schoolboy Rowe was somewhere under the stands warming up and when it was time for the game to start he would take my place and I would go sit on the bench."[39]

Came 2 p.m. and a crowd of nearly 50,000 packed chilly Municipal Stadium for the game of the year in Cleveland. Although it was Ladies Day at the ballpark, there was nothing lady-like about this mob. They had read the newspaper accounts of how the Indians were treated in Detroit and were itching for payback. Rotten fruit and catcalls greeted the Tigers as they took the field for batting practice.

The game was halted in the bottom of the first when the fans littered left field with garbage as Hank Greenberg was in the process of catching a fly ball. Home plate umpire Bill Summers threatened a forfeit if the fans continued their unruly behavior—but has there ever been born an umpire who would have the guts to forfeit the biggest game of a big league season? Summers knew if he forfeited the game to the Tigers, there weren't enough police in all of Ohio to protect him. The game must go on, regardless of fan behavior.

The bottom of the first also contained a hint of the misery to come for the Indians. Ben Chapman reached on a walk from Giebell and Lou Boudreau ripped a line drive down the first base line that appeared to be headed for extra bases. But Rudy York snagged the drive and was able to double Chapman off first. A similar play occurred in the third inning, with the game still scoreless. An error and a single put two Cleveland runners on base. Roy Weatherly followed by slashing a line drive to center, but right at Barney McCosky.

Then came the fourth inning. With one out, Feller walked Charlie Gehringer, one of eight walks he would issue this afternoon. "Rapid Robert" bore down to strike out Hank Greenberg, much to the delight of the crowd. He then faced the dangerous Rudy York. York got under a Feller fastball and hit a high, lazy fly ball down the left-field line. Had the game been at League Park instead of Municipal Stadium, it would have been an easy out, for it was 370 feet down the line there. But it was only 320 feet at Municipal, and York's ball kept carrying and carrying, sailing over left fielder Chapman's outstretched glove and over the nine-foot wall just to the right of the foul pole, landing in the first row of the bleachers. The Tigers, stunningly, had a 2–0 lead.

Could Giebell make that lead stand up? He put two Cleveland runners on base in the bottom of the fourth, but got out of the jam by striking out Ray Mack. Two more Cleveland runners reached in the fifth, this time with no outs, but Giebell struck out Chapman, retired Weatherly on a pop fly and struck out Boudreau. Again in the seventh, the Indians got two runners aboard, but Giebell struck out Chapman for the third time in the game. Higgins then made a fine play on a hard grounder by Weatherly to end the inning.

Meanwhile, Feller was nearly untouchable following York's home run. He allowed only one hit over the final five innings. But it wasn't quite enough. On this day Feller struck out only four Tigers, while Giebell finished with six Ks. What were the odds of that happening?

Giebell retired the final nine Cleveland batters in order, getting pinch-hitter Jeff

Heath to ground out to Rudy York to end the game. The Tigers, other than Giebell, reacted with joy, immediately and en masse. For a moment, Giebell stood on the mound, not knowing quite what to do. Then he was mobbed by York, Sullivan and a host of Tigers who had exploded out of the dugout, led by Bobo Newsom. For Feller, it was a disastrous end to what had been a great season. Spent physically and mentally, Feller remembered thinking just one thing: I want to go home.[40]

Feller defeated the Tigers six straight times in 1939, but lost five of eight decisions to the Bengals in 1940. The reason was clear. "Baker, who coached third, was tipping off my pitches to the batters," Feller wrote in *Strikeout Story*. "He studied a pitcher's throwing habits closely and soon discovered the things he did differently when he was going to throw a fastball or a curve."[41]

The two teams still had two games to play, but for the veteran Tigers players, especially Newsom, it was party-time. Using reserves, the Tigers lost those final two games, finishing at 90–64 and exactly one game ahead of Cleveland. The Yankees, with ten wins in their final 11 games, finished third, two games back.

For Giebell, the pennant clincher was the highlight of his life. The tall right-hander from West Virginia was ineligible for the Tigers' World Series roster. He pitched briefly, and ineffectively, for the Tigers in 1941 and then faded from the baseball scene. But not before receiving the loudest ovation of all the players during a victory celebration in downtown Detroit on Sunday night as the triumphant Tigers returned to the Motor City from Cleveland.

Later on, Newsom would claim it was his idea to start Giebell against the Indians. Given the wild turn of events and Baker's trait of listening to his players' suggestions, it's a possibility. More importantly, Newsom accepted the choice of Giebell without complaint and led the cheers for the rookie from the dugout. Never truer was Milton's adage that they also serve who only stand and wait than it was on that chilly late September afternoon on the shores of Lake Erie.

The 1940 World Series was scheduled to begin on Wednesday, October 2, in Cincinnati. The Tigers would be facing the Reds, making their second straight World Series appearance. Most sportswriters and baseball fans favored the Tigers, largely because American League teams had won five straight World Series and ten of the past 13. In truth, as Del Baker knew, the Tigers and Reds were evenly matched. Detroit had a more potent offense, but the Reds' one-two pitching punch of Paul Derringer and Bucky Walters—both 20-game winners for the second consecutive year—presented a big challenge for a Tigers' pitching staff which now had only one physically sound veteran starter: Bobo Newsom. The Reds were also superbly managed by Bill McKechnie.

Having Monday and Tuesday off enabled the Tigers to rest up from the exhausting pennant drive. Meanwhile, big plans were being made back in Newsom's hometown of Hartsville. Newsom's dad Quill was ailing, in fact had not been feeling well all summer. The years of toil running the farm had taken a toll. Fronnie, his second wife, decided the World Series games at Cincinnati would be the perfect time to arrange both a vacation and reconciliation between father and son.[42]

The occasion would finally enable Quill to see his son pitch in a major league game. Quill hadn't seen Bobo pitch since the summer of 1929 when Bobo was with Macon. In fact, the two had rarely spoken in the past ten years. But Fronnie, a dynamic personality who was well-liked by all the Newsoms, decided it was high time for a family reunion. What better place than at the World Series? Fronnie was joined in her efforts by Newsom's sisters, Aline and Lilly Belle, and by Bobo's wife, Lucille. That quartet managed to convince Quill to travel north, although the elder Newsom had severe doubts, both about his health and about how he would be received by his now-famous son. By Monday night, plans were in place for the Newsom family to stay in Cincinnati. Bobo procured tickets for them for Games One and Two, and was able to talk team management into picking up their hotel tab.

With the Newsoms in attendance, along with nearly 32,000 others, for Game One, the Tigers jumped on Cincinnati ace Paul Derringer for five runs in the second inning. Bruce Campbell added a two-run home run in the fifth, and Bobo Newsom cruised the rest of the way to a 7–2 victory. It was a sensational World Series debut for Bobo and made for a memorable day at the ballpark for Newsoms young and old.

The official family reunion was held that night over dinner in the hotel restaurant, and continued in Bobo Newsom's suite. It was, by all accounts, a joyous occasion, although Daddy Quill admitted the excitement of the game left him very tired. He and

Buck Newsom and Paul Derringer shake hands prior to Game One of the 1940 World Series in Cincinnati. Newsom outpitched Derringer for an 8–3 victory. These images were used on Newsom's and Derringer's gum cards in the 1941 "Double Play" set (the Ray Medeiros collection, used by permission).

Fronnie retired early, while Bobo continued to celebrate the victory. Since childhood, Newsom's ultimate dream had been to star in the World Series. Now, not only had he won a World Series game, he did it in front of his father. Daddy Quill was an eyewitness, indeed a captive audience, to the wisdom of his son's career choice. Bobo was not a spiteful person but at this moment he was filled with pride. And as he may have remembered from his Sunday School lessons on Proverbs, pride goeth before a fall.

That night in his hotel room, HQB Newsom, age 64, gentleman farmer from South Carolina, died of a massive heart attack.

Immediately, the Newsom family began to make arrangements to return Daddy Quill's remains to his home turf. Bobo Newsom would not be at the ballpark on this day. He took Daddy Quill's passing hard. While there had been reconciliation between the two, there were so many things left unsaid, so many questions left unanswered. Ultimately, it was decided Bobo would not accompany the rest of the Newsom family back to Hartsville for the burial. Instead, he would do his mourning and retrospection in private.[43]

Newsom wasn't around the next day to see the Reds beat the Tigers, 5–3. No one knew exactly where he was—he had checked out of the Cincinnati hotel—or when he would rejoin the team. Schoolboy Rowe started for Detroit but he lasted only three-plus innings, giving up four runs. Cincy's Bucky Walters made that lead stand up, pitching a three-hitter.

The Series moved to Detroit's Briggs Stadium for Games Three, Four and Five. Newsom was still not in attendance on Friday, October 4, when the Tigers broke open a 1–1 game with four runs in the seventh, thanks to home runs by Rudy York and Pinky Higgins. Tommy Bridges hung on for a 7–4 triumph, barely. Bridges, worn out from the pennant drive, gave up three runs in the final two innings. While Detroit now held a 2–1 edge in the best-of-seven Series, it was clear that neither Rowe nor Bridges could be counted on for additional duty.

Newsom was the scheduled starter for Game Four, but he again was unable to make it to the ballpark. Baker decided to give the youthful Dizzy Trout a try, hoping Trout would be able to duplicate Floyd Giebell's heroics against the Indians. Instead, Trout gave up three runs in the first three innings and Cincy ace Paul Derringer held that lead, winning 5–2 and squaring the Series.

It remained unclear if Newsom would be able to start Game Five, but it was clear the Tigers were in increasingly desperate circumstances. Baker was able to track down Newsom, and the two met in Baker's hotel room on Saturday night. While Newsom remained distraught over his father's death, he agreed to give it a go the next day. News of Newsom's start spread rapidly the next morning, and by game time Briggs Stadium was filled to capacity. A record crowd of 55,189 was packed into the place. What they, and the Cincinnati Reds, witnessed was one of the greatest pitching performances in World Series history.

Newsom was barely able to communicate before the game, and there remained a very real question whether he would be able to pitch. But once the game began, it was obvious that Newsom was focused on only one thing: beating the Reds. It was also obvious that he had his best stuff. His fastball was alive, and his slider was breaking as sharply as it ever had. All the innings over all the years, all the hard knocks and criticism, all the doubts and distractions, all were pushed aside. This was Bobo's game, what he believed he was born to do. He could never escape being his father's son, but he could do something that would forever etch the Newsom name in baseball history. There were no antics this day. There was no arguing with a manager or an umpire or the other team. Just the pitching of a baseball, fast and charged with a purpose.

Newsom fired a three-hit shutout against the Reds, no Cincinnati runner advancing past second base. A four-run Detroit rally, highlighted by a three-run home run by Hank Greenberg, in the fourth inning gave Newsom plenty of runs to work with. He finished an 8–0 winner. Afterward, he broke down.

Between sobs, he proclaimed he had dedicated the game to his father. Later, all manner of maudlin comments were attributed to Newsom. Most likely, all he said was "That one's for dad." Whatever other thoughts he had that day, about his mother Lillian, about the rivalry between father and son, about the passage of time and the burning of bridges and the roads not taken, remained unspoken.[44]

The Tigers now held a 3–2 series lead, with the series going back to Cincinnati. Baker hoped to wrap things up in Game Six, since he lacked an able-bodied starter if there was a Game Seven. Rowe, called upon to gut it out one last time, did the best he could do with his aching right shoulder. It wasn't much. He was knocked out in the first inning, allowing two runs. That was enough, for Cincy's Bucky Walters was on his game and pitched a five-hit shutout for his second complete-game victory of the Series. Walters was a right-handed sinkerball pitcher, and that type gave the Tigers fits all year. Walters' deliveries negated Greenberg and York, who both tended to uppercut and liked the pitch up in the strike zone. You can't uppercut a sinker, as Walters once again proved that day. It also didn't do any good to tip the pitches,

Newsom winds up for a pitch during his 8–0 victory over the Cincinnati Reds in Game Five of the 1940 World Series, the highlight of Newsom's 28-year professional career (the Ray Medeiros collection, used by permission).

for Walters was basically a one-pitch pitcher, the pitch being a sinking fastball.[45]

Walters' heroics set up a Game Seven, the first time since the 1934 matchup of the Cardinals and Tigers that a World Series had gone seven games. There was no doubt about the Reds starter: Paul Derringer, who would be pitching on two-days' rest, was Bill McKechnie's only option. The Reds had no one else of championship caliber. Newsom, learning that Derringer would start for Cincy, volunteered to give it a shot for the Tigers. "I think we would have shot Baker if he had started anyone other than Bobo," Bartell said.[46]

Newsom would be pitching on only one day's rest, but many times had taken the mound on short notice. He had also recovered somewhat from the emotional fog following his father's death. So it would come down to Cincy's top pitcher versus Detroit's top pitcher for the world championship. Despite the obvious drama of the situation, there was a threat of rain that morning, prompting a quick-spreading rumor, erroneous as it turned out, that the game had been postponed. This turn of events kept the crowd down to a less-than-capacity 27,000 at Crosley Field, one of the smaller turnouts in World Series history. Those who did show up were witnesses to a classic pitching duel.

Rain or shine, Detroit's Baker was ready. He had noticed that Reds catcher Jimmy Wilson, a 40-year-old who was activated when Willard Hershberger committed suicide in August, was having trouble squatting to give the signs. In fact, as he gave the signs Wilson's fingertips were visible from a certain angle in the Tigers dugout. Thus, going into the game, Tigers hitters knew they would know every pitch Derringer threw, before he threw it. It was the sort of edge that Baker dreamed of, a little thing that made a big difference for the Tigers all year long. Unfortunately, on this day the Tigers were unable to capitalize.[47]

"Damn it, we knew everything that was coming up," Hank Greenberg remembered 40 years later. "Of course, stealing the signals was one thing, hitting the ball was another."[48]

Greenberg, who loved to be tipped off on the pitches, came to bat in the third inning with the Tigers already ahead, 1–0. Derringer had already put two men on base and was struggling with his control. He threw three straight balls to Greenberg. Normally, "Big Greenie" would be taking on a 3–0 count, but since Baker had the signs and since he signaled to Hank that a fastball was coming, Greenberg took a mighty hack ... and fouled off the pitch. The next pitch, same result. Baker signaled fastball, Greenberg got the fastball, and fouled it off. The third pitch, Baker again signaled fastball, Greenberg got the fastball ... and swung and missed.

"I can see it now," Greenberg said in a 1982 interview. "I can just see myself hitting a home run. The score would have been 4–0 and Bobo would have won that final game."[49]

Instead, the Tigers never scored again. It appeared Detroit had another run in the fourth inning, when with Higgins at second base and two outs, Newsom slapped a hard grounder headed for left field. However, Higgins, running on the play, didn't see the ball in time and was struck by it, ending the inning. Higgins later said that, in all his years in the game, it was the only time that ever happened to him, and was in fact the only time he had ever seen it happen.[50]

The game was scoreless in the third inning when the Tigers were able to push across a run. That gave Newsom an edge, and on this day it looked like it might be enough. While he didn't have the overpowering stuff he exhibited in Game Five, he was sharp. He had allowed only four hits and was still clinging to that 1–0 lead going into the bottom of the seventh. However, if the ground ball hitting Higgins was an omen, it was a whopper.

Frank McCormick led off the last of the seventh with a double. Jimmy Ripple followed with a drive to right-center. Perhaps, had the Tigers had a better defensive right fielder available, the ball would have been caught. But in right field was Bruce Campbell, he of the lame back. Campbell misjudged the ball and then was unable to jump up and make a play on it. The ball hit the fence and rebounded right back to him.

McCormick would have been the slowest runner in the game were it not for the presence of teammate Ernie Lombardi, who may have been the slowest runner in major league history. McCormick got no jump off of second and then inexplicably held up, apparently believing that Campbell would catch the ball. Meanwhile, the Tigers knew Campbell wasn't going to be able to make the catch, and shortstop Dick Bartell ran out into short right field for the relay throw. While Bartell was watching Campbell, second baseman Charlie Gehringer and third baseman Pinky Higgins were watching McCormick and realized he was caught in no-man's land.

Campbell made an excellent recovery, grabbed the ball after it bounced off the wall, and quickly and accurately threw it in to Bartell. Gehringer said in a 1980 interview,

> Bartell must have thought that since the ball was off the wall, the runner from second must've scored. But McCormick, who was no speed demon, was just rounding third when Bartell got the ball. I kept yelling, "Home, home, home!" Gee whiz, with Bartell's arm he's a dead pigeon. But he never did throw the ball. Even after he looked and still had a chance, he didn't throw. And to this day, I don't know why.[51]

Bartell, the most aggressive of all the Tigers, had picked the wrong moment in time to be passive. McCormick scored and Ripple wound up at second.

Next up was Jimmy Wilson, who also couldn't run a lick. He bunted, sharply and in the general direction of Newsom. But Bobo failed to break off the mound and third baseman Higgins had to make the play. Since Higgins was charging toward home plate, his only play was to throw Wilson out at first, allowing Ripple to take third. In later years, Newsom was always quick to defend Bartell, saying if he had made the play on Wilson's bunt he would have gotten Ripple at third base and the game would have remained tied.

Instead, Billy Myers drove Ripple home with a long fly to center, and the Reds took a 2–1 lead. Derringer made that stand up, retiring the final six Tigers in order. The result must have been hard to take for Newsom, but he was the picture of composure afterward. His was generous in his praise of Derringer and the Reds, and took no shots at his own teammates.

"We had the best shortstop in the game," Newsom told sportswriter Whitney Martin in the spring of 1941. "In the World Series game he is supposed to have held the ball and let a run score. Well, if he did, ol' Bobo wouldn't say a word. He could still be holding it yet and ol' Bobo wouldn't say anything. It was him that got us to the World Series."[52]

For Newsom, there were plenty of reasons to be magnanimous in his comments.

In the wake of his World Series heroics, he was now a household name across America, one of the most famous ballplayers in the country. Perhaps the crucible of the 1940 season and World Series finally mellowed him. Then again, there was his answer to a reporter's question just prior to the start of Game Seven of the World Series.

"Are you going to try to win this one for your daddy, too?" the reporter asked. Newsom pondered the question. "Why, no," he said. "No, I think I'll win this one for Bobo."[53]

Eight

Detroit to Washington to Brooklyn (1941–1942)

Bobo Newsom had lost his father and the deciding game of the World Series. Yet, in many ways, the winter of 1940–1941 was the happiest time of his life.

The off-season contained a whirlwind of activities, the manifestation of fame and fortune Daddy Quill wouldn't have dared dream about. But all glory is fleeting, and it flew from Newsom like a DiMaggio line drive. While he was to pitch professionally for another 13 seasons, he never regained the star status he held at the conclusion of the 1940 season. By the end of 1941, he was a pariah on the team he had almost pitched to a World Series title. And the year again brought the horrors of war to America. After December 7, Newsom's outlandish bragging and squabbles with management were no longer quite as amusing to the public as they were in the throes of the Great Depression.[1]

Any thoughts that the death of his father would bring a molecule of maturity to Newsom were quickly dispelled. The parties began early that winter and never stopped. Newsom's off-season began with not one, but two homecoming galas, one in Hartsville and one in Cheraw.[2] At these events, he proudly displayed his World Series check, a sum of $3,533, for all to see. He was actually able to

With the Tigers in 1941, Newsom's earned run average, and body weight, went up dramatically, likely because of his late-night gambols (the Ray Medeiros collection, used by permission).

keep the check in his wallet for a couple months before he was forced to cash it to buy Christmas gifts for family members. During that time, friends estimated he displayed the check to nearly half the adults in Darlington County, including total strangers he bumped into on the street.

In January, he was summoned back to Detroit for contract talks. Ordinarily, Newsom would have his guard up, but these talks promised big things. In fact, he was to sit down not with general manager Jack Zeller but with team owner Walter O. Briggs, Sr. Newsom arrived, fashionably late, for his appointment at Briggs' office, dressed to the nines in a new suit he purchased especially for the occasion (and which he charged to the team). He was greeted by Briggs' son and chief assistant, Walter O. Briggs, Jr. "Step aside, Little Bo," said Newsom as he brushed past. "Big Bobo wants to see me."[3]

The "Big Bobo" did indeed desire an audience with Newsom. It had been reported that Bob Feller was to receive a $30,000 contract for the 1941 season, and that was the starting point for the negotiations. Newsom felt the time had come that he be paid more than the Indians' ace. Newsom's argument: "Bob Feller is a good pitcher, but all he has is a fastball. Me, I've got stuff. I've got color." Briggs agreed, and made Newsom an offer of $31,000. Newsom made a counteroffer of $32,500. And $32,500 it was.[4]

"If Mr. Briggs says I'm making more than Bob Feller, then you can depend on it because he's a very truthful man," Newsom told sportswriter Shirley Povich as the pair rode the train northward from Florida to the Carolinas in April of 1941. "I don't have anything against Feller, he helped me get the kind of dough I'm getting. Mr. Briggs told me before last year's World Series that I'd be the highest-paid pitcher in the league this season and he didn't go back on his promise."[5]

Newsom also talked Briggs into throwing in a new Cadillac, since the one Newsom was driving was getting a tad threadbare. The two car buffs debated the merits of various models, and it was decided that Newsom could go to the factory and have the car specially designed to his tastes. Since his tastes in automobiles ran toward the expensive, he ultimately opted for a Cadillac with a V-12 engine and custom body and interior. After all was said and done, the cost of the car exceeded $5,000, an incredible sum for an American auto in 1941. It had, among its many features, a built-in bar.[6]

Newsom lingered in Detroit a few days, waiting for the finishing touches to be put on his car. When it was finally

When it came to being photographed, Newsom had an odd quirk: frequently, he would look away from the photographer. This is also from a family snapshot of Newsom taken at Detroit (courtesy Hartsville Museum).

ready he headed back to South Carolina. Those are those in Hartsville who still remember his grand entrance, driving the new car down the main drag at about five miles an hour—"Cadillac-ing" in the parlance of the ballplayers—and occasionally sounding its horn (which played, appropriately enough, "Hold That Tiger").[7] He was followed by two other vehicles with hired drivers at the wheel. One was his old Cadillac, the other his Plymouth station wagon. Both were loaded down with Newsom's worldly possessions: trophies, wardrobe and all manner of items that fans and admirers had given him. In the station wagon resided a pair of goats and a half-dozen chickens, gifts from a Michigan farmer. Those portions of the car's interior that the chickens hadn't ruined, the goats had eaten.

"After that, we had to take that thing right to the junkyard," Hoot Gibson remembered. "Even if it could have been repaired, we would have never gotten the stink out of it."[8]

A few days later, Newsom showed up at W. W. Shirley's barbershop, carrying a shoe box under his arm. He sat and waited patiently while Shirley performed his tonsorial tasks. He seemed unusually quiet. Finally, one of the assembled regulars asked about the shoe box. Newsom instructed Shirley to lock the front door and pull the shades down. Only then would he open the box. With the unveiling, the box was filled to the brim with $100 bills. After the customary whooping and backslapping, an argument ensued as to what the cash would look like if it were spread out instead of being confined within the cardboard. Newsom obliged, spreading the bills out over the floor of the barber shop. "Those suckers covered every square inch of my daddy's shop," said Bob Shirley. "I never did hear how much money was in the box, but it had to be thousands. Bobo was in his glory that day, just like a little kid. I can still see him, slapping down those hundreds and laughing."[9]

Later that winter, someone in town asked Newsom what he would be making for the 1941 season when all the fringe benefits and endorsements were added to the $32,500 contract. Newsom was momentarily stumped, then did some figuring with a grease

In his never-ending quest for more cash, Bobo Newsom was finally able to top Bob Feller as the highest-paid pitcher in the American League for the 1941 season. This happened despite Rapid Robert's clear statistical edge over him. Bobo's counter-argument? "Feller, all he has is a fastball. Me, I've got stuff, I've got color" (the Ray Medeiros collection, used by permission).

Newsom with his custom-made Cadillac in spring training, Lakeland, Florida, 1941. On the dashboard in gold-leaf lettering is his signature. Note the "transoceanic" radio in the center of the dashboard. Newsom loved to listen to the radio, with "Amos & Andy" being his favorite show (courtesy Special Collections, Lakeland Public Library, Lakeland, Florida).

pencil on the mirror behind a bar and came up with the sum of $50,000. For a change, his creative accounting methods actually arrived at a fair approximation. But the most important thing to him was that he was now the highest paid pitcher in baseball. He had reached the top of his profession. The threat of going back to work on the farm was definitely, unequivocally over.[10]

Newsom's personal favorite among the many endorsements was a deal touting Hi-Speed Gas. For several years, the endorsement enabled him to fill his cars with fuel for free. This was no small consideration considering the amount of driving he did, the speeds he hit on a regular basis, and the fact that his luxury vehicles rarely achieved even ten miles per gallon.

Adding to Newsom's high-octane spirits that off-season, his restaurant in Hartsville opened in early 1941, fulfilling a long-standing dream. He was anything but a silent partner in the deal, although he put up little beyond his name in the capitalization process. Someone else owned the land and building, and held first dibs on the profits.[11]

To Newsom, the main attractions of the restaurant were that it gave him a place to hold court and to try out his culinary skills. It also made an excellent hide-out from Lucille. By the spring of 1941, their marriage was definitely heading toward "splitsville," to borrow a phrase from Walter Winchell. Bobo was rarely home these days, and when he was within shouting range Lucille's lectures on taking care of his family and his money fell on deaf ears. After 15 years of co-existing with Bobo, Lucille was nearing the end of her patience. She had two small children to take care of and didn't need a man-child as a husband.[12]

A contest was held in the *Hartsville Messenger* to name the new restaurant, the winning entry being the "Diamond Star Grill." However, it quickly became known to townsfolk as Buck's Place. It was essentially a fast-food restaurant, and its location wasn't exactly ideal for such bill of fare. On the northern outskirts of Hartsville, the Diamond Star was removed from the busy downtown, Hartsville High School and Coker College. The one business advantage of the rather remote address was that, in a "dry" city, it gained a reputation as a spot where a thirsty individual could procure a jar of moonshine—by going around to the back door, of course.[13]

After a couple of months hanging around the restaurant, slinging hash and gabbing with guests, Newsom was ready to head south for spring training. He was looking forward to rejoining his Tigers teammates and decided to drive his custom-made Cadillac from Hartsville to Lakeland, FL, to show it off. Lucille and the kids were to follow in the older Caddy.

The trip south included a disquieting incident for Newsom, one that foreshadowed what proved to be his most difficult season in pro baseball. While driving his new car in south Georgia, Newsom stopped to pick up a hitchhiker, since he hated to drive alone. This hitchhiker was a teenage boy. Newsom quickly struck up a conversation, trying to steer the topic to baseball. The teen seemed uninterested. Newsom changed the subject to the car. The lad's interest seemed to pick up. Newsom pointed out all the vehicle's custom features, and the teen seemed impressed. "And how 'bout that!" said Newsom, pointing to the gold "Buck Newsom" autograph embedded in the dashboard. "Yeah, that's really something," the teen said. "I don't think I've ever ridden in a Newsom. Who makes 'em?"[14]

Newsom, appalled at the boy's ignorance, stopped the car and kicked him out. "Anybody who don't know a Buck Newsom is me and not a car is too stupid to ride with me," he told a teammate upon his arrival at Lakeland.

In reality, there probably were very few teenage boys in the U.S. in the spring of 1941 who did not know who Newsom was. Articles on Newsom, many of them quite fanciful, appeared in newspapers across the country. His photo was in many of the magazines on the newsstands. Newsom's opinion of himself was at an all-time high, and the "ignorant" hitchhiker rankled.

Newsom's new car was definitely an attention-getter in Lakeland. Perhaps too much so. A few days into camp, Newsom came up to a teammate and asked for a ride into town. "Where's the Cadillac?" the teammate asked. "Don't know," said Newsom. "When will it be back?" the teammate asked. "Don't know," said Newsom. "Who's got it?" asked the teammate. "Some dame," Newsom answered. "Who is she?" the teammate queried. "Damn, do you expect me to know everything?" Newsom replied.[15]

On that occasion, the car was eventually recovered. But the final whereabouts of the "Buck Newsom" Cadillac are a bit of a mystery. The legend handed down by Newsom's cronies in Hartsville is that he kept it in Detroit throughout the 1941 season, and then embarked on the long trip home to Hartsville. While driving through a remote area of West Virginia the Cadillac ran out of gas, not surprising since it only got about six miles to the gallon. An angry, antsy Newsom waited by the side of the road on a raw, rainy October day for about an hour before a farmer driving an ancient Ford pickup truck happened by. Newsom was so impatient to move on down the road that he traded the farmer the Cadillac for the pickup truck, straight up. It could well be that by that time Newsom regarded the expensive vehicle as a hoodoo wagon. Reportedly, the "Newsom" was last spotted in the 1960s, the farmer having converted it into a chicken coop.[16]

An incident with the media on Newsom's first day in Lakeland also proved irksome. He was holding court and talking about the 1940 season and what a great year he had. "Who had a better year than me?" Newsom crowed at one point. One of the sportswriters offered the opinion that Bob Feller had the superior 1940 season. "How do you figure?" bellowed Newsom. The scribe produced a *Sporting News Guide* and rattled off Feller's numbers, comparing them with Newsom's. In virtually all categories, Newsom had gotten the short end of the statistical stick. Finally, he could stand no more. Grabbing the offending guide, he ripped it up, asking, "Who are ya gonna believe, me or some God-damn book?"[17]

It was understandable that Newsom was a tad testy in spring training. Despite his new-found wealth, star status and comfortable surroundings at the exclusive Terrace Hotel in Lakeland, his marriage was falling apart and he wasn't willing or able to put it together again. He made it clear to Lucille that he intended to spend the season in Detroit alone, and that if she wanted to visit to make sure to give him advance notice ... plenty of advance notice. Daddy Quill was now gone, but it seemed to Bobo that Lucille had taken up his war club of reason.[18]

In truth, the entire Tigers organization was on edge that spring. Their star slugger, Hank Greenberg, held a low draft number and was in imminent danger of being whisked away by Uncle Sam. He was one of only a handful of major leaguers in that position— "the president of his draft board must be a Yankees fan," quipped Newsom—and losing him would seriously damage the Tigers' hopes for a repeat AL title. Not only was "Hammering Hank" indispensable in the Tigers' lineup to protect Rudy York so the opposition couldn't pitch around him, Greenberg was also a calming influence in the clubhouse. Nowhere was that influence more noticeable than with Newsom.

The Tigers assembled at League Field in Lakeland for their first day of spring practice with virtually the identical cast that won the 1940 AL title. Earl Averill had been sold to the Boston Red Sox, but rookie Pat Mullin looked fully capable of taking over the role of reserve outfielder. Newsom's old pal from the Pacific Coast League, Tuck Stainback, was also on hand to lend depth to the outfield. Otherwise, all the familiar faces were back, with the added bonus that young pitchers Hal Newhouser and Dizzy Trout now had a full year of experience under their belts.[19]

But it quickly became obvious that second baseman Charlie Gehringer, age 38, and shortstop Dick Bartell, age 33, were struggling. Del Baker decided early on that Bartell's aching ankles prevented him from playing shortstop on an everyday basis. Instead, he put Frank Croucher in that role. Croucher, nicknamed "Dingle," had been impressive in his rookie year with the Tigers in 1939, but played only sparingly in 1940. Now, he was going to have to carry the load at shortstop. Bartell was sold on waivers to the New York Giants in May, having played only five games for the Tigers. Publicly, the team presented a united front on Bartell's contributions in 1940. Privately, there was a lingering bitterness over his gaffe in Game Seven of the World Series and his prickly nature. The fact that Bartell was one of the few Tigers players who wasn't a Del Baker believer also hastened his departure.

Similarly, Gehringer was just about spent. His back troubles, described in the press as lumbago but likely something more serious, slowed his reflexes considerably, and only his mental quickness kept him in the lineup.

Newsom was also slow to round into shape that spring, and some would argue that he never did. He didn't make an appearance in a game until March 23, near the end of the Tigers' time in Lakeland. On that date, he pitched three innings against the Senators before an overflow crowd at League Field, the word having got out that Bobo would pitch that day. Afterward, he pronounced himself ready to start the season.

The Tigers trekked north at the end of March and the beginning of April, playing exhibition games in Charlotte, NC, and Greenville, SC, before heading west to open the regular season in St. Louis. Reportedly, during the Tigers' stop-over in Greenville Newsom paid a call on "Shoeless" Joe Jackson, one of his boyhood heroes. This entailed quite a bit of intrigue, as both Jackson and Newsom were afraid Commissioner Landis would find out about their socializing and Newsom would wind up being banned from baseball. He was at the game at Charlotte but missed the game at Greenville, instead spending that afternoon in Hartsville in a half-hearted attempt to mend his marriage. That night, he traveled to Greenville to rejoin the Tigers. But not before stopping to see Shoeless Joe.[20]

Jackson, living in disgrace if not destitution, was unwilling to meet Newsom in public. Twenty years into his lifetime banishment from baseball, Jackson still followed the game and knew well of Newsom's accomplishments. But the Commissioner's power was considerable, and Jackson didn't want Newsom drawn into Landis' crosshairs any more than he already was.

Certainly, the two talked baseball. Whether or not Jackson warned Newsom about the fickleness of fame isn't known.

In St. Louis, the regular season opened on a sour note for the Tigers, as Newsom lost to the St. Louis Browns, 8–1, thoroughly out-pitched by Elden Auker. Even so, the Tigers hung together until the morning of May 7. There was even a morale-lifting 10–1 victory by Newsom over the New York Yankees on May 4, a game in which Newsom held Joe DiMaggio to a double in four at-bats. "I got this guy's number now," Newsom bragged afterward. But fortunes turned quickly for the Tigers, for the Yankees and especially for Newsom and DiMaggio.

On May 7, 19 games into the season, Hank Greenberg was drafted and left the team, not to return until the summer of 1945. His loss was immediately felt, as the Tigers dropped six games in a row to fall to an 11–14 record. They rebounded slightly and were above the .500 mark, at 30–26, and in fourth place on June 15. But the Bengals endured an eight-game losing streak in early July, ending all possibilities of a miracle September akin to the one of 1940. The 1941 Tigers limped home at 75–79, fourth place in the AL.

There was more than enough blame to go around. Croucher was a disaster at shortstop, making 44 errors in 136 games. He hit .254 with little power (two home runs, 34 RBI) but with a tendency to strike out (72 times in 489 at-bats). Gehringer hit only .220, easily the worst season of a Hall of Fame career, and while he made only 11 errors in 116 games at second base, he lacked the range to make any but the most routine plays and could no longer turn the double play with proficiency. The Tigers turned only 129 double plays, fewest in the league and 67 fewer than the Yankees. Croucher's backup, Boyd Perry, hit .186. Gehringer's backup, Dutch Meyer, hit .190.

There were positives. Pinky Higgins was again solid at third base, as were the catching tandem of Birdie Tebbetts and Billy Sullivan and the outfield play of Barney McCosky and Bruce Campbell. Veteran Rip Radcliff, purchased from St. Louis to fill the void in left field left when Greenberg was drafted, did so admirably, hitting .317 in 96 games. But York, not surprisingly, had a rough go. His batting average fell from .316 to .259, his home runs from 33 to 27 and his RBI from 134 to 111.

Victories for Newsom in 1941 were few and far between. He lost his 20th game on September 24, again getting beat by the lowly Browns, this time 3–1 at Sportsman's Park. He finished with only 12 victories. His complete games fell from 20 to 12, and his earned run average soared from 2.83 to 4.60. When he pitched well, his teammates didn't support him with runs or quality defense. And there were days, as evidenced by his Opening Day start, when he simply was ineffective.

No one else on the staff emerged to pick up the slack. Veteran Al Benton had a quality year, going 15–6, but veterans Tommy Bridges and Schoolboy Rowe weren't much help, Bridges finishing at 9–12 and Rowe at 8–6. "Schoolie" also managed to incur the wrath of upper management by skipping several starts in the late going, pleading a tired arm. Among the younger set, neither Hal Newhouser nor Dizzy Trout had the breakout season expected of them. Newhouser finished with a 9–11 record, while Trout came in at 9–9.

Despite his lack of success on the field, or maybe because of it, Newsom escalated his off-the-field activities dramatically.[21] He rented a suite at the city's best hotel and booked a permanent reservation for a table for two at the city's swankiest restaurant. In Lucille's absence, he did not lack for female companionship. For the first time,

Although he's smiling in this 1941 photograph, the 1941 season was anything but a laughing matter for Newsom. It proved to be his last stand with the Tigers (the Ray Medeiros collection, used by permission).

his alcohol consumption may have had an adverse effect on his ability to struggle out of bed the next day and pitch a baseball. But there was no reining him in, especially once "policeman" Greenberg left.[22] On those occasions when Newsom failed to find a date, he and a teammate would often indulge in late-night gambols. Often as not, Rudy York was that teammate. All of this rather public behavior quickly came to the attention of the Tigers' front office—and Lucille back home in Hartsville.

Newsom's behavior became so outlandish, and his lack of pitching success so pronounced, that during the summer of 1941 he was summoned to the offices of Commissioner Landis in Chicago. Landis, in his 20th year as undisputed ruler of baseball, had by now learned of Newsom's visit to Joe Jackson that spring. But the main reason for the summons was that Landis had received reports Newsom was placing big bets on horse racing. "Newsom, you can't be betting on the ponies," scolded the Judge. "You have to keep your mind on baseball. Suppose you're batting in the ninth inning of a tight game and you've got a $50 bet on a horse; are you up there thinking about baseball or are you worried about your bet?"

Newsom was not stumped for a snappy comeback. "Judge, if it's a close game, I ain't even gonna be batting! Some pinch-hitter's gonna take ol' Bobo's turn."[23]

The answer defused the situation, for the time being. But Newsom was now definitely suspect as far as Landis was concerned, and future encounters between the two were increasingly unpleasant for Newsom.

Newsom also didn't help team unity by insisting that Sullivan, not Tebbetts, catch him. As things unfolded, there came a time when Sullivan was injured and Tebbetts was forced to catch him. Not surprisingly, Newsom got into a rumble with the home plate umpire and started toward home plate to argue his case. Tebbetts waved him back, yelling "stay where you are, you big galoot. That was a lousy pitch."[24]

By virtue of their hefty contracts and general mischief, Newsom and York became upper management's scapegoats But statistics can be misleading, and the pair's seasons weren't quite the disasters that Tigers management made them out to be. York, despite a series of minor injuries and considerable carousing, played in every game. Newsom, now an acknowledged king among carousers, never missed a start, 36 of them. He was also used seven times in relief, holding leads in two contests. York's 27 home runs and 111 RBI were the best power numbers of any first baseman in the major leagues. Newsom allowed 235 hits in 1940, 265 hits in 1941; 110 runs in 1940, 140 in 1941. The increases in both could as easily be attributed to awful infield play as to him being too hung over to pitch properly. And the jump from five losses to 20 losses had a lot to do with the absence of Hank Greenberg's booming bat and calming influence.

Were either York or Newsom able to avail themselves of an agent, or if the current baseball labor rules been in effect in 1941, the bitter contract negotiations between the pair and Detroit management would have been avoided. Management won the contract battles, of course, but in Newsom's case lost the war. Newsom was ultimately banished, the Tigers receiving nothing in return other than money, which they had to begin with. Had the Tigers retained Newsom, it is possible they would have won pennants in addition to the one they did capture in 1945. For Newsom, the difference between pitching for the Tigers in 1942–1945 and pitching for the teams he wound up with might have cost him a spot in the Hall of Fame.

The lesson the Tigers' hierarchy should have taken away from the 1941 season was just how remarkable the 1940 team's accomplishments were, and how little margin for error that team had. In 1940, everything worked perfectly, everybody stayed relatively healthy and everybody gave 100 percent, and the result was 90 wins and a one-game edge in the standings. In 1941, one crucial piece of the machine was taken away—Hank Greenberg—and the rest of the unit never functioned properly.

The Tigers led the majors in runs in 1940 with 888. In 1941, they scored fully 200 less. The 1940 Tigers hit 134 home runs, the 1941 Tigers only 81. Tigers management could not be faulted for Greenberg's misfortune with the draft lottery. But they could definitely be blamed for failing to acquire adequate replacements at second base or shortstop.

Del Baker, hailed as a managerial genius in 1940, became a lightning rod for criticism in 1941. Lauded for his ability to handle "problem" ballplayers like Newsom and York in 1940, he was blasted for his inability to handle them in 1941. In reality, he was exactly the same man, doing exactly the same things. Baker, following another losing season in 1942, was fired by the Tigers. He never again landed a job as a major league manager, finishing out his 50-year baseball career as a coach for the Boston Red Sox in 1960.[25]

Tigers home attendance fell from 1,112,693 in 1940 to 684,915 in 1941. And no wonder, since the team was basically punchless and out of the pennant race by the time the warm weather of summer arrived. The 1941 Tigers were as dull as the 1940 edition had been exciting. About the only thing die-hard Tigers fans had to cheer about was that arch-rival Cleveland fell just as far, finishing with an identical 75–79 record. The Yankees once again ruled baseball, running away with the American League pennant and knocking off the Brooklyn Dodgers in five games to win the World Series.

Leading the charge for the Bronx Bombers was Joe DiMaggio, who shook off a slow start to put together his record hitting steak during May, June and July. Newsom had one chance to stop it. DiMaggio entered a June 20–22 series against Detroit having

While Newsom struggled in 1941, the Yankees' Joe DiMaggio had a huge season, hitting in a record 56 straight games. One of those games was against Newsom (the Ray Medeiros collection, used by permission).

hit in 32 straight games, at the time only notable as the longest in Yankees history. He promptly made it 33 in a row against Newsom, slashing two singles in his first two at bats in the game of June 20, which the Yankees won, 14–4. He kept the streak going with a hit in Game 34, off Dizzy Trout, and in Game 35, off Hal Newhouser. DiMaggio did not face the Tigers again during the streak, which finally ended at 56.

While DiMaggio's streak was still going, the annual All-Star Game was played on July 8 at Briggs Stadium. Newsom, with a 6–11 record, was not selected to the AL squad, the only Tigers player on the roster being Rudy York. Newsom was in attendance, however, and humbled himself by volunteering to pitch batting practice for the AL stars. The game itself had a notable finish, Boston's Ted Williams hitting a three-run home run in the last of the ninth inning to give the Americans a come-from-behind 7–5 victory.[26]

Like DiMaggio, Williams was in the middle of a breakout season. The Red Sox played the Tigers at Briggs Stadium immediately following the All-Star Game, Williams entering that game with a .405 average. However, Newsom turned in his best effort of the season, firing a six-hit shutout in out-dueling Lefty Grove, 2–0. On this day, Grove was attempting to win his 300th game. He pitched well, but Newsom pitched better. He retired Williams in all four of his at-bats to put him under the .400 mark.

Newsom was just about the only pitcher in the league to have any luck with Williams that year. In five starts against Boston, he held Williams to two hits in 14 at bats, meaning Williams hit .129 against him and .413 against the rest of the league. He finished at .406 overall, a mark like DiMaggio's hitting streak that seems to loom larger with every passing year.

"I don't think any fan or sportswriter could ever understand just how good DiMaggio was," former Yankee Tommy Henrich said. "You really had to play alongside him day after day to understand. People rave about [Ted] Williams' great eyesight, but Joe's had to be just as good. I have never seen any hitter make consis-

Ted Williams hit .413 against the rest of the league and .129 against Bobo Newsom in 1941. The net result was a .406 average, the last time a major leaguer reached the .400 level for a full season (the Ray Medeiros collection, used by permission).

tently solid contact like Joe did. I wasn't surprised he hit in 56 straight. I was surprised when he was stopped."[27]

"The team with Joe DiMaggio was going to win," said Joe Cronin. "That's the kind of difference he made."[28]

And then there are the Williams boosters. Former major leaguer Al Zarilla said,

> The pitcher always controls the ballgame. I mean, he throws when he wants to throw and what he wants to throw where he wants to throw it. But with Williams at bat, it was just the opposite. Theodore controlled the game. He was the only guy I ever saw who could hit any pitch, any time and hit it hard.[29]

Red Embree, a right-handed pitcher for the Indians, had trouble getting left-handed batters out early in his big league career. So he worked on throwing a curveball to them and experienced remarkable success, at one point retiring 20 left-handers in a row. And then came Ted Williams. Embree recalled,

> First time up, I actually struck Ted out with the pitch. Next time up, he still hadn't zeroed in on it, and popped out to left field. But the third time up, he took that thing and hit it out, about 460 feet to right-center there at Fenway Park. Once Teddy had you read, once he knew what to look for, he was deadly. He lived to hit a baseball.[30]

Although both DiMaggio's and Williams' careers would be interrupted by military service from 1943 to 1945, and Newsom's was not, even in absentia their star status seemed to climb at the same time his was plummeting.

Once the Tigers' disappointing 1941 season was over, there was no quick resolution of Newsom's 1942 contract. He knew he was going to have to take a cut, but the team delayed making an offer. Then came December 7 and the Japanese attack on Pearl Harbor, and the world changed in an instant. Suddenly, major league baseball seemed like the least of the nation's concerns.

When the Tigers' contract finally showed up in the mail, Newsom—for once in his life—was speechless. The contract called for an $11,000 salary for the 1942 season, a cut of $21,500 from 1941. The Tigers' offer to Rudy York was almost as severe, slashing him from $20,000 to $11,000. Today, such cuts are not only unheard-of in baseball, they are illegal. But in that dark winter, when there was great uncertainty whether there would even be a 1942 baseball season, Tigers management must have reckoned it had nothing to lose by attempting to recoup some of its financial losses. The White House had given America's businesses the go-ahead to do whatever they felt necessary to stay afloat in those depressing days at the beginning of World War II. For Tigers ownership, that meant putting the financial screws to Newsom and York.

War or no war, Newsom was having none of it. Once the shock wore off, he made sure everyone knew about what the "cheapskate" Tigers were trying to pull. Newsom's position, often stated to the media that winter, was that he would quit baseball rather than sign the contract. "They can cut all they please—and maybe they can look for another pitcher, too," Newsom told a reporter from the Associated Press in February. "If I don't get a better offer, I'll just stay here [in Hartsville] and run my grill."[31]

Legend has it that Newsom returned the contract to the Tigers, unsigned and torn to pieces. Also included in the package was a particularly odorous piece of cheese.

Since negotiating via the mails seemed pointless, a meeting was arranged in Detroit with Tigers general manager Jack Zeller. Zeller, in the words of John Lardner, "had a surpassingly bald head."[32] He also had a rather sore cranium, for in addition to the contract battles with Newsom and York he was still fending off media criticism for having cut loose Rowdy Dick Bartell. A year earlier, he had been burned by Commissioner Landis, who took a dim view of how Zeller was operating the Tigers' farm system and declared 92 of Detroit's top minor leaguers free agents.

Zeller's logic to Newsom regarding the huge pay cut was simple. There was a war on, and Newsom had a terrible year. "Bobo, I gotta cut your pay," Zeller pleaded. "You lost 20 games!" Newsom's reported reply: "Hell, Curly. You lost 90 of Briggs' ballplayers last year, and I don't see you taking a cut."

Clearly, cooler heads were not going to prevail. Newsom continued his holdout and escalated his attacks on Tigers management, up to and including all Briggs great and small. In doing this, he was violating two of pro baseball's top commandments: Honor thy Owner, and Honor thy Contract and Keep it Silent. While Newsom did not win this battle, he did help establish a precedent. The 66 percent cut the Tigers attempted became a horror story among major leaguers, and eventually forced Major League Baseball's owners to accept restrictions on how much a player could be cut from one season to another. From the humble start of a standardized minimum wage and a ceiling on pay cuts, the baseball labor movement began in earnest. However, that development was fully ten years in the future, far too late to help Bobo Newsom in 1942.

The longer Newsom remained in Hartsville that spring, the less likely it was he would be seen in Tigers togs for the 1942 season. Zeller finally decided to face reality and put Newsom up for sale to the highest bidder. That bidder, not surprisingly, turned out to be Clark Griffith of the Washington Senators. The winning bid was a reported $40,000. On March 31, Bobo Newsom was once again a member of the Washington Senators.

While Griffith's offer may have seemed a tad foolish, given the current events of that time, Griffith had tidbits of inside information that led him to believe the $40,000 would be money well spent. Like most folks in the know in the spring of 1942, Griffith realized this world war was going to continue for several years, with able-bodied players becoming increasingly scarce. He also knew, better than anyone else in baseball, that there would be major league baseball played during the duration of the conflict. Based on what Washington insiders were telling him, he firmly believed the war would be won, eventually, by the Allies. For Griffith, it made sense to build up his ballclub, especially since it was his sole source of income.

If others were selling, he was buying. That off-season, in addition to Newsom, Griffith picked up Bruce Campbell and Frank Croucher from the Tigers and outfielder Stan Spence and pitcher Jack Wilson from the Red Sox. Early in the 1942 season, he acquired outfielder Roy Cullenbine and pitcher Bill Trotter from St. Louis. There would be no lame-duck session for baseball's Washington Senators.

As things came to pass, the optimistic "Old Fox" was designated by Commissioner Landis to serve as baseball's chief lobbyist at the White House. Landis hated President Roosevelt, both for his politics and his unbridled ego. These clashed with Landis' politics and unbridled ego. FDR felt the same way, and Landis was not welcome at the White House. But Griffith was. Since Griffith had long been a regular visitor to 1600 Pennsylvania Avenue, delivering free tickets to Senators games and various and sundry promotional literature on his ballclub, it made sense to use him as baseball's point man in dealings with FDR. Like Landis, Griffith wasn't especially keen on Roosevelt's politics but knew enough about the inner workings of the Capitol to seek out those who held the power. And FDR, without question, had clout.[33]

Griffith was an effective advocate, and Roosevelt became a big booster of wartime baseball, even urging owners to schedule more night games. Unfortunately, Griffith's influence over General Hershey at the Selective Service Department was nowhere near as persuasive. Griffith hoped to be able to land draft deferments for some of his key players, or at least delay their departures. In this he proved unsuccessful, and the wartime Senators were adversely affected by the military draft to the same extent as other major league teams.

In Griffith's grand plan, Newsom would serve as a key component of his wartime teams. To prove the extent of his interest, Griffith addressed Newsom's contract beef by countering the lowball Detroit offer of $11,000 with one of $20,000. This Newsom reluctantly accepted—by this time, he had no choice—and agreed to report to the Senators on April 14, the date of the season opener.

The 1942 Senators that Newsom was joining, sans benefit of spring training, were managed by Bucky Harris, to whom Newsom needed no introduction. There was a history of ill-will between the two but they managed to patch up past differences and co-exist for the season. The team was loaded with rookies, 12 of them to be exact, and Harris was just optimistic (or naïve) enough to think that Newsom might actually be able to aid in their development. Griffith felt the team was talented enough to ascend to pennant contender status. This did not happen. The 1942 Senators finished at 62–89 and in seventh place in the AL standings. The youthful pitching staff, including Early Wynn, Sid Hudson, Walt Masterson, Ray Scarborough and Bill Zuber, failed to produce consistently.[34] The team's top pitcher from 1941, Dutch Leonard, suffered a broken ankle in April and missed virtually the entire 1942 season. Leonard, a likable fellow, had developed a sensational knuckleball while laboring for the Senators—many hitters of that era regarded it as the best they ever saw—and became a consistent winner. He won 64 games for the Senators from 1938 to 1941, but when he asked for a $2,000 raise in the winter of 1941–1942 Griffith flatly refused. In this light, Newsom managing to land the $20,000 contract from Griffith once again proved the two had a mystic bond.

Unfortunately, Newsom reported to the team out of shape and never quite got into it, posting a disappointing 11–17 record. He managed to complete 15 of his 29 starts for Washington, but he had definitely lost something off his fastball. In 1941, he struck out 175 batters in 250 ⅓ innings. In 1942, he struck out only 113 in 213 ⅔ innings. Although Newsom always denied having arm problems, it is quite possible in 1942 he injured his arm but elected to play through it. He also turned 35 that summer, and his 15 years of pitching professionally had definitely begun to take a toll.

"We had some good ballplayers on that team, guys like Early Wynn and Mickey Vernon and Stan Spence and George Case, but we were young and I don't think we ever thought of ourselves as world-beaters," said Johnny Sullivan, a rookie shortstop on the 1942 team. "We were all part of Mr. Griffith's latest youth movement.... Griff brought in Newsom to be our ace, but he just wasn't effective. He did keep the clubhouse loose, however. I don't think Bucky Harris appreciated Buck's antics, but the players sure did."[35]

"When you talk about colorful characters you have to put Bobo Newsom at the top of the list," George Case told author Donald Honig. "There was only one Bobo Newsom and there never will be another one. Some people might say A-men to that but not me; I thought he was great."[36]

The players, especially the younger set, lived with the ultimate distraction throughout the 1942 season. The war wasn't going well for America, and it became increasingly clear that virtually all able-bodied males under the age of 35 were going to have to face the military draft. The players' attention was very much divided between the game and their draft boards that summer. Even Bucky Harris, the Senators manager, was weighing his options for military service. Newsom, for the time being, held a draft deferment as sole provider (in theory) for his wife and two children, as well as his step-mother. There is no indication he showed any interest in volunteering for military duty. By now, he knew himself well enough to know the Army was no place for him. His paths of glory were destined to be the base paths.

On the field, once again Newsom was unable to get through a season with the Senators without being the victim of a bizarre incident. In a game against Boston, Oscar Judd of the Red Sox—a good-hitting pitcher—lined a ball off Newsom's head. The drive wound up carrying all the way to the right-center field power alley, a considerable distance from the point where it made contact with Newsom's dome. Press accounts of the game indicate that he was knocked out momentarily. However, he was able to regain his senses—such as they were—and finish the final three innings of the contest, which he won. His comment afterward, while sporting a large ice pack on his head, was that events of the day just proved he was a better pitcher unconscious than most guys conscious.

The topper to the incident occurred that evening, as a still fuzzy-headed Newsom was holding court for sportswriters in the lobby of a Washington hotel. A young writer walked in with a pretty gal in tow. "Bobo, I want to introduce you to my new bride," the writer said. Newsom rose and gave a courtly bow. "A pleasure, madam," he said. "Would you like to feel my lump?"[37]

In addition to holding audiences for the faithful in hotel lobbies, one of Newsom's favorite activities as a ballplayer was entertaining his teammates on the long train rides then very much the norm. He gradually worked up a stand-up comedy routine with impressions, including one of FDR. "He was very, very good," said Johnny Sullivan. "A lot funnier than most of these guys you see now on TV. Buck had a real gift for humor, just a natural talent."[38]

One of the ballplayers' favorites was a routine Newsom did in the persona of an African American preacher. He was a master of the dialect, and for the occasion would borrow a book to serve as a hymnal and a pair of glasses, to add spice to the impersonation. Newsom could stretch this routine out for nearly a half-hour, working teammates into the sketch as "converts."[39] The young Newsom's enforced stint in Sunday School at the Hartsville Methodist Church had not been entirely in vain; "He could quote hundreds of verses from the Bible," attested former Senators teammate George Myatt.[40] As Newsom became increasingly taken by the "spirit of da Lawd" his voice rose and his gestures became oversized.

Called upon to do "The Preacher" on a long train ride late in the 1942 season, Newsom quickly borrowed a novel and a pair of reading glasses, ripped from the person of a very surprised Bucky Harris. On this occasion, Newsom really got worked up during his "sermon" and while he made a point to the assembled "sinners," the glasses sailed off his head and smashed against the back of a seat, breaking them beyond redemption. Harris was not amused by the goings-on, and it is conceivable it was at that moment he decided to leave the hazardous job of being Newsom's keeper for a commission in the U.S. Navy reserves.

Being in the presence of Newsom was always an adventure. George Case remembered a time in 1942 when the Senators made their first trip into Detroit. It seems that Newsom still had untapped reserves in the city and made a bee-line for a bank. He returned to the team's hotel later that afternoon. There he spotted Bob Repass, his roommate and a reserve infielder who just happened to be the lowest-paid player on the Senators, in the lobby. "Bob, ya got change for a ten?" Newsom yelled.

"Repass went into his pocket and pulled out a couple fives," Case remembered. "Bobo handed him a ten, but it wasn't a 10-dollar bill. It was a *ten-thousand* dollar bill. In typical Newsom fashion, instead of getting his money in a bank draft, he got it in cash.... We just all stood around with our mouths open, looking at that piece of paper. I'd never seen one before and I've never seen one since."[41]

During the season, Griffith was invited to lunch at the White House and decided to take along a ballplayer. Naturally, he chose his best pal, Newsom. Arriving at 1600 Pennsylvania Avenue at the appointed time, the pair was ushered into the ultra-posh Executive Dining Room. FDR was not in attendance that day, but a couple of members of his cabinet were, along with about four U.S. Senators and assorted other dignitaries. Newsom took it all in and proceeded to study the menu, which included five different entrees and assorted side dishes. After pondering the list for some time, a concerned Newsom turned to Griffith and asked, "Are we gonna have to pay for all this?" Assured they would not be billed, Newsom proceeded to eat with gusto.[42]

By August, it was obvious the 1942 edition of the Senators wasn't going to challenge for the pennant. Harkened by the news that pitching ace Dutch Leonard was going to recover from his broken ankle, and doubly so by the news that the injury made Leonard permanently 4-F, Griffith weighed his options and decided Newsom might indeed be expendable. Based on past experience, the "Old Fox" balked at dealing him to another American League team. But an unexpected suitor came a-calling, in the person of Dodgers President Larry MacPhail.

MacPhail's Dodgers had won the National League pennant in 1941 and looked like a lock to repeat. That is, they looked that way until mid–August, when the St. Louis Cardinals started winning like nobody's business. The Cards were matching the Dodgers win for win and gradually gaining ground. MacPhail did what he seemed to do best— panic. While Brooklyn didn't need more pitching, MacPhail reasoned the acquisition of a veteran such as Newsom might provide the psychological lift the Dodgers needed to hold off the Cardinals. Thus it was that, on August 30, the Dodgers purchased Newsom from the Senators for a reported $25,000. From MacPhail's viewpoint, even if Newsom wasn't needed down the stretch he would come in handy when the Dodgers faced the Yankees in the World Series that fall.

The move was ballyhooed in the New York newspapers as a tremendous coup for MacPhail. Newsom added to the ballyhoo by, reportedly, sending MacPhail a telegram reading, "Congratulations on buying the 1942 N.L. pennant" or words to that effect. In reality, it's doubtful that Newsom sent any such telegram—for one thing, it represented an unnecessary expense. But it gave the media something to bandy about, and Newsom's arrival on the Dodgers was loudly trumpeted.[43]

His initial start with his new team, on September 3, was indeed something special. In the first meaningful game he had pitched since the seventh game of the 1940 World Series, Newsom shut out the Cincinnati Reds 2–0. It was a curious flashback to his first go-around with the Dodgers, way back in 1929. And this go-around had a similar denouement. Newsom was much less effective in his next four starts for Brooklyn, losing two of them, and the hard-charging Cardinals caught and passed the Dodgers in the final two weeks of the season. The Cards moved ahead of the Dodgers to stay on September 13 when they split two games and the Dodgers dropped a doubleheader to the Reds. Newsom played a part in that dark day for Brooklyn, being outpitched by Cincy's Bucky Walters in a 6–3 loss in the nightcap. Even though Brooklyn won its final eight games, including a 4–2 victory by Newsom over the Philadelphia Phillies on September 20, St. Louis stubbornly hung on to its lead by winning seven of its final eight contests.

The 1942 Dodgers represented the best ballclub Newsom ever pitched for, winning a team-record 104 games. The Cardinals won 106, including 30 of their final 36 contests. It was an exciting, and ultimately heart-breaking, finish for Dodgers fans. A major league season can rarely be boiled down to one play, but the 1942 National League pennant race certainly hinged on an event at Sportsman's Park on July 19. In the 11th inning of a game between the Dodgers and Cards, Enos Slaughter hit a long drive to center. It appeared that Pete Reiser, the Dodgers' All-Star center fielder, had the play, and indeed he caught the ball just as he crashed into the wall. The ball popped loose and before it could be retrieved Slaughter circled the bases for an inside-the-park home run and a 7–6 St. Louis victory. Had the Dodgers won the game, the two teams would have finished the regular season with identical 105–49 records. Much worse,

By the time he arrived in Brooklyn in September of 1942, Newsom was definitely showing his age. Problems with his marriage, his draft board and his bank account no doubt contributed to his decline, and his increasing reliance on alcohol after games (the Brace photograph collection, used by permission).

from the Dodgers' viewpoint, was that Reiser suffered a severe concussion on the play and was never again the same player. Rushed back into the lineup by manager Leo Durocher, Reiser's batting average fell all the way from .350 to .310.[44]

While Newsom's presence failed to clinch first place for the Dodgers, as had been advertised, he was happy to be a member of a first-class ballclub again. On the Dodgers, he was reunited with old friend Schoolboy Rowe and found a kindred soul for partying in the person of fellow South Carolinian Kirby Higbe. Higbe was, along with Whit Wyatt, one of the Dodgers' top pitchers. Thus, Newsom reckoned that if he conducted his nocturnal rambles with Higbe he would be protected from the wrath of Durocher. That September, Durocher let the pair ramble, figuring they needed to blow off steam from the red-hot pennant race. No one knew how to blow off steam better than Higbe, who had an amazing gift for attracting the opposite sex.[45]

Newsom opted to head back to South Carolina that October, accompanied by Higbe. It was a memorable trip, even by Newsom's exacting standards. From Brooklyn to South Carolina normally took a couple days. For Bobo and Hig, it took two weeks. Virtually every tavern and roadhouse along the way was graced by the pair's presence. Higbe, like Newsom, was married. But that didn't slow down his quest for female companionship. While Newsom ate and drank, Higbe fornicated.

Eventually, the pair ran out of cash. They survived the rest of the way by a bit of skullduggery. Newsom would drive up to a diner, engage the owner in talk of baseball, and then go to the trunk of his Caddie and produce the baseball he had used to pitch the Tigers to victory in a 1940 World Series game. This treasure he would trade for two meals. By Newsom's reckoning, he swapped about 20 "World Series" balls for food and drink on the trip. In reality, the spheroids were discards from Brooklyn batting practice sessions.

Newsom belatedly arrived in Hartsville, hung over, broke and plum out of baseballs. Lucille was not amused. She was even less amused when one of Newsom's suitcases turned out to be filled with ladies' lingerie. The items in question had been collected by Higbe but unfortunately wound up in Newsom's baggage. The argument had just begun in earnest when a process server showed up at the door. He handed Newsom legal papers indicating he was the target of a paternity suit filed by a woman in Detroit.

The twin barrels of lingerie and legalities shot down the troubled marriage, then and there.[46]

While his marriage was doomed, Newsom at least had a sense of security regarding his career. MacPhail indicated he wanted to keep the Dodgers together for another run at the pennant in 1943 and would do so by paying his players top dollar. But America was an uncertain place in the winter of 1942–1943, and events abroad would adversely impact Newsom's career in ways even he could not imagine.

Nine

Brooklyn to St. Louis to Washington (1943)

Bobo Newsom, baseball's ultimate iconoclast, and Brooklyn, the most irrepressible borough in the cosmos, appeared to be an ideal combination. As *Time* magazine commented at the time of his acquisition by the Dodgers in September 1942, "Buck Newsom ... is, by instinct, a natural member of the Daffiness Boys." Certainly, all indications were that Newsom was looking forward to pitching for the 1943 Brooklyn Dodgers. The spring training roster included many of his best buddies, and as a bonus featured the talent and experience necessary to contend for the National League pennant. Unfortunately for Newsom and Dodgers fans, the impulsiveness of Dodgers President Larry MacPhail threw a major league-sized monkey wrench into the Brooklyn dream machine.

MacPhail, who had served in the Army in World War I, grew incensed over the faltering U.S. war effort as well as his team blowing the National League pennant. He abruptly quit as Dodgers president at the conclusion of the season and re-enlisted for active duty. It wasn't a difficult decision. MacPhail's patriotism offered a refuge from the frustrations of dealing with an increasingly tight-fisted ownership. Helping grease MacPhail's exit was the late-arriving knowledge on the part of the Dodgers' board of directors that the reported $25,000 paid for Louis Norman Newsom's September cameo was in reality $60,000.[1]

After a series of consultations between Dodgers officials and National League President Ford Frick, it was decided that the Dodgers would hire Branch Rickey—on the outs in St. Louis with Cardinals owner Sam Breadon—to replace MacPhail.[2]

The fact that Rickey was the antithesis of MacPhail did not bode well for Newsom. MacPhail drank; Rickey was fanatical in his opposition to alcohol. MacPhail could be very generous to his hired hands; Rickey pinched pennies until Lincoln was blue in the face. MacPhail loved to socialize with the players; Rickey preferred the players' side of any conversation be limited to "Yes, Mr. Rickey." MacPhail was willing to overlook idiosyncrasies; Rickey had little patience for anyone's opinion save his own. In addition, Newsom had run afoul of Rickey in St. Louis, in 1934 when Rickey was the de facto boss of the Browns' front office and the pair clashed over—what else?—money.

Newsom's year began on a sour note when he received what he felt was a substandard contract from Rickey, calling for a 1943 salary of $15,000, a sizable downgrade from the $20,000 he received in 1942. His reaction was to refuse to report to spring training. Since there was a war on, the Dodgers were training close to home in Bear Mountain, NY. Newsom was comfortably ensconced in the considerably warmer climes of South Carolina. To him, it made little sense to head north. Newsom explained to sportswriters his rationale for hanging around home until just before the start of the regular season. "Birds go south in the winter, and if it's good enough for them, it's good enough for me," he said.[3]

By this point in his career, Newsom was firmly convinced there was no need to train, in the spring or any other time of the year. His arm was healthy and he was ready and willing to pitch on a moment's notice. Willing, that is, if he were paid to throw a baseball. Since players were not on salary during spring training, Newsom had no incentive to be in camp. His marriage to Lucille was now all over except the shouting (he had moved out of their Hartsville home and was residing in nearby Cartersville), and she was in the process of obtaining a divorce. All things considered, South Carolina was a secure place to be.[4] He was exercising by pushing a pool cue. He was improving his eyesight by looking for an inside straight. He was getting in his roadwork by driving his latest Cadillac at breakneck speeds on Carolina's back roads. And he was observing a strict training table, by never refusing a free meal or drink. Who needed spring training?

For Rickey, the notion of a player disputing a contract was anathema. Further, Newsom not reporting for training set a horrid example. No talk of money would be tolerated until Newsom brought his large body northward and deposited it at Bear Mountain.[5]

There the matter rested through most of March. With the manpower shortage brought on by the war, Newsom figured he was in like Flynn in the Dodgers' scheme of things. On paper, he was no worse than their No. 2 pitcher, behind veteran Whitlow Wyatt. With players being called into the military every day, there was no telling how high Newsom's value might rise by the time the pennant drive rolled around in September. Thus, he felt sure he could talk Rickey into giving him a raise. It turned out to be one of the more foolish notions in a life filled with them. For, unbeknownst to Newsom and most of the Dodgers players, Rickey had a different direction in mind for the franchise. Rickey's grand plan eventually collided with the pennant aspirations of his veteran players, a collision that nearly led to the first labor shutdown in National League history.

In the spring of 1943, that explosion was still months away. March did not come in like a lion for Newsom's hopes of a raise. In fact, after an initial exchange of letters, negotiations abruptly ended. All was silent between Rickey and Newsom, and silence did not suit either man, a lull warning of the coming storm. Newsom clung to his belief that he was, at long last, an indispensable man. And Rickey wasn't worried, for in the mind of "The Mahatma" Newsom was already as good as gone.

Sans Newsom, the Dodgers proceeded to train in Bear Mountain, spending the first few days throwing more snowballs than baseballs. Three weeks went by without further developments on the Newsom-Rickey front. Finally, on March 20, Newsom decided to break his silence and contacted Jimmie Thompson, sports editor of the *Columbia* (SC) *State* and a journalist he considered an ally. Terming his situation with the Dodgers "unsatisfactory," Newsom outlined his case to Thompson in one of the longer authentic Newsom interviews on record. "I don't want to be classed as a holdout," an articulate Newsom told Thompson via telephone from his stepmother's home in Hartsville.

All I want is satisfaction out of Mr. Rickey, and I haven't been able to get it. I haven't talked with Mr. Rickey in weeks and if I don't talk to him in three weeks more it doesn't matter to me. [The regular season was scheduled to open on April 21.]

Don't get me wrong. Mr. Rickey is a nice fellow and all that and he's a businessman. But so am I, and I can't see his side of the deal at all. I'm not asking for anything I don't honestly think I deserve. If Mr. Rickey doesn't see it that way he can write me a release right now.

That shot across the bow was answered by Rickey, in indirect fashion, three days later. Rickey sold Schoolboy Rowe, one of Newsom's cronies, to the lowly Philadelphia Phillies, a development that appeared to weaken Newsom's resolve. Further weakening it was a dwindling bank account and the looming prospect of a very costly divorce settlement. After a couple more weeks, Newsom finally agreed to report, accepting the $15,000 contract on March 31 only after insisting it included a codicil (not to be filed with the commissioner's office) calling for a $5,000 bonus should he still be with the team on July 15, the halfway point of the season and also the time his divorce from Lucille figured to be finalized. In retrospect, it's hard to understand how Newsom allowed himself to believe that he would still be with the Dodgers by that date. But Rickey could be powerfully persuasive, with the ability (in the words of columnist Westbrook Pegler) to charm an Eskimo out of his parka.

Bobo Newsom strikes a pose for George Burke in this 1943 photograph, taken at Wrigley Field in Chicago. Newsom got off to a great start with the Dodgers that year, but problems with manager Leo Durocher (and team president Branch Rickey) forced him out of Brooklyn by July. Of all the trades and unconditional releases that happened to Newsom in his career, this was by far the bitterest (the Brace photograph collection, used by permission).

The Newsom-Rickey power summit, as rendered by several New York sportswriters, included the following long-distance exchange:

> Rickey (in Bear Mountain): "Please report to camp Louis. We need you."
> Newsom (in Hartsville): "No way am I going to report without a contract."
> Rickey: "But we need you here. Leo Durocher, your manager, needs you here."
> Newsom: "I don't care what Leo needs, I need a new contract."
> Rickey: "But your teammates miss you, my boy. They ask about you every day."
> Newsom: "Gee, they are a swell bunch of guys. They miss me, huh?"

Rickey: "Most definitely. We all miss you. In fact, just today I had nine photographers in here asking for you."

Newsom: "Nine of 'em, huh? I guess I better get up there, hate to let the newspaper boys down."

Rickey: "A very wise decision, my boy. We'll be waiting for you tomorrow."

(Both parties hang up.)

Rickey to his secretary: "Call around town and get me nine photographers. Tell them to be here tomorrow."[6]

That exchange almost assuredly did not occur. The Bobo Newsom of 1933 might have fallen for it, but not the Bobo Newsom of 1943. There is no doubt that he had an oversized ego and enjoyed media attention. But Newsom's reasons for reporting to Bear Mountain boiled down to money, as did Rickey's reasons for wanting him in camp. As Rickey well knew, there isn't much of a market for a player who's refusing to sign his contract.

According to John Lardner, during Newsom's holdout Rickey attempted in vain to convince Leo Durocher of the wisdom of bumping Newsom off the roster. Durocher balked at the thought of losing one of his best pitchers.[7] Not that Durocher had any illusions about being able to dictate to Newsom. He knew full well what Newsom could be like, based on the few weeks Newsom spent with the team in the fall of 1942 and on his long and very public record of questioning authority and missing curfews. But "Leo the Lip" believed the 1943 Dodgers could win the NL pennant with the assembled herd of veteran players, most of them already classified 4-F and at least one of them—Kirby Higbe—far wilder than Newsom at his worst.[8] Of course, the herd had been rounded up by Larry MacPhail. Rickey was determined to put his own brand on the franchise.

"Leo had no qualms about having drunks around," said Bill Rigney, who played for and coached for Durocher. "If anything, Leo thought drunks were easier to handle than the sober Sams. The quiet guys were the ones he worried about. Leo had a lot of the gangster in him. [He] was the best at getting the best out of the misfits, guys nobody else wanted."[9]

While the Dodgers' roster, with its average age of 33, figured to remain intact for the duration, the Selective Service was a definite threat to the youthful St. Louis Cardinals. Rickey, of course, knew both teams inside and out. He disagreed with Durocher, not only about Newsom but also about the relative value of experience over youth. "The Mahatma" believed the Cardinals had simply out-hustled the Dodgers to the pennant in 1942. "The sleek, hungry mice beat the fat, lazy mice to the cheese" was how he painted the goings-on in the dramatic final weeks of the 1942 season. Newsom, naturally, would be one of the fat, lazy mice in this scenario.[10]

In spring training, Dodgers veterans remained in shock over not winning the pennant. They had won it in 1941 and, to a man, believed the 1942 team was even better. Durocher and his players felt that the loss of star center fielder Pete Reiser in July to injury was the reason the Dodgers came up short. Rickey disagreed, arguing that the Cardinals also incurred injuries and that injuries were a part of baseball and must be overcome by whatever means possible. Durocher saw Reiser's untimely absence from the lineup as a rationale for not winning a pennant; Rickey saw it as an excuse.

Still, with manpower shortages becoming acute throughout baseball in the spring of 1943, it was difficult not to like the Dodgers' chances. They had All-Star caliber players at every position except third base: catcher Mickey Owen; first baseman Dolf Camilli (the league's Most Valuable Player in 1941); second baseman Billy Herman; shortstop Arky Vaughan; and outfielders Dixie Walker, Augie Galan and Joe Medwick. Veterans Paul Waner and Frenchy Bordagaray could have started in the outfield for any other team; on the Dodgers, they were key reserves. The starting rotation, in addition to Newsom, included Whit Wyatt, coming off a 19-win season, Kirby Higbe, coming off a 16-win season, and Curt Davis, coming off a 15-win season. Ed Head, Max Macon, Rube Melton and Les Webber gave Brooklyn a reliable bullpen. It was a team good enough to win a pennant, in wartime or peacetime. Durocher, for all his quirks, was a proven strategist. And Rickey could, if the spirit moved him, pull off a key trade to bolster any weaknesses.[11]

Contrast that Opening Day roster to one late in the season, that included the likes of Al Campanis, Billy Hart, Albie Glossop, Carden Gillenwater, Dee Moore and Pat Ankenman. What in the world had happened in Flatbush?

The answer was simple: Branch Rickey.

Al Campanis, competing for a job in spring training of 1943, realized going in that the odds were against him. His best position, second base, was already manned by the veteran Billy Herman, a perennial All-Star. After a few days, he received the dreaded notice to report to Mr. Rickey. Rickey told him he was being sent to the minors, that he lacked the ability to be a major league player.

"He could see I was upset so he changed the pace, began to talk to me like father to son," Campanis said. "He knew I had gone to college, unlike most of the players back then. So we talked about that for a while. And then he lowered his voice and said something I'll never forget: 'Look around you, young man. See all those old warhorses out there on the field, those ruffians? I am going to get rid of every one of them, and soon.'"[12]

Rickey told Campanis that, despite the war, the Dodgers were going to step up the scouting and signing of young players and make sure they were all properly schooled in baseball fundamentals. Rickey's ideal Dodger would be young, well-educated and receptive to being taught. He urged Campanis to consider a career in the organization as a coach or in the front office rather than as a player.

As for the future of the franchise, Rickey did exactly what he said he would do. Eventually, he cleared the roster of the "warhorses" and brought in a whole new breed of player, players who would dominate the National League for the next 13 years. In September, with the team hopelessly out of the pennant race, Campanis was one of several youngsters promoted to the big club. Another was Gil Hodges, who turned out to be the rock on which Rickey built a string of championship teams. So while the veterans were only looking at 1943, Rickey was looking far beyond that point.

While Durocher and Rickey privately disagreed over the wisdom of keeping the veterans, they were on the same page regarding one very important thing: organized labor. Durocher, contrary to his rebel image, was an ultra-conservative politically, and shared Rickey's view that unions would be the ruination of the country. "Collective bargaining" were dirty words in their vocabularies. Durocher made it clear that he would not intervene on behalf of any player in a salary dispute with Rickey and always deferred to Rickey on personnel moves.[13]

Peace reigned for a few days after Newsom reported to camp, but the uneasy truce between "The Blimp" and "The Lip" was shattered the day before the start of the regular season by, of all things, a movie shoot.

MGM Studios had arranged with MacPhail to use Ebbets Field as a backdrop for the latest Red Skelton vehicle, "Whistling in Brooklyn." Rickey inherited the contract and wasn't exactly in love with the idea of Hollywood using the Dodgers' home for its own purposes, especially for a comedy. But MGM was paying for use of the field, and the day of filming did fall on an open date for the team.

According to Skelton, the original plan was to use extras as players and Leo Durocher as manager and commentator on Skelton's gaffes. However, upon arrival in Brooklyn the film crew discovered the Dodgers players were going to be working out at Ebbets Field at the same time as the filming. MGM was using a real baseball stadium, so why not real players? Besides, the cost to the studio per player was only $25 for the day, well within budget for a well-to-do movie studio.[14]

The date of filming, the day before the start of the season, was a bitterly cold one in Brooklyn. Despite advance notice, there was scarcely a soul in the park, so crew members ran around the surrounding neighborhood rounding up whoever they could find, paying them $5 to go to Ebbets. Reportedly, among the brave folks who did show up for the shoot was Hilda Chester, Dodgers fan deluxe. Skelton said,

> I go out and start to warm up with the players. I had to wear a beard for the scene, I'm supposed to be playing with a House of David team ... and the players just give it to me. And we're laughing and goofing around and this big guy—I didn't know one player from another—is razzing me and, you know, he's funny as hell. Our director, he was there in the dugout running lines with Durocher, looks out and says what the hell is going on? And I say, it's this fat guy, he's funny.[15]

So a quick re-write was ordered, creating a scene for Bobo Newsom and his batterymate, Mickey Owen. This necessitated taking lines away from Durocher and giving them to Newsom. It also meant that Newsom and Owen would get $250 apiece for the shoot instead of $25. This created two happy players and one unhappy manager.

"Here's what you need to know about Durocher," Skelton said. "He took his acting very seriously. He had the same agent as George Raft, and the funny thing is George didn't care if he never acted in another movie and Leo was just constantly pushing for parts. And he always wanted to run the show, just like in baseball."[16]

Eventually, Skelton learned the "fat guy" was Bobo Newsom. He thought Newsom displayed potential as a comedic actor and encouraged him to consider a second career in the movies. He even recommended him to MGM for his side-kick when Rags Ragland, who had been playing that role, died suddenly. However, shortly thereafter Skelton was drafted into the Army, the director of the "Whistling" series, L. Sylvan Simon, took ill, and the studio scrapped the series.[17]

The upshot of the movie shoot was three-fold: First, the other players were jealous over Newsom and Owen getting the extra $225 and complained to Rickey. Second, once Rickey saw the finished film he thought it poked fun at the national pastime and banned any further movie shoots at Ebbets Field, a ban that was continued by Walter O'Malley even after the team moved to Los Angeles.[18] Thirdly, Durocher was pushed firmly into the anti–Newsom camp. He felt Newsom had shamelessly stolen his cinematic thunder. For someone who took himself and his second career as a thespian very seriously, it was an unforgivable sin.

Once the season began, several Dodgers pitchers were slow to get untracked—not a surprising development considering the wretched weather during spring training at Bear Mountain. But Newsom was in top form, making quality start after quality start. He won seven of his first nine decisions and saved another game in relief. Due in no small measure to those exploits, the Dodgers were in first place, at 42–26, on June 30.

Typical of the way things were going for Newsom that spring was a game on June 4 at Wrigley Field in Chicago. He was not scheduled to pitch that day, and his services looked even less likely when the Dodgers scored seven runs in the top of the first inning against the Cubs. However, Brooklyn starter Rube Melton couldn't throw strikes. He walked three batters and allowed a single to Eddie Stanky. With no outs and the bases loaded, Durocher abruptly yanked Melton and inserted Newsom. Newsom went the rest of the way, coming away with an 18–5 victory. He also had his best day ever with the bat, getting three straight singles, driving in two runs and scoring twice. He ended his busy afternoon with an exclamation mark, striking out Cubs slugger Bill Nicholson on a high-arcing changeup for the final out. He took the return throw from the catcher, stuffed the ball into his hip pocket, and swaggered to the Dodgers dugout.

Newsom wasn't shy about holding court with the New York media after every victory. Soon the papers were full of Bobo quotes, Bobo philosophy, and Bobo folklore. Dodgers fans took a fancy to the rotund right-hander, who was impossible to miss in the friendly confines of Ebbets Field. All of this did nothing to lighten Durocher's load. "The guy thought he was a combination of John J. McGraw and Judge Landis," Durocher remembered. "I couldn't tell him a thing. He knew all the answers. He was a bad influence on the younger players."[19]

Clearly, Brooklyn wasn't big enough to hold the egos of both Durocher and Newsom. Newsom regaling reporters and fellow players before and after games constantly irked his manager, who also didn't appreciate Newsom referring to him as Lippy, on those rare occasions he referred to him at all. Of course, with Newsom, there were highlights along the way.

One such moment occurred early in the season when Newson was detailing his many honors to those assembled. "They love ol' Bobo in South Carolina," he raved. "Why, I've been given the key to just about every city down there. Hartsville held a day for me, Cheraw held a day for me, Darlington held a day for me …"

At this point, one of the sportswriters noticed Kirby Higbe taking all this in. "Hey Hig," said the scribe. "You're from South Carolina, too. Was there ever a Kirby Higbe Day down there?"

Higbe pondered this for a moment and then responded. "Shoot yes," he drawled. "Why jest last winter the sheriff of Columbia County gave me a day—to git outta town."[20]

Still, whatever advances in team morale Newsom may have spawned were snagged by Durocher, who was pushing his veterans hard. For their part, the Brooklyn players remained confident. They knew it was a long season and they were riding the favorite in the NL pennant race. However, there remained the strong belief among the veterans that Durocher had over-managed down the stretch in 1942 and was doing exactly the same thing in the first half of 1943. The team had abundant experience, and to the players Durocher's micro-managing and second-guessing every pitch seemed unnecessary. Gradually, the clubhouse broke into pro– and anti–Leo camps. Newsom, true to form, was in the anti–Leo camp.

Newsom's love of card playing and his friendship with Kirby Higbe also figured into his troubles with Durocher. Durocher fancied himself a world-class poker player and had no qualms about playing high-stakes games with his players. Newsom was a bit too sharp to get caught up in this action, but Higbe wasn't. Eventually, Durocher clipped Higbe for several thousand dollars, in games Newsom felt were not entirely according to Hoyle. At Newsom's urging, Higbe went to Rickey and reported both his losses and Newsom's suspicions. Rickey forced Durocher to give the money back, something Durocher claimed he was going to do anyway at the end of the season. Newsom was dubious of that claim and made sure thereafter to steer Higbe far, far away from Durocher's impromptu poker parlors.[21]

In the clubhouse, the split began to surface in earnest in early July. The Dodgers fell out of first place, for good as things turned out, on July 4 when the Cardinals came into Ebbets Field and swept a doubleheader, the Brooks scoring only two runs in 19 innings. The twin losses, and Durocher's tirade afterward, sent team morale skidding. Durocher had by now joined Rickey in thinking the team's veterans were giving less than 100 percent. He said as much in his post-game pyrotechnics.

Even though Newsom gave the team a lift on July 5 by outdueling old nemesis Paul Derringer for a 6–3 victory over Chicago, the team was clearly spinning out of control.

The first of the Durocher doubters to go—not counting Schoolboy Rowe's departure in spring training—was outfielder Joe Medwick. Reportedly, Medwick responded to Durocher's July 4 tongue-lashing with a two-word suggestion, said loud enough for everyone in the cramped clubhouse to hear. Those seven letters were more than enough to seal Medwick's fate in Brooklyn. He was clearly not the player he had been in the 1930s, but was still one of the most feared right-handed hitters in the league. Rickey, who had a running battle with Medwick over money matters when both were in St. Louis, sold "Ducky" to the New York Giants on July 6. No players were obtained in return. The sale confirmed the worst fears of many Dodgers, who believed that Rickey and Durocher were far more interested in settling old scores than winning a pennant. The Medwick deal also revived the rumor that Rickey's contract netted him a portion of the revenue from player sales. That touched off more than a tad of paranoia among the veteran players and further alienated them from Durocher.[22]

Another area of contention, at least between Dodgers pitchers and Durocher, was his use of the inexperienced Bobby Bragan at catcher over the veteran Mickey Owen. Bragan was not a strong defensive catcher, but he was brash and confident and a Durocher favorite. But for a veteran, headstrong pitcher (such as Bobo Newsom), Bragan was a highly undesirable batterymate. Handling Newsom was a real chore, even for Owen. For Bragan, it was asking the impossible. Newsom had a history of run-ins with his catchers, dating way back to his pre-teen years with his brother Marion, and made it no secret that he much preferred Owen to Bragan.

Unfortunately for both Newsom and Bragan, they formed the Dodgers' battery in a game on Friday, July 9, at Ebbets Field against Pittsburgh. While press accounts and Durocher's version of events varied, what isn't in dispute is that Newsom was struggling with his control that day and blamed the problem on Bragan, who was having difficulty catching the pitches, let alone "framing" them for the plate umpire. Eventually, a pitch eluded Bragan altogether and rolled to the backstop. The Pirates had a runner at third, and he scored easily as Newsom failed to cover home plate, choosing instead to stand on the mound with his hands on his hips, staring darts through Bragan's backside as he chased after the ball.[23]

While Durocher's account of the incident included the information that the pitch in question was a spitball, this seems unlikely. Newsom rarely threw a spitball, since his pitches had plenty of natural movement. Further, if it was a spitball it could only have been called by Durocher himself, who certainly wasn't opposed to a little cheating. It may have been that Bragan called for a fastball and Newsom threw a slider, perhaps even an honest mistake on his part. What is evident is that, after the inning, Durocher confronted Newsom in the dugout. Bobo, being Bobo, immediately blamed Bragan for the wild pitch. Still, it appeared to be just one of those things that happen to all teams over the course of the long season. But Durocher wouldn't let the matter die, and the sniping between he and Newsom escalated. It ended with Durocher banishing Newsom to the clubhouse in the bottom of the seventh inning with the Dodgers trailing, 4–1.

"Pitching for Durocher was no barrel of laughs," said Roger Bowman, who pitched for "The Lip" as a member of the New York Giants from 1949 to 1952. "What I learned was, Leo had a pathological desire to always get in the last word. You could argue like hell with him, for minutes on end, as long as you let him get in the last word. If you replied he would get angry all over again. You had to let him end the conversation. It was just a quirk he had."[24]

Newsom simmered in the clubhouse the rest of the afternoon, as the Dodgers rallied from a 7–4 deficit to pull out an 8–7 victory. The cooling-off period, and the team's victory, failed to ice his injured ego, and he and Durocher resumed verbal warfare in Durocher's office. Newsom would not cease and desist and, throwing caution to the winds, hit Durocher right where it hurt most, saying he couldn't manage worth beans and all his players hated his guts. At that point, Durocher suspended Newsom indefinitely for "insubordination" and Newsom replied with words to the effect that he didn't care if he never pitched another inning for Durocher. It's probable that Newsom included in his critique his belief that Durocher was a lousy actor and an even worse card player.

Even then, the ugly incident might have been contained to the clubhouse had not Durocher bumped into Hugh Casey, on leave from the Navy, immediately afterward. Casey asked what all the shouting was about, and Durocher reported that Newsom had deliberately shown up Bragan by throwing a spitball that caught the young catcher offguard. Unfortunately for Durocher, sportswriter Tim Cohane of the *New York World-Telegram* overheard the conversation and reported same in that evening's editions. He also told other members of the media what Durocher said.[25]

That night, word of Newsom's suspension quickly spread to the other players, with Newsom doing the spreading. It had finally dawned on him that the suspension would, in all likelihood, cost him the $5,000 signing bonus, along with any chance of a World Series payday. By this time, the players also had a chance to read all about it in the evening newspapers, or at least Durocher's side of what happened.

The next day, July 10, was a warm one in Brooklyn but it was a hell of a lot warmer in the Dodgers clubhouse before the game. The newspaper accounts of the previous day's incident quoting Durocher struck a collective nerve among the veterans. For one, the comments violated the ancient baseball rule: What happens in the clubhouse stays in the clubhouse. Additionally, Durocher pinning all of the blame on Newsom and none on Bragan neatly dovetailed into what had been happening for several weeks, with Durocher seen as favoring the younger players at the expense of the veterans. Since the only logical source for the quotes was Durocher himself, the Dodgers skipper found himself in a pickle of the giant dill variety.

"Durocher had a real sharp tongue," Billy Herman told author Donald Honig in a 1975 interview. "Well, so did Newsom.... Newsom had been getting to Durocher for weeks, throwing in cutting little remarks. Bobo didn't mean any harm, but Leo was getting madder and madder. So finally he had a chance to stick it to Bobo, and he did."[26]

While there is ample evidence that Newsom was a special nuisance to all his managers, the one documented case where he reduced a manager to tears involved the Dodgers' Leo Durocher. Shortly thereafter, Newsom was again exiled to St. Louis (the Ray Medeiros collection, used by permission).

The press accounts struck a particular nerve with Arky Vaughan, normally the most gentlemanly of all the Dodgers. He waited for Durocher to arrive at his office that morning, and when he did Vaughan confronted him with the offending story. When Durocher denied being the source of the information, Vaughan went back to his locker, bundled up his game togs, and marched back to Durocher's office.

"Take this uniform and shove it right up your ass!" Herman reported Vaughan as saying. With that, Vaughan flung the bundle in Durocher's face. "If you would lie about Bobo, then you would lie about me and everybody else. I'm not playing for you."[27]

Thus began Leo Durocher's longest day in baseball. The stunning scene of the mild-mannered Vaughan exploding touched off a call for a players-only meeting. All thoughts of batting or infield practice were pushed aside. After the players filed out of their meeting, Durocher tried to placate Vaughan, who wouldn't even return his gaze. Dixie Walker piped up to express support for Newsom. Johnny Allen, known for his trigger temper, chimed in with "If Bobo ain't playing and Arky ain't playing, I ain't playing."[28]

Durocher went back into his office to work the phone. Eventually, he located sportswriter Cohane at his home. Cohane normally did not work Saturdays and told Durocher he had no intention of coming to the ballpark. However, Durocher yelling accusations into the phone, along with demands for a retraction, had the effect of energizing the scribe. Cohane jumped in his car and drove straight to Ebbets Field. There, he confronted Durocher in the clubhouse, before God, players and fellow sportswriters. It was a rare sight indeed and all the proof the players needed to convince them of the accuracy of Cohane's report. Several immediately joined Vaughan, Walker and Allen in threatening not to play another inning for Durocher.

Durocher responded with a plea for unity. This falling on deaf ears, he committed the psychological blunder of issuing an ultimatum. He took a stand on one side of the clubhouse and said something to the effect that he'd suspend Vaughan along with Newsom. He then dropped the "with me or against me" line and asked all those players who wanted to play for him to step to his side of the clubhouse. Only Bragan and pitcher Curt Davis did so. Durocher specifically asked veterans Walker, Dolf Camilli and Whit Wyatt to join him. That trio, respected by all in the room, refused. It was too much for Durocher, who broke into tears and locked himself in his office. There the matter stood until someone, possibly Durocher but more likely one of his coaches, called Branch Rickey and broke the news that the organization had just lost its major league team to mutiny.

At home when the call came, Rickey rushed to Ebbets Field and made a rare appearance in the clubhouse to address the players. After yet another appeal for team unity failed, Rickey played management's trump card: All players who refused to play would not only be suspended, they would be blacklisted, effective immediately. Only then did the players agree to play the scheduled game against the Pirates. Getting Durocher fired was all well and good, but losing their livelihood was something none of them could afford. Ultimately, only Vaughan stuck to his guns and refused to play.

A very angry group of Dodgers took the field, a few minutes late, and proceeded to take out their aggressions on the Pirates. Brooklyn scored ten runs in the first inning and went on to rout Pittsburgh, 23–6. Still, the developments of that day were anything but a "Much Ado About Nothing Revolt" that some sportswriters made them out to be. In fact, Roscoe McGowen of the *New York Times* found out just enough of the goings-on inside the Dodgers' clubhouse to realize the incident's historic implications. The *Times* played McGowen's (somewhat disjointed) account of the mutiny on page A1 of its July 11 editions.

Clearly, the blow-up at the ballpark was not just Newsom stirring up more trouble but the result of a deep and long-standing divide between the majority of Dodgers and Durocher. The notion of a minor disagreement between a couple of players and Durocher was purely a Rickey creation, fed to the unsuspecting media. In reality, while the players ultimately agreed to play, the ill-will generated by the incident carried over during the rest of the season. The organization had narrowly averted a work stoppage, and Rickey knew just how close a shave it had been. Promptly, he finalized his plan to get rid of Newsom, whom he viewed as the chief carcinogen in the clubhouse.

First, Rickey announced he was reducing Newsom's indefinite suspension to three days. While this seemed like good news for Newsom and his teammates, in reality it was a tactical move by Rickey. A player on the suspended list can't be traded, waived or released. Rickey jammed through waivers on Newsom (a process that normally took ten days) and on July 14—the day Newsom came off suspension and one day before his bonus was due—closed a deal with the St. Louis Browns. Newsom was sent west, in return the Dodgers receiving left-handed pitchers Fritz Ostermueller and Archie McKain. The rationale for the trade, according to Rickey, was that the team needed left-handed pitching. While that might have been the case, Ostermueller rarely pitched for the Dodgers the remainder of the 1943 season and won the grand total of one game. McKain never pitched an inning for the Dodgers.[29]

Rickey wasn't through. Johnny Allen and Dolf Camilli were next on the firing line, traded to the Giants on July 31 for three second-stringers. The loss of Newsom, Allen, Camilli, Medwick and Rowe, with nothing of value gained in return, put the kibosh on any thoughts of a pennant race involving Brooklyn. The Dodgers went on a ten-game losing streak, from July 28 to August 8, a skid that buried them behind the Cardinals in the standings. St. Louis went on to win the NL title at 105–49, Cincinnati came in second at 87–67 and Brooklyn faded to third, at 81–72. And the news got worse for Brooklyn fans in the off-season. Vaughan did return to the Dodgers lineup after his one-game strike, but most definitely did not forgive either Durocher or Rickey, especially because Rickey docked him one day's pay. The All-Star shortstop played out the season and abruptly retired, staying retired until he was finally coaxed back by Rickey in the spring of 1947. With all the player losses and lingering distrust in the clubhouse, the Dodgers plunged to the bottom of the National League standings in 1944, finishing in seventh place.[30]

For Newsom, it was difficult to say which news hurt more, the loss of his $5,000 signing bonus or the fact he was once again headed to the Browns. Newsom's reaction to the events was succinct: "I just got the rawest deal in the history of baseball," he complained to sportswriters. "It's the worst thing that's ever happened to me. I'm going to retire."[31]

A couple of days later, it got worse for Newsom. The divorce papers were served, with Lucille asking for a very sizable settlement. A divorce would also mean a change in his draft status, to 1-A. Needing an immediate influx of money and having no way to make it other than playing baseball, Newsom reneged on his vow to retire. However, he did take his sweet time reporting to St. Louis.

The Browns anxiously awaited his arrival. Against all odds, St. Louis had been elevated to the status of American League pennant contender due to the circumstances of the war. Team president Bill DeWitt certainly had reservations about bringing Newsom back into the Brownies fold, but he was a proven winner and clearly the best pitcher available on the open market. Further, he remained a gate attraction in the Gateway City, someone guaranteed to give the Browns media attention in a town that had gone gaga for the Cardinals. DeWitt also owed his benefactor, Rickey, a few favors, and taking the mutinous Newsom off Brooklyn's hands certainly ranked as a monumental good deed.

Newsom finally checked in with the Browns on July 18. His first stop was DeWitt's office. Once there, he presented a written demand for the $5,000 bonus, his travel expenses from New York to Missouri (players of that era were not given travel money when traded from one team to another) and various and sundry amounts he claimed the Browns owed him dating back to 1934. DeWitt said he wouldn't pay; Newsom said he wouldn't play. And it wasn't merely Bobo being Bobo. This time he meant it, in fact had hired a lawyer and was threatening to go to the newspaper boys with the whole truth about his abrupt banishment from Brooklyn.[32]

Only the personal intervention of Browns manager Luke Sewell managed to get Newsom in uniform. At least, his large body got into a uniform. His soul was not into the enterprise of pitching for the Browns until the financial situation was settled to his satisfaction. He was sent to the mound that day at Sportsman's Park, gave up six runs in two innings to the Indians, and took the loss. It was an omen of things to come in Brownie Land. Joe Schultz, a catcher for the Browns, said,

> It looked like we might make a run for the pennant in 1943 when we got Bobo Newsom. But he had gotten screwed over by Rickey in Brooklyn and was just totally out of control. He spent more time in DeWitt's office, or standing around in the hallway outside the office, complaining about his contract than he did with the team. He managed to drive DeWitt crazy, which I guess was what he was trying to do in the first place. But he didn't help us a bit.[33]

"Bobo Newsom. What a character," said Al Zarilla, a rookie outfielder on the 1943 Browns. "First thing he says to me, 'Rook, hold out for all you can get.' Here I am, a young kid just glad to be in the big leagues, and he's lecturing me on how to negotiate a new deal. Sad thing was, he could have really helped the Browns. But he and Mr. DeWitt tangled, it got real personal, and Bobo had to go."[34]

DeWitt finally agreed to pay Newsom $1,500 in hush money. That didn't placate him, whose bad attitude was affecting his pitching. The bonus brouhaha reached the Commissioner's office, no doubt pushed along by Newsom's very public utterances on the subject. Judge Landis fined both the Dodgers and Browns undisclosed amounts for their handling of the matter. It was a Pyrrhic victory for Newsom, since Landis also ruled the $5,000 bonus was illegal to begin with and would not be paid.

On the field, instead of threatening the Yankees and Senators in the AL pennant race, the Browns fell apart. Only seven games out of first place when Newsom arrived with the expressed aim "to pitch them to the pennant," they finished at 72–80 and in sixth place. A large reason for their summer swoon was Newsom. He started nine games for the Browns and lost six of them. In 52⅓ innings, he gave up 45 runs on 69 hits. He won the grand total of one game for the Browns, exactly the same production the Dodgers got from Fritz Ostermueller.

"[Newsom] just didn't materialize for us," pitcher Nelson Potter told author William Mead in an interview for *Even the Browns*. "They knocked him out nine straight times. He'd start, and I'd relieve him. I came out of the clubhouse one day and said 'Say, Buck, when are you and I pitching again?'"[35]

Potter and several Browns players recall that Newsom was having family troubles and was being pursued by both lawyers and bill collectors. After he had been knocked out several times, the story goes that when he finally finished a game a sportswriter quipped that he must've seen a sheriff in the stands and was afraid to leave the field.[36]

During his 1943 stint with the Browns, Newsom abruptly demanded a change of uniform numbers. While the public explanation was that he wanted to change his luck, privately most teammates believed it was his attempt to throw the process servers off track. In those days, players did not wear their names on the back of their uniform, but his number switch made sense only if you didn't factor into the equation that on a baseball field he was unmistakable. Suffice to say, it was not a pleasant summer in St. Louis for Mr. Newsom.

Mr. DeWitt wasn't exactly a happy camper either. By the end of August he had seen and heard enough. With the Browns now out of the race, and as always in need of money, on August 31 DeWitt sold Newsom, fellow pitcher Johnny Niggeling and third baseman Harlond Clift to the Senators. All three had disappointing seasons in St. Louis, and DeWitt reportedly received $25,000 for their services.[37] In truth, he probably would have accepted 25 cents. Newsom and Clift, the highest-paid players on the team, were both firmly entrenched in DeWitt's doghouse. Clift, a former All-Star, had developed the bad habit of taking himself out of the lineup; Joe Schultz recalled a game in 1943 on a hot summer day in St. Louis when Clift asked to be taken out of a game due to a hangnail.[38]

Now, they were a part of an unexpected pennant contender. The deal delighted Newsom, reuniting him with his old pinochle partner Clark Griffith. He couldn't wait to get out of St. Louis, staying at Sportsman's Park just long enough to clean out his locker and unload a bundle of unpaid bills on DeWitt's secretary.

"The ballclub has been good to me," Newsom was quoted as saying upon his departure from St. Louis, with more than a touch of sarcasm. "And the newspapers have treated me fairly. But the Brownie fans have been my true friends—both of them." Reportedly, in his haste to leave he forgot his train ticket. No matter. "I'll ride the baggage car to get out of this town," he told the conductor.[39]

The Senators and Yankees were locked in a race for the AL pennant that September. Unfortunately, Newsom was still out of shape and split six decisions for Washington. One of the losses was particularly galling, a 12–3 setback to the Browns on September 23, which officially eliminated Washington from the pennant race. In Newsom's defense, he did manage to beat the powerful Yankees twice that September, once outdueling Yankees ace Red Ruffing, 5–1, on September 5.

Of the two other players acquired from the Browns, Niggeling won four of his six starts, but Clift came down with the mumps and played in only eight games for the Senators. It wasn't exactly what Clark Griffith had in mind for his $25,000. In the calm following the storm of the season, Griffith took time to reflect. Pinochle playing aside, a rational man examining Newsom's 1943 season, as well as 1941 and 1942, would arrive at the conclusion that he was on the down side of his career. Newsom was 36 years old and had pitched professionally for nearly 20 years. His off-field antics had to be taking a toll on his well-being. Keeping him around represented a very expensive hobby, as evidenced when DeWitt forwarded the bundle of unpaid bills to Griffith.

About the only positive for Newsom during his latest stay in D.C. was that he struck up a friendship with Senators second baseman Jerry Priddy. Priddy mentioned he was going to play in a series of exhibitions in Los Angeles that fall. Newsom, sensing a payday the likes of the one he experienced back in the winter of 1933, asked to tag along. He needed to be in the general vicinity of Las Vegas anyway, since the twice-postponed divorce hearing was set there in November.[40]

Arriving in Los Angeles on October 5, Newsom and Priddy joined a team that included major leaguers Peanuts Lowrey, Johnny Lindell, Lou Novikoff, George

Metkovich and Roy Partee. While there was no winter league per se, as in years past, the big leaguers did find solid competition, including games against a team of Negro Leagues All-Stars led by Satchel Paige, Terris McDuffie and Buck Leonard. Promoter of the games was Joe Pirrone, who had also promoted Newsom's successful 1933 winter league season.[41] It looked like easy money to Newsom, who desperately needed to squirrel away a large nest egg in advance of his divorce. Well aware that Lucille's legal beagles were on his financial trail, Newsom insisted on being paid in cash.

Another legal mind was also watching. Judge Landis decreed that the major leaguers' participation in the series was to end ten days after the conclusion of the World Series. However, as in year's past, most players ignored this edict, claimed that the games were for charity, or simply played under assumed names. Indeed, the games may well have benefitted all players involved, were it not for Newsom's antics.

Newsom helped hasten an early conclusion to the games on a cold, damp October night at L.A.'s Wrigley Field. As the starting pitcher for Pirrone's All-Stars, on a night that Paige was not pitching for the Negro Leagues All-Stars, Newsom demanded $500. The other players on both teams were to get amounts ranging from $100 to $150. Soon after the game started, fog rolled in. After two innings, the fog was so thick the game had to be stopped. Pirrone told the players to come back the next night to finish the game, and announced same to the fans. Not so fast, said Newsom. He wanted his $500, and he wanted it now. Pirrone patiently explained that if he paid Newsom, he would in fairness have to pay the other players as well. This made absolutely no impression on Newsom, who threatened to quit the series and talk Paige into leaving with him. Since the two had bonded, this was no idle threat.[42]

Pirrone finally gave in and paid Newsom the $500, in cash. The other players, reluctantly, agreed to wait for their money. The next night, Newsom was a no-show. For Pirrone, who had also paid Newsom $1,000 in cash up-front to participate in the series, the no-show was the financial last straw. He reported Newsom's stunt to Landis, who in turn brought his office's wrath down on all major leaguers participating in the games.

The most logical rationale for Newsom's unbridled greed was the upcoming divorce hearing. The much-delayed hearing finally took place in mid–November in Las Vegas. When it was done, Newsom was considerably poorer, Lucille opting for a lump sum payment rather than trusting him to come through with monthly alimony checks. She also was awarded full custody of the couple's two children.[43]

There was one final indignity in Newsom's nightmarish year. On December 13, Clark Griffith traded him to the Philadelphia Athletics. Knowing his best buddy in baseball no longer wanted him around cut deep.

Fortunately, an old man in Philadelphia and a young lady in McKeesport did want him. And that's all it took to ignite another spectacular rise from the ashes.

Ten

Philadelphia to Washington (1944–1946)

On the baseball front, the impact of World War II was felt everywhere. The military draft cut deeply into the talent pool. The quality of the major league baseball played in 1943–1945 was decidedly substandard, likely the worst of the 20th century. Excluding pitchers, of the 128 starters on Opening Day in 1945, three out of four would be on the bench or back in the minor leagues by Opening Day 1946.[1]

So how were things in Bobo Newsom's universe? Just fine, thank you. The two full years he spent with the Philadelphia Athletics were, by all accounts, the most peaceful of his stormy life. It was a time when he evolved into an elder statesman and arrived at something resembling peace with at least a few of his inner demons. He even developed a certain fondness for an authority figure, in this case A's owner-manager Connie Mack.

Part of the reason for Newsom's new-found tranquility can be traced to Mack, a kindly if

A snapshot of Newsom taken in 1946 with the Senators. Newsom normally put on his best uniform and groomed himself prior to photograph shoots, but here the photographer captures him unshaven and slightly bleary eyed (the Ray Medeiros collection, used by permission).

quirky man who by 1944 was a living legend. And part had to be attributed to Newsom's new bride. Curiously, there is almost no mention of Newsom's second wife in any of the interviews he gave over the last two decades of his life. The information he did give was unfailingly incorrect. Perhaps, as one of his relatives suggested, he realized he had "married up" and didn't want to say or do anything to jeopardize the union.

Ruth Griffiths, known by her nickname of Kay (he called her Kay-O), was 14 years younger than Newsom. He told relatives he had met her while "playing baseball" and that was undoubtedly true. She hailed from McKeesport, PA. Her maiden name, rendered in some sources as Griffith, gave rise to rumors she was related to Clark Griffith. She wasn't, although she did come from a reasonably well-to-do family.[2] One fact that isn't in dispute is that the second Mrs. Newsom was a looker, in the parlance of the 1940s American male. Bob Shirley, Newsom's longtime Hartsville acquaintance, said,

> She was a honey blond, and a real honey. Probably one of the best looking women I've ever seen. She used to wear slacks, very unusual for that time, and when she walked down the main street here in Hartsville she absolutely stopped traffic. Bobo was very proud of her. I don't know exactly what they had in common but there was definitely a physical attraction there.[3]

"[Kay was a] really beautiful person, outside and inside," said Tallulah Williams, Newsom's cousin. "I know when Buck brought her to our house to introduce her to the family you could tell he was really smitten by her. And I think she was good for him. She helped to knock some of the rough edges off him and build him up at a time he was kind of low as far as his baseball career was concerned."[4]

Newsom's marital status had undergone a war of its own until late 1943. After years of threatening to do so, Lucille finally obtained a divorce in mid–November. Lucille eventually remarried and settled in northern California.[5] For Bobo, the divorce's immediate result was twofold; it put a big dent in his bank account and changed his draft status to 1-A. The Selective Service situation was resolved when Newsom finally got around to taking the Army physical, in mid–February of 1944. He was quickly found to be 4-F due to the broken knee suffered in 1935. Newsom told Bob Shirley,

> This ol' Army doctor started looking Bobo over from the feet up. He didn't like the looks of my feet, both of 'em had been broke. Then he moved up to my knee, the trick one that's always going out on me. And he fiddled around with it for a couple minutes, and then got up and looked at me and shook his head. "You play baseball? You belong in a wheelchair, not on the ballfield." Then and there, I knew I was 4-F.[6]

Draft status settled permanently, Newsom prepared for duties with his new team. Connie Mack acquired his services from the Senators for pitcher Roger Wolff on December 13 and was to introduce him as the newest Athletic at the annual baseball writers' holiday banquet in Philly. Unfortunately for Mack, at that time Newsom had other things on his mind and missed the banquet.

A whirlwind courtship of Kay culminated on either New Year's Eve, 1943, or New Year's Day, 1944. No one was sure exactly when the civil ceremony took place, since there was considerable partying at the time, but take place it did, in Darlington, SC. What is remembered was that the union of Bobo and Kay defied the naysayers and lasted until his death, 18 years later. While at first Kay was regarded by many of Newsom's cronies as a "trophy wife," she was totally devoted to him and eventually of necessity became more a nurse than a mate.

"I always felt a little sorry for Kay," said Tallulah Williams. "I don't think she fully knew what she was in for as Buck's wife. And their last few years had to be very difficult. She was still a young woman when he died. But she stuck it out and kept Buck in line, as much as that was possible."[7]

Also helping keep Newsom in line was his new manager. At first, Newsom treated Mack pretty much the same way he treated another former boss, Clark Griffith: as an equal, not an employer. When the twice-delayed press conference announcing Newsom's acquisition was finally held, in late January at Mack's office in Shibe Park, Newsom amused all in attendance by arriving late, smoking a cigar (Connie Mack was a confirmed non-smoker), commandeering Mack's chair, constantly interrupting Mack's comments, and accepting a personal phone call right in the middle of the soiree. The topper occurred when Mack began to detail plans for the A's upcoming spring training session. At that point, Newsom interjected the news that, while spring training was all well and good for his teammates, Bobo himself planned to stay put in Hartsville until the regular season opened. "A most peculiar fellow," was Mack's reported summation after this close encounter with Newsom.[8]

Probably the only man in America who called Bobo Newsom "Louis" was Connie Mack. Mack picked up Newsom in a trade in the winter of 1943 and enjoyed his pitching, if not his ability to cajole Mack into advances on his salary, which was already the highest on the team. Eventually, Mack made sure he always had a witness present when he and "Louis" discussed money matters (the Ray Medeiros collection, used by permission).

When spring training started, the Athletics en masse nearly froze to death in Frederick, MD, a site imposed on the team by World War II travel restrictions.[9] Meanwhile, Newsom was true to his word, remaining in Hartsville with his new bride in the bridal suite of the town's best hotel. There is no evidence Newsom did any training or physical activity of any sort other than the normal honeymoon marital duties. Like all players during spring training, he wasn't on salary but was to receive expense money. Dutifully (Newsom could be very dutiful when it came to spending other people's money), he sent his hotel bills, food bills and laundry bills, along with those of Kay's, northward to Mack. The blizzard of dunnage gave Mack ample reason to rue ever allowing Newsom out of his sight. Whatever was said between the two men in private, in public the diplomatic Mack would only say "Hartsville must be the most expensive city in the United States."[10]

After that experience, Mack allowed Kay to travel with the team during the season, no doubt deducing that Bobo would find a way to bill him for her room and board anyway.

The thin, gentlemanly Mack presented a stark contrast to the bulky, brash Newsom. While the two had little in common other than a love of baseball, Newsom generally behaved himself around Mack, even to the point of cleaning up some of his more colorful language. Initially, he called Mack "Connie." This upset the younger set on the Athletics, several of whom urged him to show proper deference to Philadelphia's Mr. Baseball. Newsom pondered this request and ultimately agreed to say "Mr. Mack" when addressing the Philly manager. He kept his word, although on occasion he would become excited and revert back to Connie, or even Bobo, as in "Ol' Bobo, ya gotta get this Bobo outta the game right now! Bobo is killin' us, Bobo!" Connie Mack, like Franklin D. Roosevelt before him, took it all in stride.[11]

Unfortunately, it was evident that the 81-year-old Mack had slowed down, physically and mentally. He tended to nod off during games, forgetting the number of outs, and was prone to posting the wrong lineup card before games, filled with players' names from the great Athletics teams of the past. Woody Wheaton, a member of the 1944 team from spring training onward, remembered an incident that summer in a Cleveland hotel lobby when Mack came over and asked, "Young man, you look familiar. Do I know you?"[12]

Increasingly, coaches Earle Bruckner and Earle Mack (Connie's youngest son) took over running the team on the field. Unfortunately, Earle Mack was as absent-minded as his father and possessed none of Connie's vast baseball knowledge. It was a highly awkward situation for the players, who felt compelled to kowtow to the younger Mack despite his obvious lack of ability as a major league coach.[13]

Still, there were days when Connie Mack was his old self, strong and clear-headed. On those days, he showed a genius for the game he had been a big part of for over 50 years. His positioning of fielders—accomplished by a flick of his ever-present scorecard—was notably brilliant. He also retained a firm knowledge of pitching, dating back to his days as a major league catcher in the 1880s. Newsom loved to talk about pitching to anyone, anywhere, and especially enjoyed his strategy sessions with Mack. The drawback to all this was that the discussions often took place on the bench during a game, when Mack was in theory supposed to be managing the team.

Jesse Flores remembered a game he pitched during which a dugout debate broke out between Mack and Newsom. Subject: the best way to pitch to Babe Ruth. The tête-à-tête took place over the course of several innings, with Mack and Newsom becoming totally engrossed, along with several other players on the bench. Unfortunately for Flores, in the meantime he was getting pounded and was receiving absolutely no guidance, or relief, from Mack. By the time Mack and Newsom agreed on the one and only true way to strike out Ruth—who had retired years earlier and wasn't likely to be making a comeback anytime soon—Flores had given up several runs.[14]

Connie's concept was to have son Earle take over as field manager, enabling Connie to concentrate on the business side of baseball. Toward that goal, Connie gave the younger Mack considerable tutoring over the course of several years, but it became increasingly clear this acorn had fallen far, far from the tree. Earle Mack never quite absorbed how to manage a ball team. In particular, he couldn't get over being intimidated by the players.

It was no secret that Newsom hated to be taken out of a game. However, there came a time on a hot summer afternoon in 1944 when Newsom was getting hammered by the opposition and it was evident to even Earle Mack that he just didn't have it. It was also a day on which Connie had entrusted son Earle with the running of the team. Earle put off and put off going out to give Newsom the hook until Connie finally urged him to do so. Gingerly, Earle walked to the mound, where stood a very hot, very angry Newsom.

"Daddy says you have to come out now," Earle said to him.

"Tell Daddy to go screw himself," Newsom replied.

Back to the dugout went a red-faced Earle Mack. Newsom finished the game.[15]

It was remarkable that Newsom retained whatever sanity he had left while pitching for the 1944 and 1945 Philadelphia Athletics. As the undisputed ace of the A's pitching staff, Newsom posted a combined 21–35 win-loss record in those seasons. Newsom's earned run average for the two seasons was right at three runs a game, and it's no stretch of imagination to project him as a two-time 20-game winner with anything resembling a major league team supporting him.

Flores, a native of Mexico, was leery of having Newsom as a teammate, knowing Newsom hailed from South Carolina and that many of the southerners in baseball were "hard-asses" about racial matters. However, no problems developed on or off the field. "As for Buck, I got along with him fine," Flores said. "The only thing was that he never got it through his head that I was Mexican, not Cuban. He thought I was Cuban. But he never remembered anybody's name either, so I didn't take offense."[16]

Entering the 1944 season, the Athletics had nowhere to go but up. They had finished 1943 with a 49–105 record, worst in the major leagues. The dismal season included a stretch of 20 straight losses. Connie Mack, for all his baseball genius, was no visionary in the Branch Rickey mold. He hadn't cultivated a minor league farm system and resisted signing young players during the war or spending money on anything but the bare necessities. Virtually the only promotional literature the team issued from 1943 to 1945 was a list of A's players in the military service. Touting players who weren't there was not a strategy designed to attract fans to the ballpark. Attendance at A's home games slipped from 525,000 in 1941 to 375,000 by 1943.

At the infamous news conference in Connie Mack's office, Newsom was asked about the Athletics' declining attendance. He was quick with an answer. "That's not gonna be a problem," he told the assembled scribes. "If all the God-damn Philly fans who came out to the ballpark the past ten years to boo my ass come back out here to cheer for me, we'll fill the God-damn place every game." That quote was cleaned up a tad for consumption by the citizens of Philadelphia.[17]

With Bobo Newsom, there was no question the team now owned an ace pitcher and a legitimate gate attraction. The 1944 Athletics were virtually identical to the 1943

Athletics, other than Newsom and 40-year-old rookie pitcher Joe Berry, but those two clearly made a big difference. The 1944 A's improved to 72–82, good enough for fifth place in the American League. Attendance climbed to 505,000.

The 1944 A's weren't going to scare opponents with their bats. First baseman/outfielder Dick Siebert led the team with a .306 average, outfielder Bobby Estalella was next at .298, third baseman George Kell hit .268 and catcher Frankie Hayes, playing in all 155 games, came in at .248. None in that group was a true power hitter or fleet of foot, so the Athletics had difficulty scoring runs. But the pitching was solid, top to bottom as good as any staff in the league. Newsom finished at 13–15, with an excellent 2.82 earned run average. Russ Christopher, coming off a 5–8 season, went 14–14. Lum Harris, who was 7–21 in 1943, was 10–9 in 1944 prior to entering the military service halfway through the season. Don Black improved from 6–16 to 10–12. Flores, the ace of the staff in 1943 at 12–14, went 9–11 in 1944.[18] "Jittery" Joe Berry, so named for a multitude of nervous mannerisms on the mound, turned out to be one of the top relief pitchers in baseball, appearing in 53 games with a 10–8 record, 12 (retroactive) saves and a 1.94 earned run average.[19]

The Athletics' pitchers could have sued for non-support. The A's scored a major-league low 525 runs, an average of 3.4 per game. Philadelphia hit only 36 home runs and stole only 42 bases. It all meant A's pitchers had virtually no margin for error. Flores said,

> The biggest plus having Bobo was that he worked a lot with the young pitchers. He had the reputation as a self-centered guy but he sure didn't show that with us. He taught our guys to pitch aggressively, which you have to do to win in the big leagues. I can still hear him yelling from the dugout, "knock him on his ass!" It probably upset Mr. Mack but, hey, we were winning a few ballgames for a change so what could Connie say?[20]

"You spend your first six years in baseball learning how to pitch," Newsom told Ed Pollock of the *Philadelphia Evening Bulletin* early in the 1944 season, "and the next six years wishing you'd known it from scratch."

Newsom, no doubt via the travails on and off the field during his 1941, 1942 and 1943 seasons, had mellowed. While still a certified egomaniac, he now could identify with the younger Athletics players, especially the pitchers. He offered them advice on baseball, finances and women, not necessarily in that order. For many, he was a savior financially. In addition to Flores and Wheaton, published memoirs by Phil Marchildon, Bob Savage, Lum Harris and Marion Fricano all attest to Newsom's noblesse oblige. Savage recalled,

> Bobo Newsom and I were close friends on the Athletics. He took a liking to me in spring training and spoke up for me to Mr. Mack on many occasions. He got Dorothy (Savage's new bride) and me a cellar apartment at his apartment house, and we drove to the ballpark together. Bobo took very good care of us.[21]

Newsom, clearly, was at ease in his new surroundings. It also proved helpful that Connie Mack was an old hand at handling eccentrics. Mack had worked his magic on the likes of Rube Waddell, and Waddell became one of the top pitchers of his era. Newsom was no less, or more, sane than Waddell, and Mack's kinder, gentler approach produced malleability in him, a quality rarely induced by others.

Responding to Mack's request, Newsom deferred to Lum Harris for the honor of starting the Athletics' 1944 season opener. Harris, who hadn't pitched more than six innings all spring due to the dismal weather in Frederick, MD, was told by Mack he would only pitch three innings. Instead, he pitched the first nine innings of a game the Athletics eventually won in 12 innings. Newsom, who hadn't pitched at all in the spring unless you count pitching and wooing Kay, started 1944's third game and turned in a complete-game 5-hitter.[22]

In mid-season 1944, Harris was called to active duty in the Navy.

"The other players knew I was leaving," Harris said. "Led by my good friend Bobo Newsom, they gave me a Navy duffel bag filled with a hundred one-dollar bills."[23]

Newsom bragged to Connie Mack about what the players had done, and Mack came through with an extra $500 as the team's going-away gift to Harris. Mack might have done this anyway, but Newsom's pointed comments about stingy owners did Harris' financial cause no harm.

Newsom's solid 1944 season led to his selection to the American League All-Star team. Since the team was managed by longtime nemesis Joe McCarthy, he didn't expect to pitch in the game, held at Forbes Field in Pittsburgh. However, the other AL hurlers were roughed up by the National League stars and Newsom was pressed into service to get the final out in the eighth inning. This he did with a minimum of complaint, a far cry from his earlier All-Star Game tantrums directed at McCarthy. It was his final All-Star appearance. The 1945 game was canceled due to wartime travel restrictions, and Newsom was never again invited to the mid-season classic.

Unquestionably the highlight of the year for Newsom, and Athletics fans, occurred on August 4. The occasion marked Connie Mack's 50 years as a major league manager. As a tribute to the "Tall Tactician," sportswriter Ed Pollock organized a slam-bang evening at Shibe Park. The event drew a crowd of over 30,000, despite a public transit strike and the threat of a federally imposed blackout. Numerous local politicos were on hand, broadcaster Ted Husing, acting as master of ceremonies, read a telegraph from President Roosevelt concluding with "long may your scorecard wave" and pre-game entertainment was provided by Abbott and Costello.[24]

The game matched the Yankees and the A's, and Newsom and New York's Hank Borowy were both at the peak of their abilities. Newsom had a no-hitter for four innings, and struck out six of the first 12 Yankees he faced. The game was scoreless going into the top of the ninth, when two infield singles and a double-play grounder botched by A's second baseman Irv Hall brought in the go-ahead run. Not surprisingly, the A's went out 1–2–3 in the last of the ninth, saddling Newsom with yet another one-run loss.

Still, it had been a great show and Newsom enjoyed himself immensely. For the occasion, Pollock managed to assemble members of Connie Mack's all-time All-Stars, and Newsom got to rub shoulders with the likes of Babe Ruth, Walter Johnson, George Sisler, Tris Speaker, Honus Wagner and "Home Run" Baker. He had no trouble fitting into the elite company.

The 1–0 loss to the Yanks on Connie Mack Night typified the Athletics' 1944 season. The team consistently found a way to lose close games. Meanwhile, the St. Louis Browns, of all teams, managed to find a way to win them. The A's witnessed this firsthand in a three-game series at St. Louis on September 22–24. A's pitchers held the Brownies to only 16 hits in the three games. However, St. Louis won all three, part of a string of ten wins in their final 11 games that netted the Browns their first, and last, pennant. Newsom pitched the opener of the series and allowed only five hits, but an A's error led to an unearned run in a 4–2 St. Louis triumph. Don Black allowed only four hits in six innings pitched in Game Two of the Series, but the A's bats were silent in a 3–1 loss.

The final game featured one of those beyond-belief endings. Behind Flores, the A's led, 2–0, with two outs in the ninth. Then the Browns managed to get runners at first and second. Mark Christman hit a line drive at center fielder Bobby Estalella. Estalella, trying for a one-handed catch, misjudged the ball and it carried past him. Tex Shirley, a pitcher who had been pressed into service as the pinch-runner at first base, barreled all the way around the bases, running through the coach's stop sign at third. He stumbled halfway to home plate, fell down, and wound up crawling plate-ward on his hands and knees. The A's had him dead to rights, in fact could have rolled the ball to home plate to retire him and end the game. Instead, the cutoff man cranked up and gunned his throw well over the head of the catcher and all the way to the backstop. This gave Shirley ample time to get up and score to tie the game up. Christman advanced to third base on the errant throw. The next Browns batter hit a routine fly to center, where Estalella called for it, gloved it—and dropped it, allowing Christman to trot home with the winning run. Estalella was disconsolate after the game but Newsom, of all people, was the first to console him.[25]

While Newsom's temperament and ego may have mellowed, another side of his personality became increasingly pronounced during his years with the Athletics. Always superstitious, he seemed to acquire more and more rituals the longer he played baseball, while never quite shedding the older ones. As a younger, better-educated breed of ballplayer entered the majors in increasing numbers, Newsom's quirks became standouts. "Crazy Bobo" was how teammate Phil Marchildon described him.

For many years, Newsom followed the conventional player modus operandi of not stepping on the foul lines while entering and exiting the field. During his days with the A's, for some reason he decided to alternate: first inning, step on foul line; second inning, don't step on foul line. While it made little sense to others, Newsom took this, and all his superstitions, very seriously.

It all began in the clubhouse before the game. Newsom had a certain way of getting out of his street clothes, as a reporter from *Time* magazine found out when he attempted to interview him prior to a game in New York. The reporter was especially fascinated by the way he very carefully took off his socks, and then dangled them by their garters over his street shoes until they swung into the shoes without Newsom guiding them in any way. This procedure, akin to working an Ouija board, could take as long as five minutes, but Newsom would allow no interruptions until it was completed.[26] Once Newsom began to put his uniform on, it had to be in a certain order, belt buckle always fastened in exactly the same way, socks and baseball cleats last to go on, left foot first and then the right. If he was on a winning streak, he didn't want the uniform washed or touched by anyone else. This led to some rather unpleasant experiences for teammates sitting next to him in the dugout on hot summer days in Philadelphia.[27]

Putting on the uniform was only the start of Newsom's peculiar mannerisms. On days he was pitching, he refused to tie his own shoes, his thinking being he might injure himself while bending over. Given his medical history, this ritual made some semblance of sense. After a teammate or coach or the trainer attended to his footwear, he was ready to enter the arena. Supposedly, there came a time in Philadelphia when everyone forgot about tying his shoes and headed out onto the field. Newsom stood rock-still in front of his locker for 15 minutes until someone finally noticed his absence during warm-ups. The batboy was sent back to the locker room to tie those shoes. "Otherwise, he'd still be there," commented Flores.[28]

Approaching the mound, Newsom would always pick up a pinch of dirt on the first base side and deposit it on the third base side. He would fiddle around with the rosin bag until it was placed in exactly the right spot behind the mound. Before making his first pitch, he would lightly touch the bill of his cap, a salute to his long-dead mother. Then he would spit into the pocket of his glove. And he would never throw a pitch, even in warm-ups, if there were any scraps of paper on or in the general vicinity of the mound. The latter fetish was so important to him that he was known to sit down on the mound and refuse to pitch until every bit of paper was cleaned up. On at least two occasions, this behavior led to his ejection from a major league game by an impatient home plate umpire. Opponents were not above the tactic of deliberately scattering paper scraps on the field, knowing it would infuriate him and distract him from the task at hand. There is evidence that the Yankees' Joe McCarthy was the originator of this tactic, which further explains why he and Newsom were not exactly nuzzling buddies.[29]

Newsom's glove—and he used the same glove for years—had to be in its proper place at all times. When he finished an inning, he would flip his glove to his favorite spot on the third base side of the infield (this in the days when players left their gloves on the field). If the flip wasn't accurate, or if the glove didn't land palm down, he would pick up the glove and try again. No one else was permitted to touch his glove at any time.

Nothing better illustrates Newsom's adherence to superstitions than his choice of uniform numbers. While it is impossible to know with a certainty all the different numbers he wore in his hyperactive career, the ones that are known are revealing. When he first came up with the Browns in 1934, he chose uniform number 21, an obvious choice for someone who loved card games. In 1936, he decided to change his luck and reversed the numbers, wearing No. 12 (reportedly, his late mother's lucky number) from that season until joining the Dodgers late in the 1942 season. There, No. 12 wasn't available so Newsom took No. 8. In his tumultuous 1943 season, he wore No. 8 with the Dodgers, dumped that for No. 15 with the Browns, dumped that for No. 33 while in the midst of a long losing streak, and, upon joining the Senators late in the year, chose 00. The double zeroes, Newsom was quick to point out, didn't reflect his ability, his IQ or his value to the team. Rather, they were his lucky spot on the roulette table. He is believed to be the first professional athlete to wear "double zero" and it certainly was an attention-getter, which of course was the main reason Newsom wanted it.

Moving on to the Athletics in 1944, Connie Mack was not receptive to the 00 idea, so Newsom chose No. 16. Or rather, it was chosen for him, since by the time he joined the team in April it was the only A's uniform left that fit him (it had been Roger Wolff's in 1942 and 1943). Besides, Larry Rosenthal was already wearing No. 12 and Don Black No. 21. Rejoining the Senators in 1946, Newsom promptly reverted to his beloved 00. When he joined the Yankees in 1947, management specifically forbade Newsom from wearing 00. He settled on No. 34, mainly because it was the closest available to his old No. 33 and the digits added up to seven—another lucky number. He was back to No. 12—reverse 21—for his homecoming with the Senators in 1952. He switched to No. 20 for his final two seasons with the Athletics, since Pete Suder already wore No. 12 and Sam Zoldak No. 21 and both rejected his pleas to change numbers.

When asked why he did all these strange things, Newsom replied, "Just so folks will watch me pitch." But it was more than that. Some of the mannerisms dated all the way back to his childhood days. And while Newsom was in some ways an enlightened man, the rituals came to rule him, becoming almost as important as the game itself. He never quite got over the farm-boy sensibility that the fates were fickle in the extreme and nothing must be done to rile them up. Hoot Gibson, his friend in Hartsville, remembered that Newsom always smoked Chesterfields, with a certain way to open the pack, a certain way to light the cigarette, and the throwing away of the first and last "coffin nail" in a pack. Nothing could prevent him from following this ritual. The habit made no sense, yet it made perfect sense.[30]

The Athletics, thanks to their competent 1944 season and the fact that the St. Louis Browns—of all teams—had won the 1944 AL pennant, entered the 1945 season with honest-to-goodness pennant hopes. But those sand castles began to crumble in early 1945 when Newsom broke his left collarbone. Officially, the injury occurred either (a) when he took a tumble while hunting in the hill country to the north of Hartsville or (b) in a car accident on his way to church. Unofficially, most of his Hartsville confidants believed he injured the collarbone in a particularly rough barroom brawl. Whatever the cause, the injury led to Newsom missing spring training—yet again—and limited his effectiveness for most of the season.[31]

Newsom, true to his nature, balked at the initial Philadelphia contract offer. Connie Mack dismissed Newsom's complaints with the comment that "sometimes Louis pouts like a big overgrown boy." Newsom was having none of that. "I may be actin' like a little boy," he told the media, "but I want a grown man's salary!" In due time, the contract dispute was settled and Newsom reported to the A's in time for the season opener. Newsom claimed he got a raise, while Mack claimed he would make the same in 1945 as he made in 1944. Likely, it was the $20,000 per that Newsom made the previous three seasons. The important thing was that peace once again graced the Athletics' front office.

The A's, despite the loss of several key players to the military, began the season by winning six of eight games. One of the losses was in the season opener on April 17 when Newsom was outpitched by the Senators' Dutch Leonard. Things quickly turned sour for Philly after the 6–2 start. Any chances of the team being a pennant contender were dashed in late June by a 14-game losing streak, Newsom absorbing four of those losses. For bad measure, they assembled a 10-game losing streak in July. When the curtain went down on the 1945 season, the A's were back in last place, at 52–98.

Once again, A's pitching was reasonably solid. Russ Christopher went 13–13, Jesse Flores was 7–10, and Joe Berry had another solid year as the team's top relief pitcher, going 8–7 with a 2.35 earned run average in a league-high 52 appearances. But Newsom was thoroughly snake-bit, finishing at 8–20 despite a 3.29 ERA. The A's were as punchless as ever, averaging only 3.3 runs per game. Of Newsom's eight wins, three came via shutouts. His outings included two 1–0 losses, a 2–0 loss and a 2–1 loss. In addition, he pitched seven innings in a game that ended in a 0–0 tie, halted in the 13th inning due to a wartime curfew.[32]

After winning his second start of the season, Newsom endured a 12-game losing streak, by far the longest of his career. He finally snapped it by shutting out the Browns on July 12. He won his next four games, but by then Philly was hopelessly behind in the pennant chase.

He Perhaps the highlight in an otherwise aggravating season for Newsom occurred on August 21 at Detroit. He came into town with the A's and declared he would pitch both games of the scheduled doubleheader. It was a warm, muggy day at Briggs Stadium, but he was true to his word and started both games. It was the fifth, and last, time he pitched both ends of a doubleheader in the major leagues. The twin bill drew a crowd in excess of 30,000 to Briggs Stadium. World War II was finally over and servicemen were admitted free to the games, swelling the attendance considerably. Detroit fans were also out in force to welcome back slugger Hank Greenberg from the war and to see if the Bengals could successfully continue their pennant run. Still, in Newsom's version of events, the 30,000 (he claimed it was 50,000) came out to the ballpark to see him. Who is to doubt that more than a few did?

"One of Bobo's favorite expressions was 'Gonna do it to you two times,'" recalled Hank Greenberg. "So that's what he was saying that day to us, gonna do it to you two times."[33]

The day turned out to be a microcosm of Newsom's season. He pitched six innings of the opener, leaving with a 6–2 lead. Unfortunately, the usually reliable Joe Berry gave up the tying runs before Philadelphia prevailed in 11 innings, 7–6. In the nightcap, Newsom nursed a 6–5 lead into the ninth inning, but surrendered a walk and game-tying double by Greenberg. The A's turned to Joe Berry at that point, who promptly gave up a game-winning single by Rudy York.

So, for his 14 innings, Newsom came away without a victory.

"He wasn't a rapid pitcher," Greenberg said. "He used to walk around the mound ... so that first game must have taken over three hours. He goes into the clubhouse and sure enough, he comes out to pitch the second game. That was really something! ... a Herculean task."[34]

The 1945 season was quite a trial for Newsom. He managed to keep his composure most of the way, but George Kell recalled a particularly tough loss late in the year, in which throwing errors by catcher Greek George led to the deciding runs in a 3–2 A's setback. When the Philly writers came to Newsom for a quote after the game, he erupted. "Whatta asking me for? Go talk to that son-of-a-bitch over there!" pointing to where a dejected George sat, head down, in front of his locker.[35]

The year was also a trial in that Newsom became increasingly sensitive about his age. Maybe it was because his new bride was considerably younger, maybe because his major league future was in doubt now that all those players who served in the military were returning to the major league ranks. Whatever the reason, Newsom kept fudging on his birth year, eventually moving it all the way forward from 1907 to 1911. The latter year, as well as 1908, 1909 and 1910, made it into various record books, adding yet another bit of confusion to the Newsom biography. The tendency reached its apex in the 1950s when Newsom, then pitching for Chattanooga in the Southern Association,

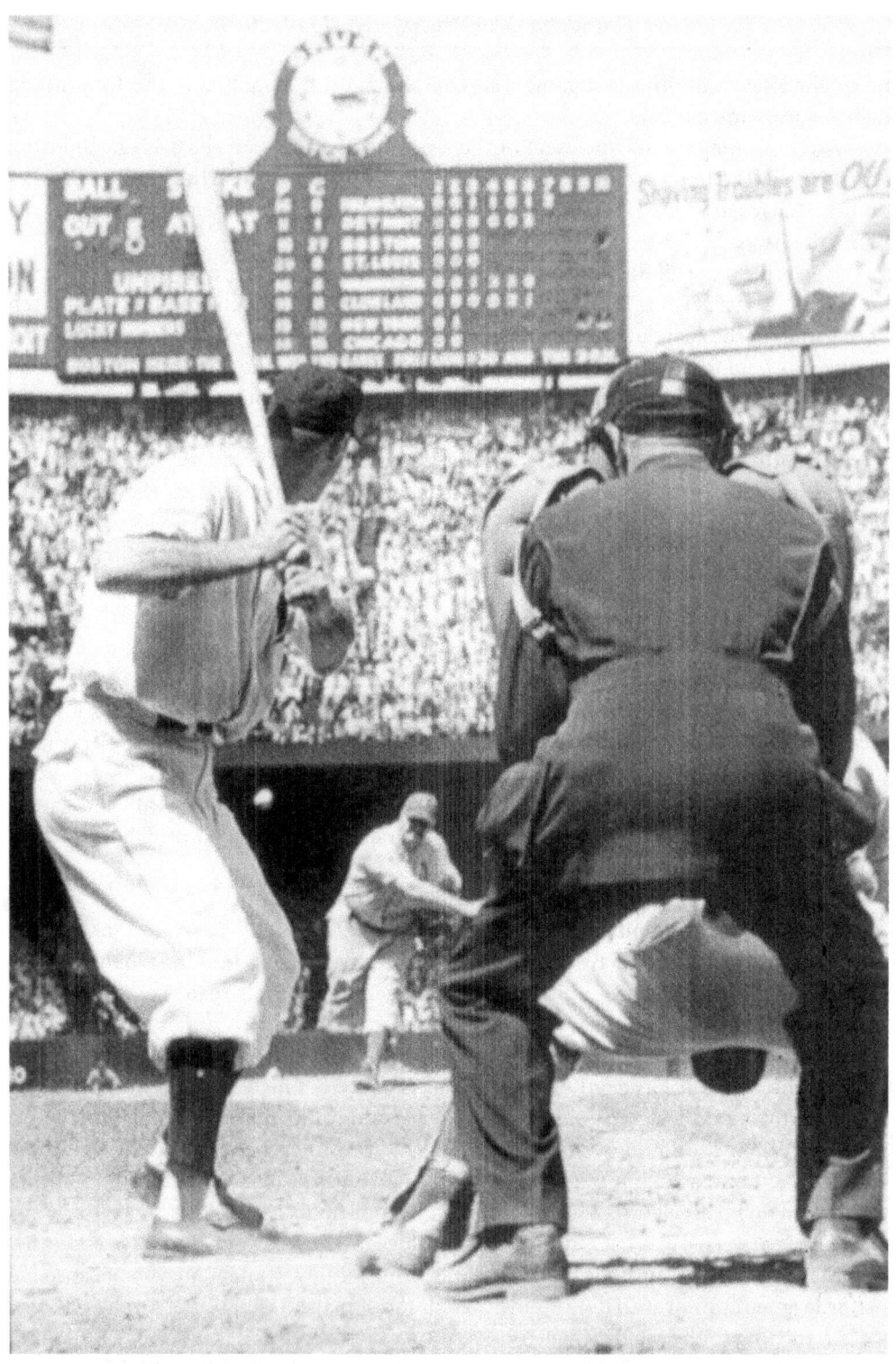

Philadelphia's Bobo Newsom pitches to Detroit's Hank Greenberg in the sixth inning on the occasion of Greenberg's return to the Tigers' lineup at Briggs Stadium on July 1, 1945. Newsom wound up walking Greenberg. Rudy York followed with a three-run home run. Newsom was saddled with his 11th consecutive loss (the Ray Medeiros collection, used by permission).

told a sportswriter that he was born on July 4, 1911, that his real name was Lawrence Nelson Newsom, that he was a graduate of Georgia Tech and that wife Kay was a former Miss Pennsylvania. It was a remarkable quartet of lies, even by Newsom's standards.[36]

Newsom also became increasingly combative with umpires. He always had difficulty with the men in blue but seemed to be hypersensitive during the war years, when some of the umpiring was as bad as the caliber of play (as evidenced by the Joe Rue-Greek George incident). Since Newsom's pitches had a lot of movement and the baseball "book" called for hitters to take Newsom's deliveries until he threw a strike, he wasn't the easiest pitcher to work with for plate umpires. This led to a lot of arguing on the part of Newsom, who admittedly brought a unique flair to his confrontations with the umps that prevented him from being tossed out of games more often than was absolutely necessary.

He got tossed once when he felt plate umpire Bill McGowan was "pinching" him, not giving him the calls on borderline pitches. McGowan finally called a strike and Newsom bounced off the mound, walked to home plate, took a deep bow and said, "Oh, thank you so very much." McGowan instantly ejected him. Flores said,

> The words were nothing to get anybody tossed. But what happened was, Bobo had a lot of goofy voices he did, and one of them was what we used to call a sissy voice. So that's what he gave McGowan. Everyone in the dugout heard it and the players all burst out laughing. I think that made McGowan even madder.[37]

A time Newsom didn't get tossed was also Lou Boudreau's favorite story about Newsom. It took place in a game in Cleveland, with Bill Summers as the plate umpire. Newsom had been working on a blooper pitch (he called it his "V-Ball") that season and Summers was already on record as saying he wasn't going to call it a strike, no matter what. With Boudreau batting, Newsom floated up his "V-Ball" and Summers called it a ball. Newsom charged home plate. Summers took off his mask and yelled "Scram!" This stopped Newsom in his tracks. "Scram?" Newsom said. "Scram? I ain't even had time to unwrap a cuss word!"[38]

An occasion when he was ejected without uttering a cuss word, or any other word, also occurred during the war years. After he jawed with the plate umpire all afternoon, a borderline 3–2 pitch was called a ball, forcing in a run. Newsom very deliberately approached the umpire, stood directly in front of him and let out a very long, very wet Bronx cheer. Exit Bobo Newsom.

Entering the 1946 season, optimism reigned at all major league training camps. The "boys" were back from the war, and the thinking among fans was that a team adding all those who served their country to the players used during the 1943, 1944 and 1945 seasons would be twice as good. Unfortunately, in the case of the A's, they were possibly twice as bad. Connie Mack had no idea exactly what players he had coming back from the war. If he couldn't remember the current players from one day to the next, how could he possibly remember players he last saw in 1941? Spring training for the Athletics was chaos, and once the bell rang for the regular season the A's were promptly buried in the AL standings. They finished the year dead last, again, with a 49–105 record.

Newsom's $20,000 contract in 1945 was one of the top war-time salaries in baseball, and with some effort he was able to convince Mack to pay him another $20,000 for the

1946 season. Mack felt uneasy about the outlay, for no matter how you sliced it statistically Newsom had lost 20 games and the A's had finished in last place. Haggling with Mack over the contract was equally unpleasant for Newsom. He was genuinely fond of Mack but was miffed that Mack's memory bank seemed to include every single one of Newsom's 20 losses but nary a one of his eight wins, or the many times a Newsom appearance lured extra fans to the ballpark. Nor were Newsom's spirits lifted that spring when he beheld yet another awful A's team in the offing.

Once the season began, Newsom pitched well enough in ten starts for Philadelphia, managing to win three of them, but it was clear the 1946 A's were yet another lost cause. After 20 years of pitching professionally, Newsom had endured a sufficient helping of lost causes. He also tracked attendance figures religiously and noticed that attendance was booming all over the majors. The owners had to be raking in big profits, and sharing the sugar with their employees seemed a small enough favor. On the other side of the labor-management equation, Mack was increasingly wary of Newsom's frequent requests for advances on his salary. Mack finally made sure a witness—usually Earle Bruckner—was present whenever he and Newsom talked money. The old man's memory may be fading, but he still had enough horse sense to know that Newsom was out for all he could get, any way he could get it.

Money matters came to a head in early June. Newsom entered Mack's office and asked for yet another advance. Mack said no. Newsom insisted he needed an extra $1,000 immediately. Mack still said no. The talk grew heated, as heated as things ever got with the soft-spoken Mack.

Finally, an angry Newsom asked if he could use Mack's phone. Mack consented. Newsom called Clark Griffith, long distance, in Washington, D.C. "Griff? Y'all need a pitcher? Wire me $1,000 and I'm all yours."[39] Mack, stunned by the gall of Newsom, agreed to release him so he could accept Griffith's $1,000 and go play for the Senators. Thus, Newsom became quite likely the first self-engineered free agent in major league history. In fact, he managed to finagle a $7,500 "signing bonus" in addition to an agreement from Griffith to pay the remaining $15,000 on his $20,000 contract. And he was to receive an additional $7,500 bonus on January 1, assuming he was alive and still on the Senators' roster on that date.[40]

The deal was remarkable for the time, more so because Newsom negotiated it all on his own. That it went virtually unpublicized wasn't surprising—Griffith had no reason to let anyone else know about the bonus, and Newsom certainly wanted to keep the information from his ex-wife, who was still seeking an increase in child support payments. But it was history-making in its way and gave other team owners pause.

Another legacy of Newsom's 1946 stint with the A's was a favorite story of Joe DiMaggio's. "The Yankee Clipper"—not known for a keen sense of humor—used this story numerous times over the years in after-dinner speeches. In reality, it never happened, or never happened quite the way DiMaggio told it. While it was true that he hit Newsom well, there is no evidence Joltin' Joe ever hit two home runs in a game against him, even in spring training.

In any event, in DiMaggio's version of events he was facing Newsom in a game at Shibe Park, placing the incident in 1946 when DiMaggio returned from the service. Supposedly, Newsom threw DiMaggio a high fastball and DiMaggio hit it into the left field stands. This provoked Connie Mack, who lectured Newsom after the inning because Mack had given specific instructions not to give DiMaggio high fastballs. "Throw him a low curve," Mack insisted. So Newsom did just that the next time DiMaggio was at bat, and DiMaggio hit it onto the roof of the left field stands.

According to DiMaggio, as he was rounding the bases Newsom walked over in the vicinity of the A's dugout and yelled, "Oh Mr. Mack! I do believe he hit your curveball a helluva lot farther than he hit my fastball!"[41]

But Newsom's days with Mr. Mack were now over. He was headed to Washington for his fourth stint with the Senators. He pitched well for them, going 11–8 in 24 appearances the rest of the 1946 season. Stimulated by the renewed presence of No. 00 in a Senators uniform, attendance jumped from 653,000 in 1945 to over a million in 1946. It also helped that the war was over and military personnel and Pentagon workers had nothing better to do than to watch baseball. Certainly, the Senators themselves, other than Newsom, weren't exactly world-beaters, finishing 76–78 under the guidance of Ossie Bluege.

The highlight of the 1946 season for Newsom occurred on September 6. The Red Sox, en route to the pennant, came to D.C. to face the struggling Senators. Newsom got the pitching nod and turned in a gem, limiting the powerful Boston attack to ten hits in a route-going, 3–2 victory in 11 innings. As a sign of pitching maturity, he did not strike out a single batter, but used his off-speed pitches to induce the Bosox into 22 ground ball outs.[42]

Afterward, he lectured Sox star Ted Williams on giving the fans proper respect. Williams at first was unreceptive and unrepentant. "Name me somebody who's been helped by this popularity stuff," Williams said (minus the expletives). "Brother, you're looking at one right now," Newsom reportedly replied. "I had losing years last year and the year before but I got raises both times. Why? Because the crowd gets a kick out of me. They laugh, they boo and they cheer. I just take it all in stride. If you only tip your hat to the customers and stop cussing them back there's no telling how great and popular you'd be."

For the season, combining his Philadelphia and Washington numbers Newsom had a very deceiving 14–13 record, but an excellent 2.93 earned run average. He completed 17 of his 31 starts, including three shutouts. It certainly represented pretty good pitching for a 39-year-old. "He could drive you crazy," Bluege told author Donald Honig, "but he was harmless and lovable and a good pitcher.... When he was out there, he had the heart of a lion."[43]

Bluege recalled a game in 1946 when Newsom was pitching on a hot day in D.C., and the home plate umpire was the easy-going Cal Hubbard. Newsom was pitching well, but bitching even better. Finally, Hubbard felt old friend Newsom had crossed the line between constructive criticism and showing Hubbard up. Hubbard called Bluege out to home plate and told him that Newsom would be thrown out of the game unless Bluege could shut him up.

So Bluege rushed out to the mound in an attempt to placate Newsom, for a tired, angry Newsom was still better than any relief pitcher the Senators had available. Unfortunately, Bluege made the mistake of agreeing with Hubbard's verdict that the previous pitch was a ball. So Newsom began jawing at him. Once that discussion reached fever pitch, Hubbard had to rush out to the mound and break it up. Newsom, by this time far angrier at his own manager than Hubbard, settled down and completed the game, a victory for the Senators.⁴⁴

For Newsom, optimism was still the mantra. On the eve of the 1946 season, he announced his own five-year plan. "I'll pitch five more years in the majors, get 250 wins, and then retire and wait for the Hall of Fame to call," Newsom said. "Ol' Bobo's got a lot of life left in him. I'm not gonna quit just when I've got my second wind."⁴⁵

Newsom proved an inaccurate prophet, although he would look back on his failure to accomplish the 250 wins (and make the Hall of Fame) by citing the always-present circumstances beyond his control.

The 1946 season ended on yet another financial high note for Newsom. In September, he was asked to join Bob Feller's All-Stars for an upcoming cross-country barnstorming tour against the Satchel Paige All-Stars. Feller even gave him a $750 advance. There is no question the tour was a windfall for the players who participated—most cleared over $3,000—and an absolute bonanza for Feller, who reportedly netted $80,000. But it was Newsom who made the easy money.

Shortly before the tour was to embark that October, Newsom discovered all travel was going to be done by plane. He also discovered that he would be playing a discordant second fiddle to both Feller and Paige. He hated to fly and hated the notion of being a supernumerary. He also hated the idea of giving back the $750. The solution was pure Bobo. He went to Clark Griffith and told the Senators owner his off-season travel

A meet-and-greet with President Harry S Truman prior to the 1947 season opener at Griffith Stadium in Washington, D.C. On this occasion, Newsom was opposed by Allie Reynolds of the Yankees, right, with Reynolds and the Yanks prevailing by a 7–0 score. The smiles in the crowd were generated by a Newsom ad lib addressed at Truman: "Oh, you're the new Bobo around here" (the Ray Medeiros collection, used by permission).

plans. Griffith laid down the law and forbade him to go. He countered by saying not going would cost him $750. Griffith agreed to pay him $750 to not go. Newsom pocketed that check, and Feller's check, figuring it was up to Griffith to discover the subterfuge and up to Feller to find a way to get his money back. Feller, busy with details of the trip, never bothered. So, for doing absolute nothing, Newsom came away with $1,500.[46]

Newsom began the 1947 season with the Senators in familiar territory: embroiled in a contract dispute. He had quickly gone through the $7,500 January bonus and wanted a raise. Instead, Clark Griffith asked him to take a pay cut, to $18,000. Apparently, in addition to the bonus, the "Old Fox" had finally gotten around to adding up Newsom's advances and "loans" over the years and realized it would take Newsom until the millennium to pay him back. By this time, he may have also discovered the flim-flam with Feller.

Newsom finally signed, only because Griffith agreed to shop him around to contending teams if the Nats failed to gel. Newsom's baseball radar had quickly detected that Ossie Bluege was managing yet another sorry Senators team, and the verbal agreement with Griffith seemed to bode well for a bigger payday come the summer.

Newsom was given the honor of starting the season opener at Griffith Stadium, and gave President Harry Truman a kick with his witty comments and unsolicited political advice in the pre-game ceremonies. But there was no Newsom magic once he took the mound. The Yankees beat him, 7–0.

After that opening-day loss, Newsom never seemed to get on track. He completed only one of his 13 starts and was increasingly bothered by aches, pains and muscle strains that kept him sidelined for days at a time. By July, he held a 4–6 record in 14 games as the Senators hovered near the AL cellar. After two decades of pitching for subpar teams, Newsom may have been experiencing something akin to burn-out. Frank Mancuso, a catcher on the Senators, said,

> [Newsom] would pitch three and four innings, and then just run out of gas. When that happened, he would argue with the umpires even more than usual, fiddle around out on the mound, talk to himself. With Bobo, it was mainly a question of focus. If he was focused, he was very, very good. If he was off the beam, for whatever reason, it was gonna be a long day at the ballpark.[47]

In retrospect, probably Newsom's chief contribution to the 1946–1947 Senators was working with a young right-hander from Florida named Early Wynn. Wynn was traded to Cleveland after the 1948 season, and there Indians manager Al Lopez and pitching coach Mel Harder helped revive his career. However, many in baseball also credited Newsom with having a strong influence on Wynn. Certainly, of all the big league pitchers in the 1950s, Wynn's pitching style bore the closest resemblance to Newsom's.[48]

While the 1947 Senators were floundering, the Yankees, Red Sox, Indians and Tigers were locked in what shaped up to be a heated pennant race. All four teams needed extra pitching help and Newsom, even at age 40, was clearly the best veteran pitcher available.

Trade rumors were rampant when Newsom took the mound for the Senators in the first game of a doubleheader on Sunday, July 6, before 30,000 fans at Fenway Park in Boston. The day was already a disaster for him. He had begged Griffith to release him so he could cut his own deal with the teams competing for his services. Griffith was having none of that and told Newsom he would go where Griffith sent him. It was the biggest blowup in the pair's rocky relationship, and Newsom was in a rebellious mood as the game began.

Knowing this was likely his swan song as a Senator, Newsom decided to use a softball windup and delivery with Ted Williams at bat in the first inning. Manager Bluege had made the comment that the way Williams was hitting, his pitchers might just as well throw underhand. So Bobo obliged.

Newsom lined himself up on the mound and launched into a windmill-style softball delivery. Williams promptly called time and stepped out of the box. The two then repeated this dance, as the Hub City fans reacted with hoots, whistles and cheers. Again, Newsom went into an elaborate softball-style windup. By this time, Williams was laughing so hard that he took the pitch, a called strike.[49]

The fandango ended when Boston manager Joe Cronin barked from the dugout to cut the comedy. Newsom shrugged his shoulders and went back to his conventional delivery. Williams stopped laughing long enough to whack the next pitch for a long out to center field. After that, the afternoon turned bleak for Newsom, for the Senators played one of their worst games of the year. They committed six errors. They were guilty of a series of base-running gaffes. Three times they loaded the bases with nobody out, and all three times they failed to score. Veteran Buddy Lewis was victimized by the hidden ball trick. Veteran catcher Rick Ferrell made a wild throw to second base. Veteran Stan Spence made a wild throw to third base. And Newsom was having trouble hitting the strike zone, walking six Red Sox batters.

Bluege yanked him from the game after five innings. Boston led, 4–2, and Newsom, angry to start with, was now as hot as the weather.

Entering the clubhouse, he ripped off his jersey top, sending buttons flying. He gave the Anglo-Saxon language a workout, describing to no one in particular just how bad his teammates were, how bad the plate umpire was, and exactly where Clark Griffith could stick both Newsom's suddenly buttonless uniform and cut-rate contract.

"Bobo Blows His Balding Top Over Nats' Messy Support" read the headline in the next morning's *Washington Post*. Meanwhile, Boston and New York papers were reporting that Newsom had already been sold—to the New York Yankees.[50]

Newsom's days as a Senator were over, for the time being at least.

Eleven

New York to Hartsville (1947–1948)

If avowed Bobo basher Joe McCarthy had still been managing the Yankees, it's safe to say Louis Norman Newsom would have never appeared in pinstripes. However, in 1947 the new Yankees manager was Bucky Harris, and Harris wasn't in a position to dictate to the front office regarding personnel moves. Harris, while not exactly delighted to see Newsom join the Bronx Bombers, held no illusions; he knew he was getting an unsecured cannon, but one that could still fire some mean munitions.

New York easily won the bidding war for Newsom. He remained persona non grata with Joe Cronin in Boston, Lou Boudreau and the front office in Cleveland, and the entire Briggs family in Detroit. Yankees owner Larry MacPhail had no such reservations and claimed Newsom off the waiver wire from Washington. The reported price was $10,000; off the record, Clark Griffith crowed that it was actually $25,000. Be it $10,000 or $25,000, MacPhail—a Newsom fancier—was glad to pay it.[1]

Newsom had no objections to joining New York. His big beef was that a Griffith, not a Newsom, got to pocket the under-the-table windfall. He tried to talk Griffith into simply releasing him so he could become a free agent and cut his own deal, as had happened the previous year. "The Old Fox" was having none of that.

"Griffith didn't do right by me," Newsom complained to Shirley Povich of the *Washington Post*. "I didn't cost him one penny, and now he sells me. That's what I call a raw deal."

Despite Newsom's dubious accounting methods, he did have a point. With no signing bonus in the offing, Newsom demanded relocation and travel expenses for the move, which neither team offered. He also wanted assurances that the Yankees would continue to allow Kay to accompany her husband on road trips. The Yanks, explaining that even the great DiMaggio didn't get that perk, refused. It was a sign of things to come in the Big Apple.

The Yankees team that Newsom was joining, on July 11, was a far cry from the powerhouses that had dominated baseball from 1936 to 1943. This Yankees team entered the season as a decided underdog in the American League pennant chase. Its top pitcher, veteran Spud Chandler, was coming off a 20-win season. However, Chandler had long endured bone chips in his right elbow and by spring training of 1947 throwing even one pitch was agony. Chandler appeared in only 17 games for the Yankees in 1947, posting a 9–5 record in what turned out to be his final year in the majors. Chandler won his ninth game on July 4, beating Washington, 7–3. He made one more start, on July 10, but was unable to get out of the third inning. After that, Chandler was limited to one token appearance in the World Series, his final pitching appearance in pro ball. Fortunately for the Yankees, Allie Reynolds, acquired in the off-season from Cleveland, picked up the mantle of staff ace. Reynolds shut out Washington, and Newsom, in the D.C season opener and finished with a 19–8 win-loss record.

After Reynolds, Harris struggled to assemble a reliable starting rotation. Rookie Frank "Spec" Shea started strong, came down with a tender arm in mid-season and missed several starts, but still managed to post a 14–5 record. Rookie Vic Raschi, up from the minors in mid-season and just learning the ropes at the big league level, posted a 7–2 record in 15 games. Hard-throwing Floyd Bevens, who won 16 games in 1946, was erratic at best in 1947. Struggling with his control all year long, Bevens finished with a 7–13 record in what proved to be his last hurrah in the big leagues. After Chandler, Reynolds, Shea, Raschi and Bevens, Harris tried youngsters Karl Drews, Don Johnson and Butch Wensloff as spot starters, but they were all inconsistent. Harris resorted to giving Joe Page a couple of starts, but Page was clearly more effective pitching in relief. Thus, Newsom filled a vital role as the fifth starter in the Yankees' rotation.[2]

The games Newsom started and innings he pitched freed up Page for bullpen duty only; Page went on to have a banner season. Newsom's work also preserved the tender young arms of Raschi and Shea. And, it must be said, his acquisition gave the Yankees a huge psychological lift. In fact, his presence on the 1947 Yankees foreshadowed Satchel Paige's role on the pennant-winning 1948 Cleveland Indians. Newsom and Paige not only pitched well, but their quote-worthy presence in the clubhouse took much of the media pressure off their teammates.[3]

Newsom joined the Yankees while they were on a winning streak and immediately contributed to prolonging the streak. Inserted in Chandler's spot in the starting rotation, he pitched New York to a 10–3 victory over Chicago on July 13, his 200th win in the major leagues. Raschi followed with a victory in the second game of the doubleheader, the sweep representing the Yankees' 13th and 14th triumphs in a row.

Make-ups of early-season rainouts forced the Yanks to play seven doubleheaders in 19 days. Despite that, New York kept winning. In the doubleheader of July 17, Newsom beat Cleveland 3–1 in the opener and Raschi won the nightcap, 7–2. Those represented the Bronx Bombers' 18th and 19th victories in a row—a team record. Newsom, acquired at the insistence of MacPhail, had already paid dividends. Raschi, promoted at the insistence of general manager George Weiss, had done likewise.

While the team's winning streak was stopped the next day, Newsom kept on winning. He won his first four decisions with the Yanks, enabling New York to pull away from the pack. He capped his 5-game winning streak on August 16 by shutting out the Red Sox, 1–0. By that time, the Yanks had taken a 13 ½ game lead in the AL standings.[4]

The Yankees finished at 97–57, 12 games ahead of second-place Detroit. Newsom cooled off after his hot start but still finished with a 7–5 record with the Yanks and an excellent 2.80 earned run average in 115 ⅔ innings.

"That old guy could still pitch," said outfielder Tommy Henrich, one of the corps of veterans on the 1947 team along with Joe DiMaggio, Phil Rizzuto, Johnny Lindell,

George "Snuffy" Stirnweiss and Charlie Keller. "He didn't have that great fastball anymore, but he really knew how to move the ball around, keep the hitters off-balance and pitch inside, which some guys never get the hang of doing."[5]

Even so, Newsom never quite clicked with his new teammates and never gained the full confidence of manager Harris. "He just didn't fit in," Henrich said. "Being a Yankee is a 24-hour deal. There's a certain way to dress, a certain way to conduct yourself, a certain way to deal with the press. Newsom always seemed out of place. To be honest, a lot of the guys on the team didn't care for him."

Henrich's biggest worry was how Newsom's presence would affect the team's star reliever, Joe Page. Page had the reputation of being a real night owl and he certainly didn't need Newsom encouraging that habit. According to Henrich, the Yanks could have had a 6 a.m. curfew and Page still would have missed it. However, Page survived the season relatively healthy and in one piece and had a sensational World Series Game Seven to lock up the championship.[6]

Henrich's concerns were well-founded. Like Page, Newsom relished the night life and, after nearly 20 years of visiting the city, he knew his way around town. As always, he hated to drink and party alone. If Page wasn't available, there were always friends and hangers-on. That summer, Newsom purchased a round-trip train ticket and arranged to have Edgar "Blue" Sommer, an old friend from Hartsville, come north to visit New York. Sommer, like Newsom a large man, had never been to a city larger than Darlington. He was also naïve to a remarkable degree, described as "just a good ol' hillbilly" by those who knew him. So Newsom made sure to meet Sommer on a Friday afternoon at Grand Central Station and escort him to his hotel. First things first; "Blue" clearly needed appropriate attire for New York City. According to Hartsville acquaintance Bob Shirley, Sommer was wearing a sports coat "that looked like a table cloth at a picnic." After a quick visit to the haberdasher and check-in at the swanky hotel in Manhattan where Newsom was staying, Bobo and Blue were off to take a big bite out of the Big Apple.[7]

All night Friday, into the wee hours of Saturday morning, the two partied, eating, drinking and taking in floor shows at NYC nightclubs. Sommer had brought a nest-egg of $127 from Hartsville, but Newsom wouldn't hear of his good buddy from down home paying for anything. The two staggered back to the hotel at four in the morning, but were up by noon on Saturday to have a light lunch and begin a new cycle of sight-seeing. Fortunately for the Yankees and the Newsom-Sommer tag team, Newsom wasn't scheduled to pitch that day.

Saturday night saw more of the same as they cut a wide swath through all the boroughs. Newsom seemed to know dozens of watering holes and thousands of people, and after 20 or 30 minutes at each nightspot he bounced up, paid for the food and beverages, left a generous tip and moved on.

Sunday morning, a very bleary-eyed Bobo and Blue managed to struggle up, get dressed and call a cab to take Sommer to Grand Central Station for his train trip home to Hartsville. At the station, Newsom made sure Sommer hadn't forgotten his ticket and knew the exact spot to wait for the train. At the last minute, he remembered the $127 and wanted to make sure Blue hadn't spent it all in New York.

"Blue, y'all got any of that $127 left to buy food on the train?" Newsom asked.

"You bet, Buck," replied Sommer. "I got me over $300!"

"$300? How did you get that?"

"Y'all know all those places we went? Well, I guess you weren't thinkin' too good, because, every time, damned if you wouldn't leave a ten-dollar bill when we left. So, every time, I would jest scoot back and pick up that ten and put down a one. So I now got me over $300." Newsom was not amused by this bit of backwoods wisdom, figuring he was now branded as a cheapskate at the majority of New York's posh establishments.

Newsom's public comments, boasting about himself and his new ballclub, became a bit much for general manager George Weiss. Weiss finally called him into his office and, basically, told him to shut up. Newsom tried it for a couple of days, explaining to the media that they could call him "Greta Garbo" Newsom from now on, after the tight-lipped actress.[8] But the New York press can be very persuasive, and it wasn't long before he was again holding court on topics ranging from sacrifice bunts to the United Nations.

A casual comment by Newsom about Joe DiMaggio, to the effect that he was great but nowhere near as great as he used to be (a not altogether false statement), came out in the press as Newsom claiming the Yankee Clipper was all washed up. DiMaggio, sensitive about his diminished talents to begin with, was livid and, according to Henrich, never spoke to Newsom thereafter.[9]

Another Newsom comment must have set ears burning in the Yankees' front office. Responding to the breaking of major league baseball's so-called color line that year with the Dodgers signing Jackie Robinson and the Indians signing Larry Doby, Newsom proclaimed that the Yankees should sign his old buddy, Satchel Paige. The notion of the iconoclastic Newsom and Paige on the same pitching staff was not a pleasing one to George Weiss.[10]

A game at Comiskey Park in Chicago in August also tempered his teammates' enthusiasm for having Newsom around. Newsom was pitching against Chicago's Joe Haynes, an old friend from their days in Washington (and related to Clark Griffith by marriage). In his first at-bat, Newsom hit a little nubber right back to Haynes. It was a hot day, and Newsom decided against running to first. Instead, he opted to pull his old trick of heading to the dugout, on the first base side of the field, and hoping Haynes would somehow forget about him. Haynes would have none of that and just stood on the pitchers' mound holding the ball. From their stationary positions, Newsom made a couple of feints toward first base, Haynes made a couple of motions as though he might throw to first, but neither man followed through on these intentions. Newsom went into the dugout, waited until he thought Haynes' attention span might have waned, and then made a mad dash out of the dugout toward first base. The sight of Newsom, all 230 pounds of him, rumbling toward first was impossible to miss and Haynes finally threw him out. To Newsom (and, presumably, Haynes) it was all in fun, just a little cat-and-mouse game to liven things up. However, such shenanigans were unthinkable on the Yankees, even under Bucky Harris, and were not well received by the team's veterans. It did not help matters that Newsom and the Yanks lost the game.[11]

As a postscript, Newsom's tendency to try this ruse helped spur a change in the baseball rule book. In the 1950s, the rule was altered to read that once the batter/runner placed one foot in the dugout he was automatically out and the play was dead.

By September, Newsom's effectiveness gradually tapered off. Bobo beat Boston, and old nemesis Joe Cronin, 11–2 on September 3 at Fenway Park to virtually lock up the pennant for the Yanks. Bobo made three more starts that month, winning one and losing two.

With the pennant secured, Harris, perhaps encouraged by George Weiss, decided he would give the team's younger pitchers several starts in September. That affected Newsom adversely, since he thrived on work and when he wasn't working he couldn't be bothered to stay in condition. Henrich estimated that Bobo put on about 25 pounds over the last two months of the season, and the weight gain is quite obvious in photos taken at the start of the World Series.[12]

Late in the season, after the Yankees had clinched the pennant, the players held a team meeting to decide how to divide their World Series shares. The older Yankees didn't lack for experience dividing up the pot. Henrich and DiMaggio, the two Yanks with the most service time, ran the meeting. Henrich read a list of several players who had joined the club during the season and said the team needed to decide whether to give them a full share or not.

"I read this list and Joe pipes up, 'give 'em a half-share.' And I'm looking at Bobo and, for once, he's struck dumb," Henrich said. After some negotiation, it was decided that Newsom would get a three-fourths share. Henrich tried to explain to him that it was actually a pretty good deal. For a guy who had gone from a last-place team where he wasn't going to get a dime, getting a check for around $3,000 wasn't anything to complain about.

Unfortunately, Newsom let the press know about not getting a full share, which put further distance between himself and his teammates and the organization. The action did nothing to increase his chances of staying with the team long-term.

After a September spent mainly on the bench, Newsom unexpectedly got the call from Harris to start Game Three of the World Series at Ebbets Field. Harris reasoned that Newsom's previous World Series experience and his dislike for his former team would be a sufficient recipe for success. But Newsom was knocked out of the game by the Dodgers in the second inning. As he hit the dugout on his way to the showers, Henrich and DiMaggio killed time in the outfield.

"Joe turns and says to me 'See, I told ya we shoulda given that bum a half-share,'" Henrich reported.[13]

Newsom's final moment in the sun in baseball's Fall Classic was indeed a sad one. Doubly so, because it is one of only a handful of games he ever pitched for which a full motion picture record still exists. Looking fat and older than his 40 years, Newsom allowed six runs on six hits and two walks. Down 6–0, the Yankees managed to battle back but never quite catch up, the Dodgers winning, 9–8.

Harris' choice for a starter in Game Four was equally questionable. He went with Floyd Bevens despite Bevens' struggles throughout the season. Bevens held the Dodgers without a hit until the final batter, but was wild and the Dodgers hit several of his pitches hard, but right at Yankees defenders. Finally, pinch-hitter Cookie Lavagetto drove a ball over Henrich's head and off the right-field wall, allowing the tying and winning runs to score.

Harris caught hell from the press (and many of his own players) for his choice of starters and for staying with Bevens for so long, no-hitter or not. Adding to the furor was the fact that he had ordered an intentional walk to Pete Reiser just prior to Lavagetto's double, thus putting the potential winning run on base.[14]

Fortunately for New York, rookie Spec Shea pitched the game of his life in Game Five and the Yankees were able to go back ahead in the Series, three games to two.

Newsom's final World Series appearance came in Game Six. The Dodgers, facing elimination, managed to knock out Yankees ace Allie Reynolds but still trailed by a run when the usually reliable Joe Page began the sixth inning. The Dodgers got to him for four runs before Newsom came out to finish the inning, but not before allowing a 2-run single by Pee Wee Reese that made it an 8–5 game. Brooklyn went on to win, 8–6, to tie the Series up.

Page, who reportedly stayed out all night drinking after the loss, somehow managed to recover for Game Seven. He came into the Series decider in the fifth inning and stopped the Dodgers cold on one hit over the last five innings.

"In those October shadows there at Yankee Stadium he was unhittable," Henrich said. "In fact, that may have been the most dominant performance by a pitcher I ever saw. Thank God for Joe Page, is all I can say."[15]

Another side of the wild and wooly 1947 World Series—the first Fall Classic to be televised by a network—was given by a member of the losing team, third baseman Spider Jorgensen.

> There was some sort of dispute between Branch Rickey and Larry MacPhail. As a result, we weren't allowed to take any batting practice at Yankee Stadium prior to the first game. Let me tell you, the ball was almost impossible to pick up there, what with the shadows and the smoke in the stadium. Those first two games, against those hard-throwing right-handers Shea and Reynolds, we were just helpless.[16]

Jorgensen and his teammates figured they would see another hard-throwing right-hander, Vic Raschi, in Game Three. Instead, they faced Newsom and quickly drove him to cover. "After facing Shea and Reynolds, it looked like Bobo was throwing beach balls up there." Jorgensen said.[17]

Newsom was not placated by the Yankees' triumph and took his beef about not getting a full World Series share to the organization's celebration party, held at NYC's Biltmore Hotel. In this report, he (a) took a swing at co-owner Del Webb; (b) took a swing at George Weiss; (c) made a pass at co-owner Dan Topping's wife; or (d) all of the above.[18]

Whether or not Newsom misbehaved, his conduct was of Boy Scout caliber compared to Larry MacPhail. MacPhail, ever the lone wolf, decided that he could no longer tolerate the troika of ownership or working with Weiss on personnel moves. Unable to get Webb and Topping to agree to fire Weiss, MacPhail used the victory celebration as a time to get roaring drunk, punch out a former employee, Joe McDonald, and make Weiss an ex-employee, firing him in a profanity-laced tirade right in front of Weiss' wife. MacPhail then took on Topping, their shouting match ending in fisticuffs. After that, MacPhail was done. He stormed out of the party and, as things turned out, out of baseball. Webb and Topping quickly did two things. First, they unfired Weiss. Then they summoned their lawyers and worked out a deal to buy out MacPhail's share in the Yankees, for a reported $2 million. By 6 p.m. the next day, MacPhail had both sobered up and signed the papers. Few, if any, team owners ever had a more public or toxic departure.[19]

Whatever Newsom did or did not do at the victory party probably didn't make much difference. MacPhail, his protector and booster, was gone, and Newsom was now on borrowed time with the Yanks. Weiss spent the winter trying to find another team to purchase Newsom's contract, hoping to recoup at least some of the money MacPhail had paid to get him. Failing that, Weiss simply fell back on not extending Newsom a contract for the 1948 season. Newsom was officially, and quietly, released in February. "He looks too fat in pinstripes" was Weiss' reported rationale for cutting him adrift.[20]

There is also the oft-repeated report that Newsom ordered his World Series ring three-quarters size: "That's my worth in this town," he supposedly said. In reality, he received the same World Series ring as the other Yankees and wore it often during his final years, along with his American League championship ring from the 1940 Detroit Tigers. And the wedding ring Kay had given him, of course.[21]

Clearly, Newsom had issues with manager Harris and general manager Weiss (as well as Yankees co-owners Topping and Del Webb). Still, his departure from the Yanks boiled down to rotten luck and a repeat of what had befallen him in Brooklyn in 1943. Since MacPhail had been the man in charge of baseball operations, and since despite Newsom's peccadilloes MacPhail remained a loyal fan, if MacPhail held onto his ownership share, Newsom would have held onto his job.

That winter, more important than any World Series ring was the fact that Newsom was suddenly unemployed. Adding up his prospects in the off-season proved discouraging. While the restaurant in Hartsville bearing his name was still in business, it wasn't bringing in much in the way of revenue to Newsom or any of the other investors. Even the addition of carhops on roller skates failed to generate much interest among Hartsville clientele, America's obsession with fast food being a decade or two in the future. Newsom's Diamond Star Grill gave him a place to hang out, entertain friends and get behind the counter to hone his culinary skills, but it was not sufficiently exciting or profitable for him to concentrate all of his considerable energies on.[22]

Newsom's playing career was stymied by his age, his now obviously declining skills, his salary demands and—most effectively—his temperament. Even Clark Griffith refused to offer him a contract for 1948, although Griffith did extend the courtesy of inviting him to work out with the Senators in Orlando during spring training. But that wasn't good enough for Newsom. He spent that winter writing and calling major league general managers, to no avail. He also ramped up his efforts to land a job in the entertainment industry, contacting radio stations with a concept for a sports talk show. Sadly, the talk show never came to fruition; it might well have been his natural métier.

"There was a point there in the winter of 1947 where I read that Newsom was available," said Jack Fournier, head scout for the St. Louis Browns. "I had seen him pitch with the Yankees and thought he still had enough left to help us. So I said to [Browns president] DeWitt, 'Bill, maybe we ought to offer this Newsom a contract.' DeWitt hit the roof. 'I'll pitch for this God-damned team before I sign that son of a bitch again!'"[23]

Late in spring training of 1948, Newsom finally got an offer. It was from the New York Giants, who at the time were struggling for attendance and attention in a town where the World Champion Yankees and exciting young Dodgers dominated newspaper coverage. The Giants contract called for $10,000, half the amount Newsom had set as his "minimum wage." But it was the only offer he had on the table, and he jumped at it. Besides, he was optimistic that the Giants might be able to break through and win the National League pennant. He felt sure he could get along with easy-going Giants manager Mel Ott, the "nice guy" in Leo Durocher's famous "nice guys finish last" theory.

Reporting to the Giants on April 11, just before the start of the season, Newsom was used only twice by Ott in the first few weeks of the season. He wasn't in tip-top shape, and Ott was trying to groom several young pitchers as starters. One of the few pluses for Newsom was that he was not the oldest pitcher on the staff; veteran left-hander Thornton Lee was one year older, at 41. Reliever Joe Beggs, at age 37, was almost their equal.[24] Still, both Newsom and Lee were older than their manager, and their presence generated a lot of "broken-down old Giants" remarks in the media and even a wisecrack by Durocher during an appearance on the Fred Allen radio show: "The only people I know older than Jack Benny are pitching for the Giants."[25]

Newsom was limited to four starts with the Giants. He went seven innings in his first start on April 25, locked in a 1–1 duel with Boston Braves ace Johnny Sain. Unfortunately, Newsom pulled a groin muscle running the bases in the eighth inning and was unable to continue. As things unfolded, that was his only moment of glory with the Giants. He failed to get past the second inning in his other three starts. His three decisions as a starter were losses. Newsom missed over two weeks of action in May when he aggravated the groin pull. When he came back, Ott relegated him to the bullpen and then forgot about him. Newsom was used only seven times in relief, losing one of those games. In his third-to-last appearance with the Giants, on June 10 at Wrigley Field in Chicago, he came on in the seventh inning of a 4–4 tie and promptly gave up two runs, enough for the Cubs to post a 6–4 victory.

Newsom repeatedly told Ott, and the media, that his pitching would get hot once the weather did but by now that was just one more boast among many. "What have you done for me lately" was the motto of baseball general managers during Newsom's time. In his case with the Giants, he hadn't done much.

Newsom's final outing, on June 18, was ignominious. On a sleepy Friday afternoon at the Polo Grounds, the Giants were getting hammered by the Cardinals, 10–0. In the ultimate mop-up assignment, Newsom was summoned from the bullpen to relieve Thornton Lee in the sixth inning. Bobo finished out the top of the inning, allowing a home run to Stan Musial, was pinch-hit for in the bottom of the inning, and St. Louis went on to post a 12–8 victory. It was the fifth loss in a row for the Giants, who saw their season record dip to 27–25. After the game, the Giants' front office, seeing another season rapidly going down the drain, decided scapegoating was in order and released both Newsom and Lee.

Clem Dreisewerd, who replaced Newsom on the Giants roster, recalled the scenario.

> [Ott] had a decent ballclub there in New York but was having some real disciplinary problems, especially with the older guys. So the management ordered him to clean house and get rid of these old coots. He calls me and asks if I would be interested in joining the team, I was pitching for the Browns at the time so I said, "Hell yes! Work out a deal and I'll be glad to pitch for you."

Unfortunately for Dreisewerd, he'd only been with the Giants a couple of weeks when Ott was fired on July 17. Since discipline seemed to be lacking on the team, Giants management decided to hire the toughest disciplinarian available, and that was Leo Durocher.

"Naturally, Durocher knew Ott was the guy who brought me in there, so my goose is cooked," Dreisewerd said. "I lasted a few days under Durocher and then was sent down to Minneapolis. Still, that was two weeks longer than Newsom would have lasted. Everybody knew that Durocher and Newsom absolutely hated each other."[26]

Attempting to offset the news of Newsom's release—sure to touch off criticism among those journalists who enjoyed having baseball's Bartlett around—the Giants announced on the same day a plan to remodel the Polo Grounds and to increase the number of parking spaces around the aging stadium.

"It's the first time I was ever cut off a roster to make room for a parking lot," Newsom told the New York press, falling back on his own egocentric logic. "I was too high-priced for 'em," he said, claiming he made $17,000 with the Giants although there is no evidence to verify that figure. "They weren't pitching me and they didn't want me warming the bench at that price."[27]

He also claimed he made sure the Giants paid him his 1948 salary in full, a claim that is probably correct given his negotiating skills and the Giants' desire to get him off the roster ASAP. Ironically, soon after Newsom was released in New York, old friend Satchel Paige finally made it to the major leagues, signing with the Cleveland Indians on July 7.

For Newsom, the only open road led back home to Hartsville. June 15, the roster lockdown date for major league teams, had come and gone, meaning Newsom was plum out of options. For the first time in over 20 years, he would spend the summer in South Carolina. For not the first or the last time, he needed money. A phone call to Dizzy Dean in St. Louis helped brighten his mood, Dean agreeing to show Newsom the ropes of doing radio play-by-play. Newsom spent a couple of weeks that September helping Dean on his broadcasts of Browns games, picking up a few hundred dollars and some valuable experience. The two men were too similar in style to work together, but contemporary reports suggest Newsom was certainly as glib in front of the mike as Dean. Unfortunately, no transcription discs or recordings of the broadcasts have survived, as is the case with much of the live radio baseball play-by-play of that era. Regardless, Newsom had officially thrown his hat into the ring for a job as a radio announcer.[28]

In Hartsville, Newsom spent most of his time driving around in a mammoth, baby blue Cadillac, his latest state-of-the-art vehicle. Hoot Gibson, who was frequently pressed into service as Newsom's chauffeur and chief mechanic, remembered that this Caddy was equipped with a trans-oceanic radio, air conditioning and a refrigerator, and was easily the most recognizable vehicle in town.[29] Newsom's athletic endeavors were limited to playing pool, although he made no money at it since by this time everybody in the county knew of his skills with the cue. Bob Shirley tells the story of Newsom driving the blue Caddy out to some tiny town, where a pool hall beckoned. Parking the gaudy car right in front of the building, Newsom said, "Do you think I can hustle some pool in here?" "Sometimes Bobo forgot he wasn't just another hick," Shirley reports.[30]

With nothing but time on his hands, Newsom was talked into driving a trio of Hartsville ministers to Darlington for a Lions Club meeting. Trapped behind the wheel in the Caddy with three men who made their living by talking, and passing judgment, he was soon made uncomfortable by their comments regarding his lack of church attendance. Unable to "unwrap a cuss word," he fell back on his last line of defense: flatulence. He then assisted the aroma by turning the car's heater on high. The three preachers made other arrangements for the return trip.[31]

Meanwhile, the town's semi-pro team—sponsored by the Sonoco paper company as in the days of Newsom's youth—was having a successful season. Newsom was persuaded to attend a couple of games, held at Hartsville High School's ballfield, where lights had been installed. It was suggested—perhaps by Newsom himself—that the team could use an experienced pitcher. Thus it was that Bobo Newsom, soon to be 41, signed on to play for his old ballclub on July 30.

"It may have seemed like a step down the ladder, a major leaguer playing on our town team, but it wasn't quite that way," said Skip Harrison, the former baseball coach at Hartsville High School. "Buck got quite a piece of change, around $2,000, to pitch for the team. Sonoco came up with the money. Of course, he was a real gate attraction. Besides, that league [the Palmetto League] was hot stuff, most of the players were ex-pros and there were also some pretty good college players thrown into the mix."[32]

With Newsom as its star pitcher, the Hartsville Sonoco team succeeded in making the playoffs. The first playoff game, against neighboring Sumter, was set for the night of September 9 at Hartsville High. Naturally, Newsom was going to pitch for Sonoco, and that news fired up the hometown fans.

"It's harder to pitch in this Palmetto League than it is in the big leagues," Newsom said in a pre-playoff quote that proved prophetic. "These boys down here will swing at anything." Bob Shirley said,

> That place was packed the night Buck pitched. There might have been 5,000 folks there, just about everybody in town. Whole truckloads of people drove in from the backwoods country, just to see ol' Buck pitch. Buck wore one of his old Senators uniforms for the game, they had a little pre-game presentation and he got a plaque from the Elks Club. Buck's wife Kay and a lot of his family were there. Buck was obviously enjoying every minute of it.
>
> Then the game starts and, damn, that other team hit everything Buck threw up there. He tried all his pitches and it didn't matter. They hit 'em. He lasted only a couple innings before he asked to come out. You talk about a sad time, that was it.[33]

It was the final indignity in a season filled with them. The Sonoco team's loss affected him for months afterward. Everyone, Newsom included, figured it was the last game he would pitch, anywhere. "I started my pitching career right here on this field," a humbled Newsom told a reporter from the *Hartsville Messenger* after the game against Sumter, "and I guess I ended it in the same place tonight. Looks like I just can't get 'em out anymore. If these country boys can knock me around like that, it's time for me to hang up my glove and spikes."[34]

Newsom's winter of 1948–1949 was one of discontent. Then came a letter from Clark Griffith, again inviting the Newsoms down to Orlando for a visit during spring training. No mention was made of a contract, or even that Newsom would be welcome to do anything other than play some catch, watch a few exhibition games and deal a few hands of pinochle with "The Old Fox." Still, it was all he needed to rekindle his baseball dreams.

Twelve

Chattanooga to Birmingham to Washington to Philadelphia (1949–1953)

Joe Engel owed Clark Griffith a ballplayer. Thus it was that, following a series of convoluted communications, Bobo Newsom became a member of a bargain-basement ensemble known as the Chattanooga Lookouts. It wasn't the major leagues, in fact it was barely pro baseball. But by the spring of 1949 Newsom didn't have the luxury of picking and choosing a place of employment.

After moping around Hartsville for a few weeks in the wake of the Palmetto League playoff debacle, Bobo had his spirits lifted by Mrs. Newsom. Kay encouraged him to write letters to major league teams, seeking either a player's contract or a job as a radio play-by-play announcer. Money was an issue; Newsom's restaurant wasn't making any (it closed its doors permanently in 1950 and was torn down in 1951).[1] The letter-writing campaign focused on a familiar victim: Clark Griffith. While Griffith did invite Mr. and Mrs. Newsom down to Orlando for a visit, he balked at putting Bobo back on his payroll since all evidence indicated Bobo could no longer get big league ballplayers out. That "The Old Fox" had shelled out about a quarter-million dollars to acquire Newsom's services and pay for his upkeep over the years no doubt spurred his sales resistance.

Newsom, in desperation, suggested that Griffith make him player-manager of the Senators' farm team in Chattanooga. There was no chance of that happening, but mention of the Lookouts did open a door. Or, from Griffith's standpoint, an escape hatch.

Griffith engineered a compromise, calling for Newsom to report to Chattanooga, a member of the Southern Association, and attempt to regain some semblance of his former pitching skills. The Lookouts were operated by longtime Griffith crony Joe Engel, who at that moment was in hot water since a player Engel sold Griffith turned up lame in spring training and had to be released. Thus, Engel owed Griffith a big favor, and the favor turned out to be to get Newsom away from the Senators for as long as humanly possible. In return for Newsom agreeing to go to the Lookouts, Griffith would pay him a yearly salary of $5,000—the current major league minimum—and Engel would pay an additional $5,000. It wasn't the greatest deal Newsom ever negotiated, representing as it did a 50 percent pay cut from what he had been making as recently as 1947. But it paid the bills and kept him in baseball.[2]

Engel was a free-wheeling buccaneer who reduced professional baseball to its base element—profit. He knew the presence of Bobo Newsom in a Lookouts uniform would bring out the fans, the only questions being how many would come out and how long they would keep coming.³ Taking the unpredictable Newsom on board was a gamble, but one worth taking. For Griffith's part of the deal, $5,000 was a cheap enough price to pay to get Newsom out of his rapidly thinning hair. For Newsom, the biggest selling point to the deal was once again pitching in the Southern Association. It was friendly turf for the South Carolina native and, at age 41, maybe it was best for him to get away from the bright lights of the big cities for a while. If he had to spend a few weeks in Chattanooga proving he could still throw a baseball, what harm was there in that?

However, it quickly became evident to Engel that Newsom was even more of a drawing card than envisioned. It also became quickly evident that the 1949 Lookouts, other than Newsom, were terrible. In the highly competitive Southern Association, the Lookouts were overmatched. The working agreement with the Senators didn't help, since the Senators lacked an abundance of talented players to share with Engel or anyone else. Engel wasn't going to spend big bucks signing good players when he could spend petty cash on bad players and still have fans pay to see them play. With Newsom pitch-

In what is obviously a staged photograph, Newsom and Chattanooga Lookouts owner Joe Engel "argue" over a contract in the spring of 1950. Newsom and Engel didn't need a press photographer, or a lawyer, to argue over money. In the end, after two seasons as Engel's "slave," Newsom had the last laugh (author's collection).

ing, Engel could "field a Class D team" and still draw big crowds, as he confided to longtime Chattanooga sportswriter Wirt Gammon, Sr.[4]

"[Engel] was the Barnum and Bailey of baseball," Calvin Griffith, who once worked for him, said. "Bill Veeck stole most of his ideas from Joe Engel. Nobody was his equal in coming up with gimmicks."[5]

Even more than P. T. Barnum or Veeck, Engel bore a remarkable resemblance to Newsom; two large, loud men who approached life as one long carnival. Engel, born in 1893 in Washington, D.C., began in baseball as a batboy for the Senators in 1907. He eventually talked his way onto the Senators' roster, as a left-handed pitcher. He was good enough to spend four seasons, 1912–1915, with the Senators but not good enough to sustain his playing career beyond 1920. Fortunately for his chances of future employment, he became friends with Senators manager Clark Griffith. When Griffith took over as Senators owner, Engel was one of his first hires, as chief scout and "go-fer." Engel's ability to find talent was keen; among those he recommended to Griffith were Bucky Harris, Joe Cronin, Buddy Lewis, Cecil Travis and a very young Buck Newsom, then pitching for the Macon Peaches.

When Griffith acquired controlling interest of the Chattanooga Lookouts in 1929, he put Engel in charge. There Engel remained until his death in 1969. He eventually became the principal owner of the Lookouts, and the ballpark was named in his honor. Like his mentor, Engel was unable to field competitive teams consistently. But he was able to keep the fans coming out to the ballpark, by shrewd use of public relations and some of the wildest stunts this side of a cut-rate flea circus.

As a result of Engel's personality, he and Newsom quickly found common ground. Both loved baseball, both loved money, both were loyal (more or less) to Clark Griffith and both were shameless self-promoters. Their frequent arguments, usually over finances, were more like family feuds. When asked about his unconventional contract with the Lookouts on the eve of the season opener in 1949, Newsom said it was a gentleman's agreement. Engel overheard and promptly shot back: "Can't be. There are no gentlemen involved here."[6]

Despite all that would happen in Chattanooga and with Engel over the course of the next two seasons, Newsom retained a certain fondness for the Lookouts owner. While Engel took advantage of Newsom in his hour of need, he did allow Newsom to be his own boss. Engel also put him to work doing public relations appearances for the team, and even some radio spots. These were things Newsom enjoyed doing, although how well the Chattanooga Rotarians received a middle-aged man called Bobo, decked out in a plaid sports jacket and a tie depicting a half-naked hula dancer, is certainly debatable.[7]

Without question, Chattanooga's baseball fans witnessed Bobo Newsom unfettered. With little at stake other than Engel's cut of the gate receipts, he could now go back to using his windmill windup, with double and triple pumps of his arms. He could throw underhand, sidearm, three-quarters or overhand. He could throw fastballs, sliders, curves, his blooper pitch and even a knuckleball or two. He could clown around on the mound, catching the catcher's return throw behind his back, juggling the rosin sack, and getting down on his hands and knees to groom the mound to his liking. And he could talk, to teammates, opposing batters, umpires and fans. While most of the time he behaved himself, there was always that chance he might launch into a tirade, or sulk, or pout and sit down on the mound right in the middle of an inning.

A remarkable thing happened in the course of Newsom's antics with the Lookouts. As the weather warmed up, so did his arm. All clowning and bragging aside, he could still throw a baseball. The relaxed atmosphere of pitching for a minor league team going nowhere enabled Newsom to slowly regain his skills.

"It was surprising how good he was," said George Myatt, his manager with the Lookouts in 1949. "Bobo's fastball still had a lot of movement on it. In fact, all his pitches moved a bit. He just never seemed to give the batter a good ball to hit."[8]

Of course, Newsom also knew that a rise from the ash pit that was the Chattanooga Lookouts would add luster to his resume. Given his nature, the clowning never stopped fully. Every game he pitched featured at least one bizarre incident. Typical was a game in Birmingham during which Newsom became increasingly unhappy over the plate umpire's strike zone. Finally, Newsom stormed off the mound and headed toward home plate. Teammates, fearing a fight, rushed to stop him. However, Newsom got to the umpire first, spun him around, grabbed the whisk broom out of his back pocket and proceeded to give home plate a thorough cleaning. When he finished, he presented the broom back to the ump as a king would present a sword to a knight. The startled ump accepted the broom—and Bobo's behavior—and the game resumed without further interruptions.[9]

For Joe Engel, who was initially reluctant to bear the burden—financial and otherwise—of Newsom, it turned out to be a sweet deal. Engel came to regard Newsom as his second-greatest gate attraction, behind only Jackie Mitchell.[10]

Mitchell happened to be a woman, actually a teenaged girl. Supposedly a protégé of former Dodgers great Dazzy Vance, Mitchell was signed by Engel in the spring of 1931. With much ballyhoo, Engel touted her talents and claimed he intended to pitch her in Southern Association games, creating a firestorm of controversy within the league that eventually reached all the way to the office of Commissioner Kenesaw Landis. However, before Landis managed to move in and quash Mitchell's career, she pitched in an exhibition game against the New York Yankees—of all teams—and struck out Babe Ruth and Lou Gehrig. Whether or not Ruth and Gehrig were playing "on the level" remains open to speculation, but Mitchell's appearance versus the Yankees hastened the sealing of her baseball fate. A couple of days after the Yankees-Lookouts game, Landis barred her from organized baseball. While Engel, undoubtedly, would have pitched her again—possibly even in an actual game—had he been allowed to, the escapade accomplished his primary goal of drumming up interest in the Lookouts.

Engel also frequently used the services of baseball clowns Nick Altrock, Al Schracht, Jackie Price and Max Patkin. When human entertainment was not available, or came at too steep a price, Engel resorted to the four-legged variety. Perhaps Engel's most famous, or infamous, stunt took place on Opening Day of the 1938 season, when he advertised a "wild elephant hunt" before the game. After a lengthy buildup, and the sound of fierce elephant trumpeting emitting from deep beneath the grandstands, the actual event—the "blow-off" in carny lingo—consisted of several men wearing baggy elephant suits being pursued by "big game hunters" wearing Frank Buck costumes and firing blanks from toy rifles. Fortunately, the good folk of Chattanooga were able to laugh at themselves for falling for the latest Engel fandango.[11]

Engel's Lookouts won the Southern Association and Dixie Series titles in 1932. They captured the SA title again in 1939, but by 1949 it was clear they were outgunned by the other seven teams in the league. Other than future major leaguer Willy Miranda, a great fielding, light-hitting shortstop, Engel's 1949 team lacked both talent and charisma. Thus, Newsom came along at exactly the right moment for Engel. Despite missing ten days in mid-season, Newsom had a banner campaign for a last-place team. He won 17 games, led Association pitchers in strikeouts with 141, completed 19 of his 33 starts and pitched 237 innings.[12] Along the way, he twice started both games of a doubleheader, pitched occasionally in relief, and was even used as a pinch-hitter, pinch-runner and third base coach. "About the only thing Bobo didn't do for Engel was sell peanuts," Newsom later said. "And he woulda had ol' Bobo doing that too, except he figured I'd eat up all the profits."[13]

Newsom made his Lookouts debut in an early April exhibition game against the parent Senators, pitching four effective innings. Asked afterward by a young sportswriter if he thought he was ready to help the Lookouts, Newsom replied, "Son, I've been ready for 20 years. They ain't got nuthin' to worry 'bout so long as Ol' Bobo's throwin' for 'um." Asked how many games he thought he could win for the Lookouts, the reporter received another reply in pure Newsom-ese: "Well, it's this way Bobo. Bobo's gonna win a passel of games for this here club and you can quote ol' Bobo as sayin' that, Bobo."[14]

The doubleheader double duty with the Lookouts warranted the attention of no less a sporting personage than New York columnist Red Smith, who devoted a full column to Newsom's latest accomplishments.[15] Attendance at games Newsom pitched, in Chattanooga and elsewhere around the circuit, zoomed. He quickly became the most popular player in the league and the most quoted. Despite a wire-to-wire last-place finish, Chattanooga home games drew over 155,000 paying customers in 1949. All in all, it was a very pleasing turn of events for Engel.

It would have been pleasing to Newsom as well, except for an unfortunate incident in July. He believed, with some justification, that his agreement with Griffith included a provision to be promoted to Washington as soon as there was an opening on the Senators' pitching staff. That event came to pass, and Griffith passed over Newsom for someone else. There may have also been a monetary element at work in the equation but, whatever the cause, Newsom jumped the Lookouts. He complained to the press that Griffith and Engel were in breach of both contract and etiquette. Griffith and Engel disagreed with this assessment and suspended him. The matter was ironed out over the course of a few days—Newsom probably needed the time off anyway—and Newsom resumed his duties for the Lookouts. The incident only added to his value as a gate attraction, and there remains speculation that he and Engel may have cooked the whole thing up for that reason. Ultimately, he wasn't promoted to the Senators that year. Not going up to Washington wasn't quite the tragedy Newsom made it out to be to the media, since the 1949 version of the Senators lost 104 games and finished dead last in the American League.[16]

The highlight of Newsom's season in the shadow of Lookout Mountain came on August 9. Chattanooga had a twilight doubleheader scheduled with Little Rock, and Engel convinced Newsom to pitch both games. Newsom, two days shy of his 42th birthday, agreed, on the condition that the other eight Lookouts in the starting lineup also play both games. By this point, he knew enough about the Lookouts' roster to know just how awful the team's reserves were. Braving the heat and humidity and porous Chattanooga defense, he hurled his team to a 10–6 victory in the seven-inning opener. After a quick shower, a change of uniform and some liquid refreshment, Newsom went right back out and went the distance in the nine-inning nightcap, winning this one, 9–6. He was carried off the field on the shoulders of his teammates, to an ovation from Lookouts fans. Engel awarded him with a new suit for the performance, a notable occurrence since Engel rarely spent his own money on anything.[17]

Over the winter, Newsom discovered the contract with "Gentleman Joe" obligated him to another year in Chattanooga. Thus was added yet another measure of discontent to the Newsom-Engel-Griffith melange a trois. In fairness to Engel, organized baseball was changing rapidly in the post–World War II era. The days of the renegade operator were just about over, and standardized contracts for all minor leaguers were now being strictly enforced. Like their major league counterparts, the minor league contracts included the dreaded reserve clause. If a major league team wanted Newsom, it was going to have to go through Engel to get him.

While Newsom pondered his baseball future, another sport came calling. As a result of his contacts in Detroit, in the winter of 1949–1950 he served as a referee for televised pro wrestling matches at the Detroit Arena. Originally, the promoter wanted him actually to wrestle, but Kay quickly vetoed that plan. Instead, he got to clown around in the ring with little or no danger to his large torso.

"Easiest job I ever had," Bobo told an associate. "All I have to do is count to three."[18]

A letter from the office of the Baseball Commissioner helped put an early end to Newsom's mat exploits. It instructed him to either give up pro wrestling—at that time ranked by the baseball establishment only slightly above appearing as a side-show freak or emcee at a strip club—or give up baseball. The letter arrived at about the same time Bobo and Kay were accosted by a group of angry, and inebriated, fans after a big match, and the experience helped convince him that maybe the job wasn't quite as easy as it first appeared.

In part due to the three months spent in Detroit, the Newsoms never got back to Hartsville that winter. Instead, in February they decided to take up residence in Winter Park, Florida. There, he worked out on a fairly regular basis with the baseball team at Rollins College.[19] As a result, he reported to the Lookouts' training camp in good shape, weighing in at 220 pounds, 30 pounds less than where he tipped the Toledos at the conclusion of the 1949 season. He wasn't thrilled with the Lookouts' contract, calling for the league maximum $5,000, but there weren't any other viable options. After much wrangling, he finagled a bonus clause out of Engel, giving him an additional $2,500 should the Lookouts hit certain attendance levels at home and on the road. At year's end, Newsom had earned that $2,500. He also earned grudging praise from Engel, who said, "Bobo's the smartest player I ever talked contract with. He's nobody's fool."[20]

As an April Fools' Day joke, Engel sent Newsom a 1950 contract calling for a salary of $100 a month. Newsom had a healthy sense of humor on most subjects, but not money. He was not amused by the low-ball offer and responded thusly: "A lousy 100 dollars? Who's Joe think he's dealin' with, the Chattanoogie Shoeshine Boy?" It was all Engel could do to straighten matters out, and keep a straight face, but untangle them he did. "When I do sign Bobo," Engel said, "I'm going to have my picture taken with my pants pockets sticking out empty." Indeed, a posed shot of Engel and Newsom haggling over a piece of paper representing a contract went out over the national news wires, no doubt prompting a series of unpleasant flashbacks in virtually all major league front offices.

Once the real contract was signed and the season began, Newsom was again the toast of the Southern Association—and the Lookouts were once again awful. Newsom compiled a 13–17 record for Chattanooga in 1950, although in many ways he pitched even better than in 1949. Included in his 16 complete games were two shutouts. He struck out 145 batters, and walked only 71, in 235 innings. In retrospect, the question of whether or not he could still get major league hitters out seemed to have been answered, since the bulk of the batters he faced—and retired—in the SA were either ex–major leaguers or youngsters on their way up to the Big Show.

"No doubt, he was one of the top pitchers in the league," said Frosty Kennedy, a member of the 1950 Atlanta Crackers. "Even at age 45, or however old he was, he had one of the best sliders I've ever seen. We had a real good club there in Atlanta, if he had pitched for us he could have won 20 games easy."[21]

Kennedy, whose time with the Crackers was curtailed due to elbow surgery, was one of two promising young players from California on the 1950 Crackers. The other was third baseman Eddie Mathews. Crackers manager Dixie Walker, a friend of Newsom's from their days in Brooklyn, decided it would be a good idea for Kennedy and Mathews to meet him and absorb some of his baseball wisdom. So a conference was arranged prior to a Lookouts-Crackers game at Atlanta.

The meeting went well. Kennedy and Mathews took to Newsom right away, especially his advice regarding contracts. "Make sure they pay you what you're worth. Not one penny less," Newsom told the young players. It was agreed the trio would meet up after the game for a meal and drinks. Kennedy said,

> So the game starts and Newsom is pitching and Mathews comes to bat in the first inning. And Eddie, like he always did, digs in there at the plate. And Bobo's just watching this. Then Bobo winds up, that great big windup of his, and throws a fastball right at Mathews' head. Then Bobo comes down off the mound and yells, "Don't ever dig in against me, you blankety-blank busher!"
>
> Then Newsom struck Mathews out. Eddie just couldn't believe our good friend Bobo Newsom would knock him on his ass. Dixie Walker cut him off. "Son, that man's been pitching longer than you've been living. You got dusted by a real major leaguer." So Eddie, and all of us, got the message.[22]

As evidence of just how strong the Southern Association was—other than Chattanooga—in 1950, Kennedy was able to break into the Crackers' starting lineup for just one game. Playing left field against Birmingham, Kennedy was the only player among the 18 starters who hadn't played in the major leagues or would play in the majors. "The only way I even got back on the active roster was for Dixie Walker to take himself off of it," Kennedy said. "A tough league, but Newsom was definitely a standout. That fat old guy could pitch."[23]

In a sign of changing times, Engel worked on a deal with Capital Airlines that would have enabled the Lookouts to fly to all their road series. For Newsom, the idea of flying was unthinkable. It wasn't just that he enjoyed riding the train. He had a definite phobia about flying, a fear that was heightened when a passenger plane crashed elsewhere in the nation that spring, killing all aboard. Thus inspired, Newsom went to work to ground Engel's plan. Ellis Clary, manager of the 1950s Lookouts, said,

> We were gonna fly, but that goofy Bobo Newsom ruined it. He stirred up the team enough so they eventually voted against flying. He would go up to the young players and say, "I had a dream last night. The plane crashed. I saw your body burned to a crisp. And your wife and kids were standing there next to your fried body, crying." He scared the daylights out of them.[24]

Newsom's final game with the Lookouts, on the last day of the 1950 season, was a perfect summation of the Newsom-Engel relationship. Newsom had a train to catch, to St. Louis to begin a new job, and wanted to skip the game. However, Engel had already advertised the event as a Bobo Newsom appearance, the only way left by that point in the season to get fans into the ballpark. Newsom threatened to bolt anyway, and only a last-minute infusion of some of Engel's cash convinced him to start the game. However, Newsom wasn't about to forfeit the price of a train ticket. Once the game began, he quickly got into an argument with the home plate umpire and managed to get himself ejected in the top of the first inning. He rushed off the field and out of the ballpark, in uniform, and caught a cab before Engel could run down from the press box and demand his money back.

Finally out from under the Chattanooga contract, Newsom spent three weeks in September announcing Browns games on KWK in St. Louis. Dizzy Dean had left St. Louis earlier that year to do Yankees games on the Mutual television network, and Newsom seemed like the next best thing. He received generally favorable notices for his relaxed Southern-style play-by-play, which owed as much to the influence of longtime Washington Senators announcer Arch McDonald as it did to Dean. The radio station offered him a contract to do Browns home games in 1951 but Newsom found it unacceptable, financially and artistically. In truth, he still hadn't given up his ultimate dream of once again pitching in the major leagues.[25]

Needing money, as always, Newsom was receptive when promoters Lew Batchelor and J. L. Wilkinson approached him with a revival of an old idea. Newsom and Satchel Paige, at that time also not under contract to any team in organized baseball, would embark on an old-fashioned barnstorming tour. Dates were hastily set up throughout the Midwest, teams were assembled and off the pair went, just like in the winter of 1933–1934. As was the case earlier, the Paige All-Stars were clearly the better team, benefiting from the presence of several Negro Leagues veterans including Cool Papa Bell and Jelly Taylor. Newsom's team consisted of minor leaguers and whatever semi-pro players could be located, although as a novelty Alice Hohlmeyer, a star from the All-American Girls Professional Baseball League, played a few games for the Newsoms.[26]

A leg injury incurred by Newsom and unusually inclement weather in late October dampened attendance at the games. The series turned out to be one of the last of its type, integration of organized baseball making the primary point of the competition moot. That these barnstorming tours between Negro Leagues and major league players—dating back to the Paige-Newsom matchups of 1933—were a major factor in promoting integration in the sport seems to have been largely overlooked by later historians, replaced by the heroic saga of Jackie Robinson and Branch Rickey. The 1950 tour did accomplish one thing; it cemented the friendship between Paige and Newsom. That most unlikely bond was renewed when both returned to the American League for the 1952 and 1953 seasons.[27]

One of the stories Newsom told about his time barnstorming with Satchel in 1950 went like this: Paige came up to Newsom and Kay in a hotel lobby. Very seriously, Paige looked at them and started to shake his head. Newsom asked what the problem was. Satchel said, "Mr. Bobo, there's one thing in life I will never understand. How does an ugly, ugly man like you get such a pretty wife?"[28]

Paige, as evidenced in a 1965 interview, shared Newsom's views on pro baseball. "I love to travel," Paige told the interviewer. "New day, new city, that's what I like. I could never figure how somebody could play for the same team for five or 10 years. The happiest time I had in baseball was barnstorming. No matter what it said across the front of the uniform, it was me who did the pitching. I get paid because I'm Satchel Paige."[29]

Bobo and Kay chose to winter again in Florida, no doubt to separate him from his Hartsville cronies. Newsom was now at the stage in life where he needed to focus his attention on sustaining his playing career and maintaining a bank balance. However, no offers came from major league teams and it became obvious the only way he was going to return to the majors was for him to prove he could still pitch, and do so with a minimum of clowning or complaining.

Against his better judgment, Clark Griffith allowed Newsom to hang around the Senators camp in Orlando in the spring of 1951. Griffith even heeded Newsom's advice and added Chattanooga shortstop Willy Miranda to the roster. Newsom insisted Miranda was the greatest shortstop he had ever seen and convinced Griffith to promote the slick-fielding Cuban.

However, for once the Old Fox resisted Newsom's siren song and refused to offer him a contract. Newsom pondered a feeler from San Diego of the Pacific Coast League—reportedly arranged by Senators manager Bucky Harris in an attempt to remove Newsom as far from the East Coast as possible—but decided instead to sign with the Birmingham Barons of the Southern Association.[30] Birmingham, unlike Chattanooga, was a first-class organization. The Barons had a working agreement with the Boston Red Sox, and the Sox organization was loaded with talented young players.

The Barons entered the season with high hopes, lifted by the presence of Newsom. Their chances improved in June when they signed another veteran pitcher, Mickey Haefner. Newsom and Haefner had been teammates on the Washington Senators in the mid–1940s, and even at ages 44 and 39, respectively, were to have banner seasons with the Barons. Haefner began the 1951 season with Seattle in the PCL but was cut loose after clashing with Rainiers manager Rogers Hornsby, making him a true kinsman of Newsom. Haefner worked with Newsom on throwing a knuckleball, and Newsom used the pitch with increasing frequency during his stay in Birmingham.

The Barons were managed by Red Marion, older brother of St. Louis Cardinals great Marty Marion. Like Newsom, the Marion brothers were South Carolina natives. Red hadn't been much of a ballplayer, but he did turn out to be an effective minor league manager, serving the Red Sox organization for 20 years in that role. The parent Red Sox supplied him with an outstanding outfield, consisting of Marvin Rackley in left,

Jimmy Piersall in center and George Washington "Teddy" Wilson in right. For the year, Rackley batted .351, Piersall .346 and Wilson .325. In addition, Piersall was nothing short of spectacular covering the huge expanse of turf in center field at Rickwood Field.

Birmingham was a first-cabin operation in all regards, including flying to other cities in the league rather than using trains or buses. As Joe Engel discovered the hard way, travel by airliner just didn't suit Newsom's style. Newsom hated the cramped quarters, the lack of freedom. The short flights around the Association rarely afforded Newsom enough time to leave his seat and wander up and down the aisles, as he had done on countless train trips. His aversion to being up in the air eventually limited his employment opportunities when the major leagues became bi-coastal in the late 1950s.

Despite the fact that Newsom insisted on driving or riding the train to road games, the Barons managed to fly high. Fans still came out to see him pitch, and he rarely disappointed them. Bobo Newsom Days were held that August in both Chattanooga and Birmingham to coincide with his 44th birthday. Attendance topped 10,000 at both events. He was always in his element at these affairs, enjoying the attention and the gifts. And, as always, there was no false modesty. "Every day I pitch, it's Bobo Newsom Day," he told Wirt Gammon. "Fans know they are gonna get their money's worth when I'm out there."[31]

The official Bobo Newsom Day at Birmingham, on the evening of August 11, was especially notable. Bobo the birthday boy pitched that night following a lengthy pregame ceremony in his honor. Understandably, since he had been standing around the infield for an hour prior to the game accepting gifts and well-wishes, he was somewhat frayed once the game began. After getting the first two Little Rock batters, Newsom forgot to cover first base on a routine ground ball to the first baseman. Perhaps he was still thinking about that play, because the next batter hit a two-run home run. Newsom then retired the final 25 Little Rock batters in order. Had he remembered to cover first base, he might have pitched a perfect game. Interestingly, in a development far too typical of Newsom's career, the Barons failed to rally from the early deficit and lost, 2–1.

The Barons wound up finishing second to Little Rock in the regular season, but that did qualify them for the Southern Association playoffs. Solid pitching and defense enabled the Barons to dominate those playoffs, beating Mobile and Little Rock in back-to-back four-game sweeps.[32]

As always, strange things happened when the moon was full and Newsom was on the mound. In the playoff opener at Little Rock, a fan dashed onto the field right before the game and waved a black cat in Newsom's face. He disposed of fan and kitty by throwing his glove and a few adjectives at them, but the Travelers disposed of him by scoring six runs in the bottom of the second inning. Pandemonium reigned at the Little Rock ballpark, but the Barons silenced the crowd by rallying for a 9–8 victory. Newsom got the final guffaw by dousing the fan who tried to jinx him with a bucket of water during a late-inning Barons rally. None of the rowdy goings-on resulted in suspensions, arrests or lawsuits, amply demonstrating the difference between baseball (and society) circa 1950 and circa 2010. "Sure hope that pussy is OK," Bobo said afterward, leaving unsaid whether he was referring to feline or fan.[33]

To Newsom went the honor of pitching the playoff clincher and gaining revenge, a 6–1 victory over Little Rock before over 11,000 fans at Rickwood Field. Teddy Wilson insured that he had enough runs to work with this time, hitting a grand-slam home run. No cats, black or otherwise, were reported in the vicinity of Rickwood that evening.

Besting Little Rock put Birmingham into the Dixie Series against Texas League champion Houston, one of the St. Louis Cardinals' top farm clubs. Birmingham won the series, four games to two. Newsom pitched a four-hitter in a 3–0 loss to Vinegar Bend Mizell in Game Three, the only runs coming on a three-run home run by Larry Miggins that Newsom claimed was just a wind-blown pop fly.

For the regular season, Newsom's Birmingham statistics were impressive, especially for a 44-year-old. He started 31 games and completed 17 of them, including three shutouts. He posted a 16–11 won-lost record, pitched 237 innings, struck out 132 and walked only 71. His earned run average was 3.04. Counting games won in the playoffs, he was once again a 20-game winner. He had accomplished all that could be expected of him in the Southern Association, pitching Birmingham to the coveted Dixie Series championship. It was time once again to look toward the major leagues.

First stop in the spring of 1952 was, of course, the Washington Senators camp in Orlando. Senators manager Bucky Harris remained dead set against the idea of Newsom joining the team, but there was a wave cresting in baseball, a high tide that helped sweep Newsom right onto the Senators roster.

The concept of a "stopper" or "closer"—a pitcher to come in the final inning or two of a game to lock up a victory—gained currency in the majors in the seasons immediately following World War II. Eventually the idea grew into using a hard-throwing youngster in the role, but in the 1950s the trend was to take an older pitcher on the downside of his career and convert him into a closer. The rationale was that pitching only an inning or two saved wear and tear on the legs and gave the veteran a chance to study opposing hitters for several innings prior to taking the mound. It also, in theory, meant the closer would likely be recovered from his prior-night activities by the time his name was called.[34]

Entering the 1952 season, the Boston Red Sox had two "graybeards" slated for the role of closer, Ellis Kinder (age 38) and Al Benton (age 41). The Browns were now using Satchel Paige as a closer, and the good Lord only knew how old he was. In the National League, the Chicago Cubs closer was knuckleballer Dutch Leonard (age 43).

Bobo Newsom's resume—listed age 41, real age 44—seemed just right for a closer's job. He always had above-average success as a relief pitcher, in part because he was able to get loose quickly, in part because he was too self-absorbed to be fazed by pressure.

"Newsom came in late there in spring training, but he could still throw," said Irv Noren, an outfielder on the 1952 Senators.

> His legs were pretty much gone, but for an inning or two he could be effective. So that's how Bucky Harris figured to use him. Of course, he was also a gate attraction, no doubt about that. It wasn't an act with Bobo. He was just an odd sort of guy. Funny talk, funny walk, a different breed of duck.
>
> I played golf with him one time there in the spring of 1952, and he was the same way on the golf course. He never stopped talking. And he was the worst cheater ever. I'm looking at his scorecard after nine holes and say, "Hey, you didn't par the last three holes." And he says, "Well, Ol' Bobo sure intended to." The best club in his bag was his pencil.[35]

Newsom preferred starting games to relieving but wasn't about to argue when Griffith finally offered him a Senators contract, fittingly, on April 1. He signed (for a reported $10,000), and his three-and-one-half-year absence from the major leagues was over.

It didn't take long for Bobo Fever to sweep the Potomac. The D.C. sportswriters dug out all their Newsom material, dusted it off and passed it along to their readers, freshened by new observations from the man himself. Newsom, of course, was delighted to be interviewed by all and sundry. Manager Bucky Harris had a particular aversion to this tendency, an aversion heightened by past history. But Newsom was unbound and now had three years of tales from the Southern Association to add to his voluminous repertoire of baseball stories.

Newsom's impact on Washington baseball was immediate, in both a negative and positive sense. In trying to show off his knuckleball to Harris in a spring training warm-up session, he uncorked a knuckler that broke about two feet. Unfortunately, the fluttering pitch also broke catcher Mickey Grasso's wrist. Since Grasso was the Senators' top catcher, the incident tended to cloud Harris' opinion of Newsom's value to the team.[36]

Not clouded was Clark Griffith's opinion, written in dollars and cents. The Brooklyn Dodgers came into town for a much-hyped exhibition game on April 10 and a crowd in excess of 25,000 showed up at Griffith Stadium (paid attendance was 21,459, a Senators record for an exhibition). While many in the crowd were on hand to see the multitude of Dodgers stars, and in particular African American pioneers Jackie Robinson and Roy Campanella, by the end of the evening there was no doubt who the star of the show was. Newsom began warming up in the bullpen in the bottom of the sixth inning, and immediately the ballpark was alive. The buzz grew louder between innings and became an ovation when Newsom went out to the mound to start the seventh inning.

Roscoe McGowen, who had covered Newsom's big league debut with the Dodgers in 1929, was on hand for the 1952 game. Writing for the *New York Times,* McGowen described what happened next: "They yelled for Bobo when he strode to the mound at the start of the seventh and the cheers grew louder as he went along to set down nine Brooks in order."[37]

The scene was repeated five days later. Newsom receiving an ovation from Senators fans when he pitched the ninth inning of Opening Day on April 15 at Griffith Stadium. Like General MacArthur, Newsom had returned. Reportedly, in the pre-game ceremonies he inquired of President Truman, "You still here, Bobo?"

Unfortunately, Harris afforded Newsom few chances to pitch in the early part of the 1952 season. The Senators were in yet another rebuilding mode and didn't hold enough leads in the late innings to give the concept of Newsom as closer much of a test. It was also clear that Newsom was unable, physically, to pitch back-to-back games anymore. He tutored some of the younger Senators pitchers, most notably Bob Porterfield, but was thoroughly flummoxed by the presence of several Cubans on the staff. This gave rise to a Newsom remark worthy of Yogi Berra: "Whatever it is they're saying ain't what I'm hearing," said Newsom of his attempts to relay his pitching knowledge to the Spanish-speaking contingent on the Senators.[38]

Harris managed to work Newsom into ten games, all in relief. Newsom saved two of those games, but also blew the lead in a game in which he became the winning pitcher. He struggled with his control, walking nine batters in 12⅔ innings, and also gave up two home runs. Increasingly, Harris went with other options.

For a change, Newsom kept his composure and in June was able to work out a deal with Griffith whereby the Senators would release him so the Philadelphia Athletics could sign him. The A's, under manager Jimmy Dykes, were entrenched in the second division and held no illusions about a youth movement, or a move of any kind except one that led out of town. Although Connie Mack owned Shibe Park, the last few seasons had seen attendance fall dramatically. It appeared that Philadelphia—like Boston and St. Louis—could not sustain two major league teams. Thus it was the A's welcomed Newsom, figuring he would boost attendance if not the team's talent level.

Dykes, who had known Newsom since Bobo was an American League rookie with the Browns back in 1934, actually enjoyed having Newsom around. Newsom became a de facto pitching coach for Dykes, and from all accounts got along swimmingly with his teammates despite the generation gap. As proof that times had indeed changed, when pitcher Bob Trice joined the A's in September 1953 he became Newsom's first African American teammate.

As was the case all his professional life, once the weather warmed up Newsom started to pitch more effectively. Newsom split six decisions in 14 appearances for the A's in 1952. Dykes managed to give him five starts, and he even completed one of them, an 11–3 victory over the Browns on July 15.

He was also called upon, on occasion, to keep Athletics owner Connie Mack company. Newsom, for all his bombast, had a gentle side that came out around the very young and very old. Mack, now in his 90s, was in failing health. His memory, for the most part, had already failed. But he remembered Newsom, and the pair was able to enjoy traversing a memory lane that only they could follow.

Most days, Newsom sat in the A's bullpen, using a fungo bat as a make-believe microphone and describing the play-by-play as it unfolded before him.

"You gotta give Bobo credit, he knew what he wanted to be after he retired as a player," Gus Zernial, a teammate on the 1952 and 1953 A's, said. "He really took his pretend play-by-play seriously. One time, he was there with his fungo bat and it's an exciting game and he's really into it and the call comes in to the 'pen for him to get up and get loose. He grabs the phone and tells [Jimmy] Dykes, 'Hey, get yourself another Bobo. I'm busy down here!'"[39]

Over the winter, Newsom concentrated on reviving his broadcasting career, figuring his playing career had finally run its course. But he was ready when Dykes invited him to the Athletics' spring training camp in West Palm Beach in March of 1953. It was understood, by both Newsom and Dykes, that his presence on the 1953 A's roster was largely ceremonial, that Dykes wasn't expecting Newsom to contribute anything beyond his considerable cheerleading abilities.

By late August, Newsom had appeared in only 15 games for the A's, all in relief, mostly in mop-up roles in games where the other A's pitchers had been shelled. Not surprisingly, by late August the leaders in the pennant race had long since lapped Dykes' ballclub. Bobby Shantz and Alex Kellner, the aces of the pitching staff, were ailing and there seemed little sense in sending them out to mound anymore in the 1953 season.

Thus, the stage was set for one final Newsom feat of legerdemain. Appropriately, it was to take place at Briggs Stadium in Detroit, scene of some of his greatest triumphs.

A doubleheader on August 31 between two second-division teams still managed to draw nearly 20,000 fans to Briggs. They got their money's worth. Dykes, after seeing Harry Byrd and Charlie Bishop get knocked around in the first game as the Tigers won, 9–7, decided to go with Newsom in the nightcap.

Newsom, who had celebrated his 46th birthday earlier in the month, was on his game. Despite the heat and humidity, he silenced a good-hitting Detroit team for four innings, while his teammates assembled a 9–0 lead. Sloppy fielding by the Athletics infield helped Detroit scoring three times in the fifth, but Newsom reached back for something extra, as in days of yore, and battled his way out of the inning. He pitched a scoreless sixth and then seemed to be faltering again in the bottom of the seventh when manager Dykes made a trip to the mound.[40]

"It was brutally hot out there," said Dykes. "I thought I better ask how he felt."

"I'm getting 'em out," Newsom replied, a sensible enough answer and one that was good enough for Dykes.[41]

Newsom and Philadelphia Athletics teammate Bobby Shantz clown around for the photographer in spring training of 1953 in West Palm Beach, Florida. Since Shantz was 5-feet-5 and 140 pounds and Newsom was 6-feet-3 and 240 pounds, Bobo is holding Bobby like a baby (author's collection).

Newsom stayed, and Newsom finished. It was his final complete game of 354 in organized baseball, his 200th win in the American League, his 211th win in the majors, and his 350th in pro ball. He received a curtain call from the Detroit fans as he walked off the field, a 10–4 victor. And no wonder, for Newsom had certainly put on one last great show. He even singled and scored a run in a six-run Athletics rally, his final major league hit and run scored. On the mound, he was as animated as ever, huffing and puffing and working his way out of jams. One of Detroit's four runs occurred when Newsom grooved a pitch for former teammate Freddie Hutchinson, now the Tigers' player-manager. Hutchinson hit it out and exchanged smiles with Newsom as he trotted around the bases.

Newsom also tossed up a blooper pitch and a few knuckleballs, caught the catcher's return throw behind his back, and—of course—carefully groomed the mound to his liking before the start of each inning. For one final afternoon of 135 pitches, Newsom was 21 all over again, his future shining as bright as a diamond.

The train ride back to Philly gave Newsom time to think about attempting another swan song, this one in Shibe Park. It turned out to be an ill-advised notion, for Newsom was knocked out of the box early in his final start, on September 7 against the Senators. Final score: Washington 13, Philadelphia 2. He was used in relief, briefly, on September 17, pitching the ninth inning of a 5–4 loss to Cleveland. It was his 600th major league game, his 3,759th inning.

The next day, Newsom wandered into the A's front office and requested his release, a quiet climax to a tumultuous career. Rumors were that the team was going to be sold, that Jimmy Dykes was out as manager. Asked why he quit, Newsom said, "The A's can't afford me any more."[42]

That was probably true, but it was also true that Newsom was increasingly uneasy over the changes that were sweeping baseball. The Athletics were to undergo one last, torturous season in Philadelphia before moving to Kansas City. The Braves moved to Milwaukee, the Browns to Baltimore, and the Dodgers and Giants were both destined to flee New York for the West Coast. The players were now better educated—farm boys were few and far between—and better paid. Millions were being spent on untried youngsters, the so-called bonus baby phenomena that proved to be a precursor of things to come. An effective players' union was close to becoming a reality, and already team owners were increasingly on the defensive in contract matters.

There was no longer any room in the majors for Louis Norman Newsom, and to his credit he knew it. "I had a good run at 'em, it's time for the kids to take over now," he told sportswriter Wirt Gammon in the winter of 1953–1954. "Ol' Bobo knows when he's not wanted. I got nothing to kick about. Guess Bobo fooled a lot of folks for a long, long time. It beat the hell out of life on the farm, that's for sure."[43]

For the record, Newsom pitched

Jimmy Dykes, who had faced Bobo Newsom numerous times as a player, was his final manager, in 1952 and 1953 with the Philadelphia Athletics. He found Newsom an amusing distraction from the depressingly bad A's teams (the Ray Medeiros collection, used by permission).

professionally for 28 years, the final 26 of them in organized baseball. In those 26 seasons, he changed teams 28 times. It was a whirlwind of activity that has bewildered those attempting to track his career. It even bewildered Newsom on occasion.

Prior to a game in St. Louis in the spring of 1947, Browns rookie outfielder Ray Coleman recalled an odd occurrence:

> I get to the park real early.... I'm sitting by myself in the Browns clubhouse and in comes Bobo Newsom. He goes over and sits down and starts to take off his street clothes. He sees me and says hi and starts talking. About then Doc Bauman (the Browns' trainer) comes out and says, "Hey Bobo, hate to tell you this, but you're in the wrong place. You're pitching for the Senators now." Bobo just laughed. "Damned if you're not right. Guess I got my horseshit teams mixed up." Even he couldn't keep up with all those trades anymore.[44]

In trying to find a statistical match for Newsom in baseball's record book, the closest numbers are those of Nolan Ryan. Newsom pitched 951 games in organized ball, Ryan 856. Newsom's won-lost record was 350–327; Ryan's was 346–302. Newsom pitched 5,827 innings, Ryan 5,677. Ryan, pitching in a vastly different era and against expansion teams, had a huge edge in strikeouts, 6,159 to 3,282. But "The Ryan Express" also walked more batters, 2,995 to 1,630. Ryan's career earned run average was right at 3 per game; Newsom's was right at 4. What Newsom might have done in an expanded 24-team major league and against free-swinging hitters is, of course, impossible to say.[45]

Which leaves the question: would a Bobo Newsom have even made it to the majors in the modern-day era? As in all things Bobo-related, opinion remains divided.

"Baseball, and our society, changed a lot there in the 1950s, 1960s and 1970s," said Al Zarilla, former major league player, coach and scout. "There just wasn't a place for the oddballs like Bobo Newsom anymore, no matter how much talent they had. You had to be able to conform, and he was never able to conform. You had to be able to take orders and follow directions. Bobo never followed anybody's advice but his own."[46]

"With all his antics, Bobo would be priceless in this day and age of baseball on television," countered former major leaguer Johnny Sullivan. "Sure, he was a guy who marched to a different drummer, but he was never dull. He always played to the crowds. Knowing the TV cameras were on his every move, he probably would have gone out and won 20 games every year. And he would have absolutely loved the attention, every blessed minute of it."[47]

Thirteen

Baltimore to Washington to Winter Park to Hartsville (1954–1962)

Bobo Newsom's graceful exit from the Philadelphia Athletics in September of 1953 would have been a good time to say adios to the sport he loved. Unfortunately, Newsom loved baseball too much to leave it. Besides, he possessed no other vocational skills to fall back on. Tallulah Williams, a cousin, said,

> There at the end of his life, Buck's lack of education really hurt him. All he knew was baseball. All his business contacts were in baseball. He was a very bright man, but at age 50 it's hard for any of us to learn a new profession. He just ran out of options. He didn't take very good care of his money, or his health. He let himself go.[1]

Newsom's recurring dream was of catching on with a major league team as a pitching coach, but that remained highly unlikely, given his well-earned reputation as a rounder and rabble-rouser. His best bet for employment seemed to be in broadcasting, where his personality quirks worked in his favor and not against it. Good buddy Dizzy Dean had struck it rich in broadcasting and was now doing "The Game of the Week" on national television and serving as a corporate spokesman for Falstaff Beer. With Dean's guidance, Newsom set about finding work behind a microphone or in front of a TV camera.[2]

The move of the Browns from St. Louis to Baltimore that winter created an opening. Operating under new ownership, the team was putting together a broadcast package designed to compete in the competitive East Coast market. It was decided to feature a pre-game show for the WMAR-TV telecasts modeled after the one used by the Brooklyn Dodgers. A sponsor was secured, Esskay Franks, and after a rapid series of meetings and auditions Newsom was announced as the host on January 4, 1954. He was also to serve as a corporate spokesman for Esskay as "president" of the Orioles Knot Hole Gang, a marketing ploy aimed at the younger set.[3]

On the surface, it seemed like an ideal job for Newsom. He would be talking baseball, he would be around kids and he would be promoting a food product (a natural, since his mere presence served as a walking advertisement for good food and drink). First and foremost for Newsom, he would still be in the major leagues, would be able to wear the uniform of the brand-new Baltimore Orioles even if he wasn't actually on the active player roster.

Things looked even rosier for him when Jimmy Dykes was selected as Orioles manager and Art Ehlers was named Orioles general manager. Both were on good terms with Newsom from their recent time together in Philadelphia. Dykes had no objections to Newsom hanging around the ballpark when not on camera. As far as Dykes was concerned, Newsom could throw batting practice to his heart's content and "tutor" the young Orioles pitching staff. That staff included Bob Turley, Don Larsen and Ryne Duren, three right-handers with fastballs to rival that of a young Buck Newsom. From Dykes' standpoint, what damage could Newsom do to a team that was the woeful St. Louis Browns in disguise? Once the 1954 season reached its waning stages, there seemed to be a very real chance that Newsom might even be able to pitch a few games for the Orioles, as a device to boost paid admissions. All in all, Newsom entered the season in great spirits.[4]

Even *Washington Post* sports columnist Bob Addie was enthused over the idea. "Bobo Newsom ... has proved himself a polished man with an adjective.... On TV he can talk all he wants without getting thrown out of the game."

First up came a training session with the Dodgers' Knot Hole Gang TV host, Happy Felton, in Brooklyn. Since Felton's pre-game show was, to put it kindly, amateurish, it's doubtful his helpful hints aided Newsom. Wearing thick eyeglasses and a Brooklyn baseball cap askew and looking like a bookkeeper gone to seed, Felton was definitely a talent whose appeal wasn't going to transfer to the Baltimore market. In retrospect, patterning a show after Felton's must be chalked up to be pure corporate folly. Further, while Newsom had some experience doing radio, he had no background in live television. All the rehearsals and role models in the world could not prepare him, or anyone else, for doing a non-scripted, live TV show before a studio audience of pre-teen boys.[5]

The job provoked one other unfortunate consequence. Clark Griffith knew the presence of another major league team in nearby Baltimore was going to be a threat to his Senators (ultimately, he was proven right). He saw Newsom's employment in connection with said team as a bit of a betrayal, especially since Newsom didn't consult him before taking the job. The Knot Hole Gang gig may have made him many new fans, but it strained his relationship with his oldest one. Invitations to visit "The Old Fox" in Orlando or to watch a game in his private suite at Griffith Stadium abruptly ended.

Griffith's enmity aside, it soon became evident that while being a corporate spokesman for Esskay beefed up Newsom's checkbook (he was paid $20,000 a year, a hefty raise from the $11,000 he earned with the A's in 1953), it put the clamps on his natural enthusiasm. Now he was forced to measure his words, to tone down his behavior, and be on time, every time. Even worse, he had to be ready at a moment's notice, for if a rain delay occurred in the Orioles game the engineer at the ballpark would "throw it" back to Newsom in the studio. For someone who had been a free spirit all his life, it turned out being Knot Hole Gang major domo was quite possibly the worst career choice Newsom ever made. The stress stirred up by the job took a toll on his health, greatly exacerbating his alcoholism. It also turned out to be hard work, unlike playing baseball. Ray Menchine, veteran Baltimore-area sportscaster, said,

> To be blunt, Bobo wasn't very good on that show. I watched it, of course. I'm sure every boy in town watched it. I read all these fascinating stories about Bobo Newsom, and it seemed like he'd be great doing that kind of show. But he was extremely ill at ease.

Thirteen. Baltimore to Washington to Vinter-Park to Hartsville (1954–1962) 207

The show was only a half-hour long, but it seemed like that half-hour took forever. There were only about 20 or 25 of them a season, since it only aired prior to Orioles' telecasts.

Bobo, despite the fact he was wearing an Orioles uniform, looked like an old, tired fat guy. He always had that glazed-over look. I'm sure the show seemed like a good idea at the time, but it just didn't work.[6]

Newsom attended various functions for Esskay, ranging from opening day at local Little Leagues to supermarket unveilings to banquets for company executives and their wives. He also participated in instructional clinics and advertising promotions, including TV and radio commercials. Cal Ermer, longtime minor league manager, major league coach and accomplished story teller, remembered hearing one of Bobo's spots for Esskay. "He has this gravel-y, molasses-slow drawl," said Ermer. "I remember the spot went something like 'Folks, y'all love these luscious Esskay dogs at the ol' ballpark. Heck, they'll be mighty tasty in the off-season too! Get 'um today at your neighborly Piggly Wiggly store. Take it from ol' Bobo!'"[7]

Newsom's connection to Esskay even extended to the set of baseball cards of the 1954 Orioles the company issued, as though he was a genuine member of the team. Interestingly, in a card set thoroughly lacking in superstars, Newsom's Esskay card is now highly prized by collectors. The card's existence, depicting him in full Orioles attire, extends the confusion over whether or not he actually pitched for the Orioles. Ultimately, his status as a corporate spokesman worked against rather than for his chances of pitching for the Orioles in a real game.[8]

"You know, that old boy pitched some batting practice for us and he still threw better than some of the guys on our staff," said Les Moss, a catcher on the 1954 Orioles. "He still had a decent fastball and good action on the ball. There was some talk about him pitching for us there late in the season but I heard the hot dog company he was working for thought it would be a bad idea. Jimmy [Dykes] wouldn't have cared, I know that. He loved Bobo."[9]

After the new spokesman was introduced at an early-season press conference as the "loquacious" Bobo Newsom, Dykes jumped up and said, "You better explain that to Bobo before he slugs you." It got a big laugh, even from Newsom. But he knew what loquacious meant. Delivering prepared material and speaking to adults, he did fine. It was that damned camera and those snot-nosed kids that were the problem.

Perhaps the one lasting legacy of Newsom's time in Baltimore was a hot-dog eating contest with Art Donovan, NFL lineman and famed trencherman. Despite Newsom's on-the-record fondness for his sponsor's product, Donovan won easily.[10]

Newsom made it through the season, in spite of his on-camera duties with the Knot Hole Gang. Everyone in the Baltimore organization and at the hot dog company was pleased over the fact that the Orioles, even though they lost 100 games, drew a franchise-record 1.06 million fans. That was twice as many as the neighboring Senators drew. So there was little debate about bringing Newsom and the rest of the broadcast team back for another go-around.

But any hopes of long-term happiness for Newsom in Baltimore dimmed in the off-season when the Orioles fired Dykes and hired Paul Richards as manager. Richards had a history of run-ins with Newsom, and in any event was what now would be called a control freak. He wanted full reign over the Orioles, and most certainly did not want

Bobo Newsom with four members of his Knot Hole Gang at a youth baseball event at Memorial Stadium in Baltimore in 1954. After his pitching career ended, Newsom enjoyed a second life as a pitch man for Esskay Franks. However, he was let go by the hot dog company following the 1956 season (courtesy Hartsville Museum).

any part of Newsom, let alone Newsom's habit of offering young players unsolicited advice on pitching and contracts. Jim Russo, longtime Orioles scout, said,

> Richards was one of the few people I ever met in baseball who had absolutely no sense of humor. He was all business. And he wanted total control of that team. He even complained about the vendors at Memorial Stadium. He didn't want them bothering the pitchers in the bullpen or getting too close to the Orioles dugout during the games.[11]

Much too difficult for Bobo Newsom, to be sure. Richards gradually forced him from the playing field and locker room. Newsom's Knot Hole Gang duties ended with the 1956 baseball season. It proved to be Newsom's last real job, in or out of baseball. Ron Menchine said,

> It's too bad Newsom couldn't have caught on doing play-by-play or color commentary for a major league team. He certainly had that Dizzy Dean type of reputation, funny and glib and folksy. None of that came through on the Knot Hole Gang shows, but maybe it would have in a game telecast. He never got that opportunity, so we'll never know.[12]

A television urban legend involving Newsom springs from his stint as Knot Hole Gang guru. Reportedly, he was drunk on the set one day when a thunderstorm halted action in the Orioles game and the telecast was abruptly thrown back to the studio.

Newsom stumbled through 20 minutes of sheer torture under the hot studio lights. Rumor has it comedian Johnny Carson saw this or somehow heard about it and, years later, worked it into his Las Vegas act. The sight of Carson as a kids' show host, drunk as a skunk, trying to maintain his decorum and his lunch, always got a big laugh. For Newsom, the incident, and in fact the entire time he spent hosting the show, was anything but a laughing matter.[13]

Despite the on-air gaffes and increasingly erratic off-air behavior, Bobo retained his fan base. Esskay even added a twice-a-week show on WRC-TV in D.C. for the 1956 season. Washington was again safe turf for Newsom; Clark Griffith had passed away late in 1955. The promotional ads read: "Bobo Newsom comes back to Washington for the 6th time" and depicted him wearing a Senators cap. The show, like the one in Baltimore, appealed mainly to the younger set.

Following the 1956 season, executives at the hot dog company opted to terminate Newsom's contract. While the kids may have loved him, the grownups brought home the groceries, and Esskay sales were lagging. Newsom did not complain. He would miss the personal appearances, but definitely would not miss the on-air chores.

Newsom's last glimpse of glory in Baltimore was a day in his honor at Memorial Stadium on August 25, 1956. Kids under 12 were let into the ballpark free, and Newsom was presented with gifts large and small, including a new automobile. The car, an inexpensive Chevrolet, was the last Newsom owned.

This Bobo Newsom Day didn't spark much interest among Orioles players. By late-season 1956 the team's youth movement was in full force. Most of the players were half Newsom's age and had little knowledge, or interest, in his pitching exploits. Fortunately for Newsom, old friends George Kell and Willy Miranda were on hand to help remind him of better times.

Newsom's final appearance in uniform had taken place on July 16. He was talked into pitching for the Washington Home Plate Club in that organization's annual Old Timers Game, held at D.C.'s South Ellipse park. He donned one of his many old Washington Senators uniforms and pitched one inning. Then, pleading a sore leg, he begged off. Only a couple of hundred fans were there, scarcely the sort of last hurrah Newsom had envisioned.[14]

The Knot Hole Gang misadventure did not discourage him from his dream of landing a baseball play-by-play job. One opportunity was lost in the late 1950s when Leo Durocher—yet another veteran Bobo basher—was chosen over him for a spot on the NBC network baseball telecasts. Still, Newsom kept trying. George Goodale, an executive with the team, said,

> When we started up the Angels there in the winter of 1960–61 I know Gene Autry [co-owner of the team] put a lot of time and effort into picking the broadcasters. One of the names we kicked around was Bobo Newsom. We thought he might be a good choice as our color guy to work the telecasts. We contacted Dizzy Dean, and through him we tracked Newsom down there in Florida. Bobo seemed interested, but he basically priced himself out of the job. Diz recommended both Bobo Newsom and Buddy Blattner, but Buddy was willing to work for a lot less so that's who we hired.[15]

Money aside, the Angels' deck may have been stacked against Newsom. The team's executive vice president was Fred Haney, the same Fred Haney Newsom tangled with on the Browns way back in 1939. In fact, it seemed like Newsom's allies were all dead or out of baseball, while his foes were still very much around. For example, two new National League teams were added for the 1962 season, the New York Mets—where former Yankees executive George Weiss ran the show—and the Houston Colt .45s—where Paul Richards resurfaced after leaving the Orioles. Bill DeWitt was now calling the shots in Cincinnati, Joe Cronin had become president of the entire American League, and so it went. Newsom must have felt surrounded by enemies, suddenly a leper in the game he loved.

Even the flamboyant Bill Veeck wouldn't bite on hiring him. Newsom was always something of an acquired taste, and he apparently was a tad too free-spirited for Veeck's liking. "I know the idea of Veeck hiring Buck came up back in the late 1940s when Bill owned the Indians and Buck was available," said Johnny Berardino. "I mentioned Newsom and I told Bill he ought to give the guy a look-see. His response was, 'I'm looking for showmen, not showboats.' So Bobo never got a shot to work with Veeck."[16]

Even the expansion Washington franchise said no to him. Mickey Vernon, the manager of the expansion Senators, said,

> One of our owners came to me and asked if I wanted Newsom on my coaching staff. I had played with Bobo and loved him like a brother, but having him on the team just didn't make sense to me. I was new to managing, we had a brand-new team with a lot of young players and guys from other organizations. Bobo would have been just one more distraction. I told the front office that I could handle the players, but who was going to handle Bobo? After that, they didn't ask anymore.[17]

Newsom's one remaining link to the big leagues came in the form of a pension, something he had fought for as a player. For probably the only time in his life, honesty about his age paid dividends for him when he turned 50 on August 11, 1957. That made him eligible for his Major League Baseball pension, $428 a month. Many months thereafter, it was Bobo's and Kay's only income. For someone who earned more than a million dollars pitching a baseball, it was a big step down.

Ever the optimist, Newsom stayed in touch with those in baseball who might help him land a job. He faithfully attended baseball's winter meetings, looking for work. At one of these, in December of 1956, he spent some time shooting the breeze with writer John Lardner. The result was an article, "The One and Only Bobo," that Lardner penned for "True" magazine. It was subsequently reprinted in Charles Einstein's *The Second Fireside Book of Baseball* (Simon & Schuster, 1958) and has gone a long way toward keeping the legend of Bobo Newsom alive, as well as fueling many of the myths about the man.

For the flesh-and-blood Bobo, the article didn't pay any bills. At some point an out-of-work Newsom managed to land a part-time job at an Orlando restaurant. The job involved a bit of cooking, a whole lot of socializing with the customers and very little money, but Newsom enjoyed it. Restaurant patrons are still around who can remember him flipping flapjacks and then catching them while holding the frying pan behind his back.

Despite his bleak employment status, Newsom maintained his sense of humor. *Washington Post* columnist Bob Addie remembered a day in 1958 when he and Newsom attended a World Series game together at Yankee Stadium. Afterward, it was agreed they would meet at Toots Shor's for dinner. Addie arrived first, and while waiting ran into movie actor Joe E. Brown and his son, Joe L., at the time an executive with the Pittsburgh Pirates. A few minutes later sportswriters Red Smith and Lyle Smith joined the group. A few minutes after that Harry Jones, a baseball writer for the *Cleveland Plain Dealer*, also sat in. The group enjoyed pre-meal cocktails while waiting for Newsom, who finally arrived an hour late. Addie, knowing that Newsom already knew everybody at the table, stood up and, in mock formality, said, "Bobo, I'd like you to meet Mr. Brown, Mr. Brown, Mr. Smith, Mr. Smith and Mr. Jones." Newsom, without missing a beat, shot back: "If there ain't nobody gonna give their right name, I ain't either."[18]

But nights of revelry at Toots Shor's became scarce. Mainly, he just hung around his home on Malone Drive in Winter Park except for the few weeks a year when spring training was in session. Those weeks, he could be found watching his old team, the Senators, train at Tinker Field in Orlando. For someone used to the hurly-burly of major league baseball, the pace of life as a retiree had to be a big adjustment. Cousin Tallulah Williams said,

> I remember going down to Florida and stopping by to visit Buck and Kay, this was around 1961. I was surprised to find that Buck and Kay lived in a very modest house in a neighborhood that was basically all retirees. It was one of those places where no one seemed to be under the age of 80 and where they took in the sidewalks at dusk. I don't know how Buck and Kay were able to stand that kind of a lifestyle. There really wasn't anything for him to do. For someone like Buck, that was deadly.[19]

In forced retirement, Newsom retreated to the comfort of the neighborhood bar. He became a regular at Harper's Bar in Winter Park, conveniently located within walking distance of his home. On most days Newsom opened the establishment in the afternoon and was the last to leave at night. After a couple of years of such loyalty, the bar "honored" him by having him place his footprints in a cement block, and then installing the block in the floor next to the bar at the spot where Newsom always stood.[20]

Drinking and a near-total lack of exercise drove Newsom's weight up past 300 pounds. But late in 1961, he began to unexpectedly lose weight. By the time liver disease was diagnosed, in the spring of 1962, it was too late for doctors to do anything. In an age before organ transplants and miracle drugs, liver failure was irreversible.

"Contrary to popular opinion, it isn't easy to drink yourself to death," said Ryne Duren, former major league pitcher, recovering alcoholic and recognized authority on substance abuse among athletes. "Alcohol-related cirrhosis of the liver is fairly rare ... [but] if you stop drinking before the liver is severely damaged, it can heal itself. So cirrhosis is, in a way, a slow suicide. You have to ignore all the warning signs and keep drinking until you reach the point where the liver no longer functions."[21]

Newsom's final pitched battle with the baseball establishment came in the late 1950s. In 1959, he became eligible for the Hall of Fame. At the time, he still held several major league records, although they all were of an esoteric nature. Included in those records were most teams played for (nine) and most times traded, sold or released (17). Others have since broken the most teams standard, but he is likely to retain the most times traded mark for as long as there is pro baseball. Unfortunately, to sportswriters of the 1950s being traded was a stigma, a sign that somehow you fell short of a team's expectations.

When Newsom's name appeared on the Hall of Fame ballot, he garnered little support from the sportswriters of that time, who fixated on Newsom's losing record and frequent change of address. Not helping was the lingering impression among some scribes (Bob Broeg of the *St. Louis Post-Dispatch* was an example) that—bottom line—Newsom was more buffoon than big leaguer, more skilled at bragging than pitching. Newsom campaigned for entry into the Hall, but made no headway with members of the Fourth Estate. In an era when athletes rarely engaged in non-stop self-promotion, Newsom's behavior stood out like an inflamed digit.

"I think the nickname had a lot of do with the fact Newsom didn't get much respect once he was out of baseball," Johnny Berardino said. "I mean, Bobo. It's a funny name. But Mr. Newsom was no clown once he was out on the mound. Hitting against him was no laughing matter. If he was serious, and sober, you just couldn't touch him."[22]

Newsom received only six votes in 1959 in his first time on the Baseball Writers' Association of America Hall of Fame ballot. It is fair to speculate that at least five of the six votes came from Washington/Baltimore-based sportswriters. Since most of the BBWAA membership at the time was based in New York, it's clear that he received virtually no support from the Big Apple contingent. By 1973, 11 years after his death, his vote total had risen to 33. That wasn't sufficient cause to put out a call to the plaque maker for Cooperstown with instructions on the proper spelling of Newsom. After he fell off the baseball writers' ballot, no one on the Hall of Fame Veterans' Committee went to bat for him (in fact, Frankie Frisch and several other members of the committee were decidedly anti–Bobo). There the matter rests to this day.[23]

Once Newsom's health worsened, the Hall of Fame and his employment situation became the least of his worries. His physical activities became severely limited and every day was a struggle. Most of his days were spent at doctors' offices or in the hospital. By the fall of 1962, he had little interest in the World Series, featuring two of his former teams, the Giants (now transplanted to San Francisco) and the Yankees. About the only direct connection Newsom retained with either team was Yankees manager Ralph Houk, who as a third-string catcher with the 1947 Yankees frequently warmed up Newsom in the bullpen.

Bob Addie heard about Newsom's failing health and wrote to him. Newsom promptly responded with a letter. "Don't count Ol' Bobo out," he wrote. "Remember, I'm the guy who used to pitch doubleheaders. This is only the first game."[24]

By Thanksgiving, Bobo and Kay reached a decision: their Christmas cards needed to be completed and mailed early. The Newsoms completed their Christmas greetings and had them in the mail by the time December 7—Pearl Harbor Day—rolled around.[25] That morning, Newsom began spitting up blood. An ambulance was called and he was taken to the Florida Sanitarium and Hospital in Orlando, but he was dead on arrival. Cause of death, per Florida Certificate of Death No. 62–052123, was gastro-intestinal hemorrhage, brought on by cirrhosis of the liver. For someone so accustomed to bending the truth, Newsom's death certificate was remarkably accurate, including listing his correct age—55. Item 10a, "Usual Occupation," reads: "Baseball Player." Time of death was listed at 11:30 a.m., just about the time he customarily woke up to begin his day during his glory years as a baseball pitcher deluxe.

There was an outpouring of sympathetic columns from the knights of the keyboard, and one of the best was by Newsom's old friend Bob Addie. In his December 8 column

Thirteen. Baltimore to Washington to Vinter-Park to Hartsville (1954–1962)

in the *Washington Post*, Addie wrote: "Bobo was like an itinerant actor, leaving a touch of laughter wherever he went—and he went everywhere. Bobo was a man of fierce pride.... He clowned on the mound but there was nothing funny about his high hard one. He could fire as well as any man in the game."

There was one last train to ride, taking him from the Cox-Parker Funeral Home in Winter Park north to the Brown-Pennington Funeral Home in Hartsville. A memorial was held on Monday, December 10, at Brown-Pennington, an open-casket service. The only current major leaguer in attendance was Yankees second baseman Bobby Richardson. For the record, all who actually knew Newsom were shocked by his appearance. "He looked just all worn out," said Bob Shirley. "He looked every bit his age, and then some. No doubt, this was a guy who had led a fast life."[26]

Following the service, a hearse took Newsom's casket to Magnolia Cemetery, on the outskirts of Hartsville. The vehicle drove past the downtown where he had hung out, past Hoot Gibson's auto repair shop, past Shirley's Barber Shop, past the pool hall and old post office, past the old baseball field at Hartsville High. This final trip, unlike so many in his life, was taken at a leisurely pace. There was no game that day, and no one left to talk baseball with.

Louis Norman Newsom was buried in the family plot, directly to the right of his mother's grave. His gravestone, like all those in this part of the cemetery, is quite modest. Just a name, birth and death dates and a logo with a ball, bat and glove. Only one feature sets his gravestone apart from the others: the addition of the word "Bobo" at the top of his marker.[27]

The odyssey of Louis Norman Newsom was over.

Epilogue

Bobo Newsom: Baseball's Traveling Man

A sportswriter once cautioned Bobo Newsom about his incessant bragging. "After a while, no one will listen to you," said the scribe. Newsom replied with a parable: "We once had a band in Hartsville. We found out that we had 13 pieces so we got a boy just to hold a trumpet so it wouldn't be bad luck. Now, that fellow that just stood there and held that trumpet never made a dime. Why? Because he never blew his own horn."[1]

With Newsom's death, he lost his own best press agent. Fortunately, there were those who continued to carry the torch. Sportswriters Bob Addie and Shirley Povich in Washington frequently fell back on Bobo Newsom material, as did Joe Falls in Detroit, Wirt Gammon in Chattanooga and many others. Red Smith remained an admirer. When he was a sports columnist at the *Philadelphia Record*, Smith found Newsom one of his most cooperative (if not unimpeachable) sources. Covering the woeful Athletics didn't provide much in the way of inspiration, but Smith could always count on Newsom for a story. Such verbal generosity was rare in an athlete (then and now), and Smith appreciated it.

Of course, Newsom retained a strong fan base in his hometown of Hartsville.

"Buck was definitely an unforgettable character," said Tallulah Williams, one of his many cousins still residing in the Hartsville area.

> He made quite an impression on this little town. But I guess of all the people down here who knew him and remembered him it was probably his cousin Rex [Newsome] who really kept the stories alive. Rex was kind of the unofficial historian for Buck. The two had been great pals when Buck was still alive, more like brothers than cousins.
>
> Rex could tell Bobo Newsom stories by the hour, and it didn't take a lot of encouragement to get him to do so. Sometimes, he'd embellish a bit. But he'd say, "it might be a lie but it's the truth to me."
>
> Buck had so many friends, folks like Hoot Gibson and Bob Shirley who knew him and looked on him as a hero. So, as far as Hartsville is concerned, I don't think Buck was ever forgotten, or ever will be. It would have been nice if he had been elected to the Baseball Hall of Fame, but maybe it's nicer that he is so fondly remembered in his own hometown, by the people who knew him best.[2]

Hartsville is a progressive town where the engines of commerce run strong. Gradually, the haunts Bobo Newsom knew best have been torn down. The old cotton mill, the ballfield at Hartsville High School and Shirley's downtown barber shop are now gone. Daddy Quill's farm was subdivided and eventually ceased to be a farm. In 1987, it occurred to Hoot Gibson and several others that the city should have some sort of lasting monument to Newsom. Pageland, to the north, had named a portion of State Route 151 in honor of native son Van Lingle Mungo. To Gibson, that seemed like a highly appropriate thing to do for Newsom, especially since Route 151 ran right past the old Newsom homestead. Gibson fired off a letter to the South Carolina Highway Commissioner, and gradually the wheels of bureaucracy cranked out the appropriate legislation, officially renaming a ten-mile stretch of Route 151 near Hartsville the Bobo Newsom Highway. Gibson recalls,

> We got a bunch of politicians in here, they put up some signs, and we had the grand unveiling. Well sir, Bobo himself would have had a great laugh that day. When they took the tarp off the sign, it read "Bo-Bo Newsome" Highway. But the state got right to work and corrected the thing. I think it's a nice honor for Buck, keeps his name alive. Sometimes, folks will stop here in town for a bite to eat, just to ask, "who the hell was Bobo Newsom?"[3]

The Hartsville Museum, located in the old post office building, has maintained a Bobo Newsom exhibit since the 1980s. It's a modest—certainly by Bobo's standards—but sincere tribute. Kathy Dunlap, the museum's director, said,

> We've been fortunate to have received donations, but there are so many things we would like to be able to display that just don't seem to be available. We have to compete with the sports collectors for items, often times I will see something Bobo-related on eBay but I always seem to get outbid. So I guess that's a sign that he still has a fan base out there, somewhere.
> You know, one of the real mysteries of his life is what happened to all his baseball belongings, his trophies and scrapbooks and old uniforms. He played baseball for 30 years. And we know, from talking to his friends and relatives, that he was kind of a pack rat, saving all kinds of things and then bringing them back here to Hartsville. But other than a couple trophies that his cousin Rex donated, we don't have any of that material.[4]

Probably the centerpiece of the Hartsville Museum's collection is Newsom's *Sporting News* trophy recognizing him as Outstanding Player in the Pacific Coast League in 1933. It was donated by Rex Newsome, along with a plaque from 1956 from a service club in Baltimore honoring Newsom for his work with the city's youth. Those two trophies neatly bracket Newsom's long and winding career in baseball.

Of course, the museum also has a few of Newsom's baseball cards. During his long career, Newsom appeared often on bubblegum cards. Some of these cards are highly esoteric to even the die-hard collector. What, for example, is a R313 Wide Pen or a R314 Creamy or a W751 Browns team issue? The definitive Bobo bubblegum card has become the 1953 Topps issue, showing an artist's conception of a rather handsome Newsom, even if there is a tad too much gray showing under the edge of his Philadelphia A's baseball cap. Even taking into account the ball cap, the likeness appears to be that of a Southern politician—Senator Claghorn springs readily to mind—all set to press the flesh. Reportedly, it was his favorite baseball card and the one he gave out to fans for the rest of his life.[5]

Then there are the photos. Newsom was one of the most photographed players of his era, and judging by the hundreds of black-and-white photos still in circulation was a willing participant when it came to off-beat situations and unusual groupings. Invariably, in these shots with other players (some of them teammates, some of them not) everyone is smiling. Of perhaps psychological interest, in posed mug shots Newsom is rarely smiling and is often looking away from the photographer, or eyeing him warily, as if the camera will somehow magically capture hidden secrets.

To Dunlap, more valuable that any trophy or baseball card or photo is the act of compiling and maintaining of an oral history of Newsom's life and times.

> We have been able to preserve several oral histories, and those really are invaluable. It's a way of preserving the real person, what that person was like, what he or she did, where did they go, how they fit in to the history of our town. Of course, the reality is, we are now at a point where we are rapidly losing all those who actually knew Bobo Newsom, or anyone else of his era. Rex Newsome passed away here a few years back, he was the source for so many of these stories about Bobo and I now wish we had been able to get him to sit down and record them on tape. He was an inspired story teller, just like his cousin.
>
> Unfortunately, Bobo didn't leave us an autobiography or an oral history or any letters to speak of—he wasn't the type of person who would sit down and write long letters—so it's always a race against time to preserve the memories of those who did know him.[6]

Still, those stories of Newsom's baseball memorabilia stash are intriguing.

Several friends and relatives report that Newsom rented an old house, on Home Street across from the high school, where he stored his belongings. The baseball material took up an entire room, filling it with items from Newsom's long career, everything from autographed baseballs (one everyone seems to remember was signed by Mae West) to scrapbooks and news clippings to trophies to dozens of old uniforms and caps to a huge, papier-mâché blue elephant, apparently left over from some sort of promotion for the Philadelphia Athletics. Some think Newsom's son Alan inherited the material, some think his ex-wife Lucille.[7]

"Nobody paid much attention to that stuff back then when Bobo died," said Bob Shirley. "I just always assumed the family wound up with it all, but I don't really know. I do know that, the way prices have shot up for sports collectables, it would all be worth a small fortune today. It's too bad the museum doesn't have more of it."[8]

Given that Newsom lived his life in the spotlight, it is perhaps not surprising that his spirit haunts late-night TV Land, from the mythical town of Hooterville and in the person of Pat Buttram. The sitcom "Green Acres" ran seven seasons (1965–1971) on CBS, and among the fictitious inhabitants of Hooterville (which could be read as Hartsville) was an irrepressible flim-flam man, played by Buttram. The show persists in re-runs to this day. In a 1977 interview Buttram said,

> The writers got the notion that my Mr. Haney should be like Dizzy Dean. I thought about it, and said, "No, ol' Diz ain't quite right." As I saw it, Mr. Haney isn't a braggart. He really believes he's the best gol-darn salesman in the world and his truckload of crap is pure gold. So I thought back and hit upon Buck Newsom, the pitcher who never lost a game, at least in his own mind. So I just kind of put my character together based on that. A lot of folks thought I was doing a Dizzy Dean, but it's really a Buck Newsom. Thanks, Buck.[9]

Newsom could have used a Mr. Haney to help talk him into the Baseball Hall of Fame. Eventually, the closest he made it to that hallowed shrine was in 2003, when he made the Hall's Top 200 list of "overlooked" players. Like any random grouping of pre–

1960 major leaguers, the Hall's list includes several of Bobo's ex-teammates, ranging alphabetically from Dick Bartell to Rudy York. If nothing else, the list serves as a reminder of just how fleeting fame is and just how difficult it is to create a level playing field for entry into Cooperstown.[10]

Newsom is in the South Carolina Sports Hall of Fame, an honor he would be especially proud of in light of his undying loyalty to his home state. Whenever a South Carolina newspaper or TV station compiles a list of the state's all-time best athletes, Newsom always makes the list. His moniker also shows up whenever journalists compile their versions of all-time great baseball nicknames. Or all-time baseball eccentrics. So the memories definitely remain, and the Bobo legend has taken on a life of its own.

One who remembered was President Richard M. Nixon. On the campaign trail in the summer of 1972, a reporter—apropos of nothing—asked the president to name his all-time favorite baseball players. The question stumped the president—one would like to think he had more important matters on his mind—but he was game for the challenge. He and son-in-law David Eisenhower spent the better part of the next week at Camp David compiling their all-star teams, divided by National and American Leagues and by era, putting together pre–1945 and post–1945 squads. Among the five pre–1945 AL pitchers was none other than Bobo Newsom, along with Hall of Famers Satchel Paige, Herb Pennock, Lefty Grove and Red Ruffing. Nixon's teams received quite a bit of publicity at the time they were unveiled, in July of 1972. His selection of Newsom created the most controversy (where, oh where, was Bob Feller?). But the president stuck to his guns, defending Newsom's presence on the team by praising his great courage and his willingness to pitch any time, anywhere. The 1972 election and the events that followed gave the president considerably deeper concerns than the inclusion of Louis Norman Newsom on a mythical baseball team.[11]

Flash forward 20 years. The former leader—as part of a fund-raiser at the Nixon Presidential Library in Yorba Linda, CA—was asked to create a new set of all-time All-Star teams. He updated and altered his original lists considerably, but stuck with Newsom as one of his pre–1945 pitchers. Judging by Nixon's comments, he obviously identified with the slings and arrows that Newsom faced during his long and controversial career in the public arena. So Newsom has been enshrined, in a sense, in one Hall of Fame, that of Richard M. Nixon. For the record, there is no evidence the two men ever met.[12]

Newsom's reputation, to the current-day fan, rests largely on his unique statistical record and the colorful stories told by his contemporaries. He has become something of a cult icon to some, a concept that would mystify Bobo, who never thought of himself as the least bit peculiar.

In the years just prior to Red Smith's death, the sports columnist and his cronies formed a highly informal baseball discussion group, which met semi-regularly at a restaurant in Greenwich Village. Members included fellow writers Lawrence Ritter, Jim Bouton, Donald Honig and John Leo. The group quickly agreed on a name: The Bobo Newsom Memorial Fan Club. Beyond that, they rarely agreed on anything. Novelist David Markson, largely by default, was named Bobo Commissioner. Markson gussied that up a tad for his entry in *Who's Who in America*, proclaiming himself president of the Louis Norman Newsom Society.[13]

Newsom is certainly remembered by journalists who covered his exploits and by many of his ex-teammates. Newsom stories abound in many player autobiographies and sportswriters' memoirs. The fact that many of these stories are untrue would bother Bobo not one whit, although it's a trend to be reckoned with for a biographer. Several writers have attempted a full-length biography of Newsom, starting with John Lardner in the late 1950s. Unfortunately, Lardner died suddenly in 1960, depriving Bobo of his best Boswell. After Lardner's death, Newsom half-heartedly cast around for another biographer, but no doubt his mountain of confusing and conflicting press clippings ultimately served as discouraging words, as did the fact that any quotes from Newsom himself would have to be taken with more salt than even Morton could supply. Still, the project remained intriguing and several writers were reported to be working on a Newsom biography as the 21st century dawned.

At least one of these projects was completed, by George Fergusson of Tallahassee, FL. An admitted fan of Newsom—Fergusson saw him pitch in a spring training game in Florida in 1953—Fergusson spent considerable time and trouble putting together his book. Upon completion, Fergusson realized what he had written was more akin to a travelogue than a biography. It is an enjoyable, breezy read, although anyone looking for an objective viewing of Newsom is going to be sorely disappointed. Fergusson's work remains unpublished.

"It was fun to do," Fergusson said. "I probably learned more about myself than I did about Bobo, but I think the biggest thing that I came to know about Bobo was that he never gave up. And, yes, he really was a nut."[14]

As with all things Bobo, the man himself has to have to final word.

"The only thing I ever wanted to be was a baseball player," Newsom told a fellow player late in his career. "I ain't gonna retire until they tear this uniform off of me. After that, y'all know what all these owners will say? 'There's a lot of empty seats in the park today, I sure miss ol' Bobo.' But there ain't gonna be any more Bobos. I'm the last of the breed."[15]

Chapter Notes

Introduction

1. "The Senators' $12,500 pitcher...": from "This Morning with Shirley Povich," *Washington Post*, June 28, 1948, 10.
2. Newsom's pitching records are derived from Carlos Bauer and Bob Hoie, *The Historical Register* (San Diego/San Marino: Baseball Press Books, second printing, May 1999), 392–93.
3. "For a game on August 20...": Frederick Turner, *When the Boys Came Back: Baseball and 1946* (New York: Henry Holt, 1996), 187–88.
4. "He's the only man...": from "Arthur Daley's Sports of the Times" May 28, 1943, as accessed on *New York Times* database, October 15, 2006. Daley was not the first to use this line. The phase was originally used by an anonymous sportswriter circa 1905 to describe Chicago White Sox star pitcher Ed Walsh.
5. Povich's evaluation of Newsom: from "This Morning with Shirley Povich," *Washington Post*, May 30, 1935, 15.
6. "Psychic fallout from the South's loss...": Paul Hemphill, *Lovesick Blues: The Life of Hank Williams* (New York: Penguin, 2006), 15.
7. "I'd rather be lucky...": from "Arthur Daley's Sports of the Times," *New York Times*, May 28, 1943.
8. "I thought he was great...": Author's interview with former major leaguer Johnny Sullivan, June 15, 2004.
9. "We were out driving...": Author's interview with Bob Shirley of Hartsville, SC, August 4, 2004.
10. "erratic natural force": John Lardner, "The One And Only True Bobo," reprinted in *The Second Fireside Book of Baseball*, ed. by Charles Einstein (New York: Simon & Schuster, 1958), 222.
11. "the black sheep": Author's interview with Newsom's cousin John Newsome, August 4, 2004; author's interview with Newsom's cousin Tallulah Williams (sister of John Newsome), August 5, 2004.

Chapter One

1. Best available documentation that 1907 is correct birth year for Newsom: 1920 Federal Census, 7B, Bethel (School) District, Darlington County, SC, taken on January 20, 1920, which lists Norman Newsome, age 11, son of H. Q. B. Newsome; and Florida Certificate of Death for Louis Norman Newsom, registered December 10, 1962, State File No. 62–052123, that lists August 7, 1907, as date of birth and 55 as Newsom's age at time of death.
2. Jake Newsome as the source of "Buck" nickname is mentioned in several sources, and was confirmed by author's interviews with Newsom family members. For example, see 1953 edition of *The Sporting News Baseball Register* under Louis Norman Newsom listing for note on nickname.
3. Some sources list Newsom's birth name as Norman Louis Newsome. Existing legal and U.S. Census documents fail to confirm this. Family members report Newsom disliked the name Louis (from an antecedent on his father's side of the family) and rarely used it except when signing contracts.
4. Origin of Bobo: Author's interview with Tallulah Williams, April 20, 2006.
5. Information on H. Q. B. Newsome and family and Lillian Hicks and family is contained in Newsome file at Darlington (SC) County Historical Commission Museum in Darlington, SC. Information also confirmed in author's interviews with surviving members of the Newsom/Newsome family.
6. History of Newsome Corners and the Newsome farm: *Milestones: Hartsville Centennial 1891–1991* (edited and republished by the Hartsville [SC] Museum, 2000).
7. "There are Newsoms...": Author's interview with John Newsome, August 4, 2004.
8. "From looking at...": Author's interview with Drew Case of Hartsville, SC, August 3, 2004.
9. "A plantation": Tom Deveaux, *The Washington Senators, 1901–71* (Jefferson, NC: McFarland, 2001), 132.
10. "At that time, the sharecroppers...": Author's interview with Tallulah Williams, May 25, 2006.
11. Newsom's academic misadventures: Ibid. Also, interview with L. L. "Luke" Sparrow conducted by Kathy Dunlap, March 22, 1996, on file at Hartsville (SC) Museum. Used by permission.
12. Newsom attending Georgia Tech: Records at the university show no Norman Newsome enrolled in the 1920s. Further, the Georgia Tech athletic department has no record of a Newsom or Newsome pitching for the university's baseball team during that decade. Per exchange of emails with Chris Copo, Georgia Tech sports information director, March 22, 2004.
13. A detailed description of life in Hartsville, circa 1915, is contained in *Milestones: Hartsville Centennial 1891–1991* (edited and republished by the Hartsville [SC] Museum, 2000).
14. Southerners in the major

leagues: Using records in *The Sports Encyclopedia: Baseball*, by Donald S. Neft and Richard M. Cohen (New York: St. Martin's Griffin, 1996), 92–121 and 230–264, players born in the 11 states comprising the Confederacy totaled 115 out of 1,530 major leaguers in the period 1901–1919 (7.5 percent). By the period 1920–1945, the period in which Newsom was in his prime, those numbers had increased to 250 out of 2,605 (9.5 percent).

15. Ty Cobb being highest-paid player: Jonathan Fraser Light, *The Cultural Encyclopedia of Baseball* (Jefferson, NC: McFarland, 1997), 639.

16. The existing legal documents (including depositions and sworn court testimony), along with contemporary newspaper accounts and a study of play-by-play of the 1919 World Series, fail to support the alleged non-involvement of Joe Jackson in the throwing of games. The author is persuaded, by the preponderance of evidence, that Jackson did participate in the "fix" and received money for same.

17. Quill Newsome's success as a farmer: Author's interviews with John Newsome, August 4, 2004, and Tallulah Williams, August 5, 2004.

18. "After that, he...": Bobo Newsom quote on his brother Marion from Dick Farrington, "It Was Just a Breeze for Windy Buck Newsom," *The Sporting News*, October 27, 1938. Also, author's interview with John Newsome, August 4, 2004.

19. "It's safe to say...": John Newsome interview, Ibid.

20. "Buck never met...": Author's interview with Tallulah Williams, August 5, 2004.

21. Newsom's views on race: Professional baseball was integrated in 1946. Newsom did not play on an integrated team until 1952. In contrast to, for example, Bill Veeck, Jr., Newsom is nowhere on record decrying segregation (in or out of baseball). He also is nowhere on record (as are several of his contemporaries) decrying Jackie Robinson's breaking the so-called color line. Suffice to say, even as a young man he was not reluctant to associate with African Americans, and his participation in at least five off-season exhibition series versus Negro league players remained a source of pride for him. Author's interview with Tallulah Williams, May 25, 2006; author's interview with Bob Shirley of Hartsville, SC, August 4, 2004.

22. "Bobo's old man...": Ibid.

23. Information on Lillian Hicks Newsome: Author's interview with Tallulah Williams, May 25, 2006.

24. Newsom's fascination with automobiles: Author's interview with Hoot Gibson of Hartsville, SC, August 6, 2004.

25. "Oooh, he could throw...": Interview with L. L. "Luke" Sparrow, conducted by Kathy Dunlap, March 22, 1996, on file at Hartsville (SC) Museum. Used by permission.

26. Newsom's abbreviated stint in high school: There is no Norman Newsome listed in newspaper accounts of the Hartsville High graduating classes of 1925 or 1926. On the 1940 U.S. Census, Newsom listed his level of education as "2 years of high school."

27. "Shoot, doc...": Interview with L. L. "Luke" Sparrow, March 22, 1996. This was also one of Rex Newsome's favorite stories.

28. "He did want you...": Sparrow interview.

29. "he just didn't...": Ibid.

30. Newsom sent to boarding school: Author's interview with Bob Shirley, August 4, 2004; see also Brenda Lowe, "The Bobo Newsom Story," *Pee Dee Magazine*, II, no. 3 (1990), 15.

31. Carlisle Fitting School: The institution is now known as Camden Military Academy. Information on the history of Carlisle Fitting School is available on the school's Web site: www.camden-military.com.

32. Several newspaper clippings relating to the death of Lillian Hicks Newsome are available in Newsome family file at Darlington (SC) County Historical Commission Museum, Darlington, S.C. However, the most complete account of her death in the file is from an undated (January of 1925?) church bulletin from the Wesley Methodist Church in Hartsville, SC. The Newsoms were members of the church.

33. "Frankly, I'm not sure...": Author's interview with Tallulah Williams, May 25, 2006.

34. Newsom's interlude with the carnival: Author's interview with Bob Shirley, August 4, 2004; author's interview with John Newsome, August 4, 2004; In contrast to the vagabond lifestyle of Bobo Newsom, his brother Marion (who retained the Newsome spelling of the family name) worked for the South Carolina state highway department for over 40 years, older sister Aline was a schoolteacher and younger sister Lilly Belle owned and operated a beauty shop. All of Newsom's siblings are now deceased.

35. Newsom's participation with the Cheraw team is probably most accurately detailed in Dick Farrington's article in *The Sporting News*, October 27, 1938.

36. The first and last names of Newsom's first wife appear in print in various spellings. Lucille is also rendered as Lucile, and her maiden name as Arent, Arants, Arrant and Arrent. Author's research indicates that Arant is most likely correct. The date and site of the Newsome-Arant wedding is from the Newsome family Bible, as accessed by Tallulah Williams.

37. Uncle Jake's intervention: Author's interview with John Newsome, August 4, 2004; author's interview with Tallulah Williams, August 5, 2004.

38. Newsom's aborted tryout with the Columbia Reds is mentioned in several sources, probably most accurately in October 27, 1938, *The Sporting News* article by Dick Farrington. Farrington was able to verify specifics by interviewing Gabby Street, then the Browns manager.

39. Georgia Tech story: Another myth that continues to surface in published accounts of Newsom's life, including one issued by The Society for American Baseball Research (SABR). Per exchange of e-mails with Chris Copo, Georgia Tech sports information director, March 22, 2004.

40. Some accounts have the Brooklyn Dodgers signing Newsom and then assigning his contract to Raleigh. Newsom himself claimed he signed directly with Raleigh, and that seems most likely. It also appears that the Macon Peaches had some sort of arrangement with Wilmington of the East Carolina League, so it's possible that Newsom became property of the Brooklyn Dodgers at some point during the 1928 season.

Chapter Two

1. Raleigh statistics: Newsom's seasonal and career statistics used in this book are from Bob Hoie and Carlos Bauer, *The Historical Register* (San Diego/San Marino: Baseball Press Books, second printing, May 1999), 392.

2. For an account of Newsom's

brief stint at Greenville, see John Lardner, "The One and Only True Bobo," reprinted in *The Second Fireside Book of Baseball*, ed. by Charles Einstein (New York: Simon & Schuster, 1958), 222–229.

3. The tale of Newsom being traded for $18 and two baseball bats was a favorite of Newsom's cousin, Rex Newsome. See Brenda Love, "The Bobo Newsome Story," *Pee Dee Magazine*, II, no. 3 (1990), 15.

4. Weafer's later employment by the Dodgers mentioned in John Lardner, "The One and Only True Bobo," *The Second Fireside Book of Baseball*, 223. The Greenville manager is not to be confused with his younger brother Kenneth Albert "Hal" Weafer, who pitched briefly for the Boston Braves in 1936.

5. McGraw connection in Brooklyn purchasing Newsom's contract: author's interview with former major leaguer Floyd "Babe" Herman, July 3, 1977.

6. John L. Lopez, "Tom 'Shotgun' Rogers: Baseball Death Jogs Painful Memory," *Houston Chronicle*, August 19, 2007, sports section.

7. Newsom going AWOL from spring training with Macon was reported in Jimmy Jones, "Peaches Lick Cards, 7–6, by Scoring Five in Ninth," *Macon Telegraph*, April 6, 1929.

8. For a full account of Macon–St. Louis game, Ibid.

9. "Aw, hell...": Newsom quoted in Russell Streur, "The Diamond Road of Bobo Newsom," *Sports Collectors Digest*, February 7, 1992, 140.

10. "Watch This Boy": from Jimmy Jones article in *Macon Telegraph*, April 22, 1929.

11. "Damn it Buck...": Cal Hubbard quote from author's interview with former major leaguer Marv Owen, April 7, 1978.

12. Newsom's dislike of Paul Richards: Author's interview with former baseball scout Jim Russo, August 12, 1988.

13. "If Buck took...": Author's interview with Bob Shirley, August 4, 2004.

14. Newsom's appearance at Grand Theater: "Newsome is Given Ovation at Grand," non-bylined article in *Macon Telegraph*, July 19, 1929.

15. Newsom's "homecoming" at Columbia: "Buck Newsome Pitches All Way for Macon for Fourteenth Win," *Macon Telegraph*, July 23, 1929; also, author's interview with Tallulah Williams, August 5, 2004.

16. Details of Newsom's call-up to the Dodgers: "Driftin' Along" column by Jimmy Jones, *Macon Telegraph*, September 14, 1929.

17. Newsom's major league debut: Jack Ryder game story from September 12, 1929, *Cincinnati Inquirer*, reprinted in *Macon Telegraph*, September 14, 1929; Murray Tynan game story from September 12, 1929, *New York Herald-Tribune*, reprinted in *Macon Telegraph*, September 14, 1929; Roscoe McGowen, "Robins are Beaten by the Reds, 4 to 2," *New York Times*, September 12, 1929, as accessed on *New York Times* database on October 15, 2006.

18. "It isn't often...": "Driftin' Along" column by Jimmy Jones, *Macon Telegraph* sports section, September 14, 1929.

19. Argument between Newsom and his father: Author's interview with Bob Shirley, August 4, 2004; author's interview with John Newsome, August 4, 2004.

Chapter Three

1. Newsom's attitude toward spring training: John Lardner, "The One and Only True Bobo," reprinted in *The Second Fireside Book of Baseball*, ed. by Charles Einstein (New York: Simon & Schuster, 1958), 223.

2. Wilbert Robinson biographical information: Jonathan Fraser Light, *The Cultural Encyclopedia of Baseball* (Jefferson, NC: McFarland, Fourth Printing, 1997), 622; *Total Baseball*, ed. by John Thorn and Pete Palmer (New York: Harper Perennial, Third Edition, 1993), 81, 1182. See also Robert W. Creamer, *Stengel: His Life and Times* (New York: Simon & Schuster, 1990), 180–181.

3. "McGraw managed...": Author's interview with former major leaguer Floyd "Babe" Herman, July 3, 1977.

4. "akin to being aboard a flouting insane asylum": Fresco Thompson with Cy Rice, *Every Diamond Doesn't Sparkle, Behind the Scenes with the Dodgers* (New York: David McKay, 1964), 4–6.

5. Newsom's attitude in 1930: Author's interview with Floyd "Babe" Herman, July 3, 1977.

6. "Throw the ball into the...": From Roscoe McGowen, "Baseball As It Used To Be," reprinted in *The Third Fireside Book of Baseball*, ed. by Charles Einstein (New York: Simon & Schuster, 1968), 305.

7. "Sure, I like...": From John Lardner, "The One And Only True Bobo," by John Lardner, reprinted in *The Second Fireside Book of Baseball*, ed. by Charles Einstein (New York: Simon & Schuster, 1958), 224.

8. Information on 1930 Dodgers roster: *All-Time Rosters of Major League Baseball Clubs*, revised edition, by S. C. Thompson with revisions by Pete Palmer (South Brunswick, NJ: A. S. Barnes, 1973), 107.

9. Thurston-Newsom connection: Author's interview with Floyd "Babe" Herman, July 3, 1977. It was unclear, from the interview, when Thurston and Newsom discussed baseball in Los Angeles, but likely it was in spring training of 1930 when they were teammates on the Dodgers. Thurston and Newsom both pitched in the California Winter League in 1933–1934.

10. Author's interview with Floyd "Babe" Herman, July 3, 1977.

11. Dazzy Vance biographical information: Jonathan Fraser Light, *The Cultural Encyclopedia of Baseball* (Jefferson, NC: McFarland, Fourth Printing, 1997), 772.

12. Vance cutting his sleeve: Author's interview with Floyd "Babe" Herman, July 3, 1977. Also see Red Smith, *To Absent Friends* (New York: Atheneum, 1982), 466.

13. "How are things going...": Author's interview with Floyd "Babe" Herman, July 3, 1977.

14. Newsom's lack of hitting prowess: Author's interview with former major leaguer Marv Owen, April 7, 1978. Also, Newsom's lifetime batting statistics as they appear on the baseballreference.com website.

15. Burleigh Grimes' comment on Newsom's running: From interview by Donald Honig, as published in *A Donald Honig Reader* (New York: Viking, 1967), 581. Grimes set the time as the spring of 1932 but that clearly can't be correct since Newsom missed spring training that year. Likely he saw Newsom run in the spring of 1930.

16. Newsom's inability to hit George Caster's knuckleball: Author's interview with former minor leaguer Forrest "Frosty" Kennedy, April 17, 1993.

17. Newsom's dislike of New York: Author's interview with Bob Shirley of Hartsville, SC, August 4, 2004.

18. Details on Newsom's three appearances with Jersey City from sports sections of *New York Times*,

various issues, June 15–30, 1930, as accessed on the *New York Times* database, October 16, 2006.

19. Wilbert Robinson's comment on Newsom jumping Jersey City team: Author's interview with Floyd "Babe" Herman, July 3, 1977.

20. Clyde "Pea Ridge" Day, in Peter Golenbock, *Bums: An Oral History of the Brooklyn Dodgers* (New York: G. P. Putnam's Sons, 1984), 23.

21. Newsom's disappointment at being cut loose by Dodgers: Author's interview with Bob Shirley, August 4, 2004.

22. Little Rock Travelers' plight: "Seeks Funds to Build Grandstand," *Arkansas Gazette*, Little Rock (AR), September 14, 1931, 8.

23. Information on 1931 Travelers' roster: Sports sections of *Arkansas Gazette*, Little Rock (AR), various issues, April 1–September 15, 1931.

24. Newsom's participation in foot races: "Foot Race Today," *The Arkansas Gazette*, Little Rock (AR), August 30, 1931, 12.

25. Rogers Hornsby recommending Newsom: Dick Farrington, "It Was Just a Breeze for Windy Buck Newsom," *The Sporting News*, October 27, 1938.

26. "Back then, Buck...": Author's interview with Bob Shirley, August 4, 2004.

27. "Like just about all...": Author's interview with Ernest "Hoot" Gibson of Hartsville, SC, August 5, 2004.

28. "There, that'll cover...": Interview with L. L. "Luke" Sparrow, conducted by Kathy Dunlap, March 22, 1996, Hartsville (SC) Museum. Used by permission.

29. This version of Newsom's 1932 car crash from interview with Rex Newsome, conducted by George Fergusson, April 5, 1995. Used by permission. The author also used accounts of Newsom's injuries and subsequent late arrival to the Cubs as reported in *The Sporting News*, various issues, February–May 1932.

30. Newsom's version of events when he joined the Cubs: Whitney Martin, "Newsom Admits He's Good; Can Imitate Roosevelt," The Special News Service, as it appeared in *The State* (Columbia, SC) sports section, March 26, 1941.

31. Newsom's contract status, 1930–1933: Figures reconstructed from various newspaper accounts of that time, including *The Sporting News*.

32. Newsom during the earthquake: Jim Vitti, *The Cubs on Catalina* (Darien, CT: Settefrati Press, 2003), 187–191.

33. Information on John Frank "Jack" Lelivelt: Richard Beverage, *The Los Angeles Angels of the Pacific Coast League* (Jefferson, NC: McFarland, 2012), 97–99.

34. Statistical information on 1933 Angels: Carlos Bauer, ed. *The Early Coast League Statistical Record, 1903–1957* (San Diego: Baseball Press Books, 2004), 155.

35. Details on Newsom's 1933 season: *The Los Angeles Times* sports sections, various issues, March–October 1933.

36. In later life, Newsom rarely missed an opportunity to claim he won 33 games, not 30, with the Angels (see, for example, John Lardner, "The One And Only True Bobo"). For the record, the *Los Angeles Times* credited him with 31 wins. A statistical review of box scores from the 1933 PCL season by Carlos Bauer in 2009 failed to find the "missing" win but did increase Newsom's saves total to seven (awarded retroactively using criteria established in 1969) and his strikeouts to 221.

37. Newsom's financial windfall in L.A.: Author's interview with Marv Owen, April 7, 1978; author's interview with Bob Shirley, August 4, 2004.

38. "No doubt, Buck...": Author's interview with former major leaguer Jimmy Reese, July 26, 1983.

39. "[Bobo] knew Joe was going...": Former major leaguer Lee Stine quoted in Kary Booher, "Birth of a Legend," *Jackson Sun* (Jackson, TN), as accessed on www.jacksonsun.com Website on March 1, 2004.

40. "Of all the guys I faced...": Author's interview with former major leaguer Ellsworth "Babe" Dahlgren, November 5, 1995.

41. The story of Newsom tagging a runner out at home appeared in print as early as 1940. It was reported at least twice in *Baseball Digest* magazine, among other sources.

42. Orv Mohler plane crash: Reported in various issues of the *Los Angeles Times*, December 1932 to April 1933. Mohler had been at football star at USC.

43. Newsom doing L.A. radio broadcasts: Russell Streur, "The Diamond Road of Bobo Newsom," *Sports Collectors Digest*, February 7, 1992, 140. Also, author's interview with Carl Bruner of Pomona, CA, March 13, 1991.

44. Joe E. Brown incident: Brown quoted in "Out Of The Mike" column by Meiklejohn, *The Pomona Progress-Bulletin* (Pomona, CA), April 15, 1935, 17. Newsom claimed to have appeared in Brown's baseball comedies but he wasn't in Los Angeles for the filming of "Fireman Save My Child" (1932) or "Alibi Ike" (1935). He may have appeared as an extra in "Elmer the Great," portions of which were filmed at L.A.'s Wrigley Field in 1933.

45. Satchel Paige-Buck Newsom series: Author's interview with Bob Hoie, July 18, 2004; also, author's interview with Carl Bruner, March 13, 1991. Hoie researched the series via Los Angeles daily newspapers of October, November, December of 1933 and January of 1934. Bruner attended the December 18 game at Wrigley Field and remembered Paige and Newsom clowning around together for the fans prior to and after the game. See William McNeil, *The California Winter League* (Jefferson, NC: McFarland, 2002) for a full history of the league.

46. Jackie Robinson having attended one of the games: Author's interview with former minor leaguer Stan Gray of Pasadena, CA, April 20, 1990. Gray and Robinson attended the game together at White Sox Park. Later they were teammates on the Pasadena (CA) Junior College baseball team.

47. "the black and white Southerners...": Jackie Robinson and Alfred Duckett, *I Never Had It Made* (New York: G. P. Putnam's Sons, 1972), 81.

48. "How can I pitch in the big leagues...": Cool Papa Bell quoted in Larry Tye, *Satchel* (New York: Random House, 2009), 86–87. In *Buck Leonard: The Black Lou Gehrig*, by Buck Leonard with James A. Riley (New York: Carroll & Graf, 1999) 158–59, Leonard refutes the story, but clearly he is referring to an incident in the 1943 Winter League season, not 1933. The context of the Cool Papa Bell quote sets the alleged incident in 1933, prior to Newsom establishing himself as a major league pitcher. See Chapter Eight for a full account of the 1943 incident.

49. "I doubt that he said that": Author's interview with Bob Shirley, August 4, 2004.

50. Newsom's unhappiness over being drafted by the Browns was mentioned in an article in October 15, 1933, editions of the *Los Angeles Times*, with Newsom being quoted

as saying he would "quit and go back to the farm" rather than play again for Hornsby. Mention was also made of Newsom's reluctance to join the Browns in *The Sporting News*, October 12, 1933, issue announcing the results of the draft.

Chapter Four

1. Conditions in Palm Beach: Author's interview with former major leaguer Jesse Flores, April 7, 1983; author's interview with former minor leaguer Forrest "Frosty" Kennedy, October 22, 1996.
2. Details on Browns' purchase of Newsom: Author's interview with former major leaguer Jack Fournier, June 18, 1970.
3. "He was a nice guy...": Fournier interview, Ibid.
4. Blaeholder's lifetime statistics were accessed on the baseball-reference.com website.
5. Babe Ruth's 600th home run is a capsule study in America's changing financial times. Ruth hit the ball out of Sportsman's Park to right-center, the ball winding up in the street where it was retrieved by a teenage boy. In return for the home run ball, Ruth gave the boy a $10 bill and a new baseball (per Associated Press account of the event).
6. Information on the slider: Author's interview with former baseball coach Ron Squire, February 19, 1973. See also Squire's book, *How to Develop the Successful Pitcher* (Englewood Cliffs, NJ: Prentice Hall, 1965).
7. Regarding Newsom's delivery, author viewed newsreel films of Newsom in action in the 1940 All-Star Game, 1940 World Series and 1947 World Series. See also Bill James and Rob Neye, *The Neyer/James Guide to Pitchers* (New York: Simon & Schuster, 2004), 20, 323. While Newsom's delivery was frequently described as "sidewinding" by the press, as a technical point his delivery (like that of Walter Johnson's) was three-quarters rather than sidearm. For comparison's sake, Ewell Blackwell and Don Drysdale threw sidearm.
8. Bob Feller, "How I Throw the Slider," reprinted in *The Baseball Reader*, ed. by Charles Einstein (New York: Bonanza Books, 1989), 113–14. Feller's essay was originally published in 1953.
9. "room service": Author's interview with Marv Owen, September 30, 1984.

10. Blaeholder's experimentation: Author's interview with Jack Fournier, June 18, 1970.
11. Rogers Hornsby biographical information: Jonathan Fraser Light, *The Cultural Encyclopedia of Baseball* (Jefferson, NC: McFarland, Fourth Printing, 1997), 348.
12. Hornsby's demeanor: Author's interview with Jack Fournier, June 18, 1970; author's interview with Jim Russo, August 12, 1988; author's interview with former major leaguer Earl Johnson, June 1, 1993. For a revealing snapshot of Hornsby, see Jim Russo and Bob Hammel, *Super Scout* (New York: National Book Network, 1992), 89.
13. "He was a miserable...": Author's interview with former sportswriter Arthur Richman, March 12, 1996.
14. Hornsby's "loans": Author's interview with former major leaguer Woody English, September 21, 1992. See also Daniel E. Ginsburg, *The Fix Is In* (Jefferson, NC: McFarland, 1995), 214–15.
15. "He didn't know how...": Charlie Grimm with Ed Press, *Jolly Cholly's Story: Baseball, I Love You!* (Chicago: Henry Regenery, 1968), 86.
16. Rickey arranging Hornsby's move to Browns: Author's interview with Jack Fournier, June 18, 1970.
17. Hornsby's trip to Hialeah Park reported in March 26, 1934, edition of *The Sporting News*.
18. Hornsby's firing in 1937: Author's interview with Jack Fournier, June 18, 1970.
19. Information on 1934 Browns roster: S. C. Thompson, *All-Time Rosters of Major League Baseball Clubs* (revised edition), with revisions by Pete Palmer (South Brunswick, NJ: A. S. Barnes, 1973), 590.
20. Rollie Hemsley's alcoholism: Bob Feller, *Strikeout Story* (New York: A. S. Barnes, 1947), 155.
21. Frank Grube's demeanor: Author's interview with Jack Fournier, June 18, 1970. There were conflicting accounts of Frank Grube's death in the New York newspapers (some accounts reporting he was shot inside his apartment). The shooter was never apprehended.
22. Oscar Melillo's illness: Red Smith, *To Absent Friends* (New York: Atheneum, 1982), 325–326. Smith reports that Melillo's illness was Bright's Disease.
23. Ollie Bejma's "Peanuts" con-

nection: Eugene Murdock, *Baseball Players and Their Times: Oral Histories of the Game 1920–1940* (Westport, CT: Meckler, 1991), 303.
24. "Cliff had been a...": Author's interview with former major leaguer Johnny Berardino, December 2, 1995 (per Berardino's request, the spelling of his last name in this book adheres to what he used during his baseball career, rather than his stage name of John Beradino).
25. Bruce Campbell's back problems: Bob Feller, *Strikeout Story* (New York: A. S. Barnes, 1947), 96.
26. Bruce Campbell's baseball career had an interesting conclusion. After playing for the Washington Senators in 1942, Campbell was drafted. Upon completion of his military service in 1945, at age 35, he requested reinstatement to the Senators. However, due to a clerical error he was left off the Senators' 1946 spring training roster. He sued Clark Griffith (under Federal law, servicemen had to be offered their old jobs back) and won a settlement that included full pay for the 1946 season. His successful lawsuit ended his career in baseball (effectively blacklisting him). See Frederick Turner, *When the Boys Came Back: Baseball and 1946* (New York: Henry Holt, 1996), 55–56.
27. "Who the hell is Buck Newsom?": Dizzy Dean quoted in *The Sporting News*, April 10, 1934. Also, author's interview with Jack Fournier, June 18, 1970.
28. Accounts of Cardinals-Browns City Series exhibitions: *The Sporting News* issues of April 10, 1934, and April 17, 1934.
29. "There were other southern boys...": Kirby Higbe quoted in Donald Honig, *Baseball America* (New York: Touchstone, 2001), 186.
30. For another Dean-Newsom comparison, see Bob Broeg, *My Baseball Scrapbook* (St. Louis: River City, 1983), 77. A revealing portrait of Dizzy Dean is contained in Irwin Silber, *Press Box Red: The Story of Lester Rodney* (Philadelphia: Temple University Press, 2003), 157–159. Much of what Rodney reports about Dean's views on player-management relations can be applied to Newsom.
31. Others comparing Newsom favorably to Dean: Author's interview with Jack Fournier, June 18, 1970.
32. Browns' financial straits: Ibid.
33. May 8 Browns-Yankees game: James P. Dawson, "Yankees Again Win From Browns, 8–3," *New York*

Times, May 9, 1934, as accessed on *The New York Times* website, October 1, 2007.

34. Jim Weaver transaction: *The Sporting News*, March 22, 1934, 43.

35. "garish, county fair...": Ira Berkow, *Red: A Biography of Red Smith* (New York: Times Books, 1986), 40.

36. Browns-Yankees game of May 27: "Yanks Routed by Browns, 16–7; Yield First Place to Indians," non-bylined article in *New York Times*, May 28, 1934, as accessed on *The New York Times* website on October 1, 2007.

37. Browns-Yankees game of June 12: "Yankees Halted by Rain in Fifth," non-bylined article in *The New York Times*, June 13, 1934, as accessed on *The New York Times* website.

38. Newsom's admiration for Babe Ruth: Author's interview with sportscaster Ron Menchine, July 1, 2004.

39. Browns-Yankees game of June 15: James P. Dawson, "Yanks Top Browns for Fourth in Row," *New York Times*, June 16, 1934, as accessed on *The New York Times* website on October 1, 2007.

40. "The Yankees are playing...": Author's interview with former major leaguer Lefty Gomez, January 22, 1982.

41. For a contemporary news account of Newsom's no-hitter, see Rich Coberly, *The No-Hit Hall of Fame* (Newport Beach, CA: Triple Play, 1985), 52.

42. "Were you there?": Author's interview with former minor leaguer "Frosty" Kennedy, November 1, 1995.

43. "No son, only one": Newsom quoted in John Lardner, "The One And Only True Bobo," by John Lardner, reprinted in *The Second Fireside Book of Baseball*, ed. by Charles Einstein (New York: Simon & Schuster, 1958), 222.

44. Season attendance figures used in this book are from *Total Baseball, Third Edition*, ed. by John Thorn and Pete Palmer (New York: Harper Perennial, 1993), 143–145.

45. Rickey-DeWitt efforts to purchase Browns: Author's interview with Jack Fournier, June 18, 1970. Also see Peter Golenbock, *The Spirit of St. Louis* (New York: HarperCollins, 2001), 111.

46. Browns showing a profit: "This Morning With Shirley Povich," *Washington Post*, May 30, 1935, 15. Povich states that the reason the Browns made a profit in 1934 was from the sale of players.

47. Browns' financial situation in the winter of 1934–1935: Fournier interview, Ibid.

48. Newsom and Dean at the commissioner: From an account in *The Sporting News*, April 17, 1935. Also, author's interview with Jack Fournier, Ibid.

49. Newsom unhappy with St. Louis management: Fournier interview, Ibid.

50. Hornsby's intolerance of talk in the dugout: Author's interview with former major leaguer Earl Johnson, June 1, 1993.

51. Newsom "christening" Hornsby's socks: Author's interview with Jack Fournier.

52. Newsom sold to Senators: Contemporary press reports list $40,000 as the price Clark Griffith paid for Newsom. In reality, that amount may have included the writing off of thousands of dollars in gate receipts owed the Senators by the Browns. The actual cash exchanging hands was probably closer to $25,000. Fournier interview, Ibid.

Chapter Five

1. "Bobo looked on Clark Griffith...": Newsom quote from The Associated Press P.M. cycle non-bylined obituary, dateline Orlando, FL, dated December 7, 1962, as accessed on TheDeadballEra.com website on February 1, 2003.

2. "I would have loved...": Author's interview with former major leaguer Johnny Sullivan, June 15, 2004.

3. "It got to be...": Ibid.

4. Clark Griffith biographical information: Jon Kerr, *Calvin: Baseball's Last Dinosaur* (an authorized biography of Calvin Griffith) (Minneapolis: Wm. C. Brown, 1990), 11–24.

5. Al Schacht's difficulties with Nick Altrock and Clark Griffith: Al Schacht, *My Own Particular Screwball: An Informal Autobiography* (Garden City, NY: Doubleday, 1955), 139–140.

6. Clark Griffith's statistical record: Bob Hoie and Carlos Bauer, *The Historical Register* (San Diego: Baseball Press Books, second printing, May 1999), 353.

7. Clark Griffith's politics: Jon Kerr, *Calvin: Baseball's Last Dinosaur*, 20.

8. "I was summoned to...": Author's interview with Johnny Sullivan, June 15, 2004.

9. "Old Griff was...": Author's interview with former major leaguer Roy Sievers, May 7, 1993.

10. Joe Cambria: Author's interview with former major leaguer and baseball executive Al Campanis, March 19, 1977. For additional information on Cambria, see John Rosengren, *The Fight of Their Lives* (Guilford, CT: Lyons Press, 2014), 40.

11. Griffith's views on African Americans: Author's interview with former major leaguer Joe Black, June 15, 1982. Also see Frederic J. Frommer, *You Gotta Have Heart* (New York: Taylor Maid, 2013), 54–55.

12. In Buck Leonard with James A. Riley, *Buck Leonard: The Black Lou Gehrig* (New York: Carroll & Graf, 1995), 98–99, Leonard reports that Griffith interviewed him and Gibson about the possibility of his signing the pair to play for the Senators but backed off, concerned about the precedent it would set and the possibility of losing the Grays as tenants. Leonard believes the interview took place in 1938 or 1939.

13. Griffith versus Veeck: Paul Dickson, *Bill Veeck: Baseball's Greatest Maverick* (New York: Walker, 2012), 216–17. According to Dickson, Griffith approved the move only after he was guaranteed Veeck was not a part of the new ownership team and only after one of the owners, Jerold Hoffenberger, agreed to have his brewery sponsor the Senators' radio and television broadcasts for a fee of $250,000 a year.

14. "It was a modest place...": David Brinkley, *Washington Goes to War* (New York: Alfred A. Knopf, 1988), 88.

15. In the somewhat complicated Griffith/Robertson family tree, Mildred Robertson was actually Calvin Griffith's sister. Clark Griffith was her uncle. However, Clark (who had no children of his own) had Calvin's last name legally changed to his own but never legally adopted him. For further information, see Jon Kerr, *Calvin: Baseball's Last Dinosaur*, 8.

16. Details of the deal involving Joe Cronin: *The Baseball Encyclopedia* (New York: Macmillan, Tenth Edition, 1996), 2551. Washington also received shortstop Lyn Lary in the deal. Some sources report the purchase price as $375,000 but that figure includes the $150,000 in salary that Boston guaranteed Cronin, over a five-year period.

17. (Griffith) "used to say that...":

Jon Kerr, *Calvin: Baseball's Last Dinosaur*, 33.
18. "Clark was trying to be...": Griffith obituary by Shirley Povich, *Washington Post*, October 28, 1955, 1.
19. Bucky Harris biographical information: Jonathan Fraser Light, *The Cultural Encyclopedia of Baseball* (Jefferson, NC: McFarland, fourth printing, 1997), 318.
20. "I thought Harris...": Author's interview with former major leaguer Irv Noren, July 17, 2004.
21. "I liked Bucky...": Author's interview with former major leaguer Tommy Henrich, July 13, 1999.
22. Origin of Bobo nickname: Bob Addie's column from December 8, 1962, sports section of *The Washington Post*.
23. "Either his control was bad or his...": Shirley Povich, "This Morning with Shirley Povich," *Washington Post*, July 22, 1935, 15.
24. Information on 1935 Washington Senators roster: S. C. Thompson, *All-Time Rosters of Major League Baseball Clubs* (revised edition), revisions by Pete Palmer (South Brunswick, NJ: A. S. Barnes, 1973), 615.
25. Information on Earl Whitehill: From SABR Biography Project Earl Whitehill entry by Bill Johnson, as accessed on SABR website on April 15, 2014.
26. Newsom being hit by Averill line drive: John Lardner, "The One And Only True Bobo," reprinted in *The Second Fireside Book of Baseball*, ed. by Charles Einstein (New York: Simon & Schuster, 1958), 225.
27. Newsom's knee injury keeping him out of the military: Author's interview with John Newsome, August 4, 2004.
28. Newsom getting a raise: Lardner, "The One And Only True Bobo," 225.
29. Information on 1936 Senators roster: Thompson, *All-Time Rosters of Major League Baseball Clubs* (revised edition), 616.
30. Newsom-Chapman relationship: Author's interview with Bob Shirley, August 4, 2004.
31. Newsom family discarding Wheaties: Author's interview with John Newsome, August 4, 2004.
32. Newsom's fondness for the Orlando area: Ibid.
33. 1936 Opening Day: See John Lardner, "The One And Only True Bobo," 226; Bob Addie's column in *Washington Post*, December 8, 1962; Shirley Povich's game story in *Washington Post*, April 15, 1936.

34. "Sign that Bobo up!": Author's interview with Bob Shirley, August 4, 2004.
35. Nixon's claim he saw 1936 opener: Press conference in 1992 at the Nixon Presidential Library in Yorba Linda, CA, to announce Nixon's all-time baseball teams.
36. Game accounts of Newsom's 1936 season from *The Sporting News*, various issues, April–October 1936.
37. Newsom facing the best pitchers: Author's interview with former major leaguer Jack Fournier, June 18, 1970.
38. Bob Considine incident: Jimmy Powers, *Baseball Personalities (The Most Colorful Figures of All Time)* (New York: Rudolph Field, 1949), 275.
39. Medical report on Newsom's alcoholism: Author's interview with John Newsome, August 4, 2004.
40. "I don't think Buck was ever...": Ibid.
41. "Oh God, you had to...": Author's interview with Johnny Sullivan, June 15, 2004.
42. Alligator story: Author's interview with Marv Owen, September 30, 1984.
43. "If restoration of harmony...": *The Sporting News*, June 15, 1937.
44. Wes Ferrell biographical information: Dick Thompson, "The Wes Ferrell Story," *The National Pastime*, January 1, 2001; as accessed on HighBeam Research website (www.highbeam.com/library) on March 10, 2004.
45. Newsom-Ferrell bet: Donald Honig, *A Donald Honig Reader* (New York: Simon & Schuster, 1988), 31. The author also accessed the transcript of a phone interview with Ferrell conducted by journalist Don Bradley on April 1, 1973. Used by permission of the Bradley estate.
46. "Nervous little old woman": Shirley Povich, "This Morning With Shirley Povich," *Washington Post*, April 4, 1941.
47. Mel Almada: A mini-biography of Mel (also known as Melo) Almada appears on Hispanic Business website (www.hispanicbusiness.com/forum). Almada was born in Sonora, Mexico, but grew up in Los Angeles and graduated from Los Angeles High School, where he was class president. He spoke English fluently. His older brother, Lou Almada, was an outfielder in the Pacific Coast League from 1928 to 1937. Mel Almada was elected to the Mexican Baseball Hall of Fame in 1972. He died in 1988 in Sonora, Mexico.

48. "Mel just didn't have...": Author's interview with former major league scout Evo Pusich, November 22, 1992.
49. Newsom-Chapman incident with Red Sox: Author's interview with former major leaguer Ellsworth "Babe" Dahlgren, November 5, 1995. Also, author's interview with Bob Shirley, August 5, 2004.
50. "171 IQ": Some sources attribute this quip to Bill Cunningham of the *Boston Globe*. Author has been unable to locate an Egan or Cunningham column in which it appears.
51. "Bobo Morris": Author's interview with Ellsworth "Babe" Dahlgren, June 29, 1992.
52. Newsom placing bets in bullpen: Nicholas Dawidoff, *The Catcher Was a Spy: The Mysterious Life of Moe Berg* (New York: Vintage Books, 1995), 324.
53. "You get back and play...": Newsom quoted in John Lardner, "The One And Only True Bobo," reprinted in *The Second Fireside Book of Baseball*, ed. by Charles Einstein (New York: Simon & Schuster, 1958), 223.
54. Cronin as manager: Author's interview with "Babe" Dahlgren, June 29, 1992. Cronin did the same thing when he managed the Washington Senators in 1933, having catcher Luke Sewell signal pitching changes. See William B. Mead, *Even the Browns* (Chicago: Contemporary Books, 1978), 169.
55. Newsom's rabbits: Jimmy Powers, *Baseball Personalities*, 274.
56. Newsom hopping down dugout steps: Glenn Stout, ed. *Impossible Dreams, a Red Sox Collection* (New York: Houghton Mifflin, 2003), 128.
57. Newsom versus Homestead Grays in Baltimore: Buck Leonard and James A. Riley, *Buck Leonard, the Black Lou Gehrig* (New York: Carroll & Graf, 1995), 142.
58. Newsom's trade to Browns: Author's interview with Jack Fournier, June 18, 1970. Fournier claims he convinced Bill DeWitt to make the trade, using the rationale that Newsom couldn't be any more difficult to handle than Vosmik.

Chapter Six

1. Barnes-DeWitt-Rickey connection: Author's interview with Jack Fournier, June 18, 1970. See also William B. Mead, *Even The*

Browns (Chicago: Contemporary Books, 1978) 56–58 for interview with Bill DeWitt, which provides details on how the Browns operated during this era and also explains the firing of Rogers Hornsby.

2. Gabby Street's firing by Cardinals: Peter Golenbock, *The Spirit of St. Louis* (New York: Harper-Collins, 2001), 121.

3. "We're in spring training...": Author's interview with Jack Fournier, June 18, 1970.

4. Information on 1938 Browns roster: S. C. Thompson, *All-Time Rosters of Major League Baseball Clubs* (revised edition), 592.

5. "He likes to strut...": Gabby Street quote from Dick Farrington, "It Was Just a Breeze for Windy Buck Newsom," *The Sporting News*, October 27, 1938.

6. Re Newsom's pitch count: Several players of this era interviewed for this book remarked on how many pitches Newsom threw. Typical of their comments is one by Johnny Berardino: "You talk about a guy who loved his work. Buck never threw one pitch when he could throw two." Author's interview with Berardino, December 2, 1995.

7. Re Gabby Street's firing: There may well have been a financial angle involved in Street's dismissal late in the 1938 season. Jack Fournier claims it was done mainly to avoid paying the final installment on Street's sizable contract. Author's interview with Fournier, June 18, 1970.

8. "He was an okay guy...": Interview with Harry Caray by journalist Don Bradley, June 19, 1987. Used by permission.

9. "Surprise me." Author's interview with Johnny Bernardino, December 2, 1995.

10. Beau Bell's decline: Author's interview with Jack Fournier, June 18, 1970.

11. Red Kress and Don Heffner: Both had been serviceable players in their younger years, Kress with the Browns (1927–1933) and Heffner with the Yankees in the mid-1930s. See Red Smith, *To Absent Friends* (New York: Atheneum, 1982), 390–392, for information on Kress and his dramatic decline as a ballplayer after a promising start. Also, author's interview with Jack Fournier, June 18, 1970.

12. "With both the Browns...": Fournier interview, Ibid.

13. "They threw at me...": Louie Almada interview conducted by Carlos Bauer, April 15, 1993. Used by permission.

14. "With that team...": Author's interview with Jack Fournier, June 18, 1970.

15. Newsom's bonus for winning 20 games: see Dick Farrington, "It Was Just a Breeze For Windy Buck Newsom," *The Sporting News*, October 27, 1938.

16. "I had just struck out...": Bob Feller quoted in Leonard Lyons, "Reverse Credit, Reverse Charges" *Baseball Digest*, April 1954, 60.

17. "Keep the sugar Bo...": This is one oft-repeated Newsom tale that happens to be true. Author's interview with Jack Fournier, June 18, 1970. See also Dick Farrington, "It Was Just a Breeze for Windy Buck Newsomm" *The Sporting News*, October 27, 1938.

18. Ill-will between Newsom and Joe McCarthy: Author's interview with Tommy Henrich, July 19, 1999.

19. Roger Peckinpaugh comments: Peckinpaugh is quoted as saying the Indians "won't hire a screwball like Newsom" in Bob Broeg, *My Baseball Scrapbook* (St. Louis: River City Publishers, 1983), 77.

20. "I hope you guys can read that!": from Dick Farrington, "It Was Just a Breeze for Windy Buck Newsom," *The Sporting News*, October 27, 1938. Farrington altered the second half of Newsom's comments, but the substance of the quote was confirmed in author's interview with Tommy Henrich, July 19, 1999.

21. "When I was going...": Mike Ross, "Hank Greenberg & Bobo," *The National Pastime: A Review of Baseball History*, 22, January 1, 2002; 125.

22. "I remember him pitching...": Charlie Gehringer quote from Richard Bak, *Cobb Would Have Caught It, The Golden Age of Baseball in Detroit* (Detroit: Wayne State University Press, 1991), 185.

23. "That's all right...": Newsom quoted in Dick Farrington, "It Was Just a Breeze for Windy Buck Newsom," *The Sporting News*, October 27, 1938.

24. "The First Century of Baseball" movie: Talmage Boston, *1939: Baseball's Tipping Point* (Albany, TX: Bright Sky Press, 2005), 209–10.

25. "Nobody really wanted...": Author's interview with Jack Fournier, June 18, 1970.

26. Baseball salaries: Determining the accuracy of baseball salaries in the pre–World War II era is nearly impossible except for a collection at the Baseball Hall of Fame Library which is currently not available. Players were notorious for inflating the figures, and general managers and team owners were equally notorious for simply refusing to divulge them. However, the figure of $40,000 as the top salary for Gehrig has been reported in several sources, and the author believes it is reliable. Feller discusses his progressively higher salaries in his autobiography, *Strikeout Story* (New York: A. S. Barnes, 1947). Jimmie Foxx discussed his top salary, and those of other stars of the 1930s, in a radio interview with Houston, Texas-based reporter R. Donald Bradley in August 1965. Transcription of that taped interview used by permission.

27. "Bobo almost always...": Author's interview with Bob Shirley, August 4, 2004.

28. Newsom's spring holdout in 1939: John Lardner, "The One And Only True Bobo," reprinted in *The Second Fireside Book of Baseball*, 225.

29. Newsom-Haney feud: Author's interview with Jack Fournier, June 18, 1970.

30. Haney-Newsom blowup: "Run-in With Haney Preceded Trading of Newsom," *The Sporting News*. May 18, 1939, 1.

31. "DeWitt realized that the only guy...": Author's interview with Jack Fournier, June 18, 1970.

32. "Unfortunately, the pitchers...": Ibid.

33. Newsom's radio show: Jim Hawkins, "Tigers in Series: From Cobb to Trammell," *Oakland (MI) Press*, October 20, 2006.

34. Del Baker's background: Frederick G. Lieb, *The Detroit Tigers* (New York: G. P. Putnam's Sons, 1946), 230–33.

35. "I liked to play for him...": Charlie Gehringer quoted in Richard Bak, *Cobb Would Have Caught It: The Golden Age of Baseball in Detroit* (Detroit: Wayne State University Press, 1991), 183.

36. "He was so quick...": Author's interview with Marv Owen, September 30, 1984.

37. "Del Baker was one...": Birdie Tebbetts, "I'd Rather Catch," *Atlantic Monthly*, September 1949, 184, no. 3.

38. Roster information on 1939 Tigers: S. C. Thompson, *All-Time Rosters of Major League Baseball Clubs* (revised edition), 496.

39. Red Smith comment on

Rudy York: Red Smith, *To Absent Friends* (New York: Atheneum, 1982), 178.

40. Biographical information on Lynwood "Schoolboy" Rowe: Patricia Zacharias, "Schoolboy Rowe, the Tigers' Southern Gentleman," *Detroit News*, as accessed on Detroit News' "Rearview Mirror" website on February 11, 2006.

41. Newsom and Rowe as roommates: Author's interview with Marv Owen, September 30, 1984.

42. "[Newsom] was a great jokester...": Charlie Gehringer quoted in Richard Bak, *Cobb Would Have Caught It*, 184.

43. First night game in Cleveland: Bob Feller, *Strikeout Story*, 158–159.

44. Newsom's reaction to 1939 All-Star Game snub: John Lardner, "The One And Only True Bobo" reprinted in *The Second Fireside Book of Baseball*, 226.

45. Newsom-Williams encounter: Elden Auker's version of events from Kevin Paul Dupont, "Legends' Tales: 'Trying to get a fastball by him was like trying to get a sunbeam past a rooster,'" sports section of *Boston Globe*, July 22, 2002. See also Elden Auker and Tom Keegan, *Sleeper Cars and Flannel Uniforms* (Chicago: Triumph Books, 2006) 143–144 for a slightly different, but still inaccurate, version of the above events. To verify the actual events in the games of May 7 and July 17, author accessed game stories and box scores for those dates from *New York Times* website.

46. "Ol' Buck was no picnic...": Author's interview with Ted Williams, July 1, 1970. See also Ted Williams and John Underwood, *The Science of Hitting* (New York: Simon & Schuster, 1970).

47. "When (Bobo) came to Detroit...": Mike Ross, "Hank Greenberg & Bobo," *The National Pastime: A Review of Baseball History*, 22, January 1, 2002; 126.

48. "Everybody took their baseball so seriously...": Hank Greenberg quote from *Hank Greenberg: The Story of My Life* by Hank Greenberg, ed. by Ira Berkow (New York: Times Books, 1989), 132.

Chapter Seven

1. Newsom's automobiles: Author's interview with Ernest "Hoot" Gibson, August 5, 2004.

2. Roster information on 1940 Tigers: S. C. Thompson, *All-Time Rosters of Major League Baseball Clubs* (revised edition), 496–497.

3. Landis freeing Tigers' "slaves": Joe Falls, *The Detroit Tigers: An Illustrated History* (New York: Prentice Hall Press, 1989), 90.

4. "Newsom was the heart...": Ibid., 94.

5. Greenberg's bonus for switching positions: Red Smith, *To Absent Friends* (New York: Atheneum, 1982), 178.

6. York's effectiveness with "called" pitches: Author's interview with Marv Owen, September 30, 1984.

7. "The big thing about...": Author's interview with Tommy Henrich, July 19, 1999.

8. York's and Greenberg's September statistics: "The Home Stretch," unpublished magazine article by George Fergusson, 1995, 9. Used by permission.

9. Baker's use of Bartell on cut-off throws: Author's interview with Marv Owen, September 30, 1984.

10. Bartell's pickoff play: Whitney Martin, "Newsom Admits He's Good," The Special News Service, as it appeared in *The State* (Columbia, SC) sports section, March 26, 1941.

11. Higgins' drinking problem: Author's interview with "Babe" Dahlgren, June 29, 1992. "Of all the guys I knew in baseball, I think Mike was probably the one most affected (by alcoholism). He really had a problem there. But the Red Sox kept him on, because he was (owner) Tom Yawkey's favorite drinking buddy."

12. Rowe's injury: Author's interview with Marv Owen, September 30, 1984. "[Rowe] was a great one, Hall of Fame stuff. But somehow he hurt himself, and no one ever figured out what exactly was wrong. Finally, Cochrane got mad, called him a 'yellow bastard' and accused him of faking (the injury). That was it for Schoolie as far as playing for Cochrane was concerned. But Baker handled it differently, and got some good mileage out of Rowe."

13. "Tommy's curveball...": Owen interview, Ibid.

14. "[Newsom] probably was on...": Charlie Gehringer quoted in Richard Bak, *Cobb Would Have Caught It: The Golden Age of Baseball in Detroit* (Detroit: Wayne State University Press, 1993), 184.

15. "[I found] he wasn't always...": Mike Ross, "Hank Greenberg & Bobo," *The National Pastime: A Review of Baseball History*, 22, January 1, 2002, 126.

16. 1940 All-Star Game: Contemporary reports indicate Joe McCarthy had quite a bit of input on selecting the American League All-Star roster (in an era when the managers picked the teams) and it could well be that McCarthy rather than Joe Cronin chose Ruffing as the AL starting pitcher.

17. "If I don't start...": John Lardner, "The One And Only True Bobo," reprinted in *The Second Fireside Book of Baseball*, 226.

18. Ruark-Newsom encounter: Ruark was 24 years old at the time of the incident. Adding to Newsom's foul mood were two factors in addition to Ruark's column: The All-Star Game snub was still on his mind, and when the Tigers arrived in Washington, Newsom found out that his father Quill had suffered a serious heart attack back home in South Carolina. See Lardner, "The One And Only True Bobo," 226.

19. Newsom's thumb injury: The best account appears in "This Morning with Shirley Povich," *The Washington Post*, August 9, 1940, 20.

20. Newsom at the World's Fair: "Auker's Submarine Ball Puzzles Pupils at Fair," non-bylined article in the *New York Times*, July 14, 1940, 61.

21. Newsom's quest for special salve: Richard "Dick" Bartell with Norman L. Macht, *Rowdy Richard* (Berkeley, CA: North Atlantic Books, 1987), 100. Bartell doesn't date the incident but circumstances indicate it took place after the loss to the Athletics that snapped Newsom's winning streak in 1940.

22. Details of 1940 pennant drive: George Fergusson, "The Home Stretch," unpublished magazine article, 1995. Fergusson researched the month of September by tracking daily game stories in New York, St. Louis and Cleveland newspapers' sports sections. Used by permission.

23. "We just were never...": Author's interview with Tommy Henrich, July 19, 1999.

24. Yankees' botched play: Author's interview with "Babe" Dahlgren, November 5, 1995. Dahlgren claimed McCarthy blamed him for not catching Gordon's throw.

25. Oscar Vitt's problems with "Crybabies": Bob Feller, *Strikeout Story* (New York: A. S. Barnes, 1947), 173–205, is probably the

best account of the Cleveland Indians' 1940 season. See also Franklin Lewis, *The Cleveland Indians* (New York: G. P. Putnam's Sons, 1949), 200–213.

26. "Sometimes I feel that": Feller, *Strikeout Story*, 180.

27. "We had a great manager...": Newsom quoted in Whitney Martin, "Newsom Admits He's Good," The Special News Service, as it appeared in *The State* (Columbia, SC) sports section, March 26, 1941.

28. Indians players' meeting with Alva Bradley: Author's interview with former major leaguer Lou Boudreau, May 28, 1980. "I wasn't at the meeting ... but I know for a fact one of the players ratted us out (to the media). I know who it was, Feller knows who it was, but (the player) is gone now so to hell with it. After that, we wound up fighting as much with ourselves as with Vitt. By the end of the year, we had guys who wanted to kill each other."

29. "How'm I doin' Edna?": Patricia Zacharias, "Schoolboy Rowe, the Tigers' Southern Gentleman," *Detroit News*, as accessed on the Detroit News' "Rearview Mirror" website on February 11, 2006.

30. Averill as a bench jockey: Author's interview with Lefty Gomez, January 22, 1982. "Baseball had a lot of rough, tough guys back then.... Earl Averill was one of those tough guys.... He had gotten into it with Vitt there in Cleveland and that bad blood carried over when Earl was in Detroit. We were kidding around at the batting cage [in the spring of 1940] and someone asked Earl if he wanted to fight Vitt. He growled, 'hell no, I wanna kill him!' Now, that's a tough guy."

31. Oscar Vitt's demeanor: Feller, *Strikeout Story*, 179. For more information on Vitt, see Franklin Lewis, *The Cleveland Indians* (New York: G. P. Putnam's Sons, 1949), 200–13.

32. "The club I fear...": Oscar Vitt quoted in "Superstitious Mr. Vitt Looks Ahead to a Victorious Season," United Press non-bylined story as published in the *Washington Post*, July 7, 1940.

33. "Trotsky Dead!": Richard "Dick" Bartell with Norman L. Macht, *Rowdy Richard* (Berkeley, CA: North Atlantic Books, 1987), 280.

34. Baker stealing signs: Author's interview with Marv Owen, September 30, 1984.

35. Rowe injured in September 17 game: Author's interview with Babe Dahlgren, November 5, 1995. "Years later, I ran into Schoolboy and he told me he did it with mirrors there in 1940. Seems he messed up his shoulder pitching in September, wanted to hang it up, but Baker hushed it up and nursed him through it."

36. Floyd Giebell: In addition to Fergusson's research, the author accessed Vince Agul, "Tigers' 1940 pennant-clincher: Game of his life," *Detroit Free Press*, September 23, 2003, on Detroit Free Press' website, www.freep.com on October 3, 2006.

37. Detroit's arrival in Cleveland: Richard "Dick" Bartell with Norman L. Macht, *Rowdy Richard* (Berkeley, CA: North Atlantic Press, 1987), 287.

38. Giebell's effectiveness: Author's interview with Marv Owen, September 30, 1984. "He had an above-average curveball, below-average fastball and not great command of either pitch. But he was a tall, lanky guy with a bizarre delivery, very unusual, and if you were facing him for the first time you were going to have trouble. After that, he was going to have trouble getting anybody out."

39. "The fans thought Schoolboy...": Giebell quoted in Vince Agul, "Tigers 1940 pennant-clincher: Game of his life," *Detroit Free Press*, September 23, 2003.

40. Feller's reaction to losing Giebell game: Feller, *Strikeout Story*, 199.

41. "Baker, who coached third...": Ibid., 201.

42. Daddy Quill's trip to Cincinnati: In addition to numerous newspaper accounts of the events of the 1940 World Series, the author has relied on interviews with Newsom relatives Rex Newsome and Tallulah Williams. By all family accounts, the opening game of the World Series was the first time Quill had seen his son pitch since the Macon-Columbia game in 1929. Also see Mike Ross, "Tragedy And Triumph: Bobo Newsom's 1940 World Series," *The National Pastime: A Review of Baseball History*, 10, January 1, 1990, 75–79.

43. Newsom's whereabouts after Game One: An account in the *Hartsville (SC) Messenger* published on October 4, 1940, reports funeral services for H. Q. B. Newsom were held October 3 at a Cincinnati mortuary and that Bobo was in attendance, along with other family members. At that time, it was still uncertain if Bobo would accompany the family back to South Carolina for burial (scheduled for October 5 in Hartsville) or rejoin the Tigers.

44. Newsom's reaction to Game Five: Some newspaper accounts indicate Newsom gave interviews afterward, others indicate he broke down in the locker room immediately after the game and that Billy Sullivan, Schoolboy Rowe and several other teammates forced sportswriters away (in some accounts, physically throwing them out of the room). See also James P. Dawson, "Newsom Shows Emotion After His Mound Masterpiece," *New York Times*, October 7, 1940, 23. According to Dawson, Newsom returned to the locker room after his breakdown and at that time talked to sportswriters.

45. Bucky Walters' effectiveness: Author's interview with Marv Owen, September 30, 1984. Also, author's interview with former major leaguer Ewell Blackwell, March 17, 1993: "Walters was a master. When he was on, he never got a pitch above the (batters') knees all day. All he threw was one pitch, but that's all he needed."

46. Baker stealing Jimmy Wilson's signs: Mike Ross, "Hank Greenberg & Bobo," *The National Pastime: A Review of Baseball History*, 22, January 1, 2002: 125.

47. "I think we would have shot...": Richard "Dick" Bartell with Norman Macht, *Rowdy Richard*, 302.

48. "Damn it, we knew...": Ibid.

49. "I can see it now...": Ibid.

50. Higgins being hit by batted ball: Author's interview with Babe Dahlgren, June 29, 1992, in which he mentioned the odd play and Higgins' reaction to it.

51. "Bartell must have thought...": Richard Bak, *Cobb Would Have Caught It: The Golden Age of Baseball in Detroit* (Detroit: Wayne State University Press, 1993), 190. In post–1940 interviews, Newsom and Greenberg defended Bartell, while Birdie Tebbetts and Mike Higgins said Bartell botched the play. In his autobiography, Bartell devotes three pages (303–05) to the play but fails to make a convincing argument for his innocence.

52. "We had the best short stop...": Whitney Martin, "Newsom Admits He's Good," The Special News Service, as it appeared in *The State* (Columbia, SC), March 26, 1941.

53. "Are you going...": John

Chapter Eight

1. Robert W. Creamer's *Baseball in '41* (New York: Viking, 1991) remains the most pertinent account of the 1941 season. It is clear that 1941 was a watershed in baseball history, in which DiMaggio and Williams replaced Gehrig and Foxx as the reigning superstars, and Feller eclipsed Lefty Grove and Carl Hubbell as the top pitcher.
2. Newsom's homecoming: The *Hartsville Messenger* reported a crowd of more than 5,000 for Newsom's return home that October, which would indicate virtually everyone in town attended the parade.
3. "Step aside little Bo...": John Lardner, "The One And Only True Bobo," reprinted in *The Second Fireside Book of Baseball*, 227.
4. Feller-Newsom salary "war": "Cream Pitchers," non-bylined article in *Time*, February 3, 1941. *Time* reported that Feller ultimately received $45,000 for 1941. This appears inflated. What is clear is that Newsom used published figures of what Feller had been paid to feather his nest with Briggs, playing the Tigers owner against Indians owner Alva Bradley. As a point of reference, Roger Kahn in his book *Joe & Marilyn*, reports that Joe DiMaggio made $32,500 in 1940 and $37,500 in 1941.
5. "If Mr. Briggs says...": "This Morning with Shirley Povich," *Washington Post*, April 9, 1941.
6. Newsom's 1941 Cadillac: A "stock" 1941 Cadillac sold new for around $2,000. Ernest "Hoot" Gibson, who drove and serviced the car, reports Newsom's Caddy was custom-made from the frame up.
7. Newsom's grand entrance: Author's interview with Ernest "Hoot" Gibson, August 5, 2004.
8. "After that, we had...": Ibid.
9. "Those suckers covered...": Author's interview with Bob Shirley, August 4, 2004.
10. Newsom's $50,000 estimate: Ibid. (Bobo may have factored his new car into this figure.)
11. Newsom's restaurant: Reportedly, Hartsville businessman Cal Jordan was the chief investor in the restaurant. Newsom's uncle Jake and cousin Rex also owned stakes in the business.
12. Newsom's marital problems: The banquets at Hartsville and Cheraw that October were two of the last appearances in public for the couple. Lucille had not spent the season of 1940 in Detroit. See Mike Ross, "Hank Greenberg & Bobo," *The National Pastime: A Review of Baseball History*, 22, January 1, 2002: 126.
13. Diamond Star Grill: The sign on the restaurant was eventually changed to read "Newsom's." The restaurant was located on U.S. Route 15, approximately two miles north of Hartsville's downtown.
14. Encounter with hitchhiker: C. Phillip Francis, "Letters from Harvey," (an interview with former major leaguer Harvey Riebe), as accessed on the www.chatterfromthedugout.com website on February 17, 2006.
15. "Where's the Cadillac?": Author's interview with former major leaguer Tuck Stainback, July 10, 1977.
16. Fate of the Buck Newsom Cadillac: Author's interview with Ernest "Hoot" Gibson, August 5, 2004.
17. "Who had a better year...": Author's interview with Tuck Stainback, July 10, 1977.
18. Lucille remaining in Hartsville: Author's interview with Bob Shirley, August 4, 2004.
19. Roster information on 1941 Tigers: S. C. Thompson, *All-Time Rosters of Major League Baseball Clubs* (revised edition), 497.
20. Newsom's visit with Joe Jackson: Shirley Povich, *All Those Mornings ... At the Post*, ed. by Lynn, Maury and David Povich (New York: Public Affairs, 2005), 75–79. Povich reports that Jackson did go to the Tigers-Reds game at Greenville, and that Newsom was not in attendance. According to Tuck Stainback, he and Newsom visited Jackson at his home. Also, author's interview with Jack Fournier, June 18, 1970.
21. Newsom's behavior in 1941 season: "The One And Only True Bobo" by John Lardner, as reprinted in *The Second Fireside Book of Baseball*, 228.
22. "Policeman" Greenberg: Author's interview with Tuck Stainback, July 10, 1977.
23. "Newsom, you can't be...": Interview with Tuck Stainback, Ibid. Stainback said, "[Things] got so bad there (in 1941) that Judge Landis actually called Bobo on the carpet, to make sure he wasn't throwing games."
24. "Stay where you are...": Birdie Tebbetts quoted in *The Detroit Tigers* by Frederick G. Lieb (New York: G.P. Putnam's Sons, 1946) 254.
25. Del Baker's fall from grace: Author's interview with former major leaguer Red Embree, June 20, 1992: "I played for him at San Diego (in the PCL) and thought he was outstanding at inside baseball, strategy, that kind of stuff. Why he wasn't managing in the majors, and why some of the guys I played for up there were, was a mystery to me. I think Del had gone through a lot of crap at Detroit and just decided he didn't want that kind of hassle again."
26. 1941 All-Star Game: In some of the news photos of the celebration for Williams at home plate, Newsom can be seen (in street clothes) in the background.
27. "I don't think any...": Author's interview with Tommy Henrich, July 19, 1999.
28. "The team with Joe DiMaggio...": Joe Cronin quoted in *Joe & Marilyn: A Memory of Love* by Roger Kahn (New York: William Morrow, 1986), 116.
29. "The pitcher always controls...": Author's interview with former major leaguer Al Zarilla, October 15, 1990.
30. Red Embree's curveball: Author's interview with Red Embree, June 20, 1992.
31. Newsom's salary cut: Newsom himself was the "leak" in the contract negotiations. Judging by the sheer volume of interviews quoting him in the newspapers during the winter of 1941–42, it appears he simply got on the phone and called sports editors to report the Tigers' offer.
32. "Surpassingly bald head": "The One And Only True Bobo" by John Lardner, as reprinted in *The Second Fireside Book of Baseball*, 228.
33. Griffith's role as baseball's lobbyist: *Calvin: Baseball's Last Dinosaur* by Jon Kerr (Minneapolis: Wm. C. Brown Publishers, 1990), pp. 34–35; also see *Even The Browns* by William B. Mead (Chicago: Contemporary Books, 1978), 24–27.
34. Roster information on 1942 Senators: *All-Time Rosters of Major League Baseball Clubs* (revised edition) by S.C. Thompson, 618.
35. "We had some good...": Author's interview with Johnny Sullivan, June 15, 2004.

36. "When you talk about...": George Case quoted in *A Donald Honig Reader* by Donald Honig (New York: Simon & Schuster, 1988), 293–294.
37. "Bobo, I want to introduce...": "The One And Only True Bobo" by John Lardner, reprinted in *The Second Fireside Book of Baseball*, 222.
38. "He was very, very good": Author's interview with Johnny Sullivan, June 15, 2004.
39. Newsom as "preacher": *A Donald Honig Reader* by Donald Honig, 294.
40. "He could quote...": Interview with former major leaguer George Myatt conducted by George Fergusson, March 15, 1995. Used by permission.
41. "Bob, ya got change...": *A Donald Honig Reader* by Donald Honig, 294.
42. Newsom at the White House: Author's interview with Tuck Stainback, July 10, 1977.
43. Newsom's telegram to Dodgers: This was reported, after the fact, in several New York newspapers. Red Smith renders the telegram as "Have No Fear, Bobo is Here." Author's interview with former sportswriter and Dodgers executive Lee Scott, July 30, 1977: "With Newsom in town, the writers had a ball. They could make up anything and he wouldn't deny it. In fact, you could convince him he *did* say it. The telegram story was a phony, some writer made that up and everyone else jumped on it."
44. Dodgers-Cardinals game of July 19: Author's interview with Enos Slaughter, August 2, 1981: "[That play] is what killed 'em. Without Reiser, they [the Dodgers] were about half the team they had been. He was that good."
45. Newsom-Higbe connection: Kirby Higbe quoted in Russ Mellotte, "Bobo Sent His Christmas Cards Out Early," *The State* (Columbia, SC), December 8, 1962. Of all the obituaries of Newsom that appeared in print, Mellotte's was probably the most accurate. It was written with the assistance of Newsom family members.
46. Newsom's marital problems: Author's interview with Bob Shirley, August 4, 2004.

Chapter Nine

1. Dodgers' purchase price for Newsom: Fresco Thompson with Cy Rice, *Every Diamond Doesn't Sparkle: Behind the Scenes with the Dodgers* (New York: David McKay, 1964), 55–56. Thompson was a member of the Dodgers' front office at this time.
2. Rickey hired by Dodgers: Author's interview with Al Campanis, March 22, 1977. See also Peter Golenbock, *Bums* (New York: G. P. Putnam's Sons, 1984), 79–84; and Fresco Thompson, *Every Diamond Doesn't Sparkle*, 52–59.
3. "Birds fly south for the winter...": John Lardner, "The One And Only True Bobo," reprinted in *The Second Fireside Book of Baseball*, 226.
4. Newsom's troubled marriage: Author's interview with Tallulah Williams, August 4, 2004.
5. Newsom absent in spring training: Jimmie Thompson, "Bobo Will Ask For Release If Not Satisfied," *The State* (Columbia, SC) sports section of March 21, 1943.
6. Rickey-Newsom exchange: Author's interview with former sportswriter and Dodgers executive Lee Scott, July 30, 1977.
7. Rickey seeking Newsom's removal from roster: John Lardner, "The One And Only True Bobo," reprinted in *The Second Fireside Book of Baseball*, 227.
8. Kirby Higbe's behavior: Author's interview with former major leaguer Spider Jorgensen, February 22, 1995: "The modern players all think they invented sex. But the champion (expletive) of all time had to be Kirby Higbe. He could just look at a gal and get her in bed. He's the only guy I know that literally (fornicated) himself right out of baseball."
9. "Leo had no qualms...": Author's interview with former major leaguer Bill Rigney, August 3, 1984.
10. "The sleek, hungry mice...": Author's interview with Lee Scott, July 30, 1977.
11. Information on 1943 Dodgers roster: S. C. Thompson, *All-Time Rosters of Major League Baseball Clubs* (revised edition), 113.
12. "He could see I was upset...": Author's interview with Al Campanis, March 22, 1977.
13. Rickey-Durocher views on unions: Author's interview with Lee Scott, July 30, 1977.
14. Filming of "Whistling in Brooklyn": Author's interview with Red Skelton, April 11, 1983. See also Leo Durocher, *The Dodgers And Me* (Chicago: Ziff-Davis, 1948), 150.
15. "I go out and start...": Skelton interview, Ibid. According to Skelton, the baseball bits used in the movie were devised by Buster Keaton. Keaton is not listed in the film's credits.
16. "Here's what you need to know...": Skelton interview, Ibid.
17. Newsom as Rags Ragland's replacement: Ibid.
18. Ban on filming at Ebbets Field: Author's interview with Al Campanis, August 1, 1977. Also, author's interview with Lee Scott, July 30, 1977. According to Scott, Walter O'Malley was actually the Dodgers executive who decided on the ban, and enforced it (with rare exceptions) until he stepped down as team president in 1970.
19. "The guy thought...": Leo Durocher, *The Dodgers and Me* (Chicago: Ziff-Davis, 1948), 63.
20. "They love ol' Bobo...": Red Barber, *1947: When All Hell Broke Loose in Baseball* (New York: Da Capo Press, 1982), 157–58.
21. Durocher's card playing: Peter Golenbock, *Bums* (New York: G. P. Putnam's Sons, 1984), 107–08.
22. Joe Medwick's departure: Author's interview with Lee Scott, July 30, 1977.
23. Events of July 9 game: Some accounts claim the dispute between Newsom and Durocher arose due to Newsom's pitch selection to the Pirates' Vince DiMaggio. The author is persuaded that the dispute came about due to the pitch that got away from Bobby Bragan. For various accounts of the incident and its aftermath, see Leo Durocher, *The Dodgers And Me* (Chicago: Ziff-Davis, 1948), 160; Gerald Eskenazi, *The Lip: A Biography of Leo Durocher* (New York: Wm. Morrow, 1993), 172–74; Donald Honig, *A Donald Honig Reader* (New York: Simon & Schuster, 1988), 128–29; Peter Golenbock, *Bums* (New York: G. P. Putnam's Sons, 1984), 54.
24. "Pitching for Durocher...": Author's interview with former major leaguer Roger Bowman, June 15, 1992.
25. Cohane overhearing Durocher and Casey: Author's interview with Lee Scott, July 30, 1977. Scott said the reason Cohane was not in attendance at the Saturday game was because, as a Jew, he was observing the Sabbath.
26. "Durocher had a real sharp...": Billy Herman quoted in Donald Honig, *A Donald Honig*

Reader (New York: Simon & Schuster, 1988), 128.

27. "Take this uniform and...": Vaughan quoted by Billy Herman in *A Donald Honig Reader*, 128.

28. "If Bobo ain't playing...": Author's interview with Lee Scott, July 30, 1977. Al Campanis (who was not with the team in July) identified Johnny Allen as the most vocal "rebel." While the mutiny has been reported numerous times, including Roscoe McGowen's initial account in the *New York Times*, it is clear that probably only Durocher knew all of the particulars. For example, some sources say Newsom was not at Ebbets Field for the game of July 10, while others report he and Arky Vaughan sat together in box seats near the Dodgers dugout. Unfortunately, in Durocher's 1976 autobiography, *Nice Guys Finish Last* (co-written with Ed Linn) the incident is not mentioned.

29. Newsom's trade to the Browns: The speed at which Branch Rickey was able to accomplish the deal leads one to speculate it was already in the works prior to events of July 9–10. Given the shortage of quality pitching in the majors in 1943, it is amazing that all seven of the other National League teams, along with at least four American League teams, passed on acquiring Newsom's services.

30. Vaughan's retirement: Red Smith, *To Absent Friends* (New York: Atheneum, 1982), 92–94.

31. "I just got the rawest...": Newsom quoted in several sources, including John Lardner, "The One And Only True Bobo." Newsom was outspoken about what happened to him, blaming his ouster on Rickey's reluctance to pay the $5,000 bonus and not on his tirade against Durocher after the game of July 9.

32. Newsom's demands to DeWitt: Author's interview with Jack Fournier, June 18, 1970. See also William B. Mead, *Even The Browns* (Chicago: Contemporary Books, 1978), 113.

33. "It looked like we might...": Author's interview with former major leaguer Joe Schultz, November 11, 1993.

34. "Bobo Newsom, what a character...": Author's interview with former major leaguer Al Zarilla, October 15, 1990.

35. "[Newsom] just didn't materialize...": William B. Mead, *Even The Browns* (Chicago: Contemporary Books, 1978), 113.

36. Actually, Newsom did not record a complete game for the 1943 Browns.

37. Newsom's sale to the Senators: Some sources break down the sales of Newsom, Niggeling and Clift as separate deals, on different dates. Author's sources indicate they were all part of the same transaction.

38. Harlond Clift's departure from Browns: Author's interview with Joe Schultz, November 11, 1993.

39. "The ballclub has been good to me...": John Lardner, "The One And Only True Bobo," reprinted in *The Second Fireside Book of Baseball*, 229.

40. Newsom in L.A. in 1943: Author's interview with Bob Hoie, July 18, 2004. Hoie researched the abbreviated 1943 winter league season by accessing *The Sporting News* and the *Los Angeles Times*, various issues, October–November of 1943. Also see Buck Leonard and James A. Riley, *Buck Leonard, The Black Lou Gehrig* (New York: Carroll & Graf, 1995) 158–59. Leonard makes it clear the series was halted by Commissioner Landis following reports of Newsom's antics, which may or may not have included racial slurs. Hoie's research indicates the deciding factor was the fogged-out game and Newsom's demand for payment for same.

41. Participants in 1943 Winter League season: Author's interview former major leaguer Roy Partee, June 2, 1993.

42. Abrupt end to 1943 Winter League season: Ibid. Partee said the series ended when Pirrone complained to the commissioner's office about Newsom and Paige skipping out on pitching assignments for which they had been paid in advance. See also Buck Leonard and James A. Riley, *Buck Leonard, The Black Lou Gehrig* (New York: Carroll & Graf, 1995) 158–59.

43. Newsom's marriage problems: Author's interview with Tallulah Williams, August 5, 2004.

Chapter Ten

1. 1945 Opening Day rosters: Frederick Turner, *When the Boys Came Back: Baseball and 1946* (New York: Henry Holt, 1996), 10–11.

2. Ruth Griffiths Newsom: Fueling the rumor that Kay was related to Clark Griffith was the fact she was a favorite companion of Griffith in his final years. She may have also worked for the Senators in a secretarial capacity at some point. The 1940 U.S. Census confirms the spelling of her last name and her age (at that time, 18).

3. "She was a honey blond...": Author's interview with Bob Shirley, August 4, 2004.

4. "A really beautiful person...": Author's interview with Tallulah Williams, August 5, 2004.

5. Lucille's divorce action: Lucille originally filed for divorce in July 1943. Bobo was granted a delay in the trial until the season ended.

6. "This ol' Army doctor...": Author's interview with Bob Shirley, August 5, 2004.

7. "I always felt a little sorry...": Author's interview with Tallulah Williams, August 5, 2004.

8. Mack-Newsom news conference: Red Smith, *To Absent Friends* (New York: Atheneum, 1982), 30.

9. 1944 Athletics spring training: Author's interview with Jesse Flores, April 7, 1983.

10. "Hartsville must be...": Author's interview with Bob Shirley, August 4, 2004.

11. Connie Mack biographical information: Red Smith, *To Absent Friends* (New York: Atheneum, 1982), 29–31; Jonathan Fraser Light, *The Cultural Encyclopedia of Baseball* (Jefferson, NC: McFarland, 1997), 428–429.

12. "Young man, do I...": David Jordan, "Woody Wheaton Remembered" (dated 2003), as accessed on the Philadelphia Athletics Historical Society website on June 1, 2005.

13. Earle Mack's shortcomings: Author's interview with former major leaguer Ray Coleman, July 19, 1993: "Earle was totally clueless. He never knew the count or how many outs there were. An embarrassment to the team. Only out of respect for his old man did the players put up with Earle." Also, Red Smith, who had arguments with Earle Mack over media coverage of the A's, describes the younger Mack as a "moron." Quoted in Ira Berkow, *Red: A Biography of Red Smith* (New York: Times Books, 1986), 81.

14. Mack-Newsom debate: Author's interview with former major leaguer Jesse Flores, April 7, 1983.

15. "Daddy says you have to come out now": Author's interview

with Jesse Flores. Flores said Newsom's reply to Earle Mack was so loud "that the whole ballpark heard it."

16. "As for Buck...": Flores interview, Ibid.

17. "That's not gonna be a problem...": Newsom quote rendered in the media as "If all the Philly fans who came out to boo me come back out to cheer me, we'll fill the place." Author's interview with Jesse Flores.

18. Roster information on 1944 Athletics: S. C. Thompson, *All-Time Rosters of Major League Baseball Clubs* (revised edition), 571.

19. "Jittery" Joe Berry: Berry was a native of Arkansas whose given first name was Jonas. He pitched for Los Angeles in the PCL from 1936 to 1941 and, briefly, for the Chicago Cubs in 1942.

20. "The biggest plus...": Ibid.

21. "Bobo Newsom and I...": Bob Savage, "Bob Savage Tells His Story" (dated 2000), as accessed on the Philadelphia Athletics Historical Society website on June 1, 2005.

22. 1944 Opening Day: Harrington E. Crissey, Jr., "An Interview With Lum Harris," (dated 2002), as accessed on the Philadelphia Athletics Historical Society website on June 1, 2005.

23. "The other players knew...": Ibid.

24. Athletics' game of August 4, 1944: Bob Warrington, "A 1944 Tribute to Connie Mack," (dated 2005), as accessed on the Philadelphia Athletics Historical Society website on February 10, 2006.

25. September series with Browns: William B. Mead, *Even The Browns* (Chicago: Contemporary Books, 1978), 168.

26. Newsom taking off his socks: "Once a Dodger...," non-bylined article in *Time*, September 14, 1942.

27. Newsom's superstitions: Ed Pollock, "Bobo's Planned Superstition," reprinted in *Baseball Digest*, May 1944, 39–40. Also see "SABR's Baseball Biography Project: Bobo Newsom" by Ralph Berger (dated 2002), as accessed on SABR website on March 10, 2004.

28. "Otherwise, he'd still be...": Author's interview with Jesse Flores, April 7, 1983.

29. Scraps of paper trick: "Seventh Inning Stretch with Phil Rizzuto," National Baseball Hall of Fame website, as accessed on March 10, 2004. Also, author's interview with Ray Coleman, July 19, 1993. Coleman said he learned the trick from Walt Judnich, who had learned it when playing in the Yankees' minor league system.

30. Bobo smoking Chesterfields: Author's interview with Ernest "Hoot" Gibson, August 5, 2004.

31. Newsom's broken collarbone: Author's interview with Bob Shirley, August 4, 2004.

32. Roster information on the 1945 Athletics: S. C. Thompson, *All-Time Rosters of Major League Baseball Clubs* (revised edition), 572.

33. "One of Bobo's favorite...": Mike Ross, "Hank Greenberg & Bobo," *The National Pastime: A Review of Baseball History*, 22, January 1, 2002, 126.

34. "He wasn't a rapid...": Ibid., 126.

35. "Whatta asking me for?": Author's interview with Jesse Flores, April 7, 1983.

36. Newsom lying about his age: Author's interview with sportswriter Wirt Gammon, Sr., July 13, 1975.

37. "Well, the words were...": Flores interview, April 7, 1983.

38. Newsom's V-Ball: Author's interview with Lou Boudreau, May 28, 1980.

39. "Griff, y'all need a pitcher?": Author's interview with Johnny Sullivan, June 15, 2004. Also, author's interview with former major leaguer Frank Mancuso, April 11, 1992, supports the fact that Newsom basically declared himself a free agent.

40. Newsom's 1946 contract with Senators: The exact details of the contract were not known to the author until Newsom's copy of the contract appeared in the online auction website eBay.com in early 2014. The signing bonus and the bonus Newsom was to receive in January of 1947 were contained in a clause in the contract, presumably at the request of Newsom.

41. DiMaggio's two home runs: Tom FitzGerald, "Joltin' Joe Has Left And Gone Away" (obituary), *San Francisco Chronicle*, March 9, 1999, D5.

42. Newsom's victory over Red Sox on September 6: Ernest Barcella, "Don't Be Crude When You're Booed, Bobo Tells Williams," United Press, September 8, 1946, as published in the *Washington Post* sports sections.

43. "He could drive you...": Ossie Bluege quoted in Donald Honig, *A Donald Honig Reader* (New York: Simon & Schuster, 1988), 610.

44. Cal Hubbard encounter: Ibid., 611.

45. "I'll pitch five more years...": Russell Streur, "The Diamond Road of Bobo Newsom," *Sports Collectors Digest*, February 7, 1992, 143.

46. Bob Feller's 1946 barnstorming tour: Bob Feller with Bill Gilbert, *Now Pitching Bob Feller* (New York: Citadel Press, 2002), 233–35. Also see coverage in *The Sporting News*, various issues, September–November 1946.

47. "He'd last three or four innings...": Author's interview with Frank Mancuso, April 11, 1992.

48. Early Wynn's success: Author's interview with former major leaguer Mike Garcia, January 21, 1980. "Lopez and Harder were always given credit for (Wynn's) success, but the guy Early told me he patterned himself after was Buck Newsom."

49. Newsom's final game with 1947 Senators: Author's interview with Ray Medeiros (who was in attendance that day at Fenway Park), August 1, 2013. The author also accessed box score of July 6 game that Newsom pitched on baseballreference.com, August 2, 2013, as well as the game story in the July 7 edition of the *Washington Post*.

50. Newsom sold to the Yankees: After the July 4–6 weekend series in Boston, due to the All-Star Game break the Senators did not play again until July 9. The deal was officially announced July 10, but by that time it had already been reported as a done deal in the Boston, New York and Washington newspapers.

Chapter Eleven

1. Clark Griffith's price for Newsom: Jon Kerr, *Calvin: Baseball's Last Dinosaur* (Minneapolis: Wm. C. Brown, 1990), 25.

2. Roster information on 1947 Yankees: S. C. Thompson, *All-Time Rosters of Major League Baseball Clubs* (revised edition), 542.

3. Newsom and the media: Author's interview with Johnny Lindell, April 2, 1979.

4. Yankees' 1947 season: Author accessed game-by-game results on baseballreference.com on September 2, 2012.

5. "That old guy could...": Author's interview with Tommy Henrich, July 19, 1999.

6. "He just didn't fit...": Ibid.
7. Edgar "Blue" Sommer's visit: Author's interview with Bob Shirley, August 5, 2004. For many years, Shirley had a photo on display in his Hartsville barber shop of Newsom and Sommer, taken in New York during their three-day spree.
8. "Greta Garbo" Newsom: Author's interview with Johnny Lindell, April 2, 1979.
9. "I remember one thing...": Author's interview with Tommy Henrich, July 19, 1999.
10. Newsom wanting Yankees to sign Satchel Paige: Author's interview with Johnny Lindell, April 2, 1979. "[That summer] it seemed like everybody was talking about who was gonna sign Satchel. This Newsom guy kept talking about it. I heard that Satchel was asking for some ridiculous amount of money and that's why [George] Weiss didn't want him. Of course, I'm sure there might have been other reasons."
11. Newsom-Joe Haynes encounter: John Lardner, "The One And Only True Bobo," reprinted in *The Second Fire-side Book of Baseball*, ed. by Charles Einstein, 228. The first baseman on the play was Rudy York, another old friend of Newsom's.
12. Harris' selection of starting pitchers in 1947 World Series: Author's interview with Tommy Henrich, July 19, 1999.
13. "Lord knows we had...": Ibid.
14. "We were up two games...": Ibid.
15. Page's success in Series: Ibid.
16. "There was some sort of dispute...": Author's interview with former major leaguer Spider Jorgensen, April 3, 1997.
17. Re Joe Page: Page, a left-hander, had an outstanding fastball, but it was "straight as a string" according to Al Zarilla and several other major leaguers. Beginning in 1947, he augmented the fastball with a greaseball, hiding the illegal substance behind his belt. This gave his pitches extra movement and made him highly effective. See Red Smith, *To Absent Friends* (New York: Atheneum, 1982), 254–256.
18. Newsom's behavior at World Series party: Author's interview with Johnny Lindell, April 2, 1979.
19. Larry MacPhail's departure from Yankees: Robert W. Creamer, *Stengel: His Life and Times* (New York: Simon & Schuster, 1990), 209–210. See also Red Barber, *1947: When All Hell Broke Loose in Baseball* (New York: Da Capo Press, 1982), 253–55. Reportedly, Red Smith is the author of the famous description of Larry MacPhail: "With one drink, he was a genius. With two drinks, he was insane."
20. "He looks too fat...": Author's interview with Johnny Lindell, April 2, 1979.
21. Newsom's World Series ring: Author's interview with Ernest "Hoot" Gibson, August 5, 2004. Gibson recalls Newsom wearing several baseball-related rings, the 1947 World Series ring being among them. Because Newsom's fingers were so big, he had to have his rings custom fitted.
22. Newsom's restaurant: Author's interview with Tallulah Williams, August 5, 2004.
23. "There was a time there...": Author's interview with Jack Fournier, June 18, 1970.
24. Roster information on 1948 Giants: S. C. Thompson, *All-Time Rosters of Major League Baseball Clubs* (revised edition), 255–256.
25. "The only people I know...": Durocher was appearing on the Fred Allen show on NBC to promote his new book, *The Dodgers and Me*. Ironically, the book met with the disapproval of the Dodgers' board of directors and was the final straw in the team's decision to fire Durocher. Author's interview with Lee Scott, July 10, 1977.
26. "I knew Mel (Ott) real well...": Author's interview with former major leaguer Clem Dreisewerd, August 21, 1995.
27. Newsom's reaction to being released by Giants: Shirley Povich, "This Morning with Shirley Povich," *Washington Post*, June 28, 1948, 10.
28. Newsom on the radio: Newsom had begun a campaign to land a job on radio that spring. See "The Sports Show You've Been Looking For" in *Broadcasting*, March 15, 1948, 85.
29. Newsom's latest Cadillac: Author's interview with Ernest "Hoot" Gibson, August 5, 2004.
30. "Do you think we can hustle...": Author's interview with Bob Shirley, August 5, 2004.
31. Newsom versus the preachers: Ibid.
32. "It may have seemed like...": Interview with Skip Harrison, conducted by Kathy Dunlap of the Hartsville Museum, December 3, 1991. Used by permission.
33. "That place was packed...": Author's interview with Bob Shirley, August 5, 2004.
34. "I started my pitching career...": Non-bylined article in the *Hartsville (SC) Messenger*, September 11, 1948.

Chapter Twelve

1. Newsom's restaurant closing: Author's interview with Bob Shirley, August 5, 2004. Author also accessed records at the Hartsville and Darlington County museums.
2. Newsom signs with Lookouts: Author's interview with sportswriter Wirt Gammon, Sr., July 13, 1975. Some sources report that Newsom signed with the Senators, who then optioned him to Chattanooga. Based on the Gammon interview and what Newsom told other players, this is clearly incorrect.
3. Joe Engel biographical information: Author's interview with Wirt Gammon, July 13, 1975. See also Jon Kerr, *Calvin: Baseball's Last Dinosaur* (Minneapolis: Wm. C. Brown, 1990), 25–26.
4. "Field a Class D team": Author's interview with Wirt Gammon, July 13, 1975.
5. "Engel was the Barnum and Bailey...": Calvin Griffith quoted in Jon Kerr, *Calvin: Baseball's Last Dinosaur*, 26.
6. "Can't be. There are no...": Shirley Povich, *All Those Mornings.... At the Post*, ed. by Lynn, Maury and David Povich (New York: Public Affairs Books, 2005), 336. Povich has the sense of the quote right, but the context of the story wrong.
7. Newsom's colorful wardrobe: Author's interview with Tallulah Williams, August 5, 2004.
8. "It was surprising how good...": George Myatt interview conducted by George Fergusson, March 15, 1995. Used by permission.
9. Newsom "knighting" the umpire: Ibid.
10. Jackie Mitchell: Debra A. Shattuck, "Women in Baseball," in *Total Baseball* (Third Edition) ed. John Thorn and Pete Palmer (New York: Harper Perennial, 1993), 551–552.
11. Joe Engel's stunts: Jon Kerr, *Calvin: Baseball's Last Dinosaur*, 26. Calvin Griffith also remembered one of Engel's less savory stunts, involving greased pigs and members of the Lookouts' ground crew, who were African American.
12. Newsom's minor league sta-

tistics in 1949–51: Bob Hoie and Carlos Bauer, *The Historical Register* (San Diego: Baseball Press, 1999), 393.

13. "About the only thing...": Author's interview with Wirt Gammon, July 13, 1975.

14. "Son, I've been ready...": Ibid.

15. Newsom pitching a doubleheader for the Lookouts: Red Smith, *Red Smith on Baseball* (Chicago: Ivan R. Dee, 2000), 79–80.

16. Newsom suspended by Lookouts: This was reported by The Associated Press in July 1949, and also by *The Sporting News*. Wirt Gammon (author's interview, July 13, 1975) said it was one of Engel's publicity stunts. For the record, the suspension/vacation lasted ten days.

17. Events of August 9, 1949: Note that this was a different doubleheader from the one Red Smith wrote about. The "Smith" doubleheader took place in June of 1949, at Birmingham. Details of the August 9 doubleheader from the *Chattanooga News-Free Press* sports sections of August 9–10, 1949, bylined stories by Allan Morris.

18. Newsom as a wrestling referee: Author's interview with Bob Shirley, August 5, 2004.

19. Newsom training at Rollins College: Author's interview with Tallulah Williams, August 5, 2004. Williams said it was Kay Newsom's idea to move to the Orlando area, in order to help Bobo concentrate on baseball.

20. Newsom-Engel contract squabble: Author's interview with Wirt Gammon, July 13, 1975.

21. "No doubt, he was one of the...": Author's interview with Forrest "Frosty" Kennedy, March 10, 1994.

22. "What a great guy Bobo was...": Ibid.

23. "Shoot, the only way...": Ibid.

24. "We were going to fly...": Patrick Reusse, "The Baseball Man Is Gone; Tales Remain" (Ellis Clary obituary), *Minneapolis Star Tribune*, June 6, 2000.

25. Newsom on the radio: Author's interview with broadcaster Ron Menchine, July 1, 2004.

26. 1950 Paige-Newsom barnstorming tour: Russell Streur, "The Diamond Road of Bobo Newsom," *Sports Collectors Digest*, February 7, 1992, 144.

27. Impact of barnstorming tours: Author's interview with Piper Davis, April 29, 1995. Davis, who played in the Negro Leagues and with the Harlem Globetrotters, strongly felt that the barnstorming tours of the 1930s, along with basketball's touring Globetrotters, had a huge impact on the eventual integration of professional sports. "[The idea] had been tried before, but the big difference there in the 1930s was the fact both sides *wanted* the series to be publicized. Nobody was trying to hide the thing under a basket. You have to give credit to guys like Newsom and Dean and Feller for that, they're the ones who risked the most. Imagine a little white boy sitting somewhere in Georgia and reading in *The Sporting News* that the great Dizzy Dean was playing against colored folk. Now, the thinking has changed, see? He reads that and starts thinking, 'well, if it's all right for Dizzy to play with those black boys, it's gotta be OK for me, too.' That's a huge leap forward."

28. "Mr. Bobo, there's one thing...": Author's interview with Frosty Kennedy, March 10, 1994.

29. "I love to travel...": Satchel Paige interview with Houston, Texas-based radio reporter R. Donald Bradley, April 1965. Transcript of taped interview used by permission.

30. San Diego's offer for Newsom: Del Baker was managing the Padres at that time, so it is reasonable to assume that he requested Newsom's services.

31. "Every day I pitch...": Author's interview with Wirt Gammon, July 13, 1975.

32. Details on Newsom's season at Birmingham: *Bobo's Time: A Remembrance*, unpublished biography of Newsom by George Fergusson, 1995, used by permission of the author.

33. "I sure hope...": Newsom quoted by Bob Shirley, author's interview with Bob Shirley, August 4, 2004. Shirley said he attended the game at Little Rock.

34. The concept of a closer aka stopper: There is a dispute over who originated the idea, although it may have been John McGraw, as early as the 1908 season. Interestingly, Bucky Harris often used the hard-throwing Firpo Marberry as a closer during the 1924 world championship season for the Senators. As mentioned in Chapter Eleven, Harris used Joe Page as the "stopper" with the Yankees in 1947. It is generally believed that Page's noteworthy success on the 1947 and 1949 world champion Yankees teams cemented the idea of a closer in place. From that point onward, most teams employed one. For an excellent discussion of relief pitchers, see Jonathan Fraser Light, *The Cultural Encyclopedia of Baseball* (Jefferson, NC: McFarland, 1997), 608–610.

35. "Newsom came in late...": Author's interview with former major leaguer Irv Noren, July 17, 2004.

36. Newsom pitch breaking Mickey Grasso's wrist: John Lardner, "The One And Only True Bobo," reprinted in *The Second Fireside Book of Baseball*, 228. Lardner reports that in the aftermath Bucky Harris chased Bobo out of the park.

37. Senators-Dodgers exhibition game of April 10: Roscoe McGowen, "Brooklyn Downs Senators By 4–3," *New York Times*, April 11, 1952, 26.

38. "Whatever it is they're saying...": Author's interview with Irv Noren, July 17, 2004.

39. Newsom using fungo bat as a microphone: Author's interview with former major leaguer Gus Zernial, July 7, 1989.

40. Athletics-Tigers game of August 31: From Associated Press account of the game as accessed on *The New York Times* database, April 20, 2009.

41. "It was brutally hot...": Russell Streur, "The Diamond Road of Bobo Newsom," *Sports Collectors Digest*, February 7, 1992, 144.

42. "The A's can't afford me anymore...": John Lardner, "The One And Only True Bobo," reprinted in *The Second Fireside Book of Baseball*, 229.

43. "I had a good run at 'em...": Author's interview with Wirt Gammon, July 13, 1975.

44. "A game there in St. Louis...": Author's interview with Ray Coleman, July 19, 1993.

45. Ryan-Newsom career statistics: See Bob Hoie and Carlos Bauer, *The Historical Register*, 393, 417. The notable difference is, of course, that Ryan compiled virtually all his numbers in the major leagues; Newsom had nine seasons in the minors (1928–33 and 1949–51). In Lyle Spatz, ed., *The SABR Baseball List & Record Book* (New York: Scribner, 2007), Newsom has 18 entries, while Ryan has 56. (Bob Feller has 40.)

46. "Baseball, and our society...": Author's interview with Al Zarilla, May 18, 1990.

47. "With all his antics...": Author's interview with Johnny Sullivan, June 15, 2004.

Chapter Thirteen

1. "There at the end of his...": Author's interview with Tallulah Williams, October 15, 2006.
2. Dizzy Dean on TV: Dean did the National Game of the Week for Falstaff Beer for 12 years (1953–64). In 1954, Dean told Al Zarilla he was making a million dollars a year (author's interview with Al Zarilla, October 21, 1989).
3. Newsom hired for Knot Hole Gang: While the TV show was broadcast on Channel 13 and Baltimore Orioles management had some input as to its content, the sponsor had the final say.
4. Newsom's relationship with Jimmy Dykes: Author's interview with former major leaguer Les Moss, October 25, 1989.
5. Happy Felton: Reportedly, Felton had performed in vaudeville. Author's interview with Lee Scott, July 10, 1977: "I thought the show was just awful. Problem was, it caught on with the kids and this Felton character got the idea he was the cock of the walk. (He was) very demanding, very unpleasant to work with."
6. "To be blunt, Bobo...": Author's interview with Ron Menchine, July 1, 2004. See also Phil Wood, "Bobo Lacked Polish, But Not Passion," *The Examiner*, July 19, 2005, as accessed on www.examiner.com website on July 23, 2006.
7. "He has this gravel-y...": Cal Ermer interviewed by George Fergusson, March 10, 1995. Used by permission.
8. Esskay baseball cards: The 1954 Bobo Newsom card is valued at over $1,000. The cards were printed on the cardboard backing for a pack of weiners. There were also various Knot Hole Gang promotional pieces featuring Newsom, a counter display and poster as well as an 8x10-inch photo with facsimile autograph that Bobo gave out at personal appearances.
9. "You know, that old boy...": Author's interview with Les Moss, October 25, 1989.
10. Newsom-Donovan eating contest: Phil Jackman, "On The Other Hand," dated August 24, 2006, as accessed on the website www.pressboxonline.com on August 31, 2006. Despite the fact that the contest was sponsored by the hot-dog company, Donovan remembers it was turkey dinners the two ate, rather than hot dogs.
11. "Richards was one of the few...": Author's interview with former major league scout Jim Russo, August 12, 1988.
12. "It's too bad Newsom...": Author's interview with Ron Menchine, July 1, 2004.
13. Johnny Carson routine: Some sources claim Carson's kid show host routine had its origins in an incident on the Howdy Doody TV show with Buffalo Bob. Others say the origin was a local Los Angeles TV show starring a character named Sheriff John. In published interviews, both Bob Smith, aka Buffalo Bob, and John Rovich, aka Sheriff John, denied it happened on their shows. Since Carson was doing the routine by the mid–1960s, its inspiration had to pre-date that.
14. Newsom's final appearance in uniform: George Brantner, "Bobo Newsom Plays In Old-Timers' Game," *Washington Post*, July 15, 1956, C4.
15. "When we started up the Angels...": Author's interview with George Goodale, February 15, 1975.
16. "I know the idea...": Author's interview with Johnny Berardino, December 2, 1995.
17. "One of our owners came to me...": Author's interview with Mickey Vernon, August 30, 2004.
18. Newsom at Toots Shor's: Bob Addie column, *Washington Post* sports section, December 8, 1962 (Bobo Newsom obituary).
19. "I remember going down to Florida...": Author's interview with Tallulah Williams, March 10, 2005.
20. Newsom at Harper's Bar: Bob Feller with Bill Gilbert, *Now Pitching Bob Feller* (New York: A Birch Lane Press Book, 1990), 74–75.
21. "Contrary to popular opinion...": Author's interview with former major leaguer Ryne Duren, January 27, 1992.
22. "I think the nickname...": Author's interview with Johnny Berardino, December 2, 1995.
23. Hall of Fame voting totals: Voting results for all Hall of Fame elections can be accessed on the National Baseball Hall of Fame website: www.baseballhallorg/history/hof.
24. "Don't count Ol' Bobo out...": Bob Addie column, *The Washington Post* sports section, December 8, 1962.
25. Newsoms' Christmas cards: Several obituaries mention this, including the one by Russ Mellette in the December 8, 1962, sports sections of the *State News* (Columbia, SC).
26. "He looked just all worn out...": Author's interview with Bob Shirley, August 5, 2004.
27. Newsom's grave site: The Magnolia Cemetery in Hartsville is open to the public, 9 a.m. to 5 p.m. The Newsom family plot can be accessed by making a right turn at the first crossroad once you are in the cemetery proper. You will see the "Newsom" marker immediately to your left.

Epilogue

1. "After a while, no one...": Jake Penland's "Press Box" column in *The State* (Columbia, SC), February 28, 1954.
2. "Buck was definitely an unforgettable...": Author's interview with Tallulah Williams, August 5, 2004.
3. Bobo Newsom Highway: Author's interview with Ernest "Hoot" Gibson, August 5, 2004. Route 151 has a strong sports flavor: Farther north, it becomes the Van Lingle Mungo State Highway; farther south, it becomes the Harry Byrd State Highway. It also runs directly past Darlington International Speedway.
4. "We've been fortunate to have...": Author's interview with Kathy Dunlap, August 3, 2004.
5. Newsom's 1953 Topps baseball card: The 1953 Topps cards are actually photographs retouched by a staff artist. The original photos still exist in the Topps archives.
6. "We have been able...": Author's interview with Kathy Dunlap, August 3, 2004.
7. Newsom's baseball memorabilia: Brenda Lowe, "The Bobo Newsom Story," *Pee Dee Magazine*, II, no. 3 (1990), 16–17.
8. "Nobody paid much attention...": Author's interview with Bob Shirley, August 5, 2004.
9. Newsom as inspiration for Mr. Haney: Author's interview with Pat Buttram, February 17, 1977.
10. Hall of Fame list of overlooked players: The point of the 200-name list was to give those named one last chance to make it into the Hall, via a vote by the special Historical Overview Committee. Newsom was not elected.
11. President Nixon's all-time

baseball teams: Red Smith, *Strawberries In The Wintertime, the Sporting World of Red Smith* (New York: Quadrangle/*The New York Times*, 1974), 22–23. See also Nicholas Sarantakes, "Baseball: The Great Political Equalizer," ESPN 2 website, dated 2004, as accessed on July 6, 2004. Sarantakes includes background information on how Nixon came to select the 1972 teams.

12. Nixon's 1992 teams: Nixon's selections, both the 1972 and 1992 versions, are on file at the Nixon Presidential Library in Yorba Linda, Calif., along with photos of the players, some of them taken with Nixon.

13. Bobo Newsom Memorial Fan Club: John Leo, "Red Smith: a Ruthian writer," *U.S. News & World Report*, September 26, 2005.

14. "It was fun to do...": Author's interview with George Fergusson, November 19, 2004.

15. "The only thing I ever wanted...": Author's interview with Forrest "Frosty" Kennedy, June 1, 1995.

Bibliography

Books

Auker, Elden, and Tom Keegan. *Sleeper Cars and Flannel Uniforms.* Chicago: Triumph, 2006.

Bak, Richard. *Cobb Would Have Caught It, The Golden Age of Baseball in Detroit.* Detroit: Wayne State University Press, 1991.

Barber, Red. *1947: When All Hell Broke Loose in Baseball.* New York: Da Capo, 1982.

Bartell, Dick, with Norman L. Macht. *Rowdy Richard: A Firsthand Account of the National League Baseball Wars of the 1930s.* Berkeley: North Atlantic Books, 1987.

Bauer, Carlos. *The Early Coast League Statistical Record, 1903–57.* San Diego: Baseball Press, 2004.

Bauer, Carlos, and Bob Hoie. *The Historical Register.* San Diego: Baseball Press, 1999.

Berkow, Ira. *Red: A Biography of Red Smith.* New York: Times Books, 1986.

Broeg, Bob, *My Baseball Scrapbook.* St. Louis: River City, 1983.

Coberly, Rich, *The No-Hit Hall of Fame.* Newport Beach, CA: Triple Play, 1985.

Creamer, Robert W. *Baseball in 1941.* New York: Viking, 1991.

_____. *Stengel: His Life and Times.* New York: Fireside, 1990.

Durocher, Leo. *The Dodgers and Me.* Chicago: Ziff-Davis, 1948.

Dawidoff, Nicholas. *The Catcher Was a Spy: The Mysterious Life of Moe Berg.* New York: Vintage Books, 1995.

Einstein, Charles, ed. *The Second Fireside Book of Baseball.* New York: Simon & Schuster, 1958.

_____. *The Third Fireside Book of Baseball.* New York: Simon & Schuster, 1968.

Eskenazi, Gerald. *The Lip: A Biography of Leo Durocher.* New York: William Morrow, 1993.

Falls, Joe. *The Detroit Tigers: An Illustrated History.* New York: Prentice Hall, 1989.

Feller, Bob, with Bill Gilbert. *Now Pitching Bob Feller: A Baseball Memoir.* New York: Citadel Press, 2002.

Feller, Bob. *Strikeout Story.* New York: A. S. Barnes, 1947.

Frommer, Frederic J. *You Gotta Have Heart: A History of Washington Baseball.* Lanham, MD: Taylor Trade, 2013.

Gay, Timothy M. *Satch, Dizzy & Rapid Robert: The Wild Saga of Interracial Baseball before Jackie Robinson.* New York: Simon & Schuster, 2010.

Golenbock, Peter. *Bums: An Oral History of the Brooklyn Dodgers.* New York: G. P. Putnam's Sons, 1984.

_____. *The Spirit of St. Louis.* New York: HarperCollins, 2001.

Greenberg, Hank, with Ira Berkow. *Hank Greenberg: The Story of My Life.* New York: Times Books, 1989.

Grimm, Charlie, with Ed Prell. *Jolly Cholly's Story: Baseball I Love You!* Chicago: Henry Regenery, 1968.

Hartsville Museum Staff. *Milestones: Hartsville, S.C., Centennial, 1891–1991.* Hartsville, SC.: private printing, 2000.

Higbe, Kirby, and Martin Quigley. *The High Hard One.* New York: Viking Press, 1967.

Honig, Donald. *A Donald Honig Reader.* New York: Fireside, 1988.

Hornsby, Rogers. *My War with Baseball.* New York: Coward-McCann, 1962.

James, Bill, and Rob Neyer. *The Neyer/James Guide to Pitchers.* New York: Fireside, 2004.

Kahn, Roger. *Joe and Marilyn: A Memory of Love.* New York: William Morrow, 1986.

Kerr, Jon. *Calvin: Baseball's Last Dinosaur.* Minneapolis: Wm. C. Brown, 1990.

Kuklick, Bruce. *To Every Thing a Season: Shibe Park and Urban Philadelphia, 1909–1976.* Princeton, NJ: Princeton University Press, 1993.

Lieb, Fred. *The Detroit Tigers.* New York: G.P. Putnam's Sons, 1946.

Light, Jonathan Fraser. *The Cultural Encyclopedia of Baseball.* Jefferson, NC: McFarland, 1997.

McNeil, William. *The California Winter League.* Jefferson, NC: McFarland, 2002.

Mead, William B. *Even the Browns.* Chicago: Contemporary Books, 1978.

Miller, Marvin. *A Whole Different Ball Game: The Sport and Business of Baseball.* Secaucus, NJ: Carol, 1991.

Murdock, Eugene. *Baseball Players and Their Times: Oral Histories of the Game 1920–1940.* Westport, CT: Meckler, 1991.

Neft, Donald S., and Richard M. Cohen. *The Sports Encyclopedia: Baseball.* New York: St. Martin's Griffin, 1996.

Paige, Leroy. *Maybe I'll Pitch Forever: A Great Baseball Player Tells the Hilarious Story Behind the Legend.* Garden City, NY: Doubleday, 1962.

Povich, Shirley, edited by Maury Lynn and David Povich. *All Those Mornings... At the Post.* New York: Public Affairs, 2005.

Powers, Jimmy. *Baseball Personalities: The Most Colorful Figures of All Time.* New York: Rudolph Field, 1949.

Ritter, Lawrence S. *Lost Ballparks: A Celebration of Baseball's Legendary Fields.* New York: Viking, 1994.

Robinson, Jackie, and Alfred Duckett. *I Never Had It Made.* New York: G. P. Putnam's Sons, 1972.

Russo, Jim, and Bob Hammel. *Super Scout: Thirty-Five Years of Major League Scouting.* New York: National Book Network, 1992.

Schacht, Al. *My Own Particular Screwball: An Informal Autobiography.* Garden City, NY: Doubleday, 1955.

Sickels, John. *Bob Feller: Ace of the Greatest Generation.* Dulles, VA: Brassey's, 2004.

Silber, Irwin. *Press Box Red: The Story of Lester Rodney.* Philadelphia: Temple University Press, 2003.

Smith, Red. *To Absent Friends.* New York: Atheneum, 1982.

_____. *Red Smith on Baseball: The Game's Greatest Writer on the Game's Greatest Years.* Chicago: Ivan R. Dee, 2000.

Spatz, Lyle, ed. *The SABR Baseball List & Record Book.* New York: Scribner, 2007.

Spink, J. G. Taylor. *Judge Landis and 25 Years of Baseball.* New York: Thomas Y. Crowell, 1947.

Thorn, John, and Pete Palmer, eds. *Total Baseball.* 2d ed. New York: Harper Perennial, 1993.

Thompson, Fresco, with Cy Rice. *Every Diamond Doesn't Sparkle: Behind the Scenes with the Dodgers.* New York: David McKay, 1964.

Thompson, S. C., with revisions by Pete Palmer. *All-Time Rosters of Major League Baseball Clubs.* South Brunswick, NJ: A. S. Barnes, 1973.

Turner, Frederick. *When the Boys Came Back: Baseball in 1946.* New York: Henry Holt, 1996.

Tye, Larry. *Satchel Paige: The Life and Times of an American Legend.* New York: Random House, 2009.

Vitti, Jim. *The Cubs on Catalina.* Darien, CT: Settefrati Press, 2003.

Williams, Ted, and John Underwood. *The Science of Hitting.* New York: Simon & Schuster, 1970.

Magazine and Journal Articles

Considine, Bob. "They Need Me Something Terrible." *The Saturday Evening Post,* April 1, 1939.

"Cream Pitchers." *Time,* February 3, 1941.

Farrington, Dick. "It Was Just a Breeze for Windy Buck Newsom." *The Sporting News,* October 27, 1938.

Feller, Bob. "How I Throw the Slider." *Sport,* February 1953. Reprinted in *The Baseball Reader,* edited by Charles Einstein. New York: Random House, 1989.

Fergusson, George. "The Home Stretch: The 1940 A.L. Pennant Race." Unpublished article from 1995, used by permission of the author.

Lardner, John. "The One and Only True Bobo." *True,* March 1957. Reprinted in *The Second Fireside Book of Baseball,* edited by Charles Einstein. New York: Simon & Schuster, 1958.

Leo, John. "Red Smith, a Ruthian Writer." *U.S. News and World Report,* September 26, 2005.

Lowe, Brenda. "The Bobo Newsom Story." *Pee Dee Magazine* 2, no. 3 (1990).

McGowen, Roscoe. "Baseball As It Used To Be." *True,* June 1964. Reprinted in the *Third Fireside Book of Baseball,* edited by Charles Einstein. New York: Simon & Schuster, 1968.

"Once a Dodger...". *Time,* September 14, 1942.

Pollock, Ed. "Bobo's Planned Superstition." *Baseball Digest,* May 1944.

Ross, Mike. "Hank Greenberg & Bobo." *The National Pastime* 22 (2002): 124–128.

_____. "Tragedy and Triumph: Bobo Newsom's 1940 World Series." *The National Pastime* 10 (1990): 75–78.

Streur, Russell. "The Diamond Road of Bobo Newsom." *Sports Collectors Digest,* February 7, 1992.

Tebbetts, Birdie. "I'd Rather Catch." *The Atlantic Monthly,* September 1949.

Thompson, Dick. "The Wes Ferrell Story." *The National Pastime* 21 (2001): 96–124.

Web Sites

Baseball Reference: www.baseball-reference.com
SABR Biography Project: http://sabr.org/bioproject

Newspapers

Chattanooga News–Free Press (1949–1951)
Columbia (SC) State
Detroit News
Hartsville (SC) Messenger
Little Rock (AR) Gazette (1931)
Los Angeles Times (1933)
Macon (GA) Telegraph (1929)
New York Times
New York Herald-Tribune
Washington Post

Index

Abbott and Costello 167
Addie, Bob 71, 206, 210, 212, 214
Alexander, Grover Cleveland 25, 52
Alford, Gene 26
Allen, Ethan 89
Allen, Fred 186
Allen, Johnny 23, 90, 91, 112, 155–156, 157
Almada, Louie 89
Almada, Melo 79–80, 81, 89, 95
Altrock, Nick 67–68, 70, 192
"Amos & Andy" (radio show) 131
Andrews, Paul "Ivy" 54
Ankenman, Pat 150
Appleton, Pete 74, 79
Atlanta (GA) Crackers 195
Auker, Elden 99, 118, 134
Autry, Gene 209
Averill, Earl 73, 91, 97, 113, 133

Bak, Richard 92, 98, 107
Baker, Del 96, 101, 104–107, 109, 114–115, 118–119, 121, 123, 125, 134, 136
Baker, Frank "Home Run" 167
Ball, Phillip 53
Ballou, Win 44
Barnes, Donald 85, 86, 90, 93
Bartell, Dick 103, 105–106, 113, 114, 118, 125–126, 133–134, 140, 216
Baseball Hall of Fame 176, 211–212
Batchelor, Lew 196
Baxter, Frankie 71
Bean, Belve 72
Bear Mountain (NY) 147, 152
Beggs, Joe 186
Bejma, Ollie 55
Bell, Beau 88–89, 95, 97, 103, 112, 115, 117
Bell, Cool Papa 47, 48, 196
Benny, Jack 186
Benton, Al 106, 114, 135, 199
Berg, Moe 82, 83
Bernardino, Johnny 56, 88, 94, 210, 212
Berra, Yogi 200
Berry, Joe 166, 170, 171

Bevens, Floyd 180, 183
Bildilli, Emil "Hillbilly" 86–87
Bishop, Charlie 202
Bissonette, Del 29, 33
Black, Don 166, 168, 169
Black, Joe 70
Blaeholder, George 50–52, 53–54, 64, 65, 78
Blattner, Buddy 209
Bluege, Ossie 74, 75, 175, 177, 178
Bonetti, Julio 86
Bonham, Ernie 110
Bordagaray, Frenchy 150
Borowy, Hank 167
Boston Herald 114
Bottomley, Jim 25
Boudreau, Lou 112, 120, 172, 179
Bouton, Jim 217
Bowman, Roger 154
Bradley, Alva 113
Bragan, Bobby 2, 153–154, 156
Breadon, Sam 52, 146
Bressler, Rube 33
Bridges, Tommy 97, 98, 99, 106–107, 116, 118, 119, 123, 135
Briggs, Walter O., Jr. 129
Briggs, Walter O., Sr. 95, 102, 103, 104, 129
Briggs Stadium (Detroit) 111, 114, 116, 118, 123, 138, 171, 202
Brinkley, David 70
Broeg, Bob 212
Brown, Joe E. 46, 211
Brown, Joe L. 211
Bruckner, Earle 164, 173
Burke, George 39, 54, 71, 82, 95
Burke, Robert "Lefty" 72
Burns, Jack 55, 77
Bush, Guy 40
Buttram, Pat 216
Byrd, Harry 202

Cadillac La Salle 102
California State League 68
California Winter League 34, 46–48
Cambria, Joe 69
Camilli, Dolf 150, 156, 157
Campanella, Roy 200
Campanis, Al 69, 150

Campbell, Bruce 37, 56, 60, 64, 103, 105, 111, 112, 113, 122, 126, 135, 140
Cantor, Eddie 113
Capital Airlines 195
Carey, Harry 88
Carlisle Fitting School (SC) 18
Carson, Johnny 209
Case, Drew 11
Case, George 141, 142, 143
Casey, Hugh 154
Caster, George 35
Catalina Island (Calif.) 40, 43
Chance, Frank 43
Chandler, Spud 179, 180
Chapman, Ben 60, 72, 73, 74, 79–80, 81, 112, 120
Charlotte (NC) Bees 26
Chase, Hal 43
Chattanooga (Tenn.) Lookouts 189–190, 194
Cheraw, SC 19
Chester, Hilda 151
Chesterfield, SC 20
Christman, Mark 95, 168
Christopher, Russ 166, 170
Cincinnati Inquirer 28
Clark, Watty 33
Clary, Ellis 196
Clearwater, Fla. 31
Cleveland Municipal Stadium 98, 120
Cleveland Plain Dealer 113
Cleveland Press 113
Clift, Harlond 54–55, 88, 159
Cobb, Ty 12, 43
Cochrane, Mickey 96
Coffman, Dick 54, 100
Coffman, George "Slick" 100, 107
Cohane, Tim 154–156
Coker College 132
Cole, Ed 86, 88, 95
Coleman, Ray 204
Columbia (SC) Reds 15, 20
Columbia (SC) State 147
Columbia (SC) State Fair 40
Comiskey, Charles 69
Comiskey Park (Chicago) 82
Considine, Bob 77
Coppola, Hank 72

239

Cox, Bill 86
Critz, Hugh 28
Cronin, Joe 70, 79, 81, 83, 84, 108, 139, 178, 179, 183, 191, 210
Crosley Field (Cincinnati) 125
Croucher, Frank 106, 133–135, 140
"Crybaby" revolt 112–113
Cullenbine, Roy 140

Dahlgren, Ellsworth "Babe" 45, 83, 111
Daily Racing Form 82
Daley, Arthur 5, 6
Darlington, SC 11, 18, 162, 187
Davis, Curt 150, 156
Dawson, James P. 58
Day, Clyde "Pea Ridge" 36
Dean, Dizzy 4, 37, 44, 46, 56–58, 62, 64, 187, 196, 205, 216
Dean, Paul 62
DeBerry, Hank 28, 33
Derringer, Paul 121, 122, 123, 125, 153
DeShong, Jimmy 74, 79
DeWitt, Bill, Sr. 53, 63–65, 85, 86, 89, 90, 92–93, 94, 95, 157–159, 185, 210
DiMaggio, Joe 45, 50, 74, 76, 91, 93, 134, 137–139, 173–174, 179, 180, 182, 183
Dixie Series 193, 199
Dobson, Joe 112
Doby, Larry 182
Dodge, Johnny 24
Donald, Atley 111
Donovan, Art 207
Douthit, Taylor 25
Dreisewerd, Clem 186–187
Drews, Karl 180
Dunlap, Kathy 215, 216
Duren, Ryne 206, 211
Durocher, Leo 1, 2, 145, 148–151, 152–155, 157, 186–187, 209
Dykes, Jimmy 201, 202, 203, 206, 207

Eastern Carolina League 22
Ebbets Field (Brooklyn) 1, 2, 151, 156, 183
Egan, Tom 82
Ehlers, Art 206
Einstein, Charles 52, 210
Eisenhower, David 217
Elliott, Jumbo 33
Embree, Red 139
Engel, Joe 189–196, 198
Ermer, Cal 207
Estalella, Bobby 69, 166, 168
Even the Browns 158

Falls, Joe 103, 214
Farrington, Dick 87
Feller, Bob 4, 77, 82–83, 90, 93, 98, 99, 107, 108, 112–113, 117–118, 119–121, 129, 130, 133, 176, 217
Felton, Happy 206
Fenway Park 84, 109, 139, 177

Fergusson, George 218
Ferrell, Rick 62, 79, 80, 178
Ferrell, Wes 57, 61–63, 79–80, 83, 84
Fields, W.C. 33
Finn, Mickey 33
The First Century of Baseball 92
Fletcher, Artie 60, 111
Flores, Jesse 164, 165, 166, 168, 169, 170, 172
Florida Derby 53
Flowers, Jake 33
Forbes Field (Pittsburgh) 167
Ford Model T 38
Fournier, Jack 86, 89, 93, 94, 95, 185
Fox, Pete 103, 105, 118
Fox Theatre (Detroit) 109
Foxx, Jimmie 50, 80, 82, 83, 84
Frederick, Johnny 33
Frederick, MD 163, 167
French, Walter 37
Fricano, Marion 166
Frisch, Frankie 25, 86, 212

Galan, Augie 150
Gammon, Wirt, Sr. 191, 198, 214
Garms, Debs 56, 60
Garner John Nance 75
Gehrig, Lou 60, 93, 101, 192
Gehringer, Charlie 92, 96, 97, 98, 105, 106, 107, 111, 114, 116–120, 126, 133–135
George, Charles "Greek" 171
Georgia Tech 12, 21
Giebell, Floyd 116, 119–121
Gibson, Hoot 28, 130, 170, 187, 213–215
Gibson, Josh 47, 84
Gilbert, Wally 33
Gill, George 95
Gillenwater, Carden 150
Glenn, Joe 94
Glossup, Albie 150
Gomez, Vernon "Lefty" 60
Gooch, Johnny 28
Goodale, George 209
Gordon, Joe 111
Gorsica, Johnny 106, 115
Grasso, Mickey 200
"Green Acres" (TV show) 216
Greenberg, Hank 91–92, 93, 96–97, 100, 103–104, 105, 108, 109, 111, 115, 117–120, 124, 125, 133, 134, 136, 171
Greenville (NC) Tobacconists 22
Griffith, Calvin 70, 191
Griffith, Clark 4, 66, 67–71, 74, 76, 77, 78, 108, 140–141, 143, 159, 160, 162, 173, 176–177, 178, 179, 182, 185, 188, 189–191, 193, 194, 197, 200, 206, 209
Griffith Stadium (DC) 4, 68, 69, 72, 75, 109
Grimes, Oscar 112
Grimm, Charlie 42, 43, 52
Grove, Robert "Lefty" 74, 77, 82, 83, 91, 217

Grube, Frank 54–55
Gudat, Marv 44

Hadley, Bump 53–54, 64, 72, 74
Haefner, Mickey 197
Hafey, Chick 25
Hall, Irv 167
Hallahan, Bill 25
Haney, Fred 92–93, 94, 107, 209
Harder, Mel 65, 77, 112, 116–117, 177
Harper's Bar (Winter Park, Fla.) 211
Harridge, William 64
Harris, Bob 95
Harris, Bucky 71–72, 73, 75, 77, 78, 141, 142, 143, 179, 182, 183, 191, 197, 199, 200
Harris, Lum 166–167
Harrison, Skip 188
Hart, Billy 150
Hartley, Grover 53
Hartnett, Gabby 54
Hartsville (SC) cotton 10
Hartsville (SC) High School 15, 16, 132, 188
Hartsville (SC) Messenger 132, 188
Hartsville (SC) Public School 12
Hayes, Frankie 166
Haynes, Joe 182
Head, Ed 150
Heath, Jeff 112, 120
Heath, Tommy 88
Heffner, Don 88–89
Hemphill, Paul 5
Hemsley, Ralston "Rollie" 54–55, 88, 112
Henrich, Tommy 71, 104, 110, 111, 138, 180–181, 182, 183, 184
Herman, Babe 28, 31, 33, 34–35
Herman, Billy 150, 155
Hermann, LeRoy 44
Hershberger, Willard 125
Hi-Speed Gas 131
Higbe, Kirby 57, 145, 149, 150, 152, 153
Higgins, Frank "Pinky" 106, 111, 117, 118, 120, 123, 125–126, 135
High, Andy 25
Hildebrand, Oral 86, 94
Hoag, Myril 94
Hodges, Gil 150
Hohlmeyer, Alice 196
Homestead Grays 84
Honig, Donald 57, 142, 155, 175, 217
Hornsby, Rogers 13, 37–38, 40–42, 44, 48, 49, 51–53, 57–59, 60–63, 65, 72, 76, 85, 88, 100, 197
Houk, Ralph 212
Hubbard, Cal 26, 175–176
Hudson, Sid 141
Hutchinson, Fred 98, 106, 114, 202

International League 35, 41, 58, 116

Jackson, Joe 12, 134, 136
Johnson, Don 180
Johnson, Fred "Cactus" 86–87, 95
Johnson, Roy 62
Johnson, Walter 68, 70, 75, 167
Jolson, Al 76
Jones, Harry 211
Jones, Jimmy 27, 29
Jorgensen, Spider 184
Judd, Oscar 142

Kell, George 166, 171, 209
Keller, Charlie 181
Kellner, Alex 201
Kelly, Emmett 68
Kelly, George 28
Kelly, Jim 59
Keltner, Ken 112
Kennedy, Frosty 195
Kennedy, Vern 95
Killefer, Bill 53
Kimberlin, Harry 86, 95
Kinder, Ellis 199
Knott, Jack 54, 86
Kolls, Lou 62, 80
Kramer, Jack 94
Kress, Red 84, 86, 88–89, 95, 97, 106
Kuhel, Joe 74, 77
KWK Radio 196

Laabs, Chet 95
Lajoie, Nap 43
Landis, Kenesaw Mountain 27, 46, 52, 53, 64, 103, 108, 134, 136, 140, 152, 158, 160, 192
Lardner, John 6, 108–109, 140, 149, 210, 218
Larsen, Don 206
Lavagetto, Harry "Cookie" 183
Lawson, Roxie 95
Lazzeri, Tony 58–59
League Field (Lakeland) 134
Lee, Thornton 186
Lelivelt, Jack 43–44
Leo, John 217
Leonard, Buck 84, 160
Leonard, Dutch 141, 143, 170, 199
Lewis, Buddy 74, 178, 191
Liebhardt, Glenn 84
Lilliard, Gene 44
Lindell, Johnny 159, 180
Linke, Ed 72, 86
Little Rock (Ark.) Travelers 36–37
Lombardi, Ernie 126
Long Beach (Calif.) earthquake 43
Lopez, Al 33, 177
Lowrey, Harry "Peanuts" 159
Lucas, Red 28–29
Luque, Dolf 33
Lydia (SC) 17
Lyons, Ted 77

Mack, Connie 32, 161–166, 169, 170, 172–174, 201

Mack, Earle 164–165
Mack, Ray 112, 120
Macon, Max 150
Macon (Ga.) Peaches 24–25, 36
Macon (Ga.) Telegraph 25–27, 29
MacPhail, Larry 1, 2, 143, 144, 145, 146, 149, 151, 179, 180, 184, 185
Magerkurth, George 29
Mancuso, Frank 177
Marchildon, Phil 166, 168
Marcum, Johnny 94
Marion, Marty 197
Marion, Red 197
Markson, David 217
Martin, Mike 73, 75
Martin, Whitley 126
Marx, Harpo 68
Masterson, Walt 141
Mathews, Eddie 195
Mazzera, Mel 89
McCarthy, Joe 59, 71, 74, 80, 91, 94, 99, 108, 111, 112, 119, 167, 169, 179
McCormick, Frank 126
McCosky, Barney 104, 105, 116, 118, 119, 120, 125
McCoy, Benny 103
McDonald, Arch 196
McDonald, Joe 184
McDuffie, Terris 160
McGowan, Bill 80, 172
McGowen, Roscoe 29, 32, 156, 200
McGraw, John 23, 31–32, 152
McKain, Archie 157
McKechnie, Bill 121, 125
McQuinn, George 88, 93
Mead, William 158
Medwick, Joe 150, 153
Melillo, Oscar "Spinach" 55, 62, 64–65, 88, 92
Melton, Reuben "Rube" 150, 152
Menchine, Ron 206, 208
Metkovich, George 160
Meyer, Dutch 135
Miggins, Larry 199
Miller, Marvin 6
Millies, Wally 78
Mills, Buster 84, 86, 88, 89, 94
Mills, Howard "Lefty" 86
Milnar, Al 112, 115
Miranda, Willy 193, 197, 209
Mitchell, Jackie 192
Mizell, Wilmer "Vinegar Bend" 199
Mohler, Orv 46
Moore, Dee 150
Moses, Wally 103
Moss, Les 207
Moss, Ray 33
Mullin, Pat 133
Mungo, Van Lingle 215
My War with Baseball 57
Myatt, George 142, 192
Myer, Buddy 71, 77
Myers, Billy 126

Ness, Jack 45
New York Herald-Tribune 29
New York Times 5, 29, 32, 58, 156, 200
New York World-Telegram 154
Newhouser, Hal 98, 106, 133, 135, 138
Newsom, Aline 10, 122
Newsom, Fronnie 121–122
Newsom, George 11
Newsom, H.Q. B. "Quill" 10–11, 14, 18, 20–21, 27, 30, 42, 48, 50, 77, 121–124, 127–128, 183
Newsom, Kay (Ruth Griffiths) 162–164, 172, 179, 189, 194, 197
Newsom, Lillian (Hicks) 10, 14, 18, 124
Newsom, Lillian Belle 10, 122
Newsom, Louis Norman "Bobo": alcoholism onset 78; All-Star Game "snub" (1940) 108; behavior during 1933 earthquake 43; bench-jockey skills 113; bet with Wes Ferrell 80; bet with Wilbert Robinson 32; birth 9; Bobo Newsom Day at Baltimore (1956) 209; Bobo Newsom Highway 11, 215; broken jaw 75–76; broken left collarbone 170; broken left kneecap 72; broken legs 39–40; broken right thumb 109; "Buck Newsom" Cadillac 129–130, 132–133; Buck Newsom Day at Los Angeles (1933) 47; "Buck's Place" restaurant 131–132, 189; comparison to Dizzy Dean 56–57; comparison to Nolan Ryan 204; contract dispute (1937) 77; contract dispute (1939) 93; contract dispute (1942) 139–140; contract dispute (1943) 146–148; contract dispute (1945) 170; death and obituaries 212–213; death of father 123; death of mother 18; depicted on Wheaties boxes 74; dislike of cold weather 35; dislike of farming 11, 12; dislike of spring training 34; divorce from Lucille 147, 157; Dodgers players' mutiny 1–2, 153–156; exceptional running speed 35, 37; exhibition against St. Louis Cardinals 24–25; extra in the movies 46, 151–152; fear of flying 46; featured on Essay baseball cards 207; final major league win (1953) 202; first game versus Yankees (1934) 58; friendship with Hank Greenberg 100; fudging on age 171–172; Hall of Fame balloting 211–212; "homecoming" game against Columbia Reds (1929) 27; homecoming game at Columbia Reds 27; lack of ability as a hitter 35; late reporting to Cubs (1932) 40; leader of

Orioles Knot Hole Gang 205–209; learning the slider 50; lessons from Dazzy Vance 34–35; loses 1938 strikeout title to Bob Feller 90; love of automobiles 14, 15, 38; major league debut (1929) 28–29; marriage to Lucille Arant 20; marriage to Ruth (Kay) Griffiths 162; military draft status 142, 162; 1936 season opener in D.C. 75; 1929 exhibition versus Cardinals, 24–25; no-hitter versus Red Sox 60–61; number of pitches thrown in 1938 season 87; origin of nickname Bobo 10, 71; origin of nickname Buck 10; parallels between Newsom and Clark Griffith 68; pitching against Babe Ruth 60; President Nixon's all-time baseball teams 217; rabbits in his hotel room 83; radio play-by-play 46; refereeing wrestling matches 194; relationship with Commissioner Landis 64; sports memorabilia collection 216; staying with sharecroppers 11–12; stint in carnival, 19; superstitions 168–170; switching uniform numbers 169–170; thirteen-game winning streak (1940) 107–108; tryout with Columbia Reds 20; twelve-game losing streak (1945) 170–171; wins 1936 season opener in DC 75; winter league series versus Satchel Paige 46–48; World Series check (1940) 128–129
Newsom, Lucille (Arant) 19–23, 27, 42, 44, 46, 49, 95, 102, 122, 132–133, 135–136, 145, 147, 157–158, 160
Newsom, Marion 10, 13
Newsom, Norma 64
Newsome, John 11, 13, 78
Newsome, J.R. "Jake" 9, 11, 20, 40
Newsome, Rex 39, 214–216
Newsome, Willington "Willie" 11
Newsome Corners 11
Nicholson, Bill 152
Niggeling, Johnny 159
Nixon, Richard M. 76, 217
Nixon Presidential Library 217
Noren, Irv 71, 199
Novikoff, Lou 159

Oglesby, Jim 44
O'Leary, Charlie 53
O'Malley, Walter 151
O'Neill, Steve 111
Orioles Knot Hole Gang 205
Ormsby, Emmet "Red" 58
Orsatti, Ernie 25
Ostermueller, Fritz 157, 158
Ott, Mel 186
Owen, Marv 51, 96, 107
Owen, Mickey 150, 151, 153

Pacific Coast League 42, 197
Page, Joe 180, 181, 184
Pageland (SC) 215
Paige, Leroy "Satchel" 46–48, 57, 77, 81, 160, 176, 180, 182, 187, 196, 197, 199, 217
Palm Beach (Fla.) 49
Palmetto League 21–22
Partee, Roy 160
Patkin, Max 68
Peckinpaugh, Roger 91
Pegler, Westbrook 148
Pennock, Herb 217
Pepper, Ray 56
Perry, Boyd 135
Pettit, Leon 72
Phelps, Ray 33
Philadelphia Evening Bulletin 166
Philadelphia (Pa.) *Record* 214
Philadelphia Royal Giants 47
Phillie Phanatic 68
Piedmont League 21–22
Piersall, Jimmy 198
Pirrone, Joe 46, 160
Pollock, Ed 166, 167
Porterfield, Bob 200
Potter, Nelson 158
Povich, Shirley 3, 5, 71–72, 76, 77–78, 109, 129, 179, 214
Powell, Jake 72, 74
Price, Jackie 68, 192
Priddy, Jerry 159
Pusich, Ivo 81
Pytlak, Frankie 112

Rackley, Marv 197
Radcliff, Rip 135
Raft, George 151
Ragland, Rags 151
Raleigh Capitals 21
Raschi, Vic 180, 184
Reese, Jimmy 45
Reiser, Pete 105, 144–145, 149, 189
Repass, Bob 143
Reynolds, Allie 180, 184
Richards, Paul 26, 207
Richardson, Bobby 213
Richman, Art 52
Rickey, Branch, Sr. 2, 52, 53, 63–64, 85, 92, 93, 146–147, 149, 150, 153, 156–157, 165, 184, 197
Rickwood Field (Birmingham) 198, 199
Rigley, Bill 149
Rigley, Johnny 118–119
Ripple, Jimmy 126
Ritter, Lawrence 217
Rizzuto, Phil 180
Robertson, Jimmy 70
Robertson, Mildred 70
Robinson, Jackie 48, 182, 197, 200
Robinson, Wilbert 24, 28, 31–34, 36, 44
Rogell, Billy 97, 105
Rogers, Tom "Shotgun" 24–25

Rolfe, Red 111
Rollins College (Fla.) 194
Roosevelt, Franklin D. 43, 67, 70, 75, 14–41, 143
Root, Charlie 40
Rosenthal, Larry 118, 169
Ross, Mike 91, 100, 108
Rowe, Lyn "Schoolboy" 63, 74, 77, 97–98, 104, 113, 115, 117, 120, 123, 124, 135, 148
Ruark, Robert 108–109
Ruffing, Red 60, 76, 77, 99, 108, 159, 217
Russo, Jim 208
Ruth, Babe 13, 25, 45, 50, 59, 60, 91, 164, 167, 192
Ryan, Nolan 204
Ryan, Rosy 26
Ryder, Jack 28

Sain, Johnny 186
St. Louis (Mo.) Post-Dispatch 212
St. Louis (Mo.) Star 59
Sand Hill League 19
Savage, Bob 166
Scarborough, Ray 141
Schacht, Al 67–68, 70, 192
Schultz, Joe, Jr. 158, 159
Second Fireside Book of Baseball 210
Sewell, Luke 158
Shantz, Bobby 201
Shea, Frank "Spec" 180, 184
Shires, Art 29
Shirley, Bob 6, 14, 26, 38, 48, 93, 130, 162, 181, 187, 188, 213, 214, 216
Shirley, Tex 168
Shirley, W.W. 19, 130
Shor, Toots 211
Siebert, Dick 166
Sievers, Roy 69
Simon, L. Sylvan 151
Sisler, George 167
Skelton, Red 151–152
Slaughter, Enos 144
Smith, Al 112
Smith, Earl 25
Smith, Lyle 211
Smith, Red 59, 97, 193, 211, 214, 217
Solters, Julius "Moose" 65
Sommer, Edgar "Blue" 181–182
Sonoco (SC) paper plant 15, 188
South Atlantic League 24
Southern Association 37, 189–190, 195
Sparrow, L.L. "Luke" 15, 18, 39
Speaker, Tris 43, 167
Spence, Stan 140, 178
The Sporting News 2, 12, 44, 69, 79
Sportsman's Park (St. Louis) 50, 56, 59, 108, 144
Stainback, Tuck 42–44, 115, 133
Stanky, Eddie 105, 152
Statler Hotel (Detroit) 110
Statz, Jigger 44

Index

Stearnes, Turkey 47
Stengel, Casey 71
Stewart, Walter "Lefty" 90
Stine, Lee 45
Stirnweiss, George "Snuffy" 181
Stone, John "Rocky" 72, 74
Strange, Alan "Inky" 55
Street, Charles E. "Gabby" 20, 85–86, 87, 88, 92
Strikeout Story 112, 121
Suder, Pete 180
Sullivan, Billy 86, 88, 100, 103, 109, 115, 116, 119–125, 135, 136
Sullivan, Johnny 67, 69, 78, 141–142, 204
Sulphur Dell Park (Nashville) 107
Summers, Bill 120, 172
Suttles, Mule 47
Swanson, Evar 28

Tamulis, Vito 86, 87
Taylor, Jelly 196
Tebbetts, Birdie 55, 96, 103, 119, 135, 136
Terry, Bill 43
Thomas, Fay 44
Thompson, Fresco 32
Thompson, Jimmy 147
Thornwell, William 15
Thurston, Hollis "Sloppy" 33–34, 42
Tietje, Les 86
Tinker Field (Orlando) 211
Topping, Dan 184–185
Travis, Cecil 94, 191
Trice, Bob 201
Trosky, Hal 91, 112, 114
Trotter, Bill 86, 140
Trout, Dizzy 98, 106, 116, 118, 123, 133, 135
True (magazine) 210

Truman, Harry S 176–177, 200
Turley, Bob 206
Tynan, Murray 29

U.S. War Department 4

Van Atta, Russ 86, 87, 95
Vance, Dazzy 33, 34–35
Vaughan, Joseph "Arky" 150, 155–157
Veeck, Bill, Jr. 191, 210
Veeck, Bill, Sr. 38
Vernon, Mickey 141, 210
Vitt, Oscar 91, 111–114, 118, 119
Vosmik, Joe 84, 86

Waddell, Rube 29, 166
Wade, Jake 79
Walberg, Rube 62
Walker, Curt 28
Walker, Dixie 150, 155–156, 195
Walkup, Jim 86, 87, 95
Walters, Bucky 121, 123, 124, 144
Waner, Paul 150
Ward, Dick 44
Washington (DC) *Herald* 77
Washington (DC) *Post* 71, 76, 77, 178, 179, 206
Weafer, Hal 22–23
Weatherly, Roy 112, 120
Weaver, Jim 58, 59, 86
Webb, Del 184–185
Webber, Les 150
Weiss, George 180, 182, 183–185, 210
Wells, Ed 54
Wensloff, Butch 180
West, Mae 216
West, Max 108
West, Sam 56, 88, 89
West Palm Beach, Fla. 49

Wheaties cereal 74
Wheaton, Woody 164, 166
White Sox Park (Los Angeles) 47
Whitehill, Earl 72, 75, 78
Whittier College 76
Wilkinson, J.L. 196
Williams, Hank, Sr. 5
Williams, Tallulah 11, 18, 162, 163, 205, 214
Williams, Ted 50, 81, 99–100, 109, 138, 175, 178
Wilson, Jack 84, 140
Wilson, Jimmy 125, 126
Wilson, Teddy 198, 199
Winchell, Walter 132
Winter Park, Fla. 194, 211
WMAR-TV (Baltimore) 205
Wofford College (SC) 18
Wolff, Roger 162, 169
WRC-TV (D.C.) 209
Wright, Glenn 33
Wright Field (Fla.) 53
Wrigley, William, Jr. 40
Wrigley Field (Chicago) 40, 148, 152
Wrigley Field (Los Angeles) 43, 47
Wyatt, Whitlow 145, 147, 150, 156
Wynn, Early 141, 177

Yawkey, Tom 70, 79
York, Rudy 97, 100, 103–104, 109, 111, 115, 117–120, 123–124, 133, 135–136, 139, 171, 217

Zarilla, Al 139, 158, 204
Zeller, Jack 95, 102, 103, 129, 140
Zernial, Gus 201
Zoldak, Sam 170
Zuber, Bill 141

www.ingramcontent.com/pod-product-compliance
Lightning Source LLC
Chambersburg PA
CBHW060259240426
43661CB00060B/2836